LUCY
SPRAGUE
MITCHELL

Lucy Sprague (ca. 1893). Courtesy of Barbara Biber.

LUCY
SPRAGUE
MITCHELL

The Making of
A Modern Woman

JOYCE ANTLER

Yale University Press
New Haven and London

Designed by Nancy Ovedovitz and set in Goudy Old Style type by
Eastern Graphics. Printed in the United States of America by The Murray
Printing Company, Westford, Massachusetts.

LA
2317
M53A67
1987

Library of Congress Cataloging-in-Publication Data

Antler, Joyce.
Lucy Sprague Mitchell: the making of a modern woman.
Bibliography: p.
"Published works of Lucy Sprague Mitchell": p.
Includes index.
1. Mitchell, Lucy Sprague, b. 1878.   2. Educators—
United States—Biography.   3. Women educators—United
States—Biography.   I. Title.
LA2317.M53A67   1986   370'.92'4   [B]   86–11058
ISBN 0–300–03665–5 (alk. paper)

The paper in this book meets the guidelines for permanence and durability
of the Committee on Production Guidelines for Book Longevity of the
Council on Library Resources.

10   9   8   7   6   5   4   3   2   1

ƠT APR 16, 1987   4/7/87

To my mother and the memory of
my father

Contents

PART FOUR
ALONE

Preface

This book was conceived shortly after the birth of my daughter Lauren, and finished some seven years later after the arrival of her sister Rachel. As my research progressed, Lucy Mitchell's history came to serve as a model, or alternatively, as a warning, for I saw myself grappling with many of the same personal and professional struggles that informed her life. I emerged from the writing of this book with a much clearer understanding of the complicated dimensions of work/family and parent/child relationships.

The contributions of my husband, Stephen, both to this book and to the well-being of our family, have been vital. His enthusiasm for the subject and his incisive questioning of all aspects of the emerging text prodded me to refine my ideas. Above all, the resilience, verve, and good nature of my daughters and my husband allowed us to laugh together even in the midst of the most vexing family or work emergency.

The book has profited enormously from my association with many scholars and colleagues. At the Mary I. Bunting Institute of Radcliffe College, where from 1977–79 I was a Research Associate funded by the Lilly Endowment, Inc., and again, at Radcliffe's Schlesinger Library and Henry A. Murray Center, where in 1982–83 I was a fellow funded by the Mellon Foundation, I encountered many scholars whose research concerning women in American society enriched my own. Each of these institutions provided ideal working conditions for the pursuit of historical work about women, including a collegial environment that made my sojourn at Radcliffe an intense and exciting experience. Brandeis University's Mazur Fund provided a grant for travel and other research support. My colleagues in Brandeis' Department of American Studies and the Women's Studies Program offered constant encouragement and friendship.

I am especially grateful to Nancy Cott, Barbara Haber, Rosalind Rosenberg, Barbara Sicherman, and Barbara Solomon, each of whom provided invaluable advice about the entire manuscript, and to Joan Brumberg, Stanley Cavell, Allen Davis, Ellen Condliffe Lagemann, Ann J. Lane, Sonia Michel, and Steven Schlossman who gave equally beneficial counsel on various chapters. My largest debt is owed Susan Ware, whose thorough readings and expert criticisms of several drafts of the manuscript went beyond even the most exacting standards of colleagueship and friendship.

Numerous individuals gave freely of their time and their store of memories about Lucy Sprague Mitchell. Lucy Mitchell's children, Sprague Mitchell, and the late Arnold and John McClellan Mitchell, were exceedingly generous to me in their willingness to share frank recollections of the past. The late Margaret Coolidge contributed many thoughtful observations. I am also grateful to Marion Mitchell, Barbara Mitchell, Jean Schuyler, Elizabeth Coolidge Winship, Laura Sprague, and to Lucy Mitchell's grandchildren and their families: Beverly and William Corbett, Joan Watrous, Lucy Mitchell, Gregory Mitchell, Robin Mitchell, and Jack Mitchell. To Geraldine and Andrew Mitchell and their daughters, Maureen and Siobhan, I owe a special thanks for their friendship and encouragement.

Interviews with Lucy Mitchell's colleagues and former students added immensely to the portrait of Lucy I had drawn from written documents. I would like particularly to thank Barbara Biber for her many deep insights. Claudia Lewis and the late Charlotte Winsor allowed me to share their memories and wisdom on several occasions. I am also grateful to Evelyn Beyer, Rose Bliven, Eleanor Brussel, Courtney Cazden, Mary Ellen Gilder, Elizabeth Gilkerson, Edith Gordon, Sally Kerlin, Betty Miles, John Niemeyer, and the late Mary Phelps, as well as to James Black, Harriet Cuffaro, William Hooks, Gordon Klopf, Francis Rogers, Sheldon White, and Herbert Zimiles for their comments about Bank Street. The following friends, neighbors, and associates of the Mitchells also contributed their recollections: Bernie and Lora Atherton, Joan Daudon Coolidge, Huntington Harlow, Lewis Hill, Ruth Honsberger, the late Louis Kesselman, Joan Hocking Kracke, Max Lerner, the late Ellen Day Patterson, Arthur Rosenthal, Katherine and Theodore Sprague, and Peter and Roger Watson. The Hon. Arthur F. Burns and Joseph Dorfman, professor emeritus of Columbia University, gave most generously of their time to talk with me about their teacher and colleague, Wesley Clair Mitchell. Grateful acknowledgment is made to Sally Kerlin for permission to quote from her correspondence with Lucy Sprague Mitchell, and to Patricia Carlton, Sol Cohen, Emily Pond Matthews, and Martha Kransdorff, who shared sources and research in education with me.

I would also like to thank the efficient and supportive staff of the Arthur and Elizabeth Schlesinger Library of Radcliffe College for essential assistance—especially Barbara Haber, Jane Knowles, and Eva Moseley—as well as Betty Kulleseid of the Bank Street College of Education library, and the librarians at the Columbia University Rare Books and Manuscript Library, the Bancroft Library of the University of California at Berkeley, the Wellesley College Archives, the Chicago Historical Society, the Vermont Historical Society and the Vassar College Library. Throughout the course of this research, various offices at Bank Street graciously assisted my quest for sources.

To Ann J. Lane, Barbara Sicherman, Susan Ware, and Janet James—members of our Cambridge women's biography group—thanks for years of friendship and intellectual stimulation involving our common pursuits. There is no doubt that the telling of Lucy's life story has been greatly enhanced by her association with Charlotte, Alice, Molly, and Lavinia.

Gladys Topkis of Yale University Press provided enthusiastic support and expert assistance throughout: she has been an exemplary editor. In the last stages of manuscript preparation, I had the good fortune of working closely with Jehane Kuhn. Her keen perceptions and dedicated attention to detail and nuance contributed immeasurably to the final product. Above all, she shared my fascination with the life of Lucy Sprague Mitchell.

A Note on Personal Names

Lucy Sprague Mitchell preferred the use of her full three names. In this narrative, I usually use "Lucy" rather than "Mitchell," a name she did not acquire until marriage and which would not distinguish her from her husband.

Wesley Clair Mitchell was called "Robin" by Lucy, "Clair" by most other relatives, "Wesley" or "Mitchell" by colleagues. I have called him "Wesley" except when the context made "Robin" more appropriate.

Introduction

Lucy Sprague Mitchell was by any measure a woman of achievement: a writer, teacher, administrator and social reformer; an amateur architect, poet, illustrator and geographer. Her primary claim to the attention of readers today is her distinction as a builder of experimental institutions and as a leader in the education of children. She founded and directed the Bureau of Educational Experiments in New York City—now known as the Bank Street College of Education—which continues to hold a unique place in research and teacher training. Her writing for children and about teaching has had wide-ranging and long-lasting influence.

But for me, the deepest interest in this life story goes beyond Lucy Mitchell's record as a key figure in progressive education; it lies in a woman's creative struggle to resolve the conflict between demanding, innovative professional work and full engagement as a wife and mother. This abiding problem, for herself and other women, was at the center of Lucy Sprague Mitchell's life, and she was exceptionally articulate about it. In letters, articles, and notes to herself, this theme is abundantly documented—from her early thirties, when she came close to refusing marriage because she feared the conflict would be insoluble, to her last years of widowhood when she reflected on her successes and failures. The overall picture she herself presents is weighted towards optimism and self-endorsement; it has been part of my task to question her evaluation, while doing full justice to her constraining circumstances, her courage and generosity, and her lifelong demands on herself.

Born in 1878 to a wealthy and eminent Chicago family, Lucy Sprague grew up during a time when most women's lives were still circumscribed by domestic roles. Of the women who were college-educated as she was, many deliberately rejected marriage and conventional family life in favor of full-time work. The more highly educated the woman, indeed, the less likely was she to marry.[1]

Lucy Mitchell was one of a small number of college-educated women, graduating in the early twentieth century, who tried to establish an alternative lifestyle—one that combined marriage and children with full-time professional responsibilities. In this, she took a different course from that of Jane Addams, Lillian Wald, and other women of the suffrage generation who were among her role models. Her distance from these women on the issue of marriage and career exemplifies a significant shift in the aspirations of educated women.

Lucy Mitchell's struggle to define and develop a career came at a time when social supports for working women, married or not, were desperately lacking. Her education, talents, wealth and range of social contacts greatly diminished the difficulties she encountered; moreover, her way of life would have been impossible without a husband who supported her vision wholeheartedly. But these advantages did not eliminate the costs, to herself and others, of her commitment to a full-time career, and her efforts to unify the public and private spheres of her life.

Lucy Mitchell sought to work out the major issues confronting women on an individual basis, a pattern that became more common in the next generation.[2] She explicitly turned away from collective political action in the cause of women's emancipation: instead she was a pioneer of what I call "feminism as life process," a personal rather than a collective attempt by women to mold their destinies in the world and achieve autonomy.[3] In successive stages of life, the struggle is likely to be expressed in varying ways. In Lucy Sprague Mitchell's youth and early adulthood the drive for autonomy was directed to breaking away from the filial obligations that limited her opportunities: in her later life, to developing an independent professional identity as a woman and establishing intimacy within her personal relationships. The creative feminism of her old age, finally, reversed earlier patterns, for in her last decades she sought a new sense of self by breaking the bonds of dependency created both by her marriage and by her attachment to her work identity. Her personal struggles at the various stages of her life course clarify by example the experiences of a lost generation of feminist endeavor.

Because of Lucy Mitchell's exceptional openness to experience, the personal markers of her life help to illuminate larger cultural patterns regarding the situation of women. By her explicit references to the events of her own life as sources of her developing intellectual and professional ideas, she provides a vital link between individual experience and changes in the social order. She stands as a revealing transitional figure, bridging the Victorian world of her birth and the contemporary women's movement.

Eccentric in her style of dress and adornment, aristocratic in bearing and manner, Lucy Mitchell united in her outward appearance as in her character those qualities of passion and reason, artist and intellectual, that shaped her professional work. A powerful, commanding woman, gifted with a quick, brilliant mind, a vital, energetic personality, and extraordinary qualities of leadership, she was at the same time reticent and self-protective, revealing little of her inner feelings even to her closest associates. Beneath her successful public persona lay a more emotional, thin-skinned self, vulnerable to the cultural and personal contradictions her ambitions engendered.

Lucy Mitchell gave her own account of her personal history and feelings in *Two Lives: The Story of Wesley Clair Mitchell and Myself*, published in 1953, five years after her husband's death.[4] The book was first conceived as a biography of Wesley, but she soon found that she could not write about her husband without making their shared life experiences an integral part of the story. In highlighting the way their relationship had colored, supported, and favored the existence of each as independent beings, she drew attention to one of the most significant aspects of the Mitchells' lives.

Reviewing the book in the *New York Times Book Review*, Louis M. Hacker focused on the fact that both Mitchells were dedicated reformers of the species Progressive, hoping to ameliorate the urban-industrial chaos of the previous generation through innovations in their respective fields. He saw the book as an account of progressive reform in education and in economics, two parallel life stories against a broader backdrop of political and social change, and ignored almost entirely its record of an experimental "dual-career" marriage. Ernestine Evans, the *New York Herald Tribune* reviewer, on the other hand, also noted that the book offered a "better look at changing human and sex relationships than Simone de Beauvoir gives."[5] Today's readers are more likely to appreciate the contributions the Mitchells made to reform in a personal as well as a political context.

Like most autobiographers, Lucy Mitchell inevitably reconstructs her own life in the act of writing it. The shaping of events and themes is colored, furthermore, by the special premise of unity-in-duality. The newly widowed author of *Two Lives* has a strong interest in presenting herself as a sympathetic, devoted, and successful wife and mother.

The persona that emerges from this account is, inevitably, only partial. Many intimate details are provided, but others are conspicuously absent. Unusually rich documentation available to the biographer fills out this portrait: an unpublished autobiography written in 1944–45; an oral history taken in 1960; collections of material at Bank Street, New York's City and Country School, the University of California at Berkeley, and Radcliffe College; Lucy Mitchell's personal and professional papers; the diaries of her aunt, Nancy Atwood Sprague, the center of Sprague family life; and those—from 1905 through 1948—of Wesley Clair Mitchell, who kept a detailed daily account of family happenings and the events of his own professional life and of Lucy's. From these varied materials, supplemented by interviews with the Mitchells' children and grandchildren, with other relatives, colleagues, and friends, there emerges a more complex character whose self-construction responded to a dramatically changing culture. The story that unfolds is essentially that of a woman's liberation, fraught with struggle, triumph, and occasional despair.

Like every life story, however, Lucy Mitchell's is subject to varied interpretation. Mine arises out of the framework of women's studies, which looks to the history of women's lives to provide guidance for the present and seeks to present an informed, reliable discourse about that history by placing issues of gender squarely at the center along with other parameters of social and cultural organization. When both private and public life—life cycle development, parenting, and career—are viewed from the perspective of gender, new meanings emerge. I hope that Lucy Mitchell, who always welcomed "educational experiments," would have appreciated this one.

When I began work on this biography some years ago, in an interview with Lucy Sprague Mitchell's youngest son, I hazarded my view of her as a pioneer feminist who had productively brought together family and career interests. Arnold Mitchell was a writer and editor, his mother's literary executor and the child to whom she was closest. He mildly cautioned me against such an interpretation; from the children's point of view, their mother's mediation of private and public spheres had not been successful.

As I gathered evidence about Lucy Mitchell's life, I asked myself continually about the relationship of mothering to feminism. I wondered, first, if she and her children could really have had different perspectives about the quality of their family life, and if so, what generational, psychological, sociological, or cultural factors might explain the divergence. Then, as I assembled the record of her mothering, I came to question how success as a parent can be measured. Is the "good mother" in fact a myth? Finally, I asked myself whether the question of mothering was legitimate at all in considering feminist lives. To ask of a subject whose accomplishments in the world were great beyond doubt whether she was also a good mother may be to turn the focus back towards women's traditional role as keeper of the domestic flame—a role that Lucy Sprague Mitchell and others struggled to escape. If feminist biographers take a multidimensional approach in their attempt to correct the overly public and masculine bias of traditional history, will they not run the risk of setting unrealistic expectations, of wanting their subjects to achieve too much: to be great writers, businesswomen, artists, or professionals *and* great mothers, wives, or companions? If we peer too deeply into the private lives of our pioneers as well as the public faces of their achievement, are we not bound to find them wanting?[6]

It seemed clear to me that for Lucy Sprague Mitchell, the question of her self-assessment as a mother, and how far it was justified, was central to the biographer's task. Both her classroom practice and her writing on child development were inextricably linked with her experimental practice as a mother, and both had their roots, quite explicitly, in her unhappy childhood experiences. Though she was less successful as a mother than she hoped to be and believed she was, her struggle to become a responsive parent was not insulated from the work for which she was honored; it was an integral part of her adult development.[7]

Lucy Mitchell's personal and professional concerns cannot be separated: her family relationships and her educational work acted upon each other. And this interaction has consequences beyond the boundaries of her own life: her contributions to the theory and practice of early childhood education helped redefine the public dimensions of women's private sphere, while her private life gave expression to the new patterns of sex-role behavior beginning to emerge in the twentieth century.

Lucy Mitchell's style of public action may represent a larger trend. Historians have suggested that the period after 1920 marked a regression for feminism, signaled by the split between political and social reform feminists over the equal rights amendment, the failure of career women to achieve economic equality, and the disaffection of young women from feminist concerns. They claim that women turned toward personal satisfactions, finding fulfillment in marriage and domestic life or in a narrow, individualistic professionalism, and eschewed the political activism and collective goals of an earlier period.[8]

Although the paths of many women in the post-suffrage era did reflect a retreat from the public, political arena, and their representation in male-oriented professions did not keep pace with expectations, I would argue that the development of careers in such "female" fields as child development and preschool education was not a reactionary trend. Whereas an earlier generation of female educators had accepted sex-typed roles predicated on the idea of a distinctive, nurturing female temperament, Lucy Mitchell and her colleagues were drawn to early childhood education as a career not because of their belief in biologically rooted sex differences in aptitudes, but because of their eagerness for social reform. Many of them progressed naturally from concerns about women's issues before the 1910s to an interest in children's development. Furthermore, by establishing educationally sound preschools, they made it possible for later generations of women to combine motherhood with full-time work.

These educators' concerns for children had a political context that has too frequently been ignored. Lucy Mitchell, influenced by John Dewey, believed that the school was intimately related to the community— local, national, and international. She wanted to stimulate the development of emotionally secure and healthy children, in part because she was convinced that "whole" children were the best guarantors of a progressive, humanistic society. She believed that "Bank Street" should be judged by its contributions to world peace and the improvement of social welfare as well as to individual development.

Bank Street, under Lucy Mitchell's leadership, became an organization distinctive not only for its contribution to the education of children but also for its enhancement of the growth and development of faculty and student teachers. It set out to equip teachers-in-training with tools for enriching their own emotional, aesthetic, and intellectual lives and their understanding of social and economic problems.

In many respects, Bank Street exemplified the extension of a family model to a public organization, offering personal nurturance and support to its initiates in a way reminiscent of the Hull House settlement under Jane Addams. Hull House was a female institution which fostered and depended on a network of intimate relationships among unmarried women. Bank Street, established a generation later, was also predominantly a female world, whose special patterns of mentoring and guidance derived from the experiences of its Working Council. Lucy Mitchell shared her energies between Bank Street and her own family, perhaps the most significant difference from the settlement house pattern.[9] Even so, the capacity for support and nurturance she brought to Bank Street marked the character of the institution, and helped shape the careers and lives of numerous women, who in turn were mentors to others.

Bank Street was distinguished by a strong cooperative emphasis, which was also part of its political commitment. Its policy-making Working Council, chaired by Lucy Mitchell, functioned collectively as a group of peers. She refused to assume a more powerful position as president, and despite occasional conflicts between internal divisions, led her colleagues toward "joint thinking" and a "group focus." "Relatedness," a central feature of her management style, as well as of her educational theory and practice, was her favorite word.

During Lucy Mitchell's forty-year educational career, when women in male-dominated professions suffered greatly from gender-based discrimination and hierarchical control, Bank Street thus presented an alternative model of professionalism. Its empathic yet disciplined approach to children's education gave its associates status and prestige. Participation in the cooperative, nonhierarchical management of the institution provided measures of self-esteem and professional competence that were rare for women then and are far from widely available today.

During these post-Progressive years, often considered a time of decline in women's professional achievements, Bank Street and other institutions in the experimental education movement sought quiet ways to remake the world according to democratic, humanistic principles. In their ideals and programs, the activism common to women during the Progressive Era was sustained. I see their work as a continuation of the social reform movements of this earlier period, transformed by modern currents of social science and professionalism.

Lucy Sprague Mitchell did not actively support the equal rights amendment or work publicly to improve the conditions of women's labor; nor did her professional interests at Bank Street center around women as a special-interest group. But consciousness of women's plight influenced the resolution of her own problems and the unique character of the institution she founded. In her own life she challenged and eventually overcame many of the restrictions that limited women's options in the early twentieth century. A feminist point of view was implicit in her educational philosophy and practice as well as in her personal life choices. Bank Street's cooperative management suggests one dimension of this commitment. Moreover, like several of her colleagues in experimental education, she believed that the progressive classroom would herald a new mutuality between men and women. Girls and boys who had been raised with equal opportunities would use their school experience to restructure American culture. At a time when traditional education was rigidly programmed according to gender, Bank Street and its associated schools offered a new, nonbiased curriculum.

Because of the agonies of her own childhood, Lucy Sprague Mitchell focused her attentions on young children as the group in most desperate need. At the same time, she saw clearly that her own life struggles had been dictated by issues of gender. "Every stage of life has its song," she wrote in the collection of poems she assembled shortly before her death. "My song has been a woman's song."

The histories of women such as Lucy Sprague Mitchell reveal feminism not as theory but as a hard-fought life struggle. The anthropologist Ruth Benedict, a contemporary of Lucy Mitchell, wrote:

One adventure through the life of one woman who has been profoundly stirred by a great restlessness and you will comprehend more than from a library of theorizings. The theory can only be the gloss and the addenda: the urge, the power of the woman's movement does not lie in the gift of logic. It comes from the bright stinging realm of [women's] dearest desires. . . . It is a passionate attitude toward their own lives. It is a cry to be awake in their lifetime, to hazard themselves and to risk the maiming, but somehow to attain to something that may conceivably be called living.[10]

In this sense—in her passionate attitude toward life, her willingness to take chances and risk failure, to test herself to the limit, and to call into question the assumptions that constrained every woman's aspirations— Lucy Sprague Mitchell was surely a feminist, one whose life can productively illuminate the experiences of modern women and their relationship to the larger society.

PART
ONE
BEGIN-
NINGS

1

Chicago Girlhood

Lucy Sprague was born on July 2, 1878, in a four-story stone mansion on Washington Boulevard on Chicago's fashionable West Side—the fourth of the six children of Otho and Lucia Sprague. Otho Sprague was a leading Chicago citizen, one of the merchant princes who helped to build America's commercial greatness after the Civil War. He was the most dynamic of the three partners in the firm of Sprague Warner and Company, which by the time of Lucy's birth had become the largest wholesale grocery in the world. The unhesitating will that had created this corporate giant and maintained its predominance also pervaded Otho Sprague's household and shaped the family culture.

Lucy, too, would become an entrepreneur, but in the realm of social and educational reform: in her middle years she would emerge as a powerful leader, skilled and commanding like her father. In her public work and her private relationships, she would seek to reverse the authoritarian, patriarchal patterns that had dominated her childhood: but in this lifelong struggle to reject her father's values, she would call constantly on the self-discipline that he had taught her. Whenever Lucy looked back over her own life, she saw the whole drama played against the backdrop of her Chicago childhood. People never really change, she thought, they only "become more so": as she found ways to be more herself, she discovered that she was still, as much as ever, her father's and her mother's daughter.

It was not the West but New England that had molded the values and temperaments of generations of Spragues. In 1629, Ralph, Richard, and

William Sprague landed in Salem, Massachusetts, shortly after the arrival there of Governor John Endicott, who settled the region on behalf of the new Massachusetts Bay Company.[1] The brothers had come from Upway, England, a small village in Dorset where their father, a fuller, owned considerable property. Little is known of the Sprague brothers' reasons for leaving England to confront raw and desolate beginnings in America. In any event, the pioneering spirit that brought them from England also led them, once on American shores, to branch out quickly from the main settlement at Salem. They were part of the small company of men who built the "Great House" in Charlestown where the first Thanksgiving in the Massachusetts Bay Colony was celebrated by Governor John Winthrop in July of 1630.[2]

This spirit of enterprise was continued in the New World by the Spragues and their progeny. Ralph Sprague settled in Malden, where he quickly rose to prominence and wealth. His descendant Jonathan, of the fifth generation of Spragues in America, was the first to leave Massachusetts. After the Revolutionary War, he acquired a hundred acres of land north of Randolph, a small town on the White River in Vermont.[3] Jonathan's son Edward settled in East Randolph, the largest and most commercial of the villages of the township, and became one of its leading citizens.[4] He served as deacon of the radical Free Will Baptist Church of East Randolph. When he prayed, it was said, "the blessings fell right down."[5]

Like his father, Edward's son Ziba was a farmer and merchant as well as a deacon of the Free Will Baptist Church.[6] By 1850, Ziba owned approximately 250 acres of land in East Randolph; for a time he represented Randolph in Vermont's General Assembly.[7] In 1834, Ziba married Caroline Arnold, daughter of Colonel Sprague Arnold, a judge who owned the East Randolph sawmill. Their children were Albert, born in 1835; Caroline Amelia, born in 1836; and Otho Sylvester Arnold, born in 1839.

Ziba meant to prepare both his sons for college. But poor health kept Otho from attending Yale University, where Albert was enrolled. He became a clerk in the general store of H. Holden in East Randolph, and was soon able to buy an interest in the store.

With the outbreak of the Civil War, Otho Sprague—a dedicated Union supporter—enlisted in the Eighth Vermont Volunteer Regiment. During the severe winter of 1862 in Brattleboro, Vermont, he was stricken with tuberculosis and medically discharged from service just two months before his regiment reached New Orleans; he never saw battle. After his recovery, Otho joined Albert in Chicago, where the elder brother had gone in late 1861. Albert, who did not serve in the Civil War, returned to Vermont in 1862 to marry Nancy Atwood, the oldest of the twelve children of Ebenezer and Elvira Atwood from the village of Royalton, a few miles west of Randolph.

The Atwood ancestors had arrived in Massachusetts in 1634, five years after the Spragues, and the family shared the disciplined and exacting New England temperament.[8] Ebenezer—"puritanical . . . but not austere," according to his daughter Nancy—was a member of the Vermont legislature, town selectman as well as overseer.[9] But Nancy felt that her mother, Elvira, was more interesting than her father. While rearing nine sons and three daughters, Elvira somehow found the time to become one of the best educated citizens of the village, famous for "spelling down" the entire neighborhood at town spelling bees. Interested in every subject from farming to politics, she was unafraid to break into discussions of public issues to argue her own points, which she did avidly and brilliantly. "How my mother's eyes would snap," recalled Nancy, "as she seized a chance interval, during her bread-making, to dart from kitchen to sitting room, defending her side of the argument."

Though they had little money (Ebenezer once bartered a cord of wood for a new singing book) and on occasion came perilously close to losing the family farm, the Atwoods were a close and happy family. Everyone sang, with the nine brothers playing stringed instruments as well. Together, the family performed at weddings and funerals; Ebenezer led the church choir; a brother, Thomas, taught singing at a country singing school; and Lucia and her sister Lizzie, both with exceptional voices, performed at local concerts.

Lucia, born in 1849, was the family pet—a buoyant child, precocious in music. Nancy, thirteen years older, took over Lucia's care from birth: she made clothes for her "child-sister," supervised her activities, and slept in her room. When Nancy became a teacher in a neighboring district, boarding at the homes of the pupils' families, she took Lucia with her, to lighten the burden of their hard-pressed parents. The great tragedy of Lucia's girlhood was the loss of her older sister to the midwest.

All the Atwoods and Spragues filled the pews of the meeting house in Royalton that day in September, 1862, when Nancy, dressed in an ash-rose wool gown with a matching bonnet trimmed with flowers and ribbons, walked down the aisle to meet her betrothed. When the bride and groom left, a much distraught Lucia, now thirteen years old, refused to be comforted. Nancy recalled her "leaning up against the station crying as if her heart would break."[10] Four years later, Lucia came to Chicago to spend the summer with her sister and three young nieces. During those weeks, Otho renewed his acquaintance with Lucia. His engagement to another woman came to a sudden end; in 1871, in a simple ceremony in Malone, Vermont, in the home of an older brother, Lucia Atwood, now twenty-one years old, married Otho Sprague, ten years her senior.[11] Lucia's friends questioned the match, fearing that Otho was still subject to the "galloping consumption" that had already buried several members of Lucia's family.

However, the couple journeyed west full of bright hopes and enthusiasm. To Chicago—raw, uncultivated, virgin—each of them took the temperaments and talents that had been etched by two and a half centuries of the New England experience.

The Sprague brothers had emigrated to the West at a time when Chicago's basic resources of grains, lumber, and livestock, and its unrivalled position as the crossroads of the American continent, had begun to generate extraordinary commercial growth. In the economic boom that followed the Civil War, Chicago came to dominate Western commerce. Steel, agricultural equipment, wood products, ready-to-wear garments, and dry goods were shipped out of Chicago to all of the West. Chicago had numbered a mere 350 residents at the time of its incorporation in 1833. By 1890, with its population passing the million mark, it stood second only to New York. The city's vitality was expressed in its unparalleled modern architecture and its major university, leading symphony orchestra, and art institute. By the last decade of the century, Chicago's transition was complete: the frontier town had metamorphosed into a city of international standing, the commercial and cultural center of the West.[12]

The Sprague brothers' new business participated in the city's prosperity. The company had been started with $2300 that Albert Sprague borrowed from his father. After a year, his first partner retired, and Albert formed a new partnership with his Vermont schoolfriend Ezra J. Warner. In 1864, Otho was admitted as partner in charge of sales, with an investment of five hundred dollars. He was in fact, in those early days, the company's only travelling salesman. He saw, and single-handedly pursued, the opportunity for expansion of the market for wholesale groceries in the western states. He understood farming, and the needs and aspirations of farming families. Travelling by horsedrawn cart, he made contact with retailers in places not yet reached by the railroad, and won their confidence and loyalty; his own judgment as to whom to trust with credit was faultless. Both the other partners acknowledged that Sprague Warner owed its early dominance in the field to Otho's skill, foresight, and drive. It was pioneer work, as Lucy later remarked, and—given his chronic pulmonary difficulties—it bears witness to extraordinary determination that he undertook such a campaign at all.[13]

With Otho Sprague's bold vision, Ezra Warner's judicial mind and cautious banker's temperament, and Albert Sprague's talents as mediator, the firm prospered steadily. By 1871, Sprague Warner had expanded to a five-story building on Michigan Avenue north of Lake Street and was doing an annual business of nearly one million dollars. When word came at two o'clock in the morning of October 9 that fire was burning on the South Side toward the lake, the Spragues were faced with the prospect of losing the building in which they had everything invested. Hastily, Otho organized a group of men to try to save the company's vast stock of groceries. Working quickly, the rescue squad removed much of the stock and piled it up on the lake front just east of Dearborn Park, apparently a safe place because of the many vacant lots around it. By next morning, however, the fire had swept down to the water's edge, destroying everything. Only a few drayloads of tea and tobacco stored elsewhere remained unharmed. Exhausted and seriously ill from smoke inhalation, Otho went home, only to find every bed and couch occupied by people burned out of their own homes. Nan and Lucia ministered to all, making tea and changing bandages.[14]

At first the loss seemed irreparable, but Otho and his partners had circulars printed announcing the resumption of operations immediately in new quarters. Three days after the fire, Sprague Warner & Co. was back in business. Soon the firm moved back to Michigan Avenue opposite its old store. It remained there until 1876, when it moved into a large building at Randolph and Michigan Avenues opposite Dearborn Park.[15]

Year by year, the company expanded. In the 1860s and 1870s the firm added cigars and tobacco, coffee roasting, the manufacture and packaging of spices and baking powders, and the refining of syrups. By the 1880s, Sprague Warner was a mammoth establishment, importing Havana cigars, sardines, anchovies, caviar, French vegetables, truffles, fancy biscuits, prepared meats, olive oil, teas, spices, and other fancy groceries, and producing preserved fruits and vegetables under its own label. Twenty years later, the company built a modern manufacturing, warehousing and merchandising plant, the largest building in the world devoted exclusively to the production and distribution of food. "If you can't get it from Sprague Warner and Company, it isn't to be had," became the company slogan. Among its goods, for example, were two thousand varieties of tea.[16]

Within a few years, the Sprague brothers had become leading members of the city's merchant elite, many of whose names were household words, linked to products and services known across America: Marshall Field's department store, the Palmer house hotel, Armour hams, McCormick reapers, Pullman sleeping cars. These men had enormous influence over all areas of city life. "If one had to attach meaning to the raw power of Chicago," writes Hugh Duncan in his study of Chicago culture during this period, "it seemed best to fall back on 'fate,' 'determinism,' or 'historical necessity' after the fashion of Adams, and describe this new elite as some sort of primeval social force come to life in a new form."[17]

Both Sprague brothers always lunched at the Chicago Club with Marshall Field, George Pullman, Nathaniel Fairbank, John Crerar, and Franklin MacVeagh: their regular table there was known as the "millionaires' table." Both belonged to the exclusive Commercial Club, founded in 1877 to promote more "intimate friendships" among a select group of leading businessmen, with no more than two or three from each trade. Albert Sprague became president of the club in 1882. Otho was one of the founders, along with Field, Adolphus Clay Bartlett, and Martin Ryerson, of the Pelee Club, an incorporated group which sponsored fishing holidays at Pelee Island in Port Sheridan, Ontario. Between them Otho and Albert also belonged to practically all of Chicago's other elite social organizations: the Union League Club, Calumet Club, University Club, Caxton Club, Quadrangle Club, Century Club, Washington Park, and Chicago Literary Club.[18]

Lucy grew up well acquainted with her father's business friends. Most of them, like the Spragues, had roots in New England. She recalled the "sleek appearance and hard face" of Pullman; the "cold reserve" of Marshall Field (though she loved his huge emporium, a social center where friends met to shop, chat and lunch); the "gruff, almost uncouth" manner of the often outrageous R. T. Crane; the "ostentatious hideousness" of Potter Palmer's mansion; and his statuesque, elaborately dressed wife. Lucy preferred Charles Hutchinson and Martin Ryerson, who were in large part responsible for assembling the Art Institute's collection of paintings.[19]

Otho's closest friend was Clay Bartlett, a merchant whose keen business insight was the key ingredient in the success of Hibbard, Spencer, and Bartlett, the hardware company in which he was junior partner. Though constantly in poor health like Otho, he was also, like his friend, energetic and witty.[20] Lucy remembered Bartlett as "sweet and gentle and understanding . . . the kind of man on whose lap children naturally climbed."[21]

Otho Sprague himself seemed to sum up the best qualities of his business friends. He was a "daring merchant," observed a colleague, "a man of magnetic energy . . . keen perceptions, quick action, and strong will." He was among the gentlest, most respected and best liked of this adventurous, powerful group of self-made leaders; they particularly admired Otho's wit and learning. He always regretted his lack of a college education, and in compensation he assembled a huge library that was the envy of many colleagues. His collection of the autographs of Civil War heroes—particularly Abraham Lincoln—was widely admired.[22]

To Lucy, the Chicago of her youth was "a big little town" because her father and his friends thought of it as their city, in which they took enormous pride and which they felt they owned. From the marble palaces of Potter Palmer to the champagne spigots of George Pullman, there were no limits to the monuments these merchants built to themselves. It was no accident that Thorstein Veblen's analysis of conspicuous consumption emerged during his sojourn in Chicago.

But not all of Chicago's wealth was spent on private luxury. Within the two decades that followed the Chicago Fire of 1871, the city's prosperous merchants established, supported, and helped to direct the Chicago Symphony Orchestra (the first municipal symphony in the nation), the University of Chicago, the World's Columbian Exposition, the Field Columbian Museum, the Chicago Art Institute, the Newberry and Crerar libraries, and a host of municipal reform organizations.[23]

The Sprague brothers participated actively in the city's cultural and civic life. Albert was a member of the board of directors, and at one time president, of Chicago's Relief and Aid Society. He was a governing member of the Art Institute, of which Otho was a founder, and both were among the thirty founding boxholders at the new Chicago Orchestra. Otho and Albert also helped to establish the World's Fair and the University of Chicago.

Lucy remembered her father as a loyal "mugwump" who advocated reform in local and federal government. He was a strong supporter of President Grover Cleveland, whom he knew personally through his friend Walter Gresham, Cleveland's secretary of state. At home, Otho served on the executive committee of the Citizens' Association of Chicago, the nation's oldest municipal reform organization, established shortly after the Chicago Fire, and the Citizens' League.[24]

Nancy and Lucia Sprague, like their husbands, enjoyed their rapid rise in Chicago society. Both belonged to a Ladies' History Club and the Dilettante Club, at which papers on history and art were read, and in the 1890s they joined the Chicago Women's Club, which pursued various charitable and reform activities. Lucia was an ardent prohibitionist, and presumably active in the Women's Christian Temperance Union, since its stern, committed president, Frances Willard, was a personal friend. Nan and Lucia's schedule was also filled with social activities. Daily they called on friends or received calls, went to parties and dinners, held lunches or musical entertainments for the wives of Chicago leaders.[25] In the glittering, raw-edged metropolis that had become their home, Nan and Lucia learned to translate the values of their upbringing—their tradition of mutual support, and the social and musical pleasures of a frugal Vermont community—to a scale that matched their new resources. Many of the ladies they knew had come from backgrounds no more privileged than their own: the whole city was part learning, part inventing its own cosmopolitan grand style.

With the comfort and security afforded by her father's position, one might assume that Lucy Sprague's childhood was an enviable one. Yet she recalled the Sprague household as emotionally barren and joyless, and growing up there was largely a dark and forbidding experience. Lucy was anxious, frightened, and lonely throughout childhood. The contours of her unhappy girlhood influenced her adult relationships, framed her deepest conflicts, and determined her ambitions and achievements as a mature woman.

The dynamics of the family in which Lucy grew up were complex. Otho and Lucia had six children: Mary, born in 1872; Albert, 1874;

Nancy, known as Nannie, 1876; Lucy, 1878; Otho, 1880; and Arnold, 1882. Nan and Albert had one surviving daughter, Elizabeth. The two Sprague households were tightly linked by the brothers' partnership and the close attachment between the sisters; they formed a distinct family culture that both nurtured and thwarted Lucy's development.

In many respects, the Sprague home, dominated by the grim rectitude of Lucy's father, was an archetypal Victorian household. Otho, the feared and often absent father, was clearly dominant; Lucia, sharply divorced from the masculine world of Otho's business, devoted herself to family life and cultural affairs. Though Otho and Lucia came from similar backgrounds, the contrast between them could not have been more vivid. Otho, aggressive, dynamic, and active, embodied the conventional attributes of Victorian masculinity and patriarchalism. As husband and father he was stern, demanding, and authoritative. Lucia—warm and caring, shy, delicate, and often helpless—reflected a standard type of Victorian femininity. In contrast to Otho's active world of business, finance, and philanthropy, Lucia's world was limited to the confines of her home. But it was not a sphere that she occupied with confidence and authority, for Otho oversaw and overshadowed her even there.

"Father conscientiously undertook to bring up his family in the path of inexorable righteousness," Lucy explained. "And he was infallible in the eyes of his wife as well as in his own. He included his young wife along with his children as ones to be molded to his pattern. I think my mother was as afraid of him as we children were, though she loved him deeply too." Lucy noted that her mother always referred to her father as "my husband" and addressed him in letters as "my dear husband," never as "Otho." Lucy felt that much of her mother's creativity and spontaneity was stifled in the gloomy Sprague household. She perceived her mother as by nature a "gay, almost gypsy-like person" with extraordinary musical gifts and the temperament of an artist. Yet she lacked the resources to counterbalance Otho's authority and to develop avenues of autonomous action and expression. So lacking in self-confidence was Lucia, despite her substantial gifts, that although the children "enjoyed and loved her deeply . . . they never looked to her for authority—not even protection. . . . Some pity was always mixed in with our love for her." In Lucy's memories her mother was "ardent but suppressed," "delightful but tragic." Lucy was sure that marriage had prevented the flowering of Lucia's potential, and had instilled guilt and self-doubt about her natural competencies.[26]

The areas in which husband and wife were most unlike, and where
Otho tried continuously and conscientiously to reform Lucia, concerned
the display of emotion and the capacity for play. "Mother's patterns of
gypsy gaiety, of recklessness, of almost delirious pleasure in color and music and poetry were regarded as emotional indulgences by my Puritan father," Lucy recalled. Otho believed that a waste of time was the greatest
sin; Lucia, "naturally a very impulsive and a very affectionate person,"
repeatedly came up against Otho's stern sense of decorum. He had little
taste for her spontaneity, and "he disapproved of any show of affection."
Lucia thus tried to suppress spontaneous expression, "whether it was demonstrative affection or the dramatic expressions of an artist." Her gaiety
was also to be brought under control. For Lucia, music was not a discipline to be studied soberly and carefully—it was a passion. Lucy most admired her mother and was most proud of her when she sang. But for
Otho, music was a legitimate pleasure only if one took it seriously. "If
you laughed my Father scowled," Lucy recalled. "Lucia, do you think this
is an appropriately serious attitude?" he would ask. When Otho was
away, family musicales were unconstrained occasions, full of laughter, in
the Atwood tradition, and Lucia took a leading part. But in Otho's presence, Lucia was controlled and reticent. "She lost her personality and
flare," Lucy recalled. Lucy believed that her own later difficulty in expressing emotion openly, her inhibitions about play, and her deep-rooted
sense of guilt concerning her "art indulgences" sprang from her father's ri-
gidity on these issues and the example of her mother, who tried to follow
Otho's lead, but not without grave consequences. Lucia lived forever as a
tentative adult in her own household, "afraid she wouldn't live up to
[Otho's] concept of a good wife." She seemed much more like an "older
daughter" than an equal partner.[27]

Lucia was subject to severe and often incapacitating headaches. For
many women of her time, illness seems to have acted as a socially admis-
sible protest against the constraints of domesticity, a covert expression of
the conflicts and tensions engendered by patriarchal marriage.[28] Lucy
recalled being terrified by the frequent sight of black-and-blue spots on
Lucia's arms, marks caused by a rubber apparatus that was supposed to relieve pain by removing blood from the head. It was her tough, mischie-
vous son Albert who was Lucia's favored nurse during these times—
which suggests that the more sensitive children could not deal well with
her suffering. "I denied Mother's increasing headaches. . . . " she recalled, "thinking with intense concentration, 'Mother has no headache,

Mother has no headache. God is good, All is good,' over and over again. Yet all the time I might be wringing out hot wet cloths and laying them on Mother's closed eyes."[29] Doubtless Lucy made connections between Lucia's role as wife and her incapacitating illness. One of her earliest lessons was that domesticity could destroy a woman's individual capacity and will, and that if it did, it brought unrelenting suffering. Lucy's ideas of femininity were shaped by her impressions of her mother's weaknesses vis-à-vis her father's dominance in a marriage in which each appeared lovingly devoted to the other.

Life in the Sprague household was built on discipline and order. Every activity had its time and place, and for each the children were strictly accountable. Their baths, for example, taken in a big tin bathtub, were strictly scheduled for Saturday night, fifteen minutes apart. Bedtime for each of the six children was scheduled fifteen minutes apart every night. Lucy had to practice her piano twenty minutes a day, a time that seemed endless to her. Breakfast began promptly at half-past six, so that Otho could get to work by half-past seven or eight. The meal opened with Bible recitations, with each child saying a newly learned verse. Any child who did not come with a new verse was fined five cents, to be paid to a small bank in the center of the dining room table. Dunking a doughnut in milk also called for a five-cent fine, one-third of Lucy's weekly allowance. But Otho himself, without humor, would simply put a dollar in the bank and dunk a doughnut in his coffee for three weeks; Lucy found this injustice particularly cruel. Sometimes, in their parents' absence, Aunt Amelia would fine the children a penny or more for each "saucy" word. Lucy recalls that on one occasion the contents of the bank, grown heavy with time, were used to purchase a milk cow for the family. The children's sins or lack of them were registered every night in a little book: a gold star for no sin, a silver star for a small sin, a red star for a big sin. But young Lucy was passionately fond of red. She arranged the red stars in designs in the book, and if the design needed another star, she would invent another sin to confess.

Only at Sunday evening story time in the library did Otho relax his usual sternness. Every week, with Arnold and little Otho perched on his knees and the rest of the family gathered around, Otho would invent a whimsical, magical tale about a family with six offspring—children, animals or fish—whose adventures took them all over the world. Lucy thought that the stories, sometimes serialized for a year or more, were masterpieces. Yet their characters always displayed the same errant ways as the Sprague youngsters, so that the tales offered countless opportunities for moral instruction.

The rigid discipline and system of moral grading that Otho imposed upon the children successfully inculcated a deep sense of guilt. In addition to fines and stars, "really naughty" children were put in a pitch-dark closet at the end of the hallway to meditate on their sins. "Father felt that the only road to grace was through a sense of one's unworthiness," Lucy observed. He believed quite literally in original sin. Because her father was always right, she felt always wrong. "I was made to feel humble to the point of feeling guilty that I was the kind of person that I was. . . . I grew up feeling that I was not a worthy person."[30] So, apparently, did little Otho, who perpetually begged his mother to spank him. When she refused, he imposed his own punishment and hid in the hall closet, trembling with fright.

There is some evidence that Otho was not always the martinet Lucy describes. She admits that he could be a "wag" in public. The imaginative flights of fancy in his weekly stories also suggest a streak of unpredictability and humor, as did his occasional buffoonery, farce, and practical jokes. Lucy recalled one Thanksgiving celebration when Otho dressed up in her mother's skirts, a long shawl, and an old bonnet, carrying a fan in his hand to hide his moustaches, with Aunt Nan beside him in trousers.[31] Otho's colleagues considered him the most charming of companions, and Lucy acknowledged that her father had the capacity to make close and long-lasting male friendships. In her unpublished memoirs, she observed that Otho's three closest friends—his brother Albert, Clay Bartlett, and Chicago lawyer Norman Williams—all stood out for their "tender, understanding, human" quality. But although these men loved him devotedly, Lucy insisted that he himself possessed none of the same quality, "not at least within his family."[32]

In its main outlines, Lucy's portrait of Otho seems to reflect a collective family judgment. Despite his lighter moments and his public charm, Otho's private person was built upon a rigid, patriarchal moralism. As an adolescent, Lucy was well aware of her settled hostility to her father. She felt she had avoided fights with Otho, and physical punishment at his hands, by "conforming outwardly" and "rejecting inwardly."[33] Her image of herself as victim and secret rebel colored her later depiction of both her father and herself.

The guilt and sense of unworthiness that Lucy learned from her father were increased by her isolation from other children. The two oldest Sprague children attended private schools, but the four youngest were taught at home by a governess. Lucy gave two conflicting reasons for this decision. In *Two Lives*, she wrote that her parents kept her out of school after some older girls had pulled down her underpants one day during the first month of kindergarten to "examine" her.[34] In her oral history and autobiography, on the other hand, Lucy suggests that she was never allowed to go to school because her older sister Nannie used to come home battered from the many fights that erupted at the nearby public school. Her parents then decided to have Nannie, Lucy, Otho, and Arnold tutored at home. Why they could not be sent to a more suitable private school, as Mary and Albert were, is not clear in either account. In any event, Lucy felt that Miss Fisher, the governess, prepared the children very well in such subjects as reading, mathematics, American and Greek history, drawing, and music. But because Lucy made no friends of her own age and lacked the experience of classroom learning among peers, she felt that missing out on school was a "tragedy."[35]

Lucy found some solace in the company of her siblings, especially her younger brothers Otho and Arnold. The boys delighted in Lucy's storytelling talent, one she shared with her father, and she basked in their admiration. Baby Arnold, four years younger than Lucy, and "strange, high-strung" Otho, two years her junior, were the only family members she ever hugged. Their room and their company were a refuge to her.

But just as the Spragues most often paired Otho and Albert as the "little boys," so Lucy and Nannie, her elder by two years, were paired as the "little girls." The two shared a room and sometimes a bed in the crowded house, but like all the Sprague children they were trained to keep their bodies "private." They undressed in their voluminous nightclothes and were never allowed in the bathroom together. Nannie and Lucy were dressed exactly alike, except that Nannie, who had dark hair, wore red, while Lucy, with wavy blond hair and large, deep-set hazel eyes, had to wear blue. Lucy hated blue, which she felt faded quickly to dull gray, and loved the forbidden red. She would secretly pin bits of bright red yarn to her underclothes and peek at them when she could. Later, Lucy was also envious of Nannie's superiority at the piano. Despite Lucy's own abilities (Moody and Sankey evangelical hymns were her specialty), it was Nan-

nie's talent that attracted family attention. Lucy envied her sister's mature, sensitive playing and her seriousness and determination. Lucy loved
music passionately (she became so "wrought up" by the Thomas Orchestra's concerts that the "palms of [her] clenched hands were nearly bleed-
ing from the pressure in [her] nails"), but she hated to practice. She
trimmed what moments she could from practice by looking obliquely at
the minute hand of the parlor clock.

Mary, the oldest, six years older than Lucy, was more removed from
Lucy's daily life and consequently from her envy. Mary seemed to Lucy
like a princess when she emerged from her grand corner bedroom (only
Mary and Albert had their own rooms) wearing a long green cashmere
gown laced with blue silk. Her blithe spirit and spontaneity seem to have
won special indulgence from Otho; although she was subject to nervousness and headaches like her mother, she was apparently the least guilt-
ridden of the family, and she escaped the responsibilities that would normally have fallen to the oldest daughter. Lucy felt strongly the contrast
between Mary's charm and good humor and her own reticent, awkward
bearing.

Albert, four years older than Lucy, was the most rebellious child. He
held his younger brothers and sisters and most of the neighborhood children in "terrorized admiration" with his pranks and occasionally patho-
logical threats. If Lucy would not comply with his demands, Albert
would threaten to use his ever-ready jackknife to slit his own throat. To
save her brother's life, Lucy gave in. Lucy recalled that on one occasion
Albert convinced her that warm tar, which was being spread on a neighborhood street, tasted as sweet as candy, and helped her to stuff it in her
mouth. Alone of the Sprague children, Albert was beaten regularly.
Lucia would report his day's misdeeds to Otho, who would retreat with
Albert and the "fatal hairbrush" into the sewing room, where he was
spanked. Although it might have quieted any incipient rebellion in the
other children, this discipline did not seem to curb Albert's aggressive
spirit.

Lucy's fear of her father was heightened by the regular beatings he administered to her "brilliant, tempestuous and unhappy" older brother.[36]
She grew to dread her father's return home, the time of accounting and
punishment. Lucy learned that boys as well as girls suffered from patriarchal discipline, and that any rebellion against their father was dangerous.
Part of the lesson, too, was that the children's mother, though she hated
the beatings, could not prevent them.

Several other relatives played a role in the formation of Lucy's earliest attitudes and values. Most important was Nancy Atwood Sprague— Aunt Nan. The Sprague brothers were the closest of companions throughout their lives, and the Atwood sisters they had married were especially deeply attached to each other.

Nan and Albert's household was much more carefree than Lucy's own home. Albert and Nan were almost like doting grandparents to Lucy and her siblings. Their indulgence of their nephews and nieces sprang in part from their grief at having lost two daughters in early childhood. Their surviving daughter, Elizabeth, a "determined individualist" fourteen years Lucy's senior, was also an important figure in Lucy's childhood.[37]

In many respects, Albert and Nan were polar opposites of Otho and Lucia. Whereas Otho dominated Lucia and the children, Nan was the undisputed "boss" of her family and ruled gentle Uncle Albert "partly by her executive energy, which managed all things easily," Lucy recalled, "partly by her uninhibited tongue." Though Nan made "unscrupulous fun" of everything, she never used her sharp wit at the expense of her beloved sister Lucia. "Slow-going, ultraconservative" Albert had nothing but admiration for his brilliant younger brother, acknowledging that it was Otho's "imagination, his keen judgment of people, and the ready confidence he inspired," that had built up Sprague Warner so quickly. To their friends, the brothers seemed similar in their thinking and tastes, although Otho had the "more sprightly wit," it was thought, and Albert "the more literal view of life." Nancy and Lucia also had markedly different temperaments. Nan was forceful, funny, and fashionable, lavish in her affections and lifestyle. Shopping was her great passion. Under Otho's rule, Lucia was more reserved and thrifty, both in her emotions and her purchases. Yet in Nan's company Lucia could be happy and spontaneous. The sisters feared to sit next to each other in church lest they incur Otho's displeasure by fits of laughter.[38]

Just as Nan had mothered Lucia in Vermont, so she served as substitute mother to Lucia's children. When one of the children came down with a serious illness, Nan would take the others to board with her. When there were extreme disciplinary problems—as when Otho's spankings proved useless in reforming Albert—the miscreant also sought refuge at Nan's. On the occasion of each child's twelfth birthday, Nan took the celebrant to New York City for a "spree." Lucy's upbringing was guided not only by her "ardent, suppressed" mother, but by "forceful, executive," extravagant Aunt Nan.

Lucy makes no mention of the depressions and nervousness to which Nan was subject and which appear regularly in her diary. Although the diary reveals a sustained, loving relationship with Albert, throughout Nan's life she grieved over the deaths of her young daughters and became overly attached to Elizabeth, whose desire for independence caused her mother much pain. Lucy was either unaware of Nan's melancholy, or ignored it, focusing instead on the differences between her mother and her more dynamic aunt. Nan seemed to have escaped the domestic prison in which her younger sister had been trapped.

Aunt Amelia Sprague—"conscientious, conciliatory Aunt Mealy"— was the third female influence upon Lucy. Amelia had been engaged for twelve years to a brother of the Atwood girls, always hesitating to marry him. When at last she consented, it was too late: Tom Atwood's death from tuberculosis at age forty-five prevented a third Atwood-Sprague alliance. Nan and Lucia blamed Amelia for contributing to the unhappiness and illness of their beloved brother.[39] Nevertheless, both acquiesced in providing Amelia with room and board. For six months of the year, Amelia slept in the fold-up bed in Otho's library, then went to Nan and Albert's; she gratefully received a living allowance from each brother.

Amelia was a helpful, if eccentric, house guest (she had an extraordinary interest in hygiene, Lucy recalled, exemplified by her compulsive routine of washing her feet and "dressing" them for dinner); nevertheless, Lucy believed that her mother did not welcome her sister-in-law's semi-annual visits. Nor were the children enthusiastic about this humorless maiden aunt. As Lucy characterized her demeanor, "she effaced herself as far as possible" in their home.[40] The Sprague children were forever playing pranks upon Aunt Mealy—jumping on her starched bustle or locking her in a closet—and usually got away with them. Poor Amelia had "all the stigmata of a spinster" without a home of her own. Whatever the liabilities of patriarchal marriage as Lucy observed it, certainly the life of a dependent spinster offered no attractive alternative.

As Lucy looked back on her childhood, she saw herself as isolated from neighborhood children as well as from most of her family. Though the family paired her with Nannie, Nannie preferred Albert's company, at least during her growing, tomboy years. She refused to allow Lucy to join them, despite Lucia's urgings. In fact Lucy spent more of her time with Otho than with any of the others. Otho and Lucy were much alike, reading anything they could get their hands on and writing constantly. Otho filled reams of paper with his fanciful "History of the World," in which gods from Mount Olympus helped the Union side during the Civil War and a dragon in the Chicago River started the Chicago Fire. Lucy's stories were more personal and intimate. She wrote about a large imaginary family which she mothered through their trials and adventures. Lucy never played with dolls during her childhood, but in these stories she revealed her mothering instincts and her need to be mothered.[41]

"I kept to myself as much as I could in that crowded house," Lucy remembered, "and tried my best not to let anyone in on anything I cared about." Whether it was the adventure stories she told to Otho and Arnold, serials which belonged to the three of them and "bound [them] together against the world," or the notebooks in which she wrote the stories about her imaginary family, sad poetry, and allegories about such subjects as "sin, beauty, and sorrow," her creations were private. The terror of her life was that Nancy, Albert, or her father might discover her secret writings.[42]

As an antidote to her loneliness, Lucy took long walks in her neighborhood and, when she was old enough, to farther sections of the city. In these explorations, she developed an acute sense of local geography and an interest in the varied elements of city life: its streets and stores, its modes of transportation, its markets. On some days, she would wander down to the Chicago River to watch the tugboats journeying from the West Side to the city's South Side, entranced by the river traffic, its bridges and barges. She loved the graceful horsedrawn streetcars and the noisy cable cars that journeyed on neighborhood streets, as well as the Illinois Central trains on the South Side lake front, whose coal soot filtered into houses throughout the city. "I was interested in everything about me," she recalled. "I had so few playmates and so little contact with people my own age that adventure was just another way I had of exploring the environment around me."[43] She would put this habit to good use later in her professional life.

But most of all, Lucy responded to the complex family circle by retreating to the privacy of her feelings, evoking her own emotional world. The activities that were most meaningful to her were those she kept secret—writing, telling stories to her younger brothers—or ones she performed alone—like dressing up. Loneliness, privacy, and secrecy dominated Lucy's perceptions of her childhood. "My own [tragedy]," she wrote, "was extreme loneliness—loneliness within a crowd . . . perhaps the most poignant kind." "Little-Miss-Won't-Tell-'Oo," the family nickname she acquired when she was a two-year-old, was apt; even later Lucy rarely talked with others about the things that mattered most to her. According to her adult account, she spent the first years of her childhood "playing alone and crying alone."[44]

Secrecy, loneliness, repression—the sense of being an outsider—remained central themes in Lucy's adult life. The metaphor she uses in *Two Lives* to describe her childhood—the Washington Boulevard home and the larger world of Chicago as "stage set" and her large family as "cast of characters"—suggests that she saw herself acting a well-defined part in the complex Sprague family culture. Her role was that of caring, obedient daughter, who was at the same time a lonely outsider, full of secrets and private longings.

As Lucy ultimately came to recognize, she could never completely dissolve the inhibitions she developed as a consequence of her father's austere teachings, the example of her mother's passivity, and her relationships to her siblings. "Does anyone ever completely outgrow a truly engulfing experience?" she asked, referring to the emotions of late childhood.[45]

While Lucy may have exaggerated both her father's domination and her mother's powerlessness, as children often do, nevertheless her sense of her childhood as dark and lugubrious was the emotional legacy with which she struggled as an adult. Equally important to her lifelong development was her divided sense of self, a consequence of the polarities she inherited, or learned, from her parents. Lucy identified both with her mother as suffering nurturer and potential artist and with her handsome, powerful, rigid father. Otho's strict, conscientious willfullness and Lucia's light-hearted spontaneity became opposing aspects of her persona. In her deepest self, the self formed in childhood, Lucy embodied the dualities of rationalist and romantic, executive and artist, Puritan and gypsy, masculine and feminine.

When Lucy was ten, she contracted a virulent case of diphtheria. For weeks she lay in the big walnut bed in her parents' room, struggling for breath with the aid of a machine in her throat. The five other children were sent to Aunt Nan's, and a hired nurse kept vigil over Lucy. When one day her parents entered the room in tears, carrying bunches of white and red roses, Lucy was certain that she must be dying. After they had tiptoed away, the nurse told her that they would be leaving on a long trip. Otho had suffered a severe respiratory hemorrhage—a recurrent consequence of Civil War days—and his worried doctors, insisting that he stop working for a year, advised a warm, sunny climate. The Spragues planned to travel to Egypt, and from there, if Otho's health permitted, north to Europe. Anxious about her father's health, but gravely ill herself, Lucy must have felt quite abandoned by her parents' sudden, silent departure and lengthy stay abroad. In time, however, under the care and administration of Aunt Mealy, Lucy won her bout with diphtheria. From overseas came a steady stream of letters that the children read with fascination during their parents' eleven-month absence. Otho recuperated quickly as he and Lucia journeyed from the Nile to the Mediterranean, Scandinavia, Russia, and France, and Lucia blossomed at this opportunity to see the world and to share in Otho's life. At the same time, she was collecting art objects and furniture for the new house being built for the Spragues on Prairie Avenue. The long sojourn abroad was a "releasing" and transforming experience for Lucia.[46]

All the more terrible, then, for Lucia and Otho to learn on their return of the death of six-year-old Arnold—of the croup, according to Aunt Nan's diary.[47] He was their youngest and, Lucy thought, best-loved child—a gay, adorable boy. Lucia would never shake off her guilt at having left her children. For Lucy, Arnold's death marked the end of her childhood and the beginning of the swift and tragic collapse of her family. Within four years she would witness the death of a second brother, Otho, her sister Nannie's mental breakdown, the progressive deterioration of her mother's emotional and physical health, and a serious recurrence of her father's debilitating tuberculosis. With this series of events in her adolescent years, Lucy's sense of isolation inside and outside her family increased. Adolescence would mean a heightening of family tensions, the assumption of new, unwanted, adult responsibilities, and at the same time a search for new sources of self-esteem outside the family circle. For the moment, however, as her childhood came to a close, Lucy withdrew further into her private inner world.

Coming of Age

Prairie Avenue, on the near South Side of Chicago, had become the showplace of the wealthy in the 1870s, when the Pullmans, Fields, and Armours established residence there. Many Chicago millionaires and their families followed, attracted by the convenient service of the Illinois Central Railroad along the South Side lake shore. The Avenue reached the height of its prestige in the late 1880s. The Albert Spragues built a house there in 1884, and in 1890 the Otho Spragues moved from Washington Boulevard to a huge townhouse next door to Nan and Albert on the 2700 block.

Prairie Avenue had by then become the richest neighborhood in Chicago, outdoing even the wealthy exclusivity of the West and North Side elites.[1] The 2700 block was too far south to be part of the more prestigious upper avenue, which ran from Sixteenth to Twenty-second streets. Nevertheless, the "lower avenue," from Twenty-sixth Street to Thirty-first Street was inhabited by extremely wealthy families in ornate mansions, built eclectically in Greek, Gothic, and Beaux Arts styles, like those further north. It was the proximity of the lower avenue to Carville, an industrial section that housed the car shop of the Illinois Railroad, a number of breweries and distilleries, and a working-class community of German extraction, that made it less desirable. The denizens of the lower avenue were invited "to our weddings," observed one upper society matron, "not our dinner parties."[2]

Not even the exclusive upper avenue could escape the forces of industrialization. By 1893, the ready access to transportation that had drawn the elite to the South Side had become a terrible nuisance, afflicting both upper and lower residents with constant noise and coal soot from the daily passage of hundreds of trains. Lucy recalled that ladies went calling with white gloves in their handbags, to be donned only for the call itself. Window curtains were blackened within days by the soot that filtered into all the princely houses.[3] Washcloths came away from faces and necks grimy with soot.

Real estate values on the avenue were further eroded by cheap tenement housing and the gambling saloons, peep shows, houses of prostitution, pawnshops, and burlesque theaters that arose nearby during the Chicago World's Fair of 1893. Over the next decade, industry and business would make new encroachments onto the streets surrounding Prairie Avenue, transforming the neighborhood into an extensive automobile row complete with showrooms, garages, repair shops, and factories. In 1908, the Henry Dibblee mansion on nearby Calumet Avenue, built at a cost of $100,000, was sold with its lot for $33,500. Within another two decades, most of Prairie Avenue's mansions would be ripped down.[4]

For the Spragues, however, the move to Prairie Avenue in 1890, just when real estate values were at their peak, was a signpost of Otho's worldly success. With its lavish furnishings and imported objets d'art, the elegant new home enlarged the family's social life. More servants and greater spaciousness gave scope for Lucia's absorbing interest in the arts of entertainment and altered the Spragues' style of living decisively. For Lucy, the change was substantial. The gilded interiors of the Prairie Avenue house helped her to develop a new understanding of the Spragues' wealth and their social values. That awareness, and the emotional conflict it engendered, became a major lesson of her adolescence.

Lucy and Nannie were sent to Miss Loring's School for Girls on Prairie Avenue—the first time, except for her brief kindergarten experience, that Lucy had attended school. After a month or so Lucy collapsed. "I twitched constantly and uncontrollably and had those terrible pains in my legs." At home with their governess, where each child formed a grade by himself or herself, they had learned without competition. Now, each time Lucy and Nannie were sent back to school, both of them simply "went to pieces." They were taken out of school and sent for tutoring to a friend of Cousin Elizabeth Sprague, but the same breakdowns recurred. Dr. Frank Billings, the eminent Chicago physician who was the Sprague family doctor, insisted that Lucy should not be pushed, so she was kept out of school and had no tutoring. Lucy recalled: "I was desperately unhappy. I felt that I was going to grow up an ignoramus and a disgrace to myself and the family."[5] Perhaps it was her very desire to succeed at

something as important in her father's eyes as schooling, and her longing
for friends her own age, that made her tremble with anxiety when she entered a classroom.

Lucy continued to write secretly during these years—poems, stories,
and allegories that later revealed to her how "strangely divorced" she had
been from the world of most adolescents. In fact, the abstract, generalized quality of her writing from her twelfth through sixteenth years is
quite typical of adolescent writings, then and now. But given her special
isolation in these years, her recollection that the "real" world had been
far less concrete to her than her own inner world is surely accurate. "I
saw only the shadows of the outward world pass across the cave wall,"
Lucy put it.[6] Her parents sought in vain some medical explanation for
Lucy's extreme reticence, nervousness, and "offish" ways.

At the end of each afternoon, when the other children came home
from school, Lucy felt "normal" and "happy". She much enjoyed acting
in the theater that she and her brothers and sisters created for neighborhood children in the stable attached to their home. But on stage she felt
like two people—"one making up dramatic lines and rendering them
with fine action—the other listening, approving or disapproving. I was
actor and critic at the same time." Lucy continued:

I found that disturbingly true whatever I did. When I talked with Father, when I
helped Mother with household arrangements, I always heard and saw myself doing these things. I must be hopelessly insincere, I thought. But the sense of guilt
did not change me a bit. So vivid did this onlooker self become that I called it
sometimes "the-thing-in-the corner," sometimes "my other personality."[7]

In some respects, this experience of a divided self is typical of a normal
developmental stage of adolescence, the perilous transition from parental
to self-initiated behavior. Lucy's "critic" self, the "thing-in-the-corner,"
reflects her Puritan, anti-expressive conscience; as she begins to act in a
broader context, beyond her father's sphere of direct control, she takes
upon herself the responsibility for criticizing her behavior.

For Lucy, becoming an actress on her neighborhood stage opens the
second act in the family drama with which she begins *Two Lives*. Acting
in the enormous elevator of the Sprague stable was a creative, expressive
experience. With Mary and Albert away from home and Nannie uninterested, Lucy was hostess and star performer, and her shyness disappeared.
In her room she kept a photograph of Eleanora Duse. Yet the "exaltation" of public performance was followed by guilt. Though she had begun

to assert the more spontaneous side of her personality, she could not avoid the internal monitor that Otho's teaching had long ago instilled. As her adolescence unfolded, the discontinuity she experienced between her expressive and critical selves foreshadowed the main drama of her inner life.

To compensate for her lack of formal education, Lucy taught herself. She did arithmetic from a school textbook, and she set out to read her way around her father's huge library. Curled up on the comfortable leather couch that curved around the library's alcove, Lucy would start at the top of one section and read her way down to the bottom shelf, then begin the next section. This meant that she spent days reading book after book of a single author—Tolstoy, Hugo, Scott, Trollope, the Brontes, Jane Austen, Bulwer-Lytton, George Eliot, whom she particularly liked, and Dickens, whom she despised, finding his characters to be caricatures. Then, leaving the fiction section, she made her way through large quantities of archaeology and history. Though some of these books were slow going, she found that they released her from her private world "into a *real* world of *real* people."[8]

Among the works Lucy read with most interest were Green's *Short History of the English People*, Guizot's *History of France*, and John Fiske's *The Discovery of America*, which she liked best of the three. She read them each slowly and thoroughly, then again three or four times. Plato's *Republic* was a favorite, as were the fables of Rabelais, which sparked more of her own allegorical writing. Though she never finished the whole room, Lucy read her way around to the last wall by allotting herself a certain number of pages to read each day. Whenever she finished a particularly long, hard book, she allowed herself a poetry book as treat, but otherwise, except for encyclopedias and duplicates, she worked the room systematically. This was "no leisurely browsing," but a grave project undertaken in part to please her father and in part to acquire the learning she was not receiving at school.[9] Books provided "adventure, friends, new people, new problems," a path to the world outside Chicago and Prairie Avenue. The library, with its dark green paper, marble lamps, candelabra, fireplace and lounge, and its marble busts of Lincoln and Augustus, became for Lucy a cheery place, her favorite room in the new Sprague house. Yet its pleasures did not compensate for her loneliness.

The voracious reading habits that Lucy established became an important part of her daily life as an adult. Even more important, perhaps, was her failure at school and the significance it assumed in her own eyes. Lucy knew that she had read more and learned more than the average child of her age; yet she mourned her isolation from other children and felt that it condemned her to inadequacy.

As an adult, Lucy believed that school should release, rather than inhibit, childhood emotions. Undoubtedly the lonely, repressed aspects of her childhood, and her absence from formal schooling, became an important source of her deepest professional convictions.

In 1892 and 1893, two events helped Lucy to emerge from her private inner world: the opening of the University of Chicago and the World's Columbian Exposition, also known as the Chicago World's Fair. With all the Spragues and a half million other spectators in attendance, the Fair opened on May 1, 1893. "It was truly a wonderful spectacle," Uncle Albert wrote to Amelia, then traveling in Europe. "President Cleveland gave a short address, then touched a button, and as if by magic, one thousand flags on all the different buildings were unfurled. It was a day we shall long remember."[10]

The Chicago Fair was far greater in scope than any of its predecessors. It was the fifteenth World's Fair, but only the second one in America; the first had been the Philadelphia International Exposition in 1876. An entire new metropolis of fabulous buildings—a "White City"—sprouted on Chicago's Midway and lake front. The Spragues had contributed financially to build the Fair and were hosts to many out-of-town guests for whom Lucy served as guide. Otho and Charles Hutchinson, who served as Royal Greek Commissioners of the Fair, received the Order of Commander of Our Savior from King George of Greece.

Lucy, now almost fifteen, spent much time at the Fair; she prided herself on the expert tours she gave visitors. The colossal size of the buildings alone was exciting; the largest building, Manufactures and Liberal Arts, was of unprecedented dimensions with forty-four acres of floor space, and could seat 300,000 people, allowing six square feet to each. Promoters liked to inform visitors that the entire army of Russia could be mobilized on its floor, or that six games of baseball could be played there simultaneously. The decoration of the buildings, by some of America's greatest painters and sculptors, and the attention paid to landscaping the huge fairgrounds, helped make the Fair an astonishing visual experience.[11] For Lucy, who had a flair for sketching and designing, it was an endless source of interest.

Lucy loved to explore the international displays on the six-hundred-foot-wide, mile-long avenue called the Midway Plaisance. Fascinated, she saw "real people" of distant lands far removed from the Chicago she had always known: the "Street of Cairo," with 180 men and women, camels and donkeys, sword dancers, candle dancers, and a brilliant mosque where prayers were offered three times a day; a Dahoman village, a Javanese village, Greek and Turkish villages; a Viennese cafe; Eskimos; and many more.[12] The cooperative spirit and international flavor of the Fair made Lucy's reading in history and geography come alive and gave her vivid impressions of cross-cultural differences.

The thing that fascinated her most of all on the midway was the tethered balloon. Disobeying her father's orders, Lucy persuaded the attendant to let her sit in the balloon all day, going up and down on scores of rides. She was thrilled to look down on university buildings, Lake Michigan, and the picturesque sights of the Midway, and she felt that her father's inevitable lecture was a small price to pay for her "grand adventure." Lucy continued to be "airminded" throughout her life, but what counted most was the satisfaction of openly disobeying her father, the thrill of following her own decision and accepting the cost of his displeasure.[13]

Lucy makes no specific mention of having visited the Women's Building, but as she covered the Fair thoroughly it is likely that she stopped there many times. The Women's Building contained thousands of handicrafts, art works, and industrial products created by women all over the world—a tribute to women's contribution to industry, the sciences, and the arts from the beginning of time. A highly active Board of Lady Managers, headed by Chicago socialite Bertha Honoré Palmer, had struggled for several years to ensure that the Chicago Fair would include such a celebration of women's talents. Particularly likely to catch Lucy's interest was the remarkable 7000-volume library of works written by women. One shelf alone contained forty-seven different translations of Harriet Beecher Stowe's Uncle Tom's Cabin.[14]

Many international congresses convened at the Fair, the most elaborate of which was the World's Parliament of Religions, held during the last month of the Fair. Delegates from every nation of the world spent seventeen days discussing Theism, Judaism, Islam, Hinduism, Buddhism, Taoism, Confucianism, Shintoism, Zoroastrianism, Catholicism, Greek

Orthodoxy, Protestantism, Christian Science and other minor and major religions. Among the American speakers were Cardinal Gibbons, Lyman Abbot, Annie Besant, Edward Everett Hale, Richard Ely, Thomas Wentworth Higginson, Frances Willard, Antoinette Blackwell, and Mary Baker Eddy. The conference had been conceived by Rev. John Henry Barrows, the liberal pastor of Chicago's First Presbyterian Church, a close friend of the Sprague family. The Spragues and their friends were hosts to many of the delegates: Lucy came to know Dharmapala, a Buddhist from Ceylon, who gave the closing address of the congress, Swami Vivekenanda, and others who visited along Prairie Avenue.

Attending the congress, meeting delegates, and reading widely in Oriental religion and culture, Lucy felt that her access to the wider world was broadening. For this lonely, inward girl who since childhood had been concerned with the problem of sin and redemption, the juxtaposition of the world's religions was especially meaningful. About three years earlier, Lucy had begun to explore diverse religions, perhaps seeking a response to the feeling of moral unworthiness that was her constant companion. The Presbyterian Church which her own family attended ("high silk hats for Father and Uncle Albert") left Lucy unmoved. In spite of Otho's conviction of sin, Lucy was sure that organized religion was no more for him than an "outward expression of respectability," not an "inward emotional need."[15] She attended varied Protestant ceremonies, Catholic masses, and Jewish services, as well as Salvation Army revivalist meetings. She found each wanting: either it was too unfamiliar, or too emotional and hysterical, or too polished and insincere.

Then, because of her extreme shyness, Lucy had been sent to Mrs. Milward Adams, a creative Chicago teacher who taught her private students to love poetry and to use their voices and bodies expressively in reciting it. Poetry became one of the great enthusiasms of Lucy's life, and along with it, at the age of twelve, she had embraced enthusiastically the doctrine of Christian Science, Mrs. Adams's other passion. It was Mrs. Adams who helped her discover Mary Baker Eddy's *Science and Health*, which she read avidly.

"For two years I lived in a state of exalted negation," she recalled. "I remember concrete events in a haze of denial." Lucy did not discuss her conversion with any member of her family, though she scattered pamphlets around the house hoping they would be read. "Tolerance meant 'Hands off,' to Father and Mother. I had a right to my own thoughts and beliefs. They never talked to me. They just left me alone."[16]

The Parliament of Religions helped loosen the hold of Christian Science on the fifteen-year-old Lucy. This direct contact with the excitement of the outer world rechannelled some of her deepest, most inward yearnings. Yet Lucy felt that her almost automatic denial of her own illnesses later in life was a vestige of her adolescent absorption in Christian Science.

The opening of the University of Chicago in the fall of 1892 had an even more far-reaching effect on Lucy. Otho Sprague, whose own dream of a college education had never been realized, had been among the active boosters of the university. "The opening of the University was to Father a climax of his pride for the city he loved almost as a personal possession," Lucy wrote. "He regarded professors with a kind of reverence once accorded the clergy" and felt it was his civic duty as well as his personal opportunity to open his home to those of the new university faculty who were strangers in the city.[17]

At one of the elegant dinner parties her parents held for new professors, Lucy remembered meeting John Dewey, who was to be chair of a department which combined philosophy, psychology, and education. Lucy claims that henceforth she read everything Dewey wrote about education, with the immediate result that she began to question her father's attitude toward child-rearing.[18] There is no independent evidence, however, that she was at this time at all concerned with either Dewey or the education of children. Not till two decades later did Dewey's ideas begin to exert a powerful hold on Lucy's mind and aspirations.

A more immediate influence on Lucy was Alice Freeman Palmer, Dean of Women at the University of Chicago from 1892 to 1895. President Harper had originally offered her a position as professor of history as well as the deanship, and extended an offer to her husband George Herbert Palmer to head the department of philosophy. George Palmer was too attached to Cambridge to accept Harper's proposition, nor would Alice leave New England without him. But when Harper invited Alice Palmer to take the deanship on a part-time basis, requiring her to be in residence for only twelve weeks distributed throughout the year, she accepted.

Little more than ten years earlier, at the age of twenty-seven, Alice Freeman had become the second president of Wellesley College. Her accomplishments there were substantial: she raised admission standards, revamped the curriculum, assembled a unique and potent female faculty, reorganized administrative structures, and generally changed Wellesley from a domestically oriented, religiously inspired college into a first-rate academic institution. So successful was she in her aims, so skillful in wielding power and in motivating students and faculty alike, that an Alice Freeman cult arose. This "girl-president," only a few years older than the students themselves, seemed to have talents that were "magical."[19]

At George Palmer's insistence, however, Alice renounced her position as president of Wellesley when she married him five years later. Thereafter she worked only selectively, on a consulting basis. Alice Palmer was particularly interested in the Chicago position, for it seemed to her that coeducation was the goal at which most colleges should arrive. She held her post at Chicago until she believed that the position of women students there was "no less creditable than that of the men."[20]

Alice Palmer lived with the Spragues during her first stay in Chicago in 1892. Lucy found her infectious gaiety and spontaneity a sharp contrast with the ordered routines of her own household. She was "an experience for anyone," Lucy wrote in her memoirs. "To me, she seemed— and still seems—one of the great people of the world. . . . Her eager zest for life, her capacity to listen as wholeheartedly as she talked, her versatility, her light touch even in executive matters in which she was a master, made her literally unique in my experience." Alice Palmer's sharp intelligence and concern about women's education stimulated and legitimated Lucy's interest in her own intellectual development. Through her, Lucy met a number of educated women working at the university on behalf of women's interests—among them, Marion Talbot, then the Assistant Dean of Women. But it was Alice Palmer who gave Lucy, then a "withdrawn, overwrought" fourteen-year-old a "glimpse of a new world" which she later made it possible for Lucy to enter.[21] Alice Palmer always had time for the somber, moody girl. Perhaps she recognized the power and intelligence that lay beneath Lucy's unhappy exterior. She entered Lucy's life only briefly during these Chicago years, but the connection made then would later change Lucy's life.

Alice Palmer was one of two women whose achievements were to stay with Lucy throughout her life as touchstones of value. The other was Jane Addams, the Chicago pioneer of the settlement movement, whom Lucy had known since her early teens.

Jane Addams had opened the Hull House settlement in September

1889 in an old mansion on South Halsted Street in Chicago's Nine-teenth Ward, a diverse, working-class, immigrant district. Attracting college-educated women and some men as full-time residents, she estab-lished some forty clubs and activities at the settlement, including a day nursery, gymnasium, playground, dispensary, cooking and sewing courses and a cooperative boarding house for working girls. Within a few years, Hull House residents had become active on the municipal and state lev-els, helping to establish Chicago's first juvenile court, the state's first fac-tory inspection law, and numerous other reforms. A versatile lecturer and writer as well as political activist, by the late 1890s Jane Addams was widely thought of as the conscience of the nation.[22]

Lucy had come to regard Jane Addams and her work as a model of ded-icated social service. With her parent's encouragement, she had often visited Hull House and heard Addams talk about her efforts on behalf of the neighborhood's poor families. Otho, who had always recognized a duty to "uplift" the poor, admired Jane Addams' settlement work and gave Hull House financial and moral support during its early years. Ac-cording to Lucy, he was a "professional patron," more gentle to "erring or suffering humanity" than "his erring or suffering family."[23]

In 1894, an event occurred that caused Otho to alter his opinion of Jane Addams, and dramatically increased Lucy's sense of dissaffection from her family. Chicago was experiencing a new wave of labor unrest. In 1893, the city had been hard-hit by financial panic and depression. Thousands of workers were put out of their jobs, while wealthy business-men suffered severe losses. Lucy remembered the somber talks her par-ents held behind closed doors in their bedroom, talks from which Lucia emerged red-eyed and grief-stricken, Otho with "forbidding grimness." In the summer of 1894, workers at George Pullman's company town outside Chicago went on strike against newly instituted wage cuts. A national railway strike resulted, under the auspices of the American Railway Union, headed by Eugene V. Debs. "The excitement is intense," Nan Sprague wrote in her diary. "The city is in an awful way. Mobs are de-stroying property everywhere, burning cars, tearing up tracks, pulling down telegraph poles. The police [are] unable to handle them. Stock-yards are in the hands of mobs. Working people are crazy."[24] The strike was broken when President Cleveland sent in federal troops after several weeks to restore order.

Otho Sprague, a friend of Mr. Pullman and a member of the compa-ny's board of directors, sympathized wholeheartedly with management.

When teamsters at Sprague Warner went on strike in support of the rail-way workers, Albert and Otho insisted they return to work or consider themselves discharged. All but two stayed out.[25] Lucy, then sixteen, sympathized with the strikers, following the example of Jane Addams. But Otho, seething with "righteous indignation," disavowed Addams' public support of the Pullman workers and their right to strike. George Pullman was defending free enterprise, the foundation of democracy: it was a question of what was good for the country. Jane Addams, whom he had previously considered a "gracious, cultured lady," had stepped out of her place. The fact that she was a woman made him doubly indignant. "A woman cannot understand these business affairs and she should not interfere," he insisted. Lucy was convinced that Addams was right and her father wrong. Mr. Pullman stood for iniquity, the workers for a cause that was noble and just. "In a sudden flash," Lucy wrote, "I saw my father in a new light. . . . I grasped the appalling truth that Father's own busi-ness interests dominated his attitude toward people: he judged people by the amount of money they had."[26]

As a child, Lucy "had thought of the world as made up of good people and bad people, and we, of course, belonged to the good people."[27] She claimed that she never realized that her family was rich until the move to Prairie Avenue. Yet when Lucy was eight, she had been aware of the Haymarket Riot, an event that stood firmly etched in her memory and must have given her important clues to her family's place on the social spectrum. On May 4, 1886, at Haymarket Square, during a meeting called by "foreign-born anarchists" to protest the killing of a striker at the McCormick Harvester Company, a bomb thrown into the assembled crowd killed seven policemen who had been called in to break up the meeting and injured many others. Seven anarchists were condemned to death—many citizens felt unjustly—and eventually four were executed.

Lucy remembered Haymarket as the one time her mother disagreed sharply with her father. Both parents felt that the anarchist leaders ac-cused of fomenting the riot were "wicked," but Lucia deplored capital punishment, while Otho urged the hangings in order to provide a neces-sary "lesson."

With the Haymarket riot came "the beginning of the sense of an in-tangible threat to my father and to all of us."[28] Haymarket induced in Otho and his friends a state of mind "little short of terror," Lucy recalled, a terror not only of riots and bombs but of a general strike on behalf of the eight-hour day. In the family's Prairie Avenue home years later, Otho installed two panic buttons marked "Fire" and "Mob," to summon the Fire and Police departments, respectively.

For Lucy, the 1894 Pullman Strike crystallized her understanding of her father's values. As a consequence, Lucy developed a "sense of shame and guilt at being rich" which never left her. "I felt I was a 'pampered darling' bound by my father's wealth to a world of people whose standards I could not accept. . . . My adolescent conflict of loyalties became acute."[29]

Jane Addams became for Lucy a symbol of the "real world—a world of work and people that I longed to reach but could not." She was a symbol, too, of a "human, non-money point of view." In later years Lucy continued to follow Addams' work carefully and "made every cause that she stood for my cause."[30] In 1920, the first presidential election in which women could vote, Lucy voted for the Socialist candidate, Eugene V. Debs, who had led the Pullman strike.

Lucy's differences with her family expressed themselves in terms of a "social" rather than an explicitly "family" conflict, as she later understood. In order to muster her own moral autonomy, she needed her loyalty to an admired figure like Jane Addams. While she did not openly challenge her father's attitudes or his rule within the family, the opposing views she held about the Pullman strike became a turning point in her development, a stage in the gradually dawning consciousness of herself as an individual apart from her family. "Probably I never again gave my father full credit for his many fine qualities," she later admitted.[31] She could no longer identify with the model of rectitude offered by Otho Sprague or with the privileged world of Chicago society. For alternative supports and an alternative vision, she would have to strike out on her own.

Dutiful Daughter

During 1893, the Sprague family suffered the first of a new series of crushing blows that would force Lucy into a situation of greater loneliness and constraint, and cut her off from the "wider world" she had begun to glimpse in Chicago.

At the start of the year, seventeen-year-old Nannie suddenly displayed symptoms of mental collapse while she was vacationing in Sierra Madre, California, with Aunt Amelia and her younger brother Otho. The beautiful Nannie, who, according to Lucy, had always been oversensitive, had been taken ill three years earlier, and grew stranger and more irritable, until the doctors pronounced her "irresponsible." Family records do not reveal the diagnosis. ("Insanity," Aunt Nan noted tersely in her diary.) She was sent briefly to a sanitarium, and apparently recovered. But after this second attack, hospitalization brought little improvement.[1]

At the beginning of August came a second shock. While Lucy and twelve-year-old Otho were on their way to join the family on vacation in Charlevoix, Michigan, Lucy realized that Otho had a very high fever. She found a hotel room and spent the night telling the frightened boy story after story to calm him until the arrival of her parents and a doctor. Otho had typhoid; and back in Chicago, meningitis declared itself as well. He died on August 18. Lucy grieved quietly for the loss of this brother whom she loved "better than anyone else."[2]

The death of young Otho, so soon after that of his brother Arnold, left their mother physically and mentally shaken. No doubt she reproached herself, for it was while they were away from her that each of the boys had fallen ill. With Nannie's further decline, Lucia's oppression grew worse. Unable to share her feelings with family members, she withdrew into herself, sometimes remaining silent for a week or longer.

Lucia also bore the brunt of her husband's alarm at the depression and financial panic that swept the country during the summer of 1893. "Otho in the depths over the fall in stocks!" wrote Nan Sprague in her diary. "Lucia sick and discouraged! She can't help the panic—but she has to suffer for it."[3] Dr. Billings, the family physician, counseled that Lucia and Otho should leave immediately for a stay in California.

The family had been in Sierra Madre, California, only a short time when in March, 1894, Otho suffered a terrible respiratory hemorrhage. A return to Chicago's bleak climate seemed out of the question. Otho was to live as an invalid in California for the remaining fifteen years of his life. Lucy now joined her parents in their exile. As Otho had actively dominated the Sprague household when the children were growing up, so his care and maintenance dominated Lucia's later years and Lucy's young womanhood.

By the end of June, 1894, Nannie seemed to be much improved. Lucia, on a trip to New England to see Albert at Harvard, visited Miss Porter's School for Girls in Farmington, Connecticut, and enrolled Nannie there. But in the fall, after school had been in session one week, the news came back that Nannie had "gone to pieces" again. Mary, who had brought Nannie east to Miss Porter's, now took to her own bed, shocked and frightened by her sister's latest breakdown. Aunt Amelia also came down with frequent, undefined mental attacks at this time, making her own contribution to the anxiety that swept through the Sprague family that fall. Nannie spent the following year with two resident nurses at her parents' Prairie Avenue home, taking her meals next door with Aunt Nan. For the remaining few years of her life, Lucia's mental condition corresponded to the rises and dips in her daughter's mental health.[4]

Early in 1895 came "a new and terrible anxiety," as Aunt Nan described it. Albert II, now in his sophomore year at Harvard, was forced to leave school because of illness and emotional difficulties. He moved in with his aunt and uncle for the next few months, but their relations became "strained and horrid"; he was bloated and subject to fainting spells, and Lucy suspected that drinking was the cause of his problems. The Palmers, then in Chicago, were consulted; George Herbert Palmer was Albert's reader at Harvard and Alice Freeman Palmer remained an intimate family friend. It was several months before Albert could return to Harvard.[5]

Albert's wildness and hostility deepened the anxiety of the already apprehensive Spragues. His visits to Sierra Madre increased the tensions between Otho and Lucia. Albert admired his father greatly and reacted strongly to his disapproval; Lucia tried to shield Albert from Otho's wrath. Lucy admired Albert's wit and talent for mimicry; but she had never been fond of him, and as an adolescent, she thought his teasing was "gross" and "diabolical." One of his tricks was to gather bunches of petunias, geraniums and nasturtiums and put them in Lucy's room. If she was not feeling well, the harsh combination of colors was enough to nauseate her.

Oppressed by the troubles of Nannie, Albert, and Otho, Lucia daily grew more unhappy. "I watched my mother become hopeless and withdrawn," Lucy recalled. "I resented this . . . as I think my mother did, as a cruel but inevitable result of marriage."[6] ("Poor Lucia!" Nan wrote in her diary. "*Her* trouble certainly is not imaginary."[7]) Only when she was singing in the town's choir of invalids did her mood lighten. To make matters worse, Otho refused to allow her to bring her favorite furnishings from Chicago, calling such a move wildly extravagant. With Lucy's help, Lucia would continually shift furniture around the hideous house, trying to make it more comfortable. Lucy thought her own talent for arranging rooms stemmed from those unhappy days.

Lucy's own health was delicate; yet, as the least impaired member of the California household, she became primary caretaker of the physical and emotional well-being of her parents. Her competence in this role was itself a source of self-esteem and eventually of self-determination. But the catastrophic atmosphere at Sierra Madre deepened her emotional withdrawal; she had to repress her feelings of anger against those who needed her help. She hid her hostility even from herself, and instead felt guilty at her own relative well-being. Behind these feelings may have lain the fear that her own mental stability was precarious, for, like Nannie, Lucy had a nervous temperament and had always broken down when sent to school.

We know little of Lucy's actual responses except from the accounts in her memoirs, written during her old age. There she systematically portrays herself as a tireless, silently suffering martyr to family demands. Alone of all the Sprague children, she cares for her parents and gives up the companionship of peers and friendly relatives. Self-pity, resentment, and guilt are there but are only half acknowledged. "As father said," she recalled with bitter irony, "it was lucky that Lucy cared more for good books than people anyway and that she was already a good nurse."[8]

In *Two Lives*, Lucy wrote that she spent a full year in Sierra Madre nursing her family. "I was left alone in a strange land to care for a father in a virulent stage of tuberculosis and a mother in a deep depression."[9] Nan Sprague's diary indicates that actually Lucy, accompanied by her sister Mary, joined her parents in California in April, 1894, one month after Otho's severe hemorrhage, and that she began attending school away from home the following fall. Thus she spent less than six months nursing her parents, during which time Mary was sometimes present, though she seems not to have been pressed into service as nurse. This exaggeration of both the duration and the isolation of her servitude in California confirms that, as she acknowledged, her memories of that period were unusually "jumbled," saturated as they were with "confused emotions," "inner conflict," and self-pity.[10]

Even so, Lucy's version of the California years reflects the real pain and loneliness of her exile. Neither the climate nor the pristine loveliness of Sierra Madre appealed to her at first. Sierra Madre was Southern California's most famous and probably most beautiful health resort. Like the neighboring communities of Pasadena, Palm Springs, Riverside, and Altadena, this foothill settlement, with its magnificent panoramic views, was founded by health seekers who began migrating to the region in 1870. Most of them suffered from pulmonary and respiratory ailments, particularly tuberculosis. By the time the Spragues came to Sierra Madre, in 1894, it was estimated that at least one quarter of the two thousand permanent residents of the town were invalids. Almost all the rest were their relations, physicians, and other service personnel.[11]

For Otho, if not for his wife and daughter, the years in Southern California brought their own pleasures. New Englanders searching for sunshine and equable temperatures usually made Santa Barbara their resort; but most Chicagoans chose Sierra Madre and nearby Pasadena, where a migrant elite of wealthy and distinguished citizens quickly reestablished Chicago lifestyles. Along Pasadena's main streets, mansions had sprung up, duplicating in California style the exclusivity of Prairie Avenue. Otho and Lucia lived more modestly in a rented hillside house in Sierra Madre, but Otho had many old friends and acquaintances within reach, and there were dinner parties, musicales, and the usual society entertainments.

For Lucy, however, there were no friends and few pleasures. At home, there were only her parents and cousin Eleanor Atwood, fourteen years her senior. Otho Sprague had asked Eleanor, Lucia's niece, to share the benefits of Sierra Madre after she too developed a severe case of tuberculosis. Eleanor was a trained stenographer and Otho hoped that she could also help him take care of his affairs. Lucy grudgingly conceded that Eleanor did in fact bring something like "youth" into the household, with her constant gossip about family, friends, neighbors, and especially herself. Otho became the center of Eleanor's life and he enjoyed her attention. Everyone seemed to be extremely fond of this cousin, Lucy wrote, yet she declared that she could not remember a single interesting thing Eleanor had ever said. Eleanor had in fact begun to displace both Lucy and her mother in her father's emotional life, and Lucy's resentment is apparent. It was Lucy who performed tedious, hazardous nursing tasks for her father and Eleanor; it was Eleanor who shared Otho's deepest concerns and companionship during the long years of his illness.

After a few months, Lucy's life in Sierra Madre had become so circumscribed by the regimen of the invalids that even Lucia, withdrawn and unhappy herself, felt that Lucy must be removed from her custodial duties. As Lucy described it:

The household revolved around Father's schedule, which was kept to the minute. The first decision of the day depended upon the temperature. . . . The temperature decided which of three weights of underwear was to be worn. After breakfast, Father and Eleanor took up their positions in the sunshine of the porch. Then Mother and I made up the beds. . . . Then I began to empty the cuspidors. Every room except mine had at least one cuspidor partly filled with water for the use of both Father and Eleanor. I knew cleaning the cuspidors was dangerous work, for no maid was ever allowed to touch one. Father was scrupulous about protecting anyone in his employ. I half resented this job, but who else was there? I thought. It was an unpleasant job, too, and I often sent my breakfast down the toilet as a finish.

After breakfast, Lucy read aloud to her father until it was time for the patients' kumiss—a fermented drink made with milk, egg, and vegetables and kept in a hillside cellar. If the kumiss wasn't made correctly, it fermented furiously and splattered everything with a white liquid. A further hazard was involved: "Father wanted his kumiss at the appointed time," Lucy remembered. If she were late, "he never reproved me in words. Just took out his big watch that struck the hour, then quarters and remaining minutes and looked at it with a patient smile."[12]

Though Lucy loved books, reading to Otho was onerous; it could occupy as much as seven hours daily. Otho saw in his invalidism the opportunity to acquire the education he had missed. Dr. Abbot, minister of the local Congregational church, joined Otho and Lucy in a self-designed program of readings in philosophy, and the trio met weekly to discuss the thought of Greece, the Middle Ages, and eventually Descartes, Spinoza, Hume, Locke, and Kant. So heavy was the diet, Lucy recalled, and so strictly did they adhere to it that only on one occasion could she remember their taking an afternoon off to enjoy Browning's "Saul" as a lighter interlude. Otho would sometimes fall asleep as Lucy read, but if she stopped or changed the book he would awaken. Finally, she just read aloud as he dozed and told him about the book's content afterward.

Housework itself was not heavy, as Mary Carlson, the Sprague's longtime servant, had accompanied them to California with her husband, who took care of the garden and animals, and their young son. Mary Carlson shared the cooking with Lucy, who found the preparation of meals a welcome relief from more demanding nursing chores; she had rarely cooked before. Mary's special usefulness was in helping to stimulate Lucia, whom she loved and understood, Lucy thought, probably better than the family did. Mary was always running in to ask Lucia's advice about her own son or to take her to see new flowers and beautiful scenery. She understood that Lucia's passivity and silence came from too great an absorption in herself and her family, and she tried to awaken Lucia's interest in the world about her. Eventually Lucia did recover some semblance of her former self, though she continued to fall into protracted silence. Though Lucy accepted her father's preoccupation with his own health, she resented the fact that Lucia's suffering occupied so little of his attention. Lucia remained a devoted, if silent, wife; she slept next to her often violently ill husband for the remainder of her life.

While Lucy resented her own role as family nurse, her complete subordination to the needs of others seemed inevitable at the time. Otho hoped "the Lord would not lay the cross upon him of giving his dear Lucy his disease," Eleanor reported to her, but he steadfastly refused to hire a nurse.[13]

Everyone took it for granted that my job at fifteen was to stay home and take care of my parents even though I was far from strong and exposed to tuberculosis. . . . Father always said he did not need a nurse and he never did have one in his 17 years of invalidism. He said I could do all [that] was required. I accepted this as the course for a dutiful daughter. I simply did my job.[14]

Like her mother, she hid her most urgent feelings. There was no one outside the family circle, in fact, to whom she might have confided her emotional turmoil. Lucy doubted that she spoke to anyone less than twice her age during her first months in California.

"I was lonely except when I was alone," Lucy wrote of that difficult period. When she could, she escaped to the mountains—her "friends in a friendless land." In the majesty of the Sierras, she forgot her responsibilities and, for the moment, found tranquillity.

I loved the way the valley grew bigger and bigger the higher I climbed. I felt myself extending as my vision grew. Sometimes the grass was tawny, sometimes bright green with great splotches of yellow mustard and orange California poppies. Always it was beautiful; always it stretched out one's thoughts. For over the Santa Ana hills lay the Pacific and over the Pacific lay China. The Atlantic never teased my imagination as the Pacific did. . . . What did I think about? Nothing. That is what so rested me. I stopped my eternal thinking. I just climbed or sat in the sun and absorbed.[15]

This was a different kind of escape from the passionate denials of her Christian Science days, for "it was neither negation nor acceptance. It was just blessed stillness." But her peace of mind was only temporary.

I never stayed away long and the nearer I came to our house the more the sense of guilt engulfed me. What was Mother doing? Or was she just doing nothing? Had Father missed his reading aloud?. . . . I reached home in a frenzy of worry. Father smiled his sweet, patient smile and asked if I had had a good walk. And Eleanor would repeat in full what Father had said to John Carlson when he came over and what Father had answered and what she then said, and what Father and she had said after John left.[16]

And so Lucy spent this first season in Southern California, full of feelings of guilt and resentment, unable to turn for sympathy or support to her fragile mother, her self-involved yet still commanding father, or her agreeable, emptyheaded cousin. Only in a dream, one that was to recur throughout her life, could she express her misery.

I think it was in this year that the old white horse first came to me. . . . He wasn't even a memory of any flesh and blood horse so far as I know, though he looked a little like Dürer's Great Horse. But the Great Horse stands sleek and fat in his stable, and my poor old white horse looked as if no one had ever loved him. He was always climbing a hill. He was always tired, with drooping head and stumbling feet. He was always dirty, with long matted mane and tail and great yellow stains on his shaggy hair. Behind him moved a dim figure with a pitchfork. Whenever the old horse faltered, this pitchfork pricked his hind quarters and the old horse jerked forward at a faster pace.[17]

Lucy came to recognize the recurrent dream of the tired white horse and his tormentor as a barometer of fatigue. In later years, she acknowledged that the old horse might also have symbolized her suppressed self-pity. But at the time, she was not ready to recognize such feelings. "I had not yet evolved standards of my own," she recalled. "I accepted the standards of the time that daughters belonged to their families."[18]

The Marlborough School, established by Mary S. Caswell in 1889, is the oldest independent school for girls in Southern California.[19] Mrs. Caswell had been a high school teacher, author of *Letters to Hetty Heedless*, a textbook of deportment and behavior, and headmistress of an academy for girls in her native Maine, before she moved West with her seven-year-old daughter and orphaned niece in 1888. The widowed Mrs. Caswell opened the St. Margaret's School in Pasadena, which became the Marlborough School for Girls when it was relocated at the Marlborough Hotel in Los Angeles.

Long before the cause of women's education became popular, Mary Caswell championed intellectual excellence for women. At the same time she made it clear to her girls that their education, and the use to which they put it, would necessarily be different from that of men. Girls were to be trained as cultured, capable, and efficient daughters and wives-to-be, not as independent women. Nevertheless, the Marlborough School offered Lucy Sprague an escape from her life as dutiful daughter.

It was her mother, Lucy thought, who engineered her entry into Marlborough, though neither parent discussed the possibility with her. Her father, much stronger by this time, raised no objections: Eleanor could take over some of Lucy's duties, like the preparation of the mid-morning kumiss. But Lucy was filled with guilt at leaving the invalids, guilt which she "crushed down," she wrote, by remembering that she would be home on weekends and would "slave" for the family during those days and nights. Despite her guilt and "the veritable panic" she felt about attending a boarding school, Lucy was grateful and relieved at the opportunity before her. School, which had always been associated with "my nervousness, my failures, my extreme shyness, my devastatingly lonely reading," appeared now as a doorway to liberation, a crucial route to a new identity and new relationships outside the home. "I wanted desperately to go," Lucy wrote. "I wanted to get an education. I wanted young companionship. I wanted to live a normal life. And, yes, I wanted to escape from the burdens of home."[20] Perhaps the examples of Nannie's breakdown and her mother's now chronic depression frightened her into realizing that an escape from the family environment was imperative. This time, at any event, she was determined to succeed at school.

For the next two years, her sixteenth and seventeenth, Lucy boarded at the Marlborough School. Life there was "one long exciting adventure" to her. She appreciated the quality and encouragement of her teachers, who responded in kind to her enthusiasm, and she found the atmosphere of the school "freeing"; the many restrictions which bothered other students were less exacting than Lucy's family rules. A typical day at Marlborough began with prayers at half-past eight, followed by roll call, calisthenics, and then classes. After the afternoon events, students dressed for dinner, sitting in assigned places which changed every two weeks. After dinner, the girls sewed while Mrs. Caswell read to them from the classics. At half-past eight they changed to black bloomers and sweaters and worked in the gymnasium lifting weights and doing exercises.

Using Mrs. Caswell's victoria, students were required to make calls twice a month, invariably in white gloves. Attendance at theater and concerts was encouraged: Mrs. Caswell would always leave out food for students who had missed dinner to attend evening performances. On Monday and Thursday afternoons, there were special teas to which friends could be invited. And on Wednesday afternoons, Mrs. Caswell met with students to set forth her critique of their manners. Appearances, deportment, grammar and diction were scrutinized, and all manner of weaknesses noted. With Mrs. Caswell looking on, students practiced writing business letters, social invitations, and other correspondence. The relentless headmistress also quizzed them in mental arithmetic and listened to their recitations of poetry. Only after a student had achieved acceptable alertness, poise, and self-assurance at these "mind training" sessions, as one of them called Mrs. Caswell's Wednesday hours, could she graduate.[21]

The formal curriculum studied by Marlborough girls was one common to preparatory schools in the late nineteenth century: literature, composition, mathematics, history, geography, art history, language (French,

German, Latin, or Greek), Bible, and science (nature work, manual training, or physics). An unusual feature of the school was the availability of elective courses in bookkeeping and practical mathematics.[22] Generally, the curriculum was not seen as preparatory to college. With the exception of Lucy Sprague and perhaps one other girl, no Marlborough students graduating before 1904 went on to an institution of higher learning.

To her students, Mary Caswell was a powerful and inspirational force, admired for her stimulating teaching, her sense of humor, her combination of firmness and feminine warmth. Her aim, she told the girls, was to promote an active, cultured, intellectual center in each student, to spark passionate interests in each. Former students stressed the thoroughness of the training she provided, her emphasis on excellent scholarship, the freedom of mind and spirit that she attempted to pass on to her girls. Years later Lucy Sprague Mitchell described her vividly:

Mrs. Caswell, the head of the school, was terrifying yet lovable. She was very small and thin to the point of emaciation. From a face so white that it was almost luminous, looked out enormous eyes, and her thin gray hair was brushed back over an appallingly high forehead. Her trick of holding her arms crossed in front of her, each hand grasping the opposite elbow, gave an impression that she was hanging on to herself—and perhaps she was, for she was capable of explosions of temper. Her large, almost passionate mouth was in strange variance with the almost ascetic quality of the rest of her face. She spoke crisply and to the point. Everything she did and said indicated her high standards. No one would expect many concessions from Mrs. Caswell.[23]

Lucy, an adolescent struggling with competing claims, needed maternal support and example more than ever—and she saw Lucia as less than ever able to supply it. Mrs. Caswell quickly became very important to her as a teacher and role model. Lucy learned from her a vital lesson: how to appreciate herself as an individual outside her family circle.

At sixteen, however, Lucy could not completely reject her role as "dutiful daughter." From Monday to Friday she basked in the stimulation of Marlborough classes, her new circle of friends, and Mrs. Caswell. On weekends, she returned to the gloom of the Sprague household, each time resuming her place as nurse amid the circle of invalids.

I led two completely separate lives in which I was entirely different personalities. When I rode down our hill on my bicycle to take the early Monday morning train, I simply shed the family. I became a schoolgirl, absorbed in studies, in

girls, in Los Angeles, until I picked up my bicycle Friday afternoon and pumped
up the hill. Then I shed the school and became a daughter and a nurse. There
was almost no cross-referencing between my two lives, and I seldom thought of
the life I was not living at the moment.[24]

One of the most important factors in Lucy's ability to "shed" her family
and create an alternative identity was her discovery of friendship. At
Marlborough, for the first time in her life, she formed deep and loving relationships with girls of her own age. Particularly important to her were
Georgia Knight, Mrs. Caswell's niece, a brilliant, exotic young woman
"full of romance and Kipling"; Georgia Caswell, Mrs. Caswell's daughter
and administrative assistant, an outwardly serious young girl though inwardly light-hearted and eager (it was she who owned the monkeys that
frolicked on the Marlborough lawn), and above all Marion Jones, Lucy's
roommate and closest friend, daughter of the powerful senator from Nevada, John Paul Jones. Georgia Caswell, Marion and Lucy, all in the
junior class, became an inner clique at the school, joined sometimes by
Georgia Knight from the class above. In their senior year, Lucy, Marion,
Georgia Caswell, and a fourth, Harmon Spruance, constituted the staff
of *Geppo*, the school's literary magazine.

In *Two Lives*, Lucy Mitchell spent many more paragraphs describing
Marion than she did discussing the Marlborough School. Neither of the
girls had ever before attended school on a regular basis. They formed an
immediate bond that provided each with sympathy, support, and confidence. Lucy had never met anyone like Marion before. "It is hard to describe Marion without making her seem outrageous," she wrote years
later. "She was so brilliant, so talented, so intense, so full of good impulses and passionate suffering, that one always felt more impelled to
protect than to reprove her no matter what inconveniences she caused—
and she caused many."[25]

Marion was born in Nevada, where her wealthy father, who had come
West during the California gold rush of 1849, owned vast silver mines.
Because Marion suffered from heart trouble as a child, the family moved
to Santa Monica, California, where three generations of relatives lived
in a grand seaside mansion. Marion's family, fearing for her health, never
subjected her to discipline of any kind. When Lucy visited the Joneses,
she marvelled that her friend could indulge in so many temperamental
outbursts without any reproof or restraint from her elders. By the time
Marion came to Marlborough, her health problems had long since disap-

peared. She had spent many years riding horseback and playing tennis and, though of slight build, was an outstanding athlete. Several years later, she became the women's tennis champion of California.[26]

Marion provided Lucy's first introduction to the life of unrestrained, impulsive expression. Her uninhibited appreciation of music, art, and beauty astonished Lucy, whose upbringing had systematically quashed just such passionate responses. "She was full of true imagination and creativeness. Nothing seemed slight to Marion. She lived with terrifying intensity. Indeed, life for Marion was a chronic crisis."

The differences between the two only strengthened their alliance. For Marion, Lucy served as an anchor. Lucy helped Marion deal with a nervous tension so extreme that she needed two hands to steady any cup or glass she held. "In practical ways, I took her over," Lucy recalled. "I picked up the room, saw that she got her lessons and kept her appointments. . . . It was [Marion] who wept and I who comforted. It was [Marion] who told her troubles and I who listened."

For Lucy, Marion was not only an adoring, dependent, friend but a constant source of stimulation, a beacon to a life more fully lived than Lucy had known before. "When she played the violin or sang," Lucy recollected, "she was transported to the point where it was hard for her to get back to the ordinary world around her." Yet under Marion's influence Lucy learned that art was not simply to be equated with spontaneous expression; it had intellectual content.

Music, painting, sculpture became techniques to be studied and analyzed, not merely emotional escapes. Emotion itself became respectable, a power to create, not something you tried to get rid of so you could endure life. An artist climbed in my estimation to the rank of a thinker. This was new and exciting.[27]

Lucy recalled in later years that Pablo Casals once told her he would rather have Marion's criticism of his playing than anyone else's. But she felt in retrospect that Marion never exploited her extraordinary talents to the full.

The lessons of Lucy's childhood—duty, obedience, restraint—were quite the opposite of Marion's. But Lucy's own appreciation of color, her sensitivity to music, poetry, and song, were integral to her personality. "[Marion] gave me something I did not have and for which I was starved. . . . Though one paid a high price to be [Marion's] friend, it was worth the price."[28] Marion's friendship helped Lucy to begin to become acquainted with the artist in herself.

All of the Spragues returned to Chicago in the summer of 1895, where they stayed until October to attend Mary's wedding. About the time of her twentieth birthday, Mary, who was a popular Chicago debutante, had attracted the attentions of Adolph Miller, an economist who had trained at the University of California, taught briefly at Harvard, and was now an associate professor at the new University of Chicago. Adolph visited Mary and her parents in Sierra Madre during the summer of 1894 and when she returned to Chicago that fall he proposed marriage. The family was surprised that she accepted him; they thought the charming, gay young girl hardly compatible with the stiff, though stylish, professor. ("How little we can judge" wrote Nan in her diary.)[29] Yet the two seemed happy and very much in love.

Otho, much improved in health, had been given leave by his doctors to spend several months away from California, and Lucia, delighted to be reopening her beloved Prairie Avenue home for the wedding, recovered some of her gaiety. Preparing a trousseau for Mary, shopping for other members of the bridal party, and arranging for the wedding itself, she was in her element. Nannie, seemingly recovered from her terrible nervous collapse, had rejoined the family, and she and Lucy were bridesmaids, descending the long staircase of their home side by side. In their matching low-necked pink brocade gowns, Aunt Nan noted, the two were visions of extraordinary loveliness. "Nancy was radiantly beautiful," Lucy recalled, "more beautiful than anyone else I ever have seen."[30] Although she thought of herself as awkward compared with Nannie, in fact Lucy was becoming a very appealing and poised young woman, who would later know how to deploy her femininity to good effect.

After the wedding, Mary and Adolph Miller went abroad for a year, and Lucy, Nannie, and their parents returned to Sierra Madre. It was decided that Nannie, who had borne the excitement of the summer and the fall wedding so superbly, would attend the Marlborough School with her sister. She was to room with Lucy, who asserted magnanimously in her memoirs that she wouldn't have had it any other way; but Lucy also insisted that Marion Jones remain as her roommate. During her senior year, Lucy found herself trying to help them both—the "brilliant, self-centered" Marion, and "frightened, ambitious" Nannie. By winter, Nannie broke down again. Otho wanted her sent back to an institution; but Lucia argued that with nursing help she could be kept at home. The outcome this time was a compromise: a cottage was rented for Nannie at La Jolla with one of the devoted nurses who had cared for her in Chicago. But Lucia, who had rallied while Nannie was at home, sank into an even deeper depression. The family thought Lucy should continue at Marlborough since she was to graduate in the spring. Then, they said, she could come home "for good."[31]

It was at this point that Lucy rebelled. Strengthened by the experiences of the previous two years, she determined to fight the destiny that awaited her in Sierra Madre. "I was seventeen and much older than at fifteen," she recalled. "I had felt caught before but now I felt rebellious. I wrote Mary one of the most important letters of my life. I wrote that it seemed to me I should die if I had to go back to a permanent life in Sierra Madre. I wanted to go to college. But how could I leave Father and Mother? I wrote and wrote and mailed the letter to Paris."[32]

Fortunately, Lucy's letter reached Mary while Alice and George Palmer were visiting the Millers in Paris. Mary read Lucy's despairing letter to them and Alice Palmer responded immediately. Thus, Lucy received two letters in response. Mary's was sympathetic but disappointing. "Whatever I did, she would understand." Lucy wept with disappointment. "I didn't want sympathy. I wanted help."[33] Mary, the favored oldest child, now an independent matron, had been Lucy's "one hope." But unexpected help was forthcoming in the letter from Alice Freeman Palmer. Alice had been in Chicago at times when both Albert and Nannie had suffered nervous collapses and knew the family's problems. Now she wrote Lucy's parents to assure them that in college under her supervision, Lucy would not break down as Nannie and Albert had. She could enter Radcliffe as a "special" student, if need be, without a full course program that might overtax her energies. And she could live in Cambridge with the Palmers. Lucy wept for a second time, but with relief.

"That letter changed my life," Lucy recollected. "The decision was put up to me. And it was an agonizing decision to make. I took my life in my hands and said I wanted to go. Mother was glad. Father did not oppose my decision, though Eleanor kept telling me how sad it made him and how brave he was."[34]

To prepare for Radcliffe's entrance examinations (the same as Harvard's: no substitutions allowed), Lucy took special courses in physics at the University of Southern California (Marlborough had no laboratory of its own) and joined Georgia Caswell, then also preparing for college, in studying Latin. Despite her cramming sessions with Georgia and further study of Virgil and Cicero at home over the summer, she did not pass the entrance exam in advanced Latin. She was accepted at Radcliffe, with the condition that she "work off" the Latin in college.

After Lucy had taken her entrance exams at a school in San Francisco, she and a Marlborough teacher spent some time in Alaska, where they enjoyed exploring its mountain wildernesses, majestic glaciers, and Indian camps. Home again, Lucy, "delirious with happiness," prepared to leave for college. Of her family's reaction, she says in *Two Lives* only that "I hardened my heart to Father's patient smiles . . . and was frightened at its hardness while Mother and I made my new college dresses."[35] In her unpublished memoirs, however, Lucy was more explicit, admitting that her father had strongly opposed her desire to attend college. Elizabeth Coolidge Winship, a granddaughter of Lucy's cousin Elizabeth Sprague Coolidge, remembers "Aunt Lucy" telling the family that it was Otho's remark, "Oh, what a shame it is that a beautiful girl like you has to be looking after an old man like me," that finally made her angry enough to defy Otho's wishes.[36]

Lucy's insistence on leaving home in the face of her father's disapproval was indeed an act of self-determination and rebellion. "Rich girls were sent to 'finishing school'," she recalled, while a "girl who wanted to go to college [was] looked upon as a little queer . . . unfeminine . . . 'stuck up.'"[37] Her own insistence on going to college sprang from long overdue frustration at her role within the Sprague household, the new sense of her own possibilities that had been nurtured at Marlborough, and from the support of her mother, Mrs. Caswell, and Alice Freeman Palmer. Without the all-important alliance with Mrs. Palmer, Lucy could not have turned her back on Otho's pressures.

A hint of the gravity of her defiance is given in her account of her anxieties as she prepared to leave California.

Had not Browning preached the right of each person to live his own life? Over and over, I defiantly quoted Matthew Arnold's "Self-Dependence" to myself. I, too, sought the calm content of that questioner of the stars who stood "at the vessel's prow" and asked whence came their serenity. I, too, listened to the voice that replied:

Wouldst thou *be* as these are? *Live* as they. . . .
In their own tasks all their powers pouring,
These attain the mighty life you see.[38]

Excited yet apprehensive about the possibilities before her, Lucy sought the reassurance of classical authority as she dreamed of the "mighty life" that beckoned to her beyond the family circle; she legitimated her break with Otho using ideas from the shelves of his own library.

4

Meaning and
Meaninglessness:
Education at
Radcliffe College

In the fall of 1896, with a nervous excitement bordering on "panic," and a "sickly feeling that college was going to be [even] worse than the entrance exams," Lucy and the class of 1900 entered Radcliffe. "We did not know where we were, nor who we were," she recalled. "We knew we were miserable and that was all."[1]

Higher education for women was still in an experimental stage when Lucy began college. While secondary education at seminaries and normal schools had been available to women since the early nineteenth century, the idea of advanced education for women, expressly modelled after the higher standards of college education for men, was not realized in the United States until the 1870s and 1880s. The opening of Vassar College in 1865 heralded the new era. Vassar's endowment was considerably higher than those of existing female colleges, and its standards for admission and academic programs were comparable with those of men's colleges. Smith College and Wellesley, founded in 1875, as well as the later colleges for women, including Bryn Mawr (1885) and Mt. Holyoke (1888), also offered courses of study closely paralleling those of male colleges.[2] After years of agitation by leading Boston citizens to secure for women the benefits of a Harvard education, the Society for the Collegiate Instruction of Women, known as the Harvard Annex, was established in 1879. For the next fifteen years, Annex students were given ac-

cess to Harvard teaching in small, informal—but always separate—
classes. Their success led to the University Corporation's decision in
1894 to grant the Bachelor's degree to qualified women under the auspices of Radcliffe College.[3]

Lucy's sense of peculiarity in beginning college was not just her own;
Radcliffe administrators still felt in 1896 that theirs was "a questionable
enterprise." At the start of Lucy's freshman year, Agnes Irwin, dean of
the college, called in the newly elected class president to ask her to use
her influence to see that girls did not walk down Garden Street with
their arms around each other. In her welcoming remarks to freshman
girls, she urged them, too, always to wear gloves when going to the
Square; such remarks were repeated annually. It would not do to risk the
college's emerging reputation by unseemly behavior.[4]

Impeccable respectability was essential for Radcliffe if the experiment
of permitting women the advantages of Harvard training was to succeed.
And from this point of view Agnes Irwin was the ideal dean. Elizabeth
Agassiz, long-time champion of women's higher education and a leader
of the forces to regularize Annex education, was president of Radcliffe,
but in Lucy's view, Agassiz administered the institution in name only:
her only functions were to provide the prestige of her name and to host
weekly teas for students.[5] It was Agnes Irwin who was the commanding
presence at Radcliffe, from the opening of the college until her retirement in 1909. A former headmistress at a fashionable girl's school in
Philadelphia, Irwin was a forceful leader—according to her biographer
and the estimates of most contemporaries—as "conservative as Philadelphia whence she came."[6] A more liberal-minded dean would have killed
Radcliffe in its infancy, argued Irwin's supporters, but her detractors believed that Irwin's cautious and rigid approach buried many promising
opportunities. An imposing figure with a marked physical resemblance to
her ancestor Benjamin Franklin, Irwin brought to her office high Victorian standards of behavior and a regard for discipline, spiritual and moral.
She was not popular with the majority of Radcliffe students who thought
her autocratic and narrow-minded.[7]

Lucy encountered the formidable Dean Irwin shortly after arriving in
Cambridge. No Radcliffe student was permitted to live in the same residence as a Harvard student. But the Palmers were determined that Lucy
should stay with them in their Quincy Street home, along with Mr.
Palmer's nephew Eric, a Harvard freshman. It was not easy for the dean
to make an exception to her rule. Though Irwin was an acquaintance

of Lucia Sprague and was reluctant to "oppose anyone whose income reached a level," according to Lucy, still the good reputation of the budding young college came first. Despite the influence of both Palmers in educational circles and their early support of Radcliffe, it took several visits before an agreement was reached. Eric and Lucy were to continue to live at the Palmers', but Lucy was never to walk home through Harvard Yard. For four years, she walked down Massachusetts Avenue and up Quincy Street to Number Eleven, where the Palmers' lovely old colonial house stood next door to President Eliot's. The first lesson of Lucy's Radcliffe education had been learned. Higher education for women was still a separate, insulated privilege, not a free participation in the fellowship of learning.

Lucy's classmate Lucy Fuller, whose family had allowed her to attend Radcliffe only after Mrs. Agassiz persuaded her grandmother "that it really couldn't do [the girl] any harm," later recalled that Radcliffe students were advised against going to Harvard Square as well as Harvard Yard. Fuller's two Harvard cousins endorsed this rule: "It was bad enough, they contended, to have the disgrace of a cousin at Radcliffe, without running the risk of meeting her on the street and being obliged to cut her."[8]

President Agassiz treated the girls as delicate creatures whose health and femininity needed careful protection. The bouillon she sent to their examinations so that they would not lack nourishment became a Radcliffe tradition.[9] Rules laid down by Dean Irwin reinforced the model of delicate femininity. Irwin strongly disapproved of athletics, since games and practice took the students away from their studies, made them liable to injury and strain, and, above all, got them into the public press, especially when they were victorious. So great was Irwin's hostility to sports that she refused to allow the captains of Radcliffe teams to attend meetings of other captains from women's colleges. Thus, although athletics fostered self-confidence and group spirit, the message women received from college authorities was that it was not quite right, not quite feminine, to pursue athletics too vigorously.

Lucy, five feet seven inches tall, was jumping center of the class basketball team. In her junior year, as chairman of the swimming pool committee, she raised money to fill the empty swimming tank in Radcliffe's new gymnasium, but almost got expelled for it. Evidently she made the mistake of approaching some regular benefactors of the college without first receiving permission from Dean Irwin. The Dean also objected to

Lucy's role in calling a mass meeting of students on the swimming pool issue. Lucy had suggested that students might raise some of the needed
funds by giving a play, but Irwin and the Radcliffe council were eager to
have proceedings on this subject kept out of the papers.[10] At length,
however, the swimming pool was filled. It quickly became popular: "We
got our pool—and something more, too," Lucy recalled. "In the first
week of our triumph, 40 swimmers got the measles." At commencement,
Harvard's president, Charles W. Eliot, mentioned the swimming pool
fund prominently in his brief remarks, thanking the graduating students
for having raised the $1500 needed to make the pool operational. "I wish
every college in the country had a swimming tank," he declared, "and I
am sure I wish Harvard had one." One member of the class observed fifty
years later, "Perhaps [that was] the only time on record that a president
of Harvard spoke wistfully, almost enviously, of Radcliffe!"[11]

Dramatic activity also aroused misgivings on the part of Radcliffe's
cautious administration. The Idler, created in 1884 to produce "dramatic
entertainments," was Radcliffe's first and most important club. The president of the Idler, Lucy recalled, was always the leader of the girls. Sixty
to seventy Radcliffe students enrolled each year, performing plays written
by classmates as well as those of more illustrious dramatists. Several student playwrights, among them Lucy's friends Mabel Daniels, '00, and
Josephine Sherwood, '99—later Josephine Hull—went on to successful
theater careers. Although narrow quarters made performances in the Fay
House auditorium difficult, the performers and the audience were enthusiastic. Originally, students playing men's roles wore gentlemanly trousers, but Dean Irwin soon insisted that they should conceal their lower
limbs in gymnasium bloomers. Furthermore, Lucy recalled, "we could
borrow coats only from men relatives." The first time a hero came on
stage brandishing her sword and wearing gym bloomers, Mary Coes, the
Secretary of the College and its future dean, cupped her head in her
hands and laughed so hard that she cried.[12]

Harvard professors, finally, treated Radcliffe students with a mixture of
respect, scorn and condescension. Some professors were unalterably opposed to the idea of Radcliffe, feeling that it could become a "vampire,
sucking the lifeblood of the university."[13] Others taught at Radcliffe to
earn extra income but had little commitment to the school. Even the
best of intentions did not always translate into nonprejudicial treatment.
Many professors treated the women with exaggerated consideration, as a
separate species. Lewis Edwards Gates, for example, who taught the re-

quired freshman English course, used to tell his Radcliffe students that "women are the lyrical interludes in man's strenuous existence."[14] The supercilious attitude of other instructors led one Annex student to comment that "ridicule is the Harvard theory."[15]

The rules established by Radcliffe officers, in combination with the daily humiliations inflicted on women students by male students and professors, suggested to Lucy Sprague that women were a distinct class, different from, and certainly less privileged than male students. Female students had always to be alert and watchful to avoid any suspicion of impropriety. Radcliffe's hidden curriculum demanded invisibility and constraint.

Some women students came to identify with the values of Harvard men, as less privileged groups often internalize the morality of those with greater power. Student correspondence and alumnae questionnaires indicate that the majority of Radcliffe women treasured the Harvard connection. The stimulation, the intellectual freedom, and the discipline of scholarship that their access to Harvard's faculty gave them could not have been obtained elsewhere, they believed. When, occasionally, a Radcliffe student protested against women's subordinate status, her classmates usually dissociated themselves. Students denied—or accepted— the message of second-class citizenship, and retained from their Radcliffe experience only those elements that seemed to them of value.

When asked to describe the benefits she had received from Radcliffe in her class fiftieth-anniversary report, Lucy listed three: "getting free" from the narrow world of her family; finding new intellectual interests; and gaining self-confidence, which she felt equipped her to take on new responsibilities after college.[16] Elsewhere she admitted that she had been less enthusiastic about Radcliffe than many of her classmates were, partly because she was unreconciled to women's subordinate status at Harvard. Yet she did derive considerable advantage from Radcliffe as a dynamic social and intellectual world. For a further understanding of her experience, however, we must take account of what she learned from Alice Freeman Palmer and George Herbert Palmer. The relative weightings of Lucy's "new world" in Cambridge were clear to her. "I studied at Radcliffe," she declared. "I lived with the Palmers."[17]

In Cambridge, with Alice Freeman Palmer, Lucy felt a "warm comfortable glow," a sense of belonging and acceptance. Lucy found Alice Palmer "even more enchanting, abler, more human" than her memories of her from Chicago days. Alice "loved life—her profession and her home." Though her schedule was crowded with visitors and lecture engagements, Alice talked with her many callers attentively and sympathetically, and always found time to spend with Lucy, or to go on a "spree," if one were suggested.[18]

In the affectionate biography he wrote of his wife, George Herbert Palmer speculated on the source of Alice's charm. "It was as good as a circus to be with her," Palmer wrote, "for something novel was always going on." At Wellesley, her spontaneity and naturalness created a "power of instantaneous command," which had motivated students and faculty. Her approach as an educator was highly personal; she offered concrete assistance and attention to each individual, in a style that she called "heart culture."[19] She learned the name of each of her more than three hundred students, for example, helped by up-to-date notes on the girls and their characteristics. George Palmer and many of Alice's closest associates argued that the secret of her achievements lay in the perfect synthesis of sharpness of mind and sweetness of womanhood. Her girl-like spontaneity and her "emotional ardor"—the qualities her husband cited as the key to her temperament—were matched by "clear intelligence," a pragmatic "attention to business," and a "sweet" and "judicious womanhood."[20]

In spite of her withdrawal from full-time work after her marriage, Alice Palmer's power within the field of education seemed to increase not only at Wellesley but throughout the nation. She remained the power behind the scenes at Wellesley, handpicking the institution's next three presidents and dominating Wellesley politics. She served as part-time Dean of Women at the University of Chicago and advised the presidents of Harvard, Brown, Stanford, Smith, Mt. Holyoke, Vassar, and other colleges. She was instrumental in placing women deans at Oberlin, Pembroke, and the Western College for Women in Ohio, among other places. Much of her energy went into securing the establishment of Radcliffe and she later worked behind the scenes to help strengthen Harvard's commitment to the college. She served as president of the Women's Educational Association, the Association of Collegiate Alumnae, the League for the Protection of Italian Immigrants, and the Women's Home Missionary Society, and as a member of the Massachusetts State Board of Education.

Thus, though Alice was a devoted wife who enjoyed the trappings of domesticity, by no means could it be said that her private life took center stage at the expense of her public commitments. George Palmer argued that the financial and emotional security of marriage gave Alice the opportunity to choose out of the myriad enterprises that beckoned her those that most appealed to her genuine interests. The lack of an official position as college president never detracted from her influence, he felt. Alice Palmer's buoyancy convinced her admirers that she was satisfied with her chosen path of domesticity and volunteer work. Nonetheless, in giving up an institutional presidency for voluntary work in women's education, she had lost symbolic, if not real, control of her destiny. Though her schedule was busy enough to fill the calendars of at least two full-time workers, her activities were part-time and usually unpaid. In the eyes of the outside world, it was George Palmer, and the institution of marriage, that prevailed. [21]

Alice's own view of her marriage is revealed in the poetry she wrote secretly in the last five years of her life. She left instructions to burn the poems after her death; but some years later George consulted Lucy about publication. Lucy urged him to respect Alice's wishes and her privacy; but George nevertheless edited and published forty-seven of them, under the title *A Marriage Cycle*. [22] No doubt he was eager to confirm how important to Alice their marriage had been. As a whole, the poems indeed testify to the strength of the bond between them. But in "Myself" and "Suffocation," for example, she acknowledges that in marriage, a woman's identity is tied inexorably to that of her husband, and writes of her unsatisfied need to be alone. [23]

Though Alice "adored her husband," Lucy felt that she was "by no means under his thumb." She used to help Alice dress for her speaking engagements in the severe clothes George selected for her. Often she would complain that she looked like a "mooly cow." It was the placidity of her forehead, Lucy thought, and her wavy hair that gave Alice this sense of herself. Still, "there was no mooly cow about her when she got into action," Lucy asserted. "When she got mad, her small chin seemed to grow into an aggressive jaw. Mr. Palmer used to say 'God made the upper part of Alice's face, but she is responsible for the lower half.'"[24]

In spite of Alice's outgoing manner and forthrightness, she was a "private person," Lucy felt, a woman of deep reserve and modesty. Here she differed from her husband, "the little Almighty," as his sister-in-law, Mary Palmer, called him. Lucy felt that for all his protestations of modesty, "Mr. Palmer thought everything he did was too important to keep to himself."

Neither George Palmer's physical presence nor his personality appealed much to Lucy. "There never was a homelier little person," she wrote in her unpublished autobiography. Palmer was very short, she wrote (probably about five feet two inches), "with extra long arms and a gray face from which sprouted gray tufts of gray hair and gray eyebrows and a great gray mustache. His mustache flowed over his mouth like a waterfall; his eyebrows hung over extremely shortsighted eyes." Palmer refused to wear glasses, though he couldn't recognize acquaintances on the street. "Sometimes I fancied he thought glasses would injure the effect of inscrutability," Lucy commented. "I think he could not have worn them without clipping some of his eyebrows. A barber did this once, and he was furious. Perhaps his weak eyes were responsible for his habit of looking down instead of at you, as he talked."[25]

Palmer had a number of pat phrases which he repeated for many years, and which Lucy continued to quote throughout her life, phrases like "the proof of the pudding is not in the eating; that comes several hours after," or "the extraordinary man is very unusual." When he uttered one of these sayings, Lucy recalled, "he pulled down his upper lip and lowered his eyes so that he seemed like an invisible oracle behind his curtain of hair."[26]

Yet Lucy was at ease with George Herbert Palmer and learned much from him. College presidents, faculty colleagues, and students streamed through his Quincy Street living room, consulting George on appointments and curricula. Palmer, like his wife, enjoyed the role of "the power behind the throne," Lucy recalled. "I presume Mr. Palmer's finger was in nearly every college pie in the country where there was a department of philosophy."[27]

Palmer's primary success as academic power-broker came within Harvard. His support of the elective system and of President Eliot's equally controversial new graduate program was an important ingredient in the successful modernization of Harvard education. But his greatest achievement lay in his dedicated, effective promotion of Harvard's philosophy department ("the best in the world," in Bertrand Russell's judgment). Palmer was appointed full professor in 1882, and served officially as chairman during the years 1891–94 and 1898–1900. To Palmer's appreciation of quality and diversity, his active nurturance of discussion

and debate, goes much of the credit for the assemblage of genius in the
Harvard philosophy department at this time. The department included
Josiah Royce, who became professor of philosophy in 1892; Hugo Munsterberg, who came to Harvard that year for a three-year trial stint to
help William James run the psychology laboratory, returning as professor
of psychology in 1897; William James, who switched back to his old title
as professor of philosophy when Munsterberg assumed the psychology
post; and George Santayana, who began teaching in the department in
1889. Palmer's ability to reconcile differences and his commitment to
treating all department members as equals, giving each a voice in decision-making (with the notable exception of tenure questions) succeeded
brilliantly. Though he was not considered a particularly original thinker,
his own course in "moral philosophy"—later called Ethics—was taken
by generations of Harvard students and became a model for philosophy
teaching throughout the United States.[28]

On a personal level, few found George Palmer inspiring. Reticent, un-
demonstrative, aloof but unfailingly courteous, "he had himself almost
too well in hand," was the judgment of a close colleague. "The tenor
of his life was almost too even. One wished that he might occasionally
just let himself go, might, at least once, get 'swearing mad,' like other
folk."[29] But such spontaneous outbursts rarely occurred. Palmer's life was
dominated by a "passion for order that seemed total, his will was always
on duty."[30] Yet Palmer was also an idealist and esthete, with a great sensitivity to art and beauty. Throughout his life, he delighted in poetry: he
edited the works of the seventeenth century British poet George Herbert,
for whom he was named, and made a translation of the *Odyssey*.

Lucy's memories of life at the Palmers centered on scenes of domestic
contentment of which she formed an integral part—the poetry readings
several times a week in George's book-lined study, Alice lying with feet
up on the sofa, Lucy on the floor in front of the fire, George reading
aloud from the works of Blake, Kipling, or Herbert; or the Palmers holding hands in their "Fairy Ring," a wooded spot near their country home
in Boxford, where their romance had flowered years before; or the three
of them "sandpapering the woods" to make a new path (one of which was
named Lucy Boulevard in honor of her woodsmanship), or all of them
playing dominoes on the sunny porch or swimming in the brook. "Everything seemed just right when we were at Boxford," Lucy asserted.[31]

When the Spragues visited her in Cambridge, they remarked on Lucy's
unusual well-being. In spite of a chronic cough that troubled her

throughout her Radcliffe years, she seemed ebullient, fully satisfied with
school life and her residence in Cambridge. Aunt Nan noted in her diary
how devoted the Palmers were to Lucy. Mrs. Palmer, who had always regretted her childlessness, had found an "only daughter."[32] Lucy had
found a warm and supportive environment, an atmosphere of intellectual
exchange and appreciation of art and literature. As she shared their daily
lives, she learned much about the world of higher education at first hand.
Alice Freeman Palmer became a powerful role model to her, illustrating a
unique, personal style of professional "heart culture." Moreover, Alice's
synthesis of marriage and career became an example for Lucy; she learned
from both its triumphs and its limitations.

Not least of all, at the Palmers Lucy found a respite from the closed,
authoritarian, sickness-ridden family life of the Spragues, where she had
never had her share of family attention. Life with the Palmers brought
her a sense of self-worth. "Expressed affection and approval by adults was
unknown to me before I met the Palmers," Lucy wrote. In her four years
at Quincy Street, "they became a part of me and I became a part of them.
I was still shy with strangers and to an extent with the girls at college.
But with the Palmers I was as free as anyone has a right to be—foolish or
thoughtful, talkative or silent, as I felt inclined. They lived a high intellectual life and a rich human life and they took me into both. I responded to both. I fairly sprouted."[33]

Because of her close relationship with the Palmers, Lucy Sprague's experience of Radcliffe was different from that of most of her classmates.
The first Radcliffe dormitories were not built until after the class of 1900
graduated, so that students lived at home or with other family members.
Seventy percent of Lucy's classmates came from Massachusetts. In fact,
Lucy was one of only three students in her class to come from the midwest or far west, and the only one from California, which made her
something of an exotic on campus. She started out as a special student, as
many Radcliffe girls did, taking fewer entrance exams than most, but
then transferred into the regular track in her sophomore year. At the
time of her graduation, about one-third of all Radcliffe students were
"specials."[34] Many of these were schoolteachers who came to Radcliffe
for advanced training. Lucy did not come to Radcliffe seeking means to a
future livelihood. Yet, in spite of the differences in regional background,
class, and living arrangements that set Lucy Sprague apart from her

classmates, she was well liked. Though Lucy saw herself as shy and reserved, additional sources round out the portrait and suggest that she ex-
hibited a greal deal more poise than is apparent in her own account. Her
classmates were quick to accept her and to acknowledge her special qualities. She was elected vice-president of her class during her freshman year,
a position she held throughout her college career except in her sophomore year, 1897–98, when she served as class president. She had numerous friends: in addition to her own classmates Lucy Fuller and Evelyn
Livermore, she joined several women from the class of '99 in an interclass club whose members corresponded for many years after they left
Radcliffe.[35]

But the "pride of Radcliffe," as Dean Irwin often remarked, was not its
social life but its "large and liberal opportunities to learn."[36] As class historian, Lucy playfully told the visitors at 1900's Class Day, "Ink has been
a more popular beverage with us than tea. We have used during our four
years 272 pints, or 34 gallons of ink. . . . We have, you see, been eager
for knowledge."[37]

The acquisition of knowledge as the object of a Radcliffe education
was impressed upon students from the outset. The corollary was that a
Radcliffe education was every bit as good as—and *almost* identical to—a
Harvard education. Like Harvard, which pioneered a free elective system, Radcliffe students could select all of their courses, except for one
obligatory semester of English A (rhetoric and English composition) and
one semester of French or German, both in their freshman year, as well
as forensics in their sophomore year. Lucy chose to concentrate in philosophy—not surprisingly, given the influence of George Herbert Palmer
and of her father, who had always considered philosophy the basis of
learning.[38]

During the "shining years" of the Harvard philosophy department,
Lucy was taught by William James, Josiah Royce, George Santayana,
Hugo Munsterberg, and George Palmer. The brilliance of these men,
their respect for one another, and the vigorous controversies among
them, created an intellectual atmosphere that was "electric," one graduate student recalled.[39] Lucy took most of the philosophy courses that
were offered. She knew her professors outside the classroom, too, as all
were regular visitors to Quincy Street. There, an "attentive little fly on
the Palmer wall," Lucy listened carefully as "the best brains in the country" argued, debated, and plotted.[40]

Lucy was not so awestruck as to treat these luminaries and their pronouncements as sacred. She tells of an experiment she conducted to test James' theory that behavior produces emotion, and vice versa. If she behaved like her professors, would she not feel like them? So she imitated each in turn. For a week, she walked breezily, swinging her arms like William James, letting her mind and speech fly off at a tangent as he did. Then she took on Santayana and tried to act remote and slightly superior to everyone around her. Next came Munsterberg. She pretended that she was nearsighted, screwing her eyes up behind strong imaginary lenses and regarding people as physiological specimens with reflexes.

But the most revealing of all was Josiah Royce, whom she called the "baby cowboy" because of his round face covered by the huge hat he always wore. For a week, the girl with long hair and ribbons thought her head was so large that she could scarcely hold it up and imagined her face as a cross between a cherub's and a frog's. With shoulders hunched, she contemplated the problem of evil from the point of view of the mystic, the realist, and the agnostic, as Royce did. "Which was I?" she wondered.[41]

Lucy's imitation of her teachers' behavior gives us several further clues to the meaning of her Radcliffe experience. First, abstract theory proved more interesting to her when it was filtered through personal experience. James, Munsterberg, and even Royce were unusual at Harvard for their encouragement of the experimental method, which allowed for the testing of the truth of ideas by individual experience. Lucy's experiments in "becoming" her professors were definitely in the Jamesian spirit. They were part of her search for a model. Could any of these exemplars meet her own needs? Could philosophy be a future career for her?

Lucy's written work showed a bold and careful examination of her teachers' ideas. In a department of original thinkers, where empiricism flourished, her audacity did her no harm, and she was given As in most of her courses. The benefits to a student like Lucy were enormous. In her sophomore year, Lucy took an introductory philosophy course with Santayana and worked with James. In her final years (when James was away from Harvard and Santayana taught only one semester) she studied ethics with Palmer, advanced psychology with Munsterberg, and logic and metaphysics with Royce. Lucy was one of three students in her Radcliffe class to graduate with Honors and the only one to receive Honors in Philosophy. This encouragement enhanced her sense of self-worth and, along with the affection of the Palmers and the friendship of her peers, was an important aspect of her Radcliffe exerience. "Very ingenious," was a typical comment from Royce on a paper of hers. "I can't conceive of any more fruitful method of procedure."[42]

Lucy's essays provide indications of her emerging philosophical understanding. The fact that she kept her philosophy themes, when most of her other work at the college has not survived, is itself telling. The papers deal with the standard topics of philosophical inquiry at Harvard in the 1890s—the large questions of the world and the individual, the self and the other, and the distinctions between internal and external reality. Yet they also provide clues to Lucy's developing sense of self.

Lucy insists, for example, that neither reality nor knowledge exists apart from the observer's experience. In a paper for Royce, she asserts that knowledge is subjective, existing only in relation to the knower. "I believe realism to be untenable from every point of view because it is flatly self-contradictory," she wrote. This position led Lucy to deny the existence of an autonomous self. The belief that "I am what I am, do what I do, think what I think just the same, no matter what anyone else thinks," and that "I must therefore be independent of others" she condemned as solipsistic, leading to the dangerous position "I have no ties," or "I am all in all."[43]

In another paper for Royce, Lucy listed her objections to Royce's ideas about the unity between external and internal, the world (or reality "other than" myself) and the self. At the heart of her resistance to Royce's metaphysics was her belief in the impossibility of free will. "I do not believe in free will," Lucy insisted. "I seek for reality on a purely deterministic basis. . . . The question is such a very large one and I disagree so fundamentally with both Mr. Royce and Mr. Munsterberg that I will not go into it." Here, she indicated only that "the reality of evil and disappointment is one of my strongest beliefs," a belief that ran counter to Royce's idealistic notion of an ultimate reality that was benevolent and rational.[44]

Lucy speculated further about questions of freedom and independence in a paper for Palmer entitled, "To What Extent Am I Free?" Here she examined the definition of freedom given by Palmer—"Freedom means that power of self-guidance by which, for interests of our own, we narrow a future multiple possibility to a single reality"; then she discussed James's view that conduct was in some measure predictable and could be self-initiated, since beliefs cause behavior. Lucy disagreed strongly with both positions. Her own experience of conduct and of the physical world around her seemed to deny the libertarian position. "Everything points towards determinism and nothing against it," she wrote. Freedom was not only improbable, but impossible. To the question, "Am I free?" she answered emphatically "No." But "this answer will not affect my actions in the least," she continued. "The only difference . . . is that instead of having a lawless, incalculable world to live in, I shall have a rational one."[45]

In her paper for honors, written in May 1900 at the conclusion of her undergraduate career, she elaborated these ideas further. Because of her severe cough, she could not take an oral exam, and was asked to respond in twenty-four hours to the following question: "Is there any such inherent connection between my own pleasures, perfection, well-being, etc., and that of other people that the aim of one will imply the aim of the others? Or if you regard the aims as really two, how do you justify life in the absence of a single summum bonum?" Lucy's answer spoke again of the inevitable limitations on individuality, but now she allowed more independence to the self. The answer to the paradox of freedom she now believed was in the connection between the self and the other, an ultimate unity of interests postulated in both Royce's idealism and Palmer's ethics of self-determination.

"We find ourselves in a world of hopes and disappointments, of struggles and failures, of eager desires and of stern duties forbidding the fulfillment of these desires," she began. "Our plans are thus thwarted by rights or pleasures of others. . . . We are limited on every side and each one of us is separated from his fellow men by a subtle something." In spite of the "strange illusiveness [sic] of self," Lucy now argued that a separate person or self existed apart from the other. "Even if I cannot know the exact nature of myself, I can always know what is mine," she wrote.

And I always know mine as separated from yours, or someone else's. My body, my writings, my thought, my wishes, my hopes are mine and can never become yours. I am separated from the rest of the world. And this separateness it is which gives me the feeling of selfhood.

But the separate self in each individual was limited by the numerous ties binding it to the world and other people. Following Palmer's scheme, Lucy declared that the self had two aspects, "one separated from the rest of the world and one in common with the world—a private and conjunct self." Because of the intimate connection between the self and others, it was inevitable for the self to yield to other people's aims. Yet, she concluded, this renunciation of selfhood was not necessarily negative since sacrifice and disappointment were integral parts of human nature.[46]

Lucy's repeated assertions of the restrictions on knowledge, reality, freedom, and individuality deserve comment. In the first place, she denied free will in spite of the views of her professors: Palmer, who insisted that the meaning of freedom lay in the choice between "dual possibilities," between a determined, "sequential" ordering of the world and "nonsequential," interventive action; James, who equated freedom with willful behavior; and Royce, who saw no contradiction between "the one and the many" in a morally ordered universe.

Lucy, too, sought unity, harmony, and rationality in the universe, a quest that appears frequently in her papers. By the end of her Radcliffe years, she seemed to be trying to persuade herself that the inherent linkages between self and other, although they limit an individual's actions, need not be incapacitating. Part of human nature was to be found in the *"yielding,"* she wrote, in "pain, sorrow, struggle." The greatest of all paradoxes was that "true joy includes sorrow, and true goodness evil."[47] She could not avoid the truth of her own experience, that in linkages to others, in service and sacrifice, in *yielding,* lay conflict and disappointment; and yet she was sure that there was no way to happiness that escaped such bonds. Lucy's views were much more pessimistic, in fact, than those of any of her professors, whether or not she acknowledged it. Her own experience, which she invoked in her essays many times, would not allow her to share their faith in human freedom.

Nowhere in her student themes is Lucy specific about the experiences to which she refers. But on one level, her views recall the rigorous moralism of her father, whose faith was molded by the punishing unreason of a stern Puritan God. All during her childhood Lucy had submitted to Puritan notions of inevitable sinfulness.

Determinism was also more appropriate than free will to the concrete content of her childhood experiences. Otho Sprague's regime, which enforced duty, abhorred spontaneity, and punished the assertion of childhood will, in fact left little room for freedom. Obeying the mandate of service as a dutiful daughter while watching her mother grow more and more lugubrious as a dutiful wife, Lucy lived under continuous constraint. Her experience of childhood was one of individual powerlessness in an authoritarian world.

When she pondered the queries of her professors—"To What Extent Am I Free?" or "Is there any . . . inherent connection between my own pleasure . . . and that of other people?" Lucy's reference consisted in her experiences as a daughter and a woman, her experience of gender, as much as in her inheritance of Protestant moralism. Pain, sorrow, struggle, conflict, sacrifice, and disappointment—those elements which she asserted were prior in her universe to harmony and love—were consequences for women of the patriarchal culture in which she was reared.

The creed she asserted seemingly had more in common with her father's Puritanism than with the robust spirituality and individualism of the Harvard philosophers. Yet, paradoxically, the vigor with which she disagreed with her professors also suggests rejection of male authority. In her written opposition to their doctrines, Lucy found a way to displace her anger against her father. Her papers for the "Little Almighty," George Herbert Palmer—her surrogate father in Cambridge—contained her most vociferous and detailed challenge to the notion of freedom, which Palmer championed. Although, as she wrote in a paper for Royce, "I have no positive doctrine to offer myself . . . I cannot find a world which satisfies all sides of me," she would not accept any of the worlds of her teachers. Royce's great work, *The World and the Individual,* she told him, "seems to me in the nature of a threat. It says to me 'accept my conception, or you have no world.' I am sorry to say as yet I cannot reply to that threat."[48]

The Harvard philosophers by no means meant to exclude women from the sphere of their moral reasoning. In their search for answers to ultimate questions about the meaning of human existence, they posited universals that had little reference to gender. Furthermore, the empirical framework employed by James, Munsterberg, and others was intended to leave ample room to include the experiences of any specific group among the data considered. William James's faith in a pluralistic universe, his insistence on truth as "happening," rather than as absolute, and his emphasis on the practical values of ideas indicate that he, more than any other living philosopher, was concerned with bringing philosophic thought into contact with immediate experience. Even Royce's "theistic monism" appealed to individual experience as the ultimate arbiter of truth. When Lucy challenged Royce's views in a class theme, he commented about their differences, "the only way is to look for examples. . . . in your present experiences."[49]

Yet it should be no surprise that the realm of experience these men held up to students to examine was largely and perhaps exclusively male. Though many of the illustrations they drew upon were gender-neutral, the foundations and context of their moral analysis corresponded to a male-oriented perspective of life and thought. "If we are indeterminists," James wrote in a typical passage, "we lay great stress on the fact that it is just because we cannot foretell one another's conduct, either in war or statecraft or in any of the great and small intrigues and businesses of men, that life is so intensely anxious and hazardous a game."[50] It did not occur to James or his contemporaries that such language was less than universal.

One tacit lesson of Lucy Sprague's Radcliffe education, then, was that a curriculum that neglected female experience was seriously deficient. Whatever they learned about metaphysics, aesthetics, and ethics during their days at Harvard, Lucy Sprague and her classmates learned little that was relevant to their lives as women. "Never once was the word mother or child mentioned" during her four years at college, Lucy told an audience of Radcliffe alumnae in 1956.[51]

Her friend Lucy Fuller recalled one occasion in her grandmother's garden in Cambridge when Dickinson Miller, a young protégé of William James, was explaining Berkeley's idealism. "He said to Lucy Sprague and me," she recalled:

"There is nothing anywhere except as your thoughts puts it there." We said we didn't follow, and he said, "Consider that baby in the perambulator there. A moment ago it wasn't there. How did it get into our world?" Lucy and I suffered so, trying to control our giggles, that we were obliged to make a hasty exit from the garden.[52]

Though Miller surely thought he had chosen his illustration at random, the total absence of the realities of babies and the experience of sex and birth from academic philosophy was neither accidental nor indifferent. Scholars like Carol Gilligan and Jean Baker Miller have shown that because the contextual experiences of daily life have been different for women and for men, the way in which women and men frame intellectual and moral issues may also differ.[53] For a woman, a concern for relationships, for the responsibilities of affiliation and caring, has been more important than the development of a sense of independence and of the abstract principles of morality and justice, signposts of male maturation. The rituals and processes of daily life—pregnancy, birth, childrearing, illness, and death—form the context of this female associational world: this kind of rich quotidian material has found little place in philosophic thought.

On one level, the dissatisfaction Lucy felt with Radcliffe's curriculum

later in life reflects her wish to legitimate her choice of childhood education as a calling. On another, however, it is clearly true that the world of
female experience was never thought of as appropriate material for examination in philosophy or other disciplines. In her study of the Society for
the Collegiate Instruction for Women, Sally Schwager cites Barrett
Wendell, professor of literature and one of the most vehement opponents
of the education of women at Harvard, who criticized a student's paper
on Shakespeare for its references to familial experience. "I hate to dispel
illusions," he wrote, "but your argument from family examples is a terribly weak kind of thing. If there is any class of people that we don't know
in all their complexity, it is the people that we live with and care for. . . .
Your rearing, if you will permit me to say so, is charmingly feminine.
That is, you base it upon the notion of the world that exists in a well-
brought up feminine mind, and not upon the world as it is."[54] None of
the great men of Harvard's golden age of philosophy was ever as caustic
or supercilious about female experience as Wendell. Yet even William
James once told the Radcliffe Graduate Club, "Education is that which
enables us to know a good man when we see him."[55]

For Lucy, a conscious understanding of the problems of gender-defi-
cient thinking came slowly, only after leaving college. Although she
continued to take philosophy courses as a graduate student, she increasingly felt that philosophy was too sterile, too isolated from the currents of
real life, to be her main concern. There were of course male intellectuals
who had found academic philosophy dry and remote—among them the
young William James—and who had done much to bring it closer to experience. What is unusual is that the young Lucy Sprague demanded so
much from the discipline. She wanted a world "that satisfied all sides" of
her self, as she wrote to Royce, and she tried out philosophy by "becoming" each of her teachers with imagination and daring. Her ability to ask
so much of philosophy came in part from her distance as a woman from
the main currents of philosophic thought and from academia itself.

The Harvard philosophy department left an indelible imprint upon
Lucy Sprague: she drew on it selectively all through her life and work.
The precept of James and Royce, that experience is an individual's surest
guide to what is right and true, was at the heart of her work with children
in later years. The habit of intellectualizing and abstracting ideas also
continued throughout her life as counterpoint to her emphasis on experience, and was reflected in her mature career as well. Studying with the
great men of Harvard reinforced a native habit of mind.

Radcliffe also gave Lucy and her classmates opportunities to develop their interests and powers by directing their own affairs at the college. College might have been an "artificial" world, as Lucy once noted, but for many women it did indeed provide self-possession, poise, and confidence that they could operate in the world beyond home and family.[56] Socially and institutionally Radcliffe was a female world, and this in many cases contributed to the empowerment of its students, even though the empowerment might be temporary, and in conflict with other lessons learned by "Harvard women."

Lucy had enjoyed her college work and believed that she had studied with "the ablest teachers . . . to be found in any women's college." Yet she never regarded Radcliffe as "the great center of educational enlightenment," as did most of her classmates. Above all, she regretted that the Radcliffe ethos and Harvard teaching had been too abstract and "academic," too little "connected with the world."[57] In her career as an educator, she would propose that the missing link between knowledge and experience become an integral part of the curriculum. Sexuality, childbearing, childrearing—the special concerns of gender—were to provide the meanings she missed at Radcliffe.

Stasis

In June of 1900, Lucy Sprague and sixty-two classmates, the largest class ever to graduate from Radcliffe, received their diplomas and went forth into the world, not quite sure whether they were products of the nineteenth century or the first "new women" of the twentieth. "We were Victorians," one of Lucy's classmates remarked, "but we were being prepared for the twentieth century."[1] The century that lay before them promised to be a dazzling era of energy and enlightenment, ending once and for all the parochialism, sentimentality, and corruption of the Gilded Age. Beneath the restlessness and turmoil of the last decades of the nineteenth century, a new institutional accommodation to industrialism had been taking shape: the development of a new socially responsible middle class, new bureaucratic thought and procedures, and new large-scale organizations of labor, capital, and agriculture. A loose coalition of progressives—businessmen, political reformers, social scientists, and a heterogeneous women's movement—set out to remedy the recognized problems of urbanization: frequent financial crises, growing worker discontent, municipal corruption, and a rising tide of foreign immigration.

New ideas about women's roles helped shape emerging patterns of social change. While most Americans did not question conventional notions of domesticity as women's proper sphere, in the last decades of the nineteenth century a new ideology of female social activism had begun to flourish. In urban-oriented women's trade unions, consumers' leagues, social settlements and suffrage associations, and in rural-based temperance organizations, women activists began to develop comprehensive reform programs. Transmuting Christian piety into moral politics, they launched a crusade designed to make room in modern society for feminine, maternal values. In so doing, they enlarged the contemporary concept of womanhood and won an active role for themselves in public life.[2]

At the heart of the women's movement were the concerns of sisterhood as well as those of maternalism: establishing the rights of women to gainful employment and better labor conditions; providing help to women in matters of health and welfare; promoting women's political and educational equality—in every possible way, alleviating the brutalization of women and children by urban-industrial society. Waging a war of female piety against male indifference and corruption, they became potent "municipal housekeepers," cleaning the back-rooms and alleys of American cities as conscientiously as they did their own homes. The issue of alcoholism, especially, brought an army of stalwart wives and mothers into the fray. Under the leadership of Frances Willard, the Women's Christian Temperance Union (WCTU) branched out into a multiplicity of areas, in time becoming a broad-based social service and advocacy organization which actively promoted suffrage and labor legislation. Women's clubs, ranging from small town and village clubs to large, well-financed and widely influential urban associations like the Chicago Women's Club, with committees on child labor, suffrage, sexual hygiene and other reform issues, played an active role in local political life.[3] The Women's Trade Union League, Consumers' League, the National American Woman Suffrage Association, and the College Settlement Association also had enormous influence, although they enrolled a far smaller cadre of women than the General Federation of Women's Clubs. In such organizations, and especially in settlement life, many college women found a way out of the "class prison" to which their backgrounds and education seemed to condemn them.[4] Under the leadership of Florence Kelley, Jane Addams, Lillian Wald, and others, settlement workers translated maternal ideology into social practice, delivering direct services to the poor while influencing the national agenda in matters of social policy regarding urban and family life. The theory of separate spheres and of female uniqueness, which was built into socio-sexual thought in the late nineteenth and early twentieth centuries, was now used against the status quo to establish women's special influence in society at large. Here lay unprecedented opportunities for middle-class women at the start of the twentieth century.

But beneath the growing strength of the women's movement in 1900, a number of serious problems were brewing. New controversies within the movement underscored the limits of separatism as a strategy and of female exclusivity as an ideology. In 1900, the year of Lucy's graduation, the WCTU faced rising agitation on the part of members who demanded that men be allowed into full membership.[5] And in the same year, the refusal of the powerful General Federation of Women's Clubs to recognize Josephine Ruffin—the president of the Woman's Era Club, an organization of black women—as an official delegate created ripples of antagonism throughout the entire spectrum of women's organizations.[6]

The increasingly heterogeneous and often divisive constituencies of the women's movement after 1900 were reflected in the diverse views of women activists regarding suffrage. During Lucy Sprague's undergraduate years, suffrage had not been a popular campus cause. Though there was a College Equal Suffrage League at Radcliffe, Maud Wood Park, '98, one of the handful of suffragist activists at the school, had difficulty drumming up an audience for the well-known suffragist Alice Stone Blackwell when she visited campus. In the next decade, interest in suffrage increased rapidly on college campuses, as it did among the population at large.[7]

Of all the leaders in the women's education movement, only M. Carey Thomas, president of Bryn Mawr, displayed an impassioned interest in suffrage. Some educators, like Annie Nathan Meyer, founder of Barnard, were actively hostile. Alice Palmer's position was more typical. For her, suffrage, though important, was still secondary to the cause of women's higher education. As her husband explained her position: "it [suffrage] could wait, the other [higher education] could not." Although Alice Palmer was a member of the Equal Suffrage Association, she neither appeared on suffrage platforms nor urged legislatures to press for votes for women. With women's right to higher education still a controversial issue, she and other educators may have been reluctant to jeopardize their primary goal by supporting an even more radical cause. According to George Palmer, Alice believed that the suffrage movement was proceeding with "sufficient" rapidity. All the more urgent, then, was the need to shape women's minds and give them "a clearer consciousness of themselves as something more than pretty creatures of society."[8]

In the first years of the new century, the women's movement thus spoke with several voices. Though women's options had been substantially enlarged in the twenty-one years since Lucy Sprague's birth, it was not at all evident to a young woman graduating college in 1900 what the destiny of women in the new century would be—personally, politically, or professionally.

Delivering the class prophecy to the six hundred spectators who jammed Radcliffe's gymnasium on Class Day, June 20, senior Helen Ward spoke glowingly of the graduates' expectations. Radcliffe girls, she predicted, would be in the vanguard of educated women entering the business world and the professions, "waving aloft the banner of Radcliffe, and surging with a tidal wave of enthusiasm over the dry stubble of conservatism." Only six out of the sixty-three would marry, she augured; the rest would fulfill their destiny as "new women." Of Lucy Sprague, Ward prophesied she would busy herself in music, pedagogy, and the arts, "unmarried but not lonesome," since she would share "bachelor quarters" with "kindred female spirits."[9]

The prophecy was only partly right with respect to Lucy, as we shall see; nor did it entirely hit the mark with its heady forecast of the future of Radcliffe women in the larger world. Yet in the excitement of Commencement, few in the class of 1900, full of a sense of accomplishment and privilege as Harvard women, recognized the difficulties that lay ahead.

As a class officer, Lucy Sprague stood in the receiving line at the Class Day reception, next to Dean Irwin, Mary Coes, the college secretary, and President Mrs. Agassiz, in her gown of black Lyons velvet, who was leaving the college after twenty-one years of guiding Radcliffe's cautious policies. Aunt Nan, who had come to Cambridge with Uncle Albert and Lucia for the graduation festivities, remarked that Lucy seemed "quiet and sober." Even the gaiety of the evening's events, which she attended with Eric, Mr. Palmer's nephew, failed to lift her mood. The college grounds were strung with thousands of brightly colored Japanese lanterns stretched from tree to tree. Across the lawn, the Glee Club sang favorites from Radcliffe operettas and the orchestra played popular ballads. Though she had been an organizer of the day's events, Lucy did not enjoy the occasion.[10]

There was in fact much reason for discouragement. The realization that her college days and her idyllic life with the Palmers were coming to a close was painful enough. But the last months at Radcliffe had been accompanied by severe emotional upheavals that intensified Lucy's apprehension about the future. One was a romantic shock that threw Lucy into a state of confusion regarding any thoughts she had about marriage. There were also new crises in the Sprague family, unpleasant reminders of life before Radcliffe.

Before college, Lucy by her own account had been painfully shy with boys. At the Marlborough School, Marion Jones' violent love affairs frightened her away from any young men who sought her company. Although Marion delighted in interpreting Lucy's virtues to potential admirers, Lucy felt it impossible to compete with Marion for their attention. She retreated silently behind dark glasses, indoors and out.

Lucy had had at least one amorous proposition prior to college. When she journeyed to Alaska, the Marlborough schoolteacher who accompanied her "devoured" Lucy with confessions of her romantic disappointments and her appeals to Lucy to make up for them. The teacher proposed that she go with Lucy to Cambridge and keep house for her. Lucy refused. "I must have been a wholesome girl," she wrote of that strange incident.[11]

Away from home in Cambridge, Lucy was considerably more open to "love affairs," as she called them. There was a brilliant law student who wrote passionate love poems; a young naturalist who taught Lucy to follow animal trails in the woods; and in particular there was Eric, and a young man she identifies only as "Joe," both of them relatives of George Palmer. Eric lived at Quincy Street throughout Lucy's stay there; they took many of the same courses and often studied together. Eric was doggedly devoted to Lucy, and she took pleasure in his attentions, though secretly she thought him clumsy and blunt. When after graduation he fell madly in love with another woman, telling Lucy he had found the "real thing," they both found it easy to accept the view that Eric's feeling for her had been merely a mild infatuation.

With Joe, however, "it was different." He was a proud, stylish young man, determined and ambitious, who came from a poor family and resented his poverty. Joe studied mining at Harvard; he was in and out of the Quincy Street house all the time. It is not surprising that he fell in love with Lucy's deep-eyed beauty, her intelligence, and the world of graciousness and wealth she represented. For Lucy, Joe perhaps seemed to offer security as well as romance: he was interesting and mature, and as a cousin of George Palmer, he was undoubtedly trustworthy. Soon the two were spending every Sunday canoeing at Riverside. "Joe was a sophisticated lover," she recalled, "and I was very fond of him." Yet she did not have the chance to think seriously about marriage.

"In the spring before graduation came the crash," Lucy recalled. The story is a fantastic one. Certain "lewd pictures" had been circulating among Harvard students, and Mr. Palmer appointed himself detective in the matter. The trail of evidence led directly to Joe's room, where Palmer found the photographs tacked on the wall—right next to Lucy's picture.

When George Palmer first told Lucy of his discovery, she could not comprehend it.

"Who did you say was selling the pictures?" I asked. "Joe," he said. Again I asked, "Who?" Again he said, "Joe." I kept repeating my question. Finally Mr. Palmer lost his temper. "If you can't listen to me, Lucy, there's no use talking further. You don't hear a word I say."

"Oh, I heard," Lucy admitted. But "I couldn't make it seem true. To this day I can't make it seem true. It was like cheap, lurid dime-novel stuff. Joe!"[12]

Joe told Palmer he had been selling the photos to make money to marry Lucy. He was arrested, but Palmer bailed him out. On Palmer's advice, Joe skipped bail and fled to Mexico. Lucy was astounded by Palmer's action, recognizing the great struggle the professor of ethics must have had with his conscience over the decision. But a still greater shock came when Joe wrote her a bitter letter, asking her for money since she had so much. To Lucy, this was even worse than the crime from which he had been fleeing.

Lucy heard from Joe only twice again, though she suspected that her father tried to have Joe's movements traced after he left Cambridge. But the pain stayed with her for many years, making her question her own judgment in matters of love. By putting Lucy's picture next to what by nineteenth-century standards was a pornographic display, Joe had given Lucy a complicated message about sex and honor. Perhaps she felt her own erotic responsiveness to Joe was now tainted. On another level, the incident surely confirmed her discomfort about the Sprague family's wealth. Outside of her family, she never mentioned Joe's crime "to a human soul."[13]

Joe's betrayal was not the only emotional shock Lucy faced at the end of her college career. Lucy's sister Nannie, apparently recovered from her illness, had been living for the past year and a half at the rectory in Andover where Fred Palmer, George's brother, served as minister. At Andover, Nannie seemed to regain some of her intelligence and wit, though she clung to Lucy, who visited regularly on weekends, played the pipe organ and shared with Nannie in the affectionate care of Fred and his funny, lovable wife. But just before Lucy's graduation, Nannie broke down again and Lucy hastened to her side. More bad news came from Chicago. Lucy's eldest sister, Mary, was seriously ill after the birth of her first child. Lucia, though ailing herself, came in from California and brought the newborn Polly back to Sierra Madre, where she cared for her until Mary recovered. Only six months later, when Mary and Adolph Miller moved to Berkeley, was Polly returned to her mother.

All these problems—Nannie's breakdown, Mary's illness, and Joe's crash—came just before Lucy took her final examinations at Radcliffe. Despite this emotional stress and the severe coughing that made Lucy's examiners isolate her in a separate room, she did unusually well. On June 26, Lucy crossed the stage of Sanders Theater to receive her degree magna cum laude with Honors in philosophy. It was the first Honors awarded to a Radcliffe undergraduate by that celebrated department. Lucy recalled her complex feelings:

College was over. My delirious four-year vacation was over. When I walked out of 11 Quincy Street in June of 1900, I felt that I was forever walking out of the world where I had found freedom—intellectual freedom, human freedom. A new world had opened to me and now I thought it was closing forever. But I had that world inside me, I thought fiercely. Nothing can take it from me. I was nearly twenty-two and felt old and wise and experienced. I kissed the Palmers and hurried down the street. All three of us were crying.[14]

Like many female graduates around the turn of the century, Lucy Sprague experienced a profound disjunction between college life and the cultural expectations that confronted her. This dilemma was later made famous by Jane Addams in her autobiography, Twenty Years at Hull House, and her essay "Filial Relations." When graduates returned home from college eager to apply their skills to the larger social realm, Addams wrote, parents often refused to acknowledge this "social claim," and reasserted their authority. The daughter, still regarded as a "family possession" despite her years at college, submitted to the "family claim"—the "assumption that the daughter is solely an inspiration and refinement to the family"—though she felt wronged.[15] The result—an unhappy, restless woman, with her parents "unconscious of the situation"—had "all the elements of a tragedy."[16] Education served as a catalyst in women's lives, yet left them discontented outside the college context.

A popular manual "for girls" entitled After College, What?, published in 1896, described how the new graduate typically found herself at the close of four years of busy and contented college life suddenly confronted with "blank nothingness," especially if she were the daughter of wealthy parents and lived where there was "nothing going on, nothing to do, nothing to talk about" that would interest college women. What followed was several years of "deep and perplexing unhappiness" and a decided homesickness for the stimulation of college life. "What came after college?" recalled one Bryn Mawr graduate. "I didn't know."[17]

To stay at home, help one's mother entertain, perhaps take a course in domestic science—these were taken for granted. Anything more adventurous would have seemed out of the question. Our families had "spared" us for four years, to use the current phrase, and now our obligation was entirely to them.[18]

For Lucy Sprague, graduation from college at first meant a return to her role as dutiful daughter. "When college came to an end, Royce wished me to get a Ph.D. in philosophy and go into college teaching," Lucy recalled. Despite her reservations about academic philosophy, she might have followed his advice, she felt, "if family matters had not then reached a crisis." In later years, she wondered occasionally if she could have "stuck it out" as a professor of metaphysics.[19]

The first claim on Lucy was Nannie. Convinced that Nannie needed reassurance that she still belonged to the Sprague family, Lucy persuaded her reluctant doctor to allow Nannie to visit Maine, where the two sisters spent the summer in a rented cottage near a small hotel. By keeping Nannie busy with canoeing, swimming, and hiking, Lucy hoped to build her self-confidence to the point where she would be less dependent on Lucy and could begin to make her own decisions. Nannie's physician was delighted with her progress by the end of summer—but Lucy was exhausted. When Lucy left Nannie for a few weeks' rest, Nannie relapsed. Lucy's failure to bring lasting improvement to her sister left her tired and discouraged.[20]

By the fall, Lucy was far from well. Though she knew that "work was what I needed to forget Nancy, to forget Joe . . . I was too listless to fight family opposition." She yielded to her family's demand that she return to Chicago for her debut, a mandatory ritual for young women of her social class. For the next few months, she submitted to the glamour of Chicago's social life, attending dinners, dances, and teas "in a kind of a trance" of which she remembered very little.[21]

Lucy lived in the household of her older cousin, Elizabeth, the daughter of Aunt Nan and Uncle Albert, now married to a Bostonbred orthopedic surgeon, Dr. Frederick Shurtleff Coolidge, with a six-year old son, Sprague. Here she could observe the life of a young society matron at first hand. Elizabeth, a talented pianist and composer who later became one of the foremost benefactors of American chamber music, was a complicated, high-strung woman. She was always much closer to Mary than to Lucy, who probably resembled Elizabeth in personality more than she cared to admit. Elizabeth, Lucy observed, had "'social' leanings that were rather confusing to her conservative father, who greatly admired her, though a bit uncomprehendingly."[22]

During the early years of her married life, Elizabeth was frequently "morbid" and depressed. On the surface, she enjoyed the company of her husband and child, performed frequently at benefits and other entertainments, for which she often wrote her own music, and was an active member of several women's clubs, where she delivered original papers on a variety of subjects. Nevertheless she found these roles limiting. Elizabeth's many dark moods, frequent tears, and nervous illnesses are recorded in her mother's diary—surely colored by Nan's own anxieties at Elizabeth's attempts to establish her independence. A loving, ever-present mother, Nan grieved that her only surviving daughter no longer needed her. Though the Albert Spragues had built a home for the Coolidges a few doors away on Prairie Avenue, Elizabeth made it clear to Nan that she wanted to live her own life and rear her child in her own way. Much less conventional than her mother, Elizabeth found Nan's constant advice on manners, dress, and child-rearing intrusive.[23] Nan's sense of rejection and bereavement left her subject to nervous illnesses no less frequent than Elizabeth's. How much of this complex family dynamic Lucy understood is uncertain. At any rate, in the constant company of her aunt and cousin for several months, she had ample opportunity to observe that underlying the fortunate circumstances of their lives, both of these forceful and successful women harbored a deep melancholy.

On December 1, 1900, Cousin Elizabeth threw a grand reception at which Lucy "came out" as a Chicago belle. Three hundred and twenty guests thronged the hall of the Coolidge house, and Lucy received no fewer than fifty-five bouquets from admirers. One Chicago paper, noting the event, observed that Lucy Sprague was a "Radcliffe College girl and is exceedingly gifted and interesting, with a rather shy manner."[24] Lucy's ailing parents were unable to attend the event, and Nan and Albert took their place. Nan looked with pride at her lovely niece, elegant, though reserved as usual, in her white net dress, and at her own daughter, fashionably attired in black. She hoped that Lucy, the most serious and responsible of Lucia's daughters, would stay in Chicago. Watching Lucy grow up over the years, Nan was troubled by the way her niece's life had been distorted by family emergencies. Lucy deserved a chance to create a niche for herself in Chicago society. With her brooding, striking beauty and her intelligence, no doubt she would be immensely successful. Besides, Lucy was almost a daughter to Nan and would be cherished company now that Elizabeth had declared her independence from maternal control.

But this outcome was not to be. Shortly after Lucy's debut, her mother fell critically ill from an undiagnosed ailment. Otho, a chronic invalid himself, still refused to hire a nurse, and Lucy was urgently summoned back to California. After her arrival, Otho wrote to Nan that Lucy had talked freely to him, expressing great unhappiness. No relief was in sight, however, for Lucia's condition worsened. For the next few months Lucy devoted herself completely to her mother's care. In June, Lucia and Lucy came east to attend Albert's wedding to Frances Dibblee, daughter of the Henry Dibblees of Chicago and niece of Marshall Field. Nan was shocked at Lucia's appearance. Pale and desperately thin, she could swallow nothing but a few drops of liquid. Nan wondered at her hopeful manner, her refusal to be absorbed in her own pain. The family, she feared, was paying insufficient attention to Lucia's alarming condition. Lucy, who clung to her mother's side, ministering to her every need, also seemed in terrible shape. Nan was deeply worried about them both.[25]

Almost as upsetting to Nan was the behavior of the family's close friend, Alice Freeman Palmer. Mrs. Palmer was visiting Chicago that June of 1901 when Lucia and Lucy arrived en route to Albert's wedding in New York. Although she knew about the serious nature of Lucia's illness, she "neither inquired about her nor sought to see her," Nan noted in her diary. "There is decided restraint. She knows we don't like the way she and Mr. Palmer acted over Lucy."[26] Nan added nothing further, nor does Lucy take up the story in her memoirs. Circumstances suggest, however, that Lucy had sought advice and support from the Palmers and that they had proposed that she come back to them in Cambridge. Lucy's alliance with the Palmers might well have been disturbing to the Spragues throughout the troubled year after graduation. The family had been grateful to the George Palmers for their devoted attention to Lucy during her four years at Radcliffe, and to the Fred Palmers for caring for Nancy at Andover. But now the Spragues may have feared that Lucy, with the encouragement of the Palmers, was about to strike out on her own, this time for good.

For the present, at any rate, Nan could see that Lucy was faithfully attentive to Lucia. The two traveled to Rye, New York, where Albert's wedding took place in the middle of June. Though, for unexplained reasons, most of the family was less than delighted with the match, Lucy welcomed it.[27] All the family hoped that Albert had sown his wild oats for good.

Having seen Albert married, Lucia travelled to Boston with Lucy to see a Christian Science healer. Lucy, an avid reader of *Science and Health* in her teens, now reread it in "profound disbelief." She knew that her mother was dying and felt that Lucia knew it too—but Christian Science told them that only their lack of faith kept Lucia ill. Later that summer, Lucy took Lucia to a health resort in Poland Springs, Maine, where Otho, exhausted and ill, eventually joined them. Lucia wrote to Nan that "*If there were any way,* I should like to leave Lucy, but Otho will not listen to it."[28] Lucy took both parents back to Chicago on a long and terrible train ride. Doctors finally diagnosed Lucia's illness as tuberculosis of the peritoneum. There was no hope of cure. Otho recovered slightly from his own setback, but could not face the fact that his wife was dying. Lucia, suffering horribly, asked only to see Nan—she could not bear Otho in his anguish and grief. Brokenhearted, Nan marvelled anew at Lucia's patience and good humor, and tried to accustom herself to the inevitable loss of this sister who had been a companion and beloved friend throughout her life. Nan was alarmed by Lucy's worsening condition as well. "Lucy seems to be perfectly exhausted," she wrote in September. "She should never have been allowed to carry this terrible care and responsibility."[29] But Lucy's devotion never wavered. "Lucy cares for Lucia like a baby and shows how competent she is," Nan wrote in her diary, "but she is very tired. She is pretty near the end of her rope." A few weeks later, in her sister's bed next door to the Prairie Avenue home she loved, Lucia Sprague died, at the age of fifty-one. Only days after the funeral, Lucy took a train to Boxford, Massachusetts to join the Palmers. "She feels if she can only get there, she will [be] better," Nan wrote. "She is so very much pulled down."[30]

Her respite in Boxford was brief. "Now it was Father who seemed to need me," she wrote, so she returned to California to be with him. But in fact she found that cousin Eleanor was fully in charge of the invalid's regime. Both were in relatively good health and fully absorbed in building a house on Grove Avenue in Pasadena. Lucy was indignant—she called it "the last irony"—that the beautiful furniture and art objects from the Spragues' Prairie Avenue home were now going to California. How desperately her mother had wanted them about her during the years of her Sierra Madre exile, and how staunchly Otho had resisted. In protest, Lucy refused to play her mother's Liszt organ—"poor Lucia's" her father always said—in the new house. Otho was troubled by Lucy's refusal and could not understand it. In this one act lay expressed much of her anger for the many ways in which Otho had been unresponsive to her mother. Lucia was gone, a victim of tuberculosis—Otho's illness—and Otho was finding new life and interests without the wife whom his illness and his censoriousness had stifled. Perhaps that was the deeper meaning of the "last irony."[31]

Yet Lucy was not ready to turn away from her newly widowed father. Even though Otho functioned quite nicely with Eleanor's help, Lucy remained at home, trying unsuccessfully to accommodate her father's emotional needs. Over the next few months, her spirits plummeted.[32] She recalled:

I determined to get myself trained for something. But what could I do without leaving home? Architecture, which had been one dream of mine, was impossible. Land-scape gardening? Perhaps I could get a background in botany and soil analysis and later get a technical training. So I went to the Throop Institute, later to become the California Institute of Technology, and arranged with an understanding woman on the faculty to allow me to do experimental work in her laboratory. I had a vast number of seedlings, indoors and out. I faithfully experimented in soils, in moisture, in temperature. But I didn't learn much. I was untrained and too much on my own. . . . I plugged away at my experiments with plants and played bridge in the evenings or read aloud. How long? I don't even remember. I know I felt an alien in a strange land. I know I was sick. I didn't keep down half of the little food I ate. I was put on albumen water![33]

Though Lucy's family and doctors feared the onset of tuberculosis, it is possible that her sickness was mainly a response to her unhappy return to her family. Lacking outlets for both the professional ambitions and the sexual drives that had matured during her years at college, Lucy's sense of identity was in jeopardy, and her illness may have functioned as a cry for rescue.[34] Lucy's letters filled Nan with apprehension. "She ought not to stay in that gloomy atmosphere of Otho's." "She must leave her father and Pasadena and that *soon* in my opinion," she wrote in her diary. Shocked at Lucy's emaciated condition when he visited California, Un-

cle Albert took her back to Chicago to recuperate. Lucy recalled "weeks
in bed with a nurse and Uncle hovering around anxiously, bringing me
presents, joking, playing cards sitting on my bed and letting me win."[35]
Dr. Billings warned her that there was no chance of full recovery or of escape from tuberculosis if she went back to Pasadena. Lucy had had a severe cough for years, her mother had died of tuberculosis, and her father
and Eleanor were chronically ill from the disease. Lucy knew that Billings was right. Despite the fact that she showed no symptoms of tuberculosis, she worried continually about contracting it. But still she took no
decisive step. "I seemed to lack the will to plan for myself," she admitted.[36] She was caught in an especially virulent example of the postgraduate crisis described by Jane Addams. Nan and Albert had intervened to
save her from the consuming devotion to her sister, her mother, and her
father that had claimed her since graduation; now she swung to the opposite extreme and became dependent, sluggish, passive. This form of protest, though it was less directly self-destructive, could only end in tragedy
if it was not reoriented.

It was the Palmers, once again, who provided the next stage of the rescue. Now that their invitation offered an escape not from duty but from
passivity, Lucy accepted it. She agreed to accompany George and Alice
on a sabbatical trip to Europe; and if any of the Spragues objected this
time, there is no record. "Thin, constantly nauseated and coughing,"
Lucy fled to Boston to join the Palmers. "Once more I stepped into a new
world," she recalled.[37]

On the cattle steamer on which they sailed to Europe, Lucy regained
her health. Though she had been "chronically sea-sick on land for two
years," suddenly Lucy was able to keep down an astonishing amount of
food. The boat "rolled with every wave and the cattle shifted and bel-
lowed with each roll and their smell was not confined to their own quarters," Lucy remembered. Still, she loved the weeks on board and felt like
a "new creature" when at last they steamed up the Thames and landed in
London.[38]

The purpose of the Palmers' visit to England and France was not only
to sightsee, but to gather material for George Palmer's book about his
namesake, the poet George Herbert. The Palmers and Lucy attempted to
track down every spot that Herbert had visited. They saw his birthplace
in Wales, the rectory in Salisbury where Herbert had written his first

poems, and other places where Herbert had lived. In Salisbury, after some sleuthing, the trio came upon a pencil sketch after a Van Dyke portrait of Herbert that had perished in a fire years before. The owner of the sketch refused to part with it, but Lucy copied it stroke by stroke and produced a pencil drawing that could not be distinguished from the original. It hung in Mr. Palmer's study at 11 Quincy Street for many years. Lucy also sketched in the British Museum in London, where she spent hours every day with George Palmer, making notes for him on Herbert, and at the National Gallery. On weekends, Lucy and the Palmers toured the countryside with their rucksacks. During the week, they explored London's bookstores and galleries. Lucy bought several Arundel prints at Spencers, copies of works she had admired at the National Gallery, but was most excited by her purchase of an original print of Blake's "Job" at Quaritch's. Years later, she still considered it "as beautiful as anything ever drawn." Lucy also made and colored a facsimile of Blake's "Songs of Innocence and Experience." "I hugged these new treasures to my soul," she wrote.[39]

The Palmers and Lucy had their own apartment at Garlant's, a hotel near Trafalgar Square. They delighted in ordering their meals through a butler and eating in their own dining room, except when old Mrs. Garlant, looking like Queen Victoria, presided over high tea, to which all her guests were expected to come promptly. Lucy loved London but was equally impressed with Oxford, where the travellers spent two weeks visiting with Edward Caird, the Master of Balliol, and his wife. Lucy soaked up the rich atmosphere of Oxford, meeting so many famous Englishmen she knew from books that her head was awhirl. But Salisbury was best of all. In Salisbury Cathedral, in the Dean's house where Coventry Patmore had courted the young wife he immortalized as *The Angel in the House*, and at nearby Stonehenge, Lucy felt the "sweep of history."[40] Here was the English landscape she had pictured as she sat reading, curled up in the bay window of the Prairie Avenue house behind the henna silk curtains.

After finishing their research on Herbert at Salisbury, the Palmers and Lucy went to the Isle of Wight to see Tennyson's home, where they read aloud from "The Lotos-Eaters," "Ulysses," and "The Princess." Near an English lake, they found what they decided could have been the abandoned sheepfold that Wordsworth had described in his famous poem. The first *Oxford Book of English Verse* had just been published, and the

Palmers and Lucy read it together from cover to cover on these visits to England's literary shrines.

The three then journeyed to Paris, where they intended to spend a long visit before wintering in Italy. Mr. Palmer rented an apartment, and out came Lucy's Salisbury sketch of George Herbert, and Alice Palmer's two Cambridge tablecloths which she carried everywhere to make them feel at home. In the mornings, Lucy worked with George Palmer on Herbert; afternoons, evenings, and weekends they toured the city and its environs. Lucy received permission to sketch in the Louvre, where she spent hours copying.

But "an incredible lightning strike" put an end to the group's euphoric visit. Alice Palmer was suddenly taken ill with intestinal pains, and after a few days was rushed to a Parisian hospital for an emergency operation. She had had a "physiological accident," they explained: part of her intestines had telescoped another part, like the fingers of a glove hastily pulled off, and corrective surgery was required. For days George remained by his wife's side, while Lucy kept vigil at home, refusing to believe that the "gay, vital, young" Alice Palmer was dangerously ill. At three o'clock one morning, George Palmer arrived home to tell her that Alice was dead. Her last words, he said, had been, "Take care of Lucy."[41]

Less than a year after the death of her mother, Lucy thus suffered a second devastating loss. Alice Palmer had been a friend, a mentor, and much more. For Alice, Lucy had been the replacement for the young sister, Stella, whom she had lost early in life, as well as a substitute for the daughter she had never conceived. For Lucy, Alice was the steady, wise, buoyant and decisive mother-figure she had never had. Though the bonds between mother and daughter had been strong and loving, and though Lucia had intervened with Otho to send Lucy to Radcliffe and was probably responsible for her earlier attendance at Marlborough, Lucy never fully acknowledged the ways in which her mother supported her. She saw Lucia as a childlike figure, always subordinate to Otho, and viewed herself as more of an adult, caring for and protecting her mother even before the last fatal illness. It was Alice, not Lucia, who had provided Lucy with security and reliable emotional support, and who had pointed out a way of existence beyond the family claim. Alice, who had felt the emotional constraint of family obligations during much of her own adolescence, had been especially sensitive to Lucy's situation.[42] In her company, Lucy had found not only a model of a vibrant, executive woman but also a warm and rich familial environment that nurtured her intellect and emotions. In Europe with the Palmers she rediscovered the loving companionship the three had shared in Cambridge. Her astonishing physical recovery testified to its healing effect.

Now, just as Lucy had begun to vanquish the demons of her postgraduate life, came this new blow. George Palmer was stunned; Lucy braided Alice Palmer's dark hair and wound it as a crown on her head, preparing the magical "Princess," as she was always known at Wellesley, for her funeral. Barrett Wendell, the "precious, affected, supercilious" professor with whom Lucy had studied at Radcliffe, arrived in Paris and proved invaluable in helping George to arrange compliance with France's strict burial laws. Soon Lucy and George, carrying the little wooden box containing Alice's ashes, fled to England, and then home on another cattle steamer. Throughout the long voyage, George talked on and on to Lucy about his boyhood, his marriage to his first wife, Ellen, her death, and his happy fifteen years with Alice. Often Lucy would fall asleep in the early morning hours only to wake up to find Palmer still talking. The only time he stopped was to read through Alice's papers. It was there, on board ship, that he discovered her poignant "Marriage Cycle" poems.

In his grief, the sixty-year-old widower began to turn to twenty-three-year-old Lucy with "alarming dependence." They had been through terrible things together, and Palmer knew that next to himself, Lucy felt Alice's loss more than anyone else in the world. Even Katie, the Palmers' long-time Scottish housekeeper, regarded Lucy as a member of the family and assumed that now she would take charge. And so Lucy decided to stay in Cambridge. "Or rather," she observed. "I made no decision. I just stayed."[43]

Lucy remained in Cambridge through the summer of 1903, spending most of her time with George Palmer. According to an alumnae report she made some years later, she actually lived with her classmate Evelyn Livermore Prescott.[44] "Of all the abnormal situations in which I have found myself in a life which as I look back on it has held many strange situations," she recalled in her autobiography, "this life with Mr. Palmer was the most abnormal."[45]

As the time passed I knew I was caught in a vise stronger than Father ever forged for me. Mr. Palmer was subtle in his ways of limiting my life. He would say,

"Now Lucy, you need an outing. Don't worry about me. I don't want my broken life to cramp yours. I have my memories and my Herbert. Go off for an hour— go off for a whole afternoon. Don't even tell me where you are going!" I felt suffocated, torn between devotion to him and searing memories of Mrs. Palmer, and the sense that I was being drained of all capacity to live except as his shadow. What is the matter with me, I wondered desperately, that I seem incapable of finding a satisfying normal life? Why do all my relations with people seem to rob me of my own soul? Am I always to live a vicarious life?[46]

Lucy continued to spend most of her time working with Palmer on his George Herbert manuscript. But she did enroll in a graduate philosophy course at Harvard; and she also found a job as secretary to Dean Agnes Irwin and to Mary Coes, then secretary of Radcliffe. Coes, who in Lucy's view was the person really in charge at the school, became dean when Irwin retired several years later. Lucy's job, which consisted mainly of advising freshmen and handling office records, held "mild interest" for her, but she did not think of it in career terms. Nor is it likely that she intended to take an advanced degree in philosophy, as Royce had suggested. Right now her life centered on George Palmer, and she could not seem to plan further into the future.

But as the winter dragged on, Palmer changed indefinably. "Now I didn't feel suffocated," Lucy revealed in her autobiography, in a passage that was omitted from the published work, "I felt pursued." One day he held her hands tight and asked with his "eager intensity": "Do you think you could be happy to make an old man happy for the rest of his life?" Lucy felt as if she had been "struck in the face." Her "appalled silence" brought out his "sophistry," which horrified her even more. "Alice told me to take care of Lucy. How can I unless you stay with me?" he asked her. "He should not have said that," Lucy declared. "He should not have misused those precious words of my beloved Mrs. Palmer. In that moment Mr. Palmer lost his hold over me. He knew it. He tried to pretend nothing had happened. But after that I was dutiful. I was no longer loving."[47]

That summer, Lucy visited Mary and Adolph Miller; Adolph was now a professor of economics at the University of California at Berkeley. She found the atmosphere there like a fresh breeze after the "worn-out, stale prison air" of Quincy Street. Polly, Lucy's niece, was now two years old, and she and Lucy became constant companions. Mary was delighted to be relieved of much of the daily care of Polly. She and Adolph admired their friend George Palmer but were shocked at his assumption that Lucy's life belonged to him. They wanted Lucy to stay on at Berkeley.

Later in the summer, Lucy went south to visit her father. His tuberculosis had spread from his lungs to the bones of his chest, and a daily syringe was necessary, with water pouring into one hole and leaving the other. Otho refused to have a nurse even for this hour-long procedure; Lucy, again the dutiful daughter, insisted that if Eleanor had been performing this service for Otho, so could she. Handling the instruments and gloves with surgical care, she carried out the syringing operation daily when she was there, even though her clothes got drenched every time. But Lucy remembered Dr. Billings' warning that if she returned to the Pasadena household she would have no chance to escape the ravages of tuberculosis. Her father assumed that she had come home for good; George Palmer wanted Lucy to return to him, and, indeed, followed her to Berkeley and then to Pasadena. Aunt Nan, who heard about Palmer's visits from Mary, thought his behavior suspicious. "What *can* he want?" she asked herself.[48]

Lucy wanted to stay with neither her father or Palmer. "Am I becoming inhuman?" she asked herself, wondering at the way in which obligations to others seemed to overtake her life. She thought of Eleanor, who still felt privileged to serve "Uncle Otho." Her sister Nannie's life was already broken. "It would be useless to sacrifice mine for hers," she concluded. When she thought of Mr. Palmer, she longed desperately for Alice to rescue her from his grasp. Her friend Marion Jones, just married the year before to architect Robert Farquhar, seemed unhappy, and also cried to Lucy that she could not live without her. Joe had been "the one human being I might have loved enough to make me forget myself." But now no satisfying relationship seemed possible. "I must be queer," Lucy reflected, "if the only life I was capable of building was one where art and intellect took the place of people."[49]

In the end, Lucy returned to Cambridge. Though she came for a visit she stayed on, resuming her job at Radcliffe and her "vicarious" life with Palmer, although she had firmly declined his proposal of marriage. "Then the incredible happened." Benjamin Wheeler, the youthful scholar who had become president of the University of California in 1899 and whom she had gotten to know in Berkeley during her visit with the Millers, came to see her in Cambridge. "He wanted to do something with the women students at Berkeley," was the way he presented his vague proposition to her. He asked Lucy to come to Berkeley for a year or two to study the situation of women students. Then he hoped the two of them could define the duties of a dean of women in a manner that would be acceptable to Lucy. Recalling the decision, Lucy highlighted the risk Wheeler was taking in making her the offer, and her own inexperience for the job.

He knew I had no training for such a job. I knew it better than he. I wasn't quite twenty-five, had been trained at a small, man-scared woman's college and had worked there as a secretary. The University of California was coeducational, had nearly two thousand women students and many more men students and had never had a Dean of Women or a woman on the faculty. I marvel at my temerity, for I was thoroughly frightened. I told him I could never undertake to be "an influence," a Dean, unless I had some other official standing. I must teach at the University. He agreed. President Wheeler was a gambler. I was a gambler, too—a desperate one. I said I would come.[50]

Lucy had felt no special interest in a career in educational administration. She accepted the opportunity when it came because it seemed the best way out of a "personal jam," a way that her family might accept as "strange but respectable." She had taken no initiative; she proclaimed she did not *choose* her future profession. Yet Lucy made too much of her passivity and her lack of training. Despite her initial surprise at Wheeler's offer, with Palmer's advice and her own understanding of the disadvantages of female administrators on male college campuses, she bargained successfully with him for a faculty position.

In fact, Wheeler's choice of Lucy as a potential dean of women was extremely sound. As the sister-in-law of his good friend and former Cornell classmate Adolph Miller, she came from the social and intellectual circle with which Wheeler was most comfortable. Secondly, she was a California resident who had attended secondary school in the state and knew at first hand the preparation common to women college students. Thirdly, she had been an Honors student at Radcliffe, and to all who knew her, her keen intelligence and devotion to the life of the mind were her most prominent features. She had been a class officer, too, active in student affairs at Radcliffe, and for the last year had been working in an administrative capacity to improve student life at the college. In disclaiming her qualifications for the Berkeley job, Lucy had described herself as a secretary at Radcliffe, but in fact she was an assistant to Irwin and Coes, the most powerful figures at the school. The position was partly clerical, but it also gave her important knowledge of college administration.

Finally, through her association with the Palmers, two of the most influential individuals in the world of higher education, she had absorbed many progressive ideas about coeducation. Coeducation, separatism, and affiliation as competing strategies for women's education had certainly been discussed in the Palmer household while Lucy lived there. Alice had attended the University of Michigan, the first major coeducational university to admit women, and her experience there had been formative. Later at the University of Chicago, she pioneered a solution to the problem of integrating women into academic and student life at that university. She remained in constant touch with Angell of Michigan, Harper of Chicago, and other university presidents whom Lucy had met at the Palmers.

Alice Palmer had been president of Wellesley when she was twenty-six. Later she had served as a dean of women. In leaving Cambridge to take a similar job at the University of California, Lucy was following in Alice Palmer's already established path. Surely Wheeler's offer to her was less "incredible" than she painted it. Once again, Alice had rescued Lucy.

PART
TWO
ON HER
OWN

Berkeley, California: A "Heart Culture" for Women Students

Berkeley was a small town of some twenty thousand inhabitants when Lucy came to the university. Almost all the faculty came from outside California, so that the "closed-in pedantry" of many small academic towns was absent. In a way that was unique to her experience, Berkeley combined the advantages of a "small-town, closely knit, informal community, with the advantages of a city, small but cosmopolitan in atmosphere."[1] It was a stimulating, liberating environment. Lucy was a frequent guest at the dinner parties held by academic friends, wonderful occasions "full of personal and intellectual interchange" about philosophy, politics, and poetry. There were also club meetings, dances, concerts. Prominent figures came to speak at the university, among them Theodore Roosevelt and Woodrow Wilson; the actresses Sarah Bernhardt and Margaret Anglin performed at the outdoor Greek Theater. Through her official position and her friendship with President Wheeler, Lucy believed she met more world figures during her years at Berkeley than she was to encounter in the later decades of her life in New York.

Trips across the bay to San Francisco were frequent—most often to visit the city's innumerable restaurants, which Lucy enjoyed for their gaiety as much as their excellent food. She was pleased that entire families, including noisy children, dined together, a custom unheard of in the higher circles of Chicago society, and she enjoyed, too, the regular celebrations where the slightest occasion called for the throwing of confetti.

Her proper brother-in-law, Adolph, was once "scandalized" when Lucy responded to an unknown male diner's wink with her "dead-fish eye." To Lucy, the restaurants, the cable cars, the parades, the labyrinthine streets and exotic stores of Chinatown, the many touring plays that came to town with actresses like Ethel Barrymore and Mary Shaw, even the city's regular political scandals, made San Francisco a dramatic, exhilarating place.

One of the delights of Berkeley lay in its wonderful climate and its spectacular location, with San Francisco Bay to the West and the gently rounded Berkeley hills to the East. When Lucy woke up in the morning on her covered sleeping porch, she looked directly through the dramatic vistas of the Golden Gate. On the western horizon, steamers bound for China disappeared around the earth's curve; out of the north side of the Golden Gate rose majestic Mt. Tamalpais, and at the top of the Peninsula, fronting east on the Bay, stood the miracle of San Francisco, built on a hundred hills. At night the colored lights of San Francisco, Berkeley and Oakland, and of the watercraft on the Bay, made it look like "fairyland." The view from Lucy's study and living room was even more precious to her. Out of these windows, she watched the changing seasons touch the Berkeley hills.

Lucy had always loved the mountains. In her teen years she had climbed the ranges of Southern California, alone, to escape the oppressive routine of her parents' household. Now, in Berkeley, riding, hiking and mountain-climbing became social pleasures. She rode with Adolph Miller; picnics, walking and climbing parties in the Berkeley hills or the scenic redwood groves of Mt. Tamalpais were constantly being arranged, and Lucy was a sought-after companion.

Her health was not perfect, but in Berkeley her coughing fits, bronchial troubles, and loss of appetite all retreated. Overwork and strain did on occasion take their toll; in endurance and exertion she probably stretched herself well beyond the limits of the average woman of her time. Her active physical life also reflected increasing self-confidence, and her growing willingness to challenge standard Victorian definitions of femininity.

During the first few months of her residence in California, Lucy lived with Mary and Adolph Miller in their modest rented house high on a hill in North Berkeley. Miller, thirteen years older than Lucy, was a stiff, pompous man, Germanic in his upbringing and attitudes; Lucy recalled that although she found her brother-in-law tedious and oppressive, she devotedly helped in his economics work, grading papers and reporting on texts. Mary, as always, was gracious, charming, and witty, the perfect hostess and wife. She spent her days caring for her daughter Polly, visiting friends, gardening, entertaining, playing the piano, singing— activities that she and her husband agreed were wholly appropriate to her domestic life. Adolph strongly believed that women should be "caretakers" and "adornments." "The finest flower of any culture was a 'lady,'" he used to say, "and a lady never worked except in her own household."[2] Lucy knew that although he was fond of her, he disapproved of her own job—except as a stopgap until marriage.

Lucy spent much time with the Millers and with the Wheelers, their closest friends. Though she often felt like a "fifth wheel" with this older group, the two couples included her in their social activities and provided her with friendship, support, and a secure family base. President Wheeler was particularly important to Lucy. His personality was as distinctive as that of her father, George Palmer, or her brother-in-law Adolph, but he exerted his influence in a much less authoritarian way; Lucy's position as a university appointee perhaps helped her to feel more independent towards him. At the same time, he and his wife became one more set of surrogate parents to Lucy; when they took a sabbatical year in Germany in 1909 with their teenage son, they invited Lucy to accompany them.

Lucy's California circle of friends included a number of other older women and men. The most important was Sarah Hardy Gregory, known as Sadie, an economist who had trained at the University of Chicago. She taught economics at Wellesley but broke down after a brief period, and never returned to professional life. She married a wealthy San Francisco attorney, Warren Gregory, who had been a high school classmate of Adolph Miller. The Gregorys had magnificent homes in both San Francisco and the Berkeley hills. Sadie's Sunday suppers, where the most attractive course was the after-dinner conversation, were held the center of much of Berkeley's social life. Lucy visited La Loma, the Gregory's Berkeley home, so frequently that the four Gregory children called her "Tante." Sadie's friendship would become especially important to Lucy toward the end of her California stay, for Sadie was a close friend of a young economist named Wesley Clair Mitchell.

Another Berkeley friend was Winifred Rieber, or "Madonna Imp," as this uninhibited soul was affectionately called. The wife of Charles Henry Rieber, of the Department of Philosophy (later he was Dean of the University of California at Los Angeles), Winifred was a well-known artist who held regular dances at her sprawling Berkeley home where academics including Wesley Clair Mitchell waltzed and tangoed. Ernest Hocking, also of the philosophy department, and his eccentric, irrepressible wife, Agnes Boyle O'Reilly Hocking, whom Lucy had known in Cambridge, became even closer friends of hers at Berkeley, where, with their first child, Richard, they set up housekeeping in a small mountaintop home they built and furnished themselves. The distinguished philosopher George Howison, chairman of Berkeley's Philosophy Department, and his wife Lois, also became her friends. Lucy came to know Howison when she took a graduate course with him during her first year at Berkeley. He would end each session, she recounted, "by hitching his chair near me, putting his ear trumpet to his ear, and saying 'Now Miss Sprague, don't you see that Royce was wrong?'" One day Professor Howison came into Rieber's office with an essay Lucy had written in class, boasting of how well one of *his* students could write. When Rieber stopped Lucy in the hall the next day to tell her of this tribute, she gave him a stony stare and said, "The impudence of the man, and the impoliteness of you for reading it"—and strode on. It took years, Rieber later told her, for him to recover.[3] Throughout her life, Lucy reacted with unhesitating harshness to anything she saw as a personal intrusion. What to her felt like shyness, to others was often haughtiness; her privileged upbringing had given her more outward self-assurance than she could admit to.

Among Lucy's other friends were several literary scholars and their wives—George and Florence Noyes, Dryden scholars; Chauncey Wells, who taught English literature, and his wife; and John Galen Howard, a poet and architect, and his wife, Mary. These three couples (and sometimes the Hockings, the Gregorys and Walter Hart, another literary scholar and his wife) all joined the Poetry Circle that Lucy established.

Lucy was particularly fond of the Howards. John Galen Howard had come to California in 1901, after winning the Phoebe Appleton Hearst Competition for best architectural design for the university. Howard established the general plan of the Berkeley campus, designing and building the Hearst Memorial Building, the Greek Theater, Sather Gate and Sather Tower, Benjamin Ide Wheeler Hall, and other structures. Howard, who guided Berkeley's School of Architecture for thirty years, was also a classical scholar, known for his epic poems. Lucy admired his poetry tremendously (full of strange words like "coolth," she recalled) and found Mary Howard, a nonprofessional artist, to be endearing, earnest, and loving. Lucy was "Tante Lucy" to the five Howard children who ran in and out of her garden, adjoining their own backyard, as she was to her own niece, Polly Miller, and the Gregory children. These were her first and among her warmest personal contacts with young children.

It is significant that many of the relationships Lucy established with Berkeley friends extended to their children. As a "tante," Lucy made a place for herself in the hearts of several families. Her relationships with other families acted as a protective device, useful in relieving her own anxieties about her unconventional professional role. These new, less constraining surrogate families enabled Lucy to integrate her earlier, traditional role as helpful daughter with the new options offered her as an educated, aspiring twentieth-century woman.

In Cambridge, Lucy had been "a fly on the Palmer wall, watching Cambridge folk." Now she was an actor in her own right, as well as an observer. With these friends, who were not "job friends" but just "folks I liked and who liked me," she established a personal life that was "rich and satisfying" as never before.[4] Warm friendships and a wonderful "play life" made a supportive environment in which to undertake her first professional work.

The rewards of her relationships and of her own growing sociability were increased confidence and self-esteem. Slowly, the guilt and self-reproach that were constant companions of her awakening years began to fade. She discovered a new openness to risk and change. As she became aware of the ways in which her students were hampered by cultural assumptions about gender, she understood better how the constraints of her own upbringing had affected her, and she set herself consciously to overcome them. Now she began to think of making a contribution of her own to the broader problems of women's education. The emergence of this ambition marks the beginning of what she later called her "strategic years."[5]

The University of California had opened its doors in 1869, a product of the merger of the all-male liberal arts College of California (established in 1855) and the state's Agriculture, Mining, and Mechanical Arts College (founded in 1866). No one expected women to attend, but the following year, eight women registered as undergraduates. In 1879 the provision that no person should be "debarred admission to any of the

collegiate departments of the university on account of sex" was added to
the State Constitution.[6]

By the turn of the century, women at the University of California
numbered over five hundred, about half of the undergraduate student
population. Although they were numerous, in no way were they full par-
ticipants in university life. Women had few facilities, their study and
dining halls were overcrowded, they could not use the men's gymnasium
and they lacked campus housing. Most female students commuted to
classes from family homes or boarding houses in neighboring communities and were at best quiet observers at most university activities. They
could attend classes and participate in student elections, but it was the
male students who organized campus social and political life.

As coeds throughout the nation also learned, equality of access to
higher education did not necessarily mean equality of participation
within and outside the classroom. Male students, jealous of their preroga-
tives and afraid of female competition and of the bogey of "effemina-
tion," regularly teased and taunted women students and barred them
from participating in extracurricular activities. At the University of California, women students were commonly called "pelicans"—skinny, ugly,
studious creatures destined to become old maids.[7] A full fifty years after
women had first entered the university on a supposedly equal basis with
men, sexual innuendos and derogatory remarks about the women's
"cooking and sewing rallies" pervaded the humor sections of the college
yearbook. As Alice Freeman had discovered at the University of Michigan, coeducation was not for timid women.[8]

Before the turn of the century, the rowdiness of student life at the
University of California had further enforced women's marginality. Hazing, harassment, and outright physical violence and torment were part
of an interclass warfare that made sophomores and seniors the deadly en-
emies of freshmen and juniors respectively. The Academic Senate declared in 1881 that hazing would be punished by dismissal. Nevertheless,
the "rush"—in which the classes engaged in hand-to-hand combat until
one side had thrown the members of the other to the ground and tied
them up—persisted for several decades and often resulted in broken
bones. With this ritualized fracas as the centerpiece of college social life,
it is little wonder that Berkeley women remained outsiders.

When President Wheeler assumed office in 1899, he announced his
intention of transforming student life. Competitive sports helped channel student aggressiveness, but Wheeler's presentation of an alternative

vision of student mores was also an essential component of the abolition of campus violence.

Never, in fact, in its thirty-year history had the University had a president so remarkable as Benjamin Ide Wheeler. Tall, handsome, and youthful in style, Wheeler cut a striking figure as he rode through the campus on horseback; exchanges with students were punctuated with genial cries of "Bully!", after the manner of his good friend and hero, Theodore Roosevelt. "Would you like to ride?" he would often ask, and up would go a student on the president's horse.

A graduate of Brown University, where he also obtained a master's degree and taught for several years, Wheeler studied classical philology in Germany, receiving his Ph.D. from the University of Heidelberg summa cum laude in 1885. He taught German at Harvard for a year, and then spent the next eleven years at Cornell as Professor of Greek and Comparative Philology.[9] Wheeler had turned down the presidencies of at least six colleges before he accepted California's offer in 1899.[10] If it had not been for the encouragement of his friend Adolph Miller, Wheeler might well have declined the California position as well, for Berkeley's strong board of regents had a well-known habit of chewing up its presidents.

A bold, commanding, and visionary administrator, Wheeler remained as president for twenty years, ending the series of weak, short-term administrations that preceded him. Under his leadership, the university expanded until it stood second only to Columbia in the size of its student population. Strengthening the faculty, course offerings, and research and physical facilities in the university's professional, technical, and liberal arts colleges, Wheeler turned Berkeley into what was arguably the premiere academic institution of the West, rivalled only by Stanford.

Although many of the faculty found him overbearing, Wheeler was extremely popular with students. He believed that the "real university" should be like "family life," a place where relations among students, faculty, and administration were characterized by caring, concern, and freedom. In his view of the ideal college, little should divide president from faculty, students from teachers, research from instruction, or "the governed from the governing."[11]

Wheeler's commitment to this ideal was practical as well as theoretical. He inaugurated weekly meetings of the senior class, known as "Senior Men's Singing," which became vehicles for communicating student opinion and developing undergraduate policy.[12] With his encouragement, a standing committee of the student governing body, the Associ-

ated Students of California (ASC), was formed to handle questions of
student conduct and discipline. Under the honor system and the ASC's
self-governing procedures, students developed a code of student life and a
model for dealing with disciplinary cases that influenced student culture
elsewhere. Together with his achievements in administration, finance,
and educational policy-making, Wheeler's success in reforming collegiate
culture at the university won over the Board of Regents, which gave him
unprecedented support.

But although the University of California was fast becoming a nationally known laboratory of high quality public education, no way had been
found to extend the full promise of higher education to women students.
Women were pointedly excluded from the new seats of student power.
"Senior Men's Singing," the policy-making assembly, did not include
women (to compensate, a "Senior Women's Singing" was introduced),
nor did the committee that handled student discipline have any female
members. Women were similarly excluded from most academic clubs,
athletic programs, and other special activities. Like his immediate predecessors, Wheeler grew concerned about the situation of women on campus, though he was less troubled at their exclusion from general student
programs than about the lack of attention to their special needs as
women. His appointment of Lucy Sprague was the first step towards
improvement.

By 1903, when Lucy came to campus, the women students of the
University of California had already begun to organize. Recognizing that
their interests were not served by the student organization, in 1894 they
established the Associated Women Students of the University of California (AWS). Over the next few years, the AWS sponsored debating and parliamentary societies, drama and musical groups, the YWCA, and various
academic societies strictly for women. In 1901, it helped create a wom-
en's honor society, the Prytaneans (from the Greek, "those of chosen
calling"), modelled after the Golden Bear and Skull and Keys, the university's honor societies for men. Membership was open to women who
had given special service to the university as club officers or sorority
house presidents. The club dedicated its efforts to raising funds for a
women's residence hall, a women's loan fund, a student hospital, and
other causes.[13]

In short, women at the University of California were forming a sepa-
rate-but-equal social life quite apart from the male-dominated student
culture. On the one hand, separatism tended to rigidify, rather than

challenge, the sexual status quo, perhaps limiting women's choices even further. On the other hand, the creation of a separate social structure for Berkeley women was a positive response to the pervasive sexism on campus. Berkeley was not the only co-educational university that isolated and ridiculed its women students, but gender segregation seemed to flourish under the Western sun. Women students never openly attacked the tradition by which they became the butt of their classmates' humor, and in later interviews most expressed satisfaction with their student experiences. Once a year, on Washington's Birthday, the women staged a Women's Day in which they ran all campus activities—newspapers, sports, clubs, even a dance to which they escorted members of their own sex. While it celebrated women's capacities and achievements, it revealed at the same time the completeness of their isolation.

Since there were no women on the 270-person faculty, there was no one who could lead students to a more assertive and effective expression of their needs. But there were several nonfaculty women at the university who assisted women students. Phoebe Appleton Hearst, widow of the millionaire senator George Hearst and mother of William Randolph Hearst, became the university's first female regent in 1897. For several years previously, she had given her time, enthusiasm, and money to women students, establishing scholarships, holding teas, receptions, and parties. In 1900, she donated the entertainment pavilion of her Berkeley home to the university to provide a separate student center for women students—Hearst Hall. The third floor of the Hall became a gymnasium where for the first time women could receive physical education instruction. A lunchroom and meeting rooms were also provided. Mrs. Hearst had been active in all kinds of charitable ventures, but she was a former kindergarten teacher, and her priorities lay in the field of education. Women students, future mothers and teachers of children, had a special claim on her attention.[14]

University women had another influential advocate in Mary Bennett Ritter, a physician married to a professor of zoology at Berkeley. Though unsalaried, for several years Ritter examined women students, providing them with certificates of physical fitness that entitled them to use Berkeley's male gymnasium after five in the afternoon—for one hour only. In 1898 she became a part-time staff member of the university, dealing with health questions and the myriad personal problems of students. With funds provided by Mrs. Hearst, Ritter visited various colleges around the country, observing the living arrangements of women students. On her

return she persuaded Mrs. Hearst to finance two house clubs for women
and helped to start a Loan Fund to establish other residences. In many
ways, Dr. Ritter acted as an unofficial, untitled dean of women.[15]

Also important to Berkeley's women students was May Cheney, an
early graduate who began serving as appointment secretary (employment
or placement counselor) in 1902, and held that position for forty years.
The vivacious, friendly Mrs. Cheney was active in the Association of
Collegiate Alumnae, and other educational groups, and helped focus
their interests on vocational opportunities for college women. The contributions of Hearst, Ritter, and Cheney proved invaluable to Lucy
Sprague as she began her work at the university.

Lucy Sprague started out, not as dean of women, but as assistant to a
new Berkeley official, the "adviser"—in effect the dean of the two lower
classes—a position held by George C. Edwards. As assistant, Lucy's job
was "the oversight of the interests of women," especially freshmen and
sophomores. According to her recollections, she never had a single conversation with Professor Edwards, the man she supposedly assisted for two
years. May Cheney, who occupied the office next door, helped acclimate
Lucy to the problems of women students. More important, Lucy was in
constant communication with President Wheeler.

Lucy came to Wheeler with any problem she had, whether personal or
professional, and he was always respectful of her views while offering firm
advice. She believed that Wheeler was the easiest person to get along
with she had ever met, a judgment with which faculty members at the
University certainly did not concur. But Lucy felt that Wheeler gave her
the freedom she needed while providing her with direction, guidance,
and a model of managerial style. She found him courteous, thoughtful,
and kind, with a penetrating, though gentle, wit. Indeed, she "adored"
Benjamin Wheeler, Lucy later confessed—in a "seemly" way.[16] He
taught her much about universities, about administration, about people
generally.

Besides Wheeler, few people in these first two years at Berkeley knew
that Lucy's agenda went beyond seeing that students fulfilled course requirements and that their personal and social arrangements were satisfactory. All during these first years, she was carefully analyzing how students
lived, what they did, how they thought. In the fall of 1906, when she

was officially appointed Dean of Women, she put into action many of the plans she had been formulating during this learning period.

As assistant adviser, Lucy had many opportunities to get to know the women students. Every study card, sick leave, and any difficulty in which a freshman or sophomore woman might find herself came into Lucy's purview. It did not take her long to make a general diagnosis: a combination of unhelpful families, limited aspirations, ill-suited academic programs, male hostility, and lack of institutional facilities made the life of most Berkeley co-eds drab, uncoordinated, and frustrated. She began to feel that the key aspect of her job as dean would be to direct women students toward a more spirited intellectuality and a more visible presence on campus. She needed to galvanize women by sharing her ideas and passions with them. It was never a conscious strategy that she developed but an intuitive one that followed her own instincts, the cues of students, and the model set by Wheeler and, in many ways, by Alice Palmer.[17]

Before she could turn her attention to student motivation and curriculum design, however, she was confronted by a more immediate need: the problem of housing. Lagging behind most other major coeducational institutions, the University of California provided neither housing facilities nor concrete assistance in helping students find living accommodations. There were many more fraternities and clubs on campus offering housing to men students than there were sororities. Many of the students who lived in boarding homes could barely afford the rent, and accordingly scrimped on food. Not only were they often ill-nourished and in poor health, but boarding-house life kept them isolated from fellow students, without the opportunity for social contacts and unifying activities.

Lucy's approach to the housing problem was twofold. Sharing the attitudes of her generation, she felt that unsupervised and especially, "mixed" boarding houses were menaces to the "health, social manners and morals" of students. Women were more vulnerable to the dangers of unwholesome boarding arrangements, and, accustomed to parental supervision and chaperonage, they were inexperienced in dealing with the outside world. She spent a great deal of time visiting boarding houses that took women students, and placed them on an "approved" list if they agreed not to house men and to provide a downstairs reception room. But she hoped that the boarding-house solution would be temporary. Only if the university established and managed its own housing facilities would women students be assured of decent rooms, adequate nutrition, and well-supervised homes. If they lived together in student dormitories, they could also run their own facilities and develop experience in self-government.[18]

Year after year Lucy urged the president and trustees to begin to plan for the financing of dormitories. Meantime she began to encourage the formation of student-run club-houses. Under her auspices, seed money was raised to establish women's clubs, which she hoped would become self-supporting. Contributions from the California Federation of Women's Clubs, the San Francisco branch of the Association of Collegiate Alumnae, the Prytanean, and private donors (especially Mrs. Margaret Fowler, a family friend of the Spragues from Pasadena) permitted the establishment of nine club-houses. As each club-house was formed, responsibility for its policies and management was turned over to a student league, which worked in informal cooperation with representatives of the Dean's office. Lucy believed these self-governing houses were a definite improvement over the isolated boarding-house lifestyle.

One of Lucy's proudest achievements was the establishment in 1911 of "College House," a building refurbished and rented to a woman's student organization by a private group but staffed by the university with a salaried housemother under the informal supervision of the dean's office. With twenty students each paying twenty dollars a month for room and board and giving one hour a day to house duties, the club met expenses. A well-organized student league successfully played the major role in managing the home. Still, Lucy thought College House was not satisfactory as a model since the university did not directly operate it.[19] Almost two decades would pass before Lucy's dream was realized at Berkeley: the first dormitory opened in 1929. In 1946 when the university erected its first dormitory quadrangle for women, one of the buildings of the Fernwald-Residence Halls was named in her honor.[20] Twelve years later she was the guest speaker at the groundbreaking ceremony for two multistory residences on campus.[21]

In housing and other matters, Lucy was a powerful advocate of student self-government. As she observed in an article in a campus journal:

If the aim of the University is primarily to make scholars, as it is in Germany, or primarily to make gentlemen or gentlewomen, as it is in England, then self-government may not be desirable. But if the aim is primarily to make competent workers (and this is the typical American aim), to fit for the practical world which meets the college graduate, then self-government is an admirable teacher.[22]

Self-government would train students to become "inhabitants of the real world in which they will shortly become real workers," and would teach the importance of "authority" and "obedience." "It teaches a man or woman to command and to obey," she noted.[23] President Wheeler strongly influenced Lucy's belief in the benefits of self-government, but her championship of these processes also came from her instinctive sympathies with the needs of youth for active self-expression. Her own painful experiences as a child and adolescent made her wary of imposing adult models on youth. This empathy for youth, a faith in self-determined behavioral models at all ages, and a collaborative rather than authoritarian administrative style would be hallmarks of her later work.

In all her activities as dean, Lucy preferred a consultative approach. One of her chief goals was to bring together students who belonged to campus club-houses with less intellectually-minded sorority women. Lucy worked indirectly to achieve her end of healing the split between these groups, and eventually some progress was made. A former student observed years later that Dean Sprague "put responsibility on the girls, and respected the rights of the individual. She helped them to arrange committees and set the formal pattern of organization that has been kept through the years."[24]

Lucy believed that self-government would not only unify women on campus and teach them "self-control" and leadership, but would also help them to achieve greater representation and political power within the university. Lucy was distressed that women played "a distinctly minor role in the common government" of coeducational universities. Comparing her experiences at Radcliffe and Berkeley, she noted that "it is unquestionable that in a coeducational college, where the responsibility of social activities, and consequently the interests in these activities, falls in a lesser degree to the women, that the women develop self-possession less markedly than in the separate college, where they bear the undivided burden."[25] The only solution, she felt, was to give women increasing opportunities for self-direction, and ever new responsibilities. Two years later she was proud to write in her biannual report that the women of the university were "gradually solving their own problems"—self-government was becoming a reality.[26]

At a time when the women's movement in California was becoming increasingly active, it is likely that Lucy was also influenced by the example of women's participation in public discussions throughout the state. Because she was often called upon to take part in forums and to preside at campus and local events, Lucy decided it would be useful for her students and herself to learn parliamentary law and to practice public speaking on a regular basis. She organized a group called "The Critics on the Hearth" which met informally around the open fireplace at her house. She and the students would take turns making impromptu speeches; the others would criticize their use of language, delivery, and organization. Perhaps one reason this self-help group worked so well was that the young dean sat among her students, orating, laughing, and learning along with them.[27]

Lucy also paid a great deal of attention to the problem of women's social isolation at the university. At Berkeley she was particularly active in ferreting out lonely students—the ones unconnected to any campus activities other than classes—and finding ways to enrich the quality of their experience. An informal survey she conducted disclosed that in 1904, 54 percent of women students had no connection to any campus activities other than course work. The proportion of "unconnected" students decreased over the next two years, but Lucy still felt it abnormal that, on a three-year average, one-third of the women students belonged to no organization—"intellectual, social, athletic, musical, dramatic or otherwise"—through the four years they spent at college. She continually worked on the problem of reaching these students and encouraging their participation in campus activities.

"The narrowness of experience that the University offered its women students" was reflected in the students' "unconnected" housing, their isolation from each other and from male-dominated campus activities, and in the content of their courses of study. "Girls from little towns came, had a gay personal time, took the prescribed dull courses for a teacher's certificate and returned home without ever touching the big human problems by which we were surrounded."[28] Part of the problem lay in the motivation of the female students themselves, a difficulty Lucy had not encountered with Radcliffe's studious women. She found that Berkeley women had "slight intellectual interests." In her first year at Berkeley, she did a survey which showed that 92 percent of women of the graduating class had applied for teaching certificates; 81 percent received them. The proportion seeking certificates decreased over the next few years, but in 1906, 75 percent of women students still took the prescribed course sequence for teacher training. This meant, Lucy noted, that at least 72 percent of their courses were chosen in conformity to the requirements for the teaching certificate—requirements she believed were overelaborate. She felt that most of these students had no deep motivation to become teachers but simply wanted to earn a living. They were not studying for the love of scholarship or from any desire to work with children.[29] "The teacher's life is one of the few natural openings in the modern world for a woman who is forced or desires to support herself," Lucy later observed. While the achievement of a teacher's certificate was a worthy aim, the "prostitution of the teaching profession to a wage-earning trade" was not.[30]

To identify possible problems, Lucy met with each incoming freshman woman. But the class was so large that it was many months before she could see all the women, and then only on a hurried schedule. She developed the idea of entertaining freshmen women at her home, forty or so at a time, to get to know the students better and to locate the "detached" ones, as she called them. But though such assemblies were useful in sparking student spirit generally, they could not focus attention on individual problems. Essentially, freshmen women were "too much entertained and too little known." Eventually Lucy evolved a system whereby upperclassmen would befriend particular women, helping them to obtain housing and to resolve other problems. She also chose seven faculty advisers who were paid a nominal salary to work with freshmen women, and called upon the wives of these faculty as well to become personally involved with the students.[31]

In 1906, Lucy commissioned John Galen Howard to build her a house next door to his own on Ridge Road. On a hill sloping down to the west side of Euclid Avenue, with a large well-groomed garden and a huge terrace facing the Berkeley hills, the house was designed for entertaining. Each Friday afternoon, large groups of students came for refreshments and Lucy's recitals. With her lilting, dramatic inflection, she read to her visitors from the works of the English poets—Blake, Wordsworth, and Herbert—and often from an anthology of folk poems of Roumania, *The Bard of the Dimbovitza,* of which she was particularly fond. She read passionately, believing that for many of these girls from California's mining towns and farmlands, she was "throwing open doors and windows into a new world," just as George Palmer had once done for her. And like Alice Palmer, Lucy seemed a "fairy tale princess" to many of her students— strikingly beautiful, with her wide-set hazel eyes, clear, steady gaze, and brown hair curling at the nape of her neck. They loved her eclectic, elegant costumes—the long gray silk dress and the lavender mull scarf, the high-necked holland shirtwaists with many strands of beads, the multi-colored skirts, embroidered blouses, Egyptian silver chains, pins, and earrings.[32]

But not all the students responded to Lucy's charm and intensity. Some felt that the genteel, feminine Miss Sprague, with her well-bred Eastern aesthetics, could never understand life in the West, where plain-born, uncultured, ambitious women had to compete in a masculine world with whatever learning and credentials they could garner. An example came at one of her teas, when she ruefully complained of the insistent tolling of the eight o'clock bell on Bacon Hall, which had startled her from sleep that morning. Students who had risen at dawn to cross the bay, who had prepared family breakfasts or had perhaps already worked a shift as student helpers resented her self-pity. There were other criticisms of Lucy's lack of tact; of her failure to understand and empathize with the students' day-to-day problems of living.[33] Though she despised her moneyed background, it still insulated her from the reality of her students' lives.

Her negative judgment of the motivations of those students who wanted a teaching certificate simply as a means of livelihood also sprang from her own class perspectives. Ultimately, she had little sympathy for the girls of lower-middle-class origins who sought to prepare themselves at college to earn a living afterwards. Though intellectually she acknowledged the validity of their objectives, on an emotional level they were alien. In the Story Book House, in a setting of fresh flowers, fragrant burning logs, and poetry, she hoped to quicken their cultural lives.

Nevertheless, Lucy's conception of cultural enrichment did include social concerns. At these afternoons, she spoke strongly of the need for educated women to take part in social reform, discussing the minimum wage question, consumers' league strategies, and similar issues. Though she ignored the class backgrounds of her students, she made sure that they did not neglect the general problems of working-class women.

Gradually Lucy had come to believe that Berkeley's women students were isolated not only from each other but from the real world outside campus walls. The university's formal curriculum offered little that could acquaint students with the main currents of civic and social life in the surrounding community. Perhaps she was familiar with the work of teachers like Vida Scudder and Katharine Coman at Wellesley, whose offerings in English literature reflected new Progressive enthusiasms; certainly she was influenced by Jessica Peixotto, a sociologist at the University of California who touched upon contemporary concerns in her teaching. But there were not many Peixottos at the university. Lucy thought this gap in the curriculum "shocking" and set about to remedy it. Every Saturday, groups of twenty-five or thirty students would meet at her home to discuss a particular social issue, then they would go off to Oakland or San Francisco to explore the issue at first hand, returning to Lucy's house for further discussion. Among the places they visited were an orphanage, a settlement house, a children's health center and a county poorhouse. Lucy also wanted to provide experiences that could help her students understand the technological and economic aspects of community life. She took them to the San Francisco wharfs, where they could learn about shipping, and to other sites related to transportation, marketing, and finance.

In effect, the difference in class origins and educational backgrounds between Lucy Sprague and Berkeley's women students determined the nature of her informal pedagogy. With her poetry readings, her socially oriented discussions, and her fact-finding expeditions into San Francisco, she had in a sense started a settlement house within the university. To jaundiced eyes it might seem no more than a "cultural comfort station"—as Sinclair Lewis called the settlement houses—bringing beauty and truth from above to the masses: her girls.[34]

Those who disliked Lucy because of her upper-class standards appear to have been in the minority. Most accepted and responded to the sincerity of her efforts. To many students, she was, indeed, a magical princess who inspired and energized. Students also appreciated her efforts to become acquainted with them all and to remember the names of the hundreds of students who came weekly so that she could introduce any two to each other. Lucy's Fridays were modelled on both George Palmer's poetry readings and Alice Palmer's "heart culture." These receptions also recalled those of another early role model, Marlborough's Mrs. Caswell, whose Wednesday afternoons combined academic exercises with practice in deportment. Amid the arid cultural and social landscape inhabited by Berkeley's women students, Lucy's hospitality had special meaning. As Lucy put it, her house became a "stage" for her "official self." At the same time it was a place where she could be herself and "do what she wanted." Her love of poetry, color, and performance could now contribute to her professional role. She had found a mode of relationship and style of teaching that was deeply, personally satisfying.

For Lucy, trips to the city's ports and streets and to urban agencies, which enriched students' knowledge of the world, and poetry readings at the Story Book House, to stimulate their love of culture and beauty, were creative methods of countering Berkeley's failure to provide students with a challenging curriculum. Increasing self-confidence and group cohesion through self-government and shared social projects were also effective ways to mold student interests. But none of these approaches seemed to her sufficient to the task of fundamentally redirecting the nature of higher education for women at the University of California. This sense of the need for more radical change would gradually bring her to a new departure—of all her life changes, the first that was an independent initiative and not a response to a need or an invitation from someone else.

Despite her dissatisfaction with the limited potential of her job, Lucy's deanship brought her great professional and personal rewards. She also reaped much benefit from her other university role: that of faculty member. On the advice of George Herbert Palmer, Lucy had told President Wheeler that she would not take on the administrative job he offered unless she also had a faculty appointment. But she did not believe she had any qualification for a faculty position. Her graduate training had been in philosophy, yet she had no desire to teach philosophy. According to her autobiography, she was heavily under the influence of Veblen at this point in her life. At her own suggestion and with the concurrence of chairman Adolph Miller, she began her faculty career in 1903 as a Reader in the Department of Economics under Thomas Walker Page. The following year she took a course in "Economic Origins" from Wesley Clair Mitchell, recently hired from the University of Chicago. Mitchell's approach impressed Lucy with its "ferment of philosophy and ethnology" centered on a Veblenian, anthropological explanation of the economic origins of cultural institutions. She was dazzled by Mitchell's accumulation of detailed data, as well as by his creative reconstruction of those data and his vivid teaching. Evidently, Mitchell was equally impressed by his very intense, engaging student. She got an A in the course. But she did not pursue her interest in teaching that subject.

Economics challenged her mind, but poetry and writing had been passionate early loves. Although at Radcliffe Lucy had had only a beginning course in English composition, she hoped that her informal study of poetry with Professor Palmer compensated for her lack of conventional training. In 1904, she became a Reader in the English Department: then she was Assistant in English, assigned to Chauncey Wells. By 1905, she was Instructor in English, teaching a section of a prescribed writing course for freshmen. In 1906, Lucy was appointed Assistant Professor of English. In that capacity, and with the encouragement of Wells, she offered a new course in versification to seniors and graduate students. It was her first experience in teaching material so close to her heart—a subject that had been a symbol of her childhood unworthiness—and it was a profoundly liberating experience.

Lucy Sprague's only female faculty colleague at the university was her good friend Jessica Peixotto. Fourteen years older than Lucy, Peixotto had graduated from the University of California in 1894; in 1900, she earned a Ph.D. in economics—she was the second woman at Berkeley to receive the doctorate. In January, 1904, Peixotto was appointed instructor in sociology, making her the first woman to hold a formal faculty appointment at the university. She was promoted to Assistant Professor in 1907, the year after Lucy became Assistant Professor of English. In 1918, Peixotto became the first woman at the university to receive the rank of full professor. She remained at Berkeley until her retirement in 1938, teaching courses on poverty, the care of dependents, the child and the state, crime as a social problem, the household as an economic agent, and other socially oriented topics. Peixotto also organized and directed the first training program in social work in California, which eventually became an offering in the graduate curriculum.[35] After Lucy's first months at Berkeley, during which she lived with the Millers, she and Peixotto rented a small house high in the Berkeley hills, which they shared until 1906, when the Ridge Road home was built.

Lucy Sprague and Jessica Peixotto, then, were the first two women on the faculty of the thirty-five-year-old University of California, now a major educational center with over two thousand students and 268 faculty. Lucy felt that her own promotions at Berkeley had been "spectacular" and "completely unwarranted" academically. She recognized that without the support of President Wheeler they might not have happened. Although Lucy and Peixotto had a coterie of faculty admirers, the reception of the two women by the rest of the university's teaching staff was clearly cool. Lucy recalled:

It was to be expected that the great majority of the faculty should look askance—to put it mildly—at appointing a blooming, inexperienced and not very intellectual young woman to the faculty. But Jessica Peixotto was their equal in training and in intelligence, and they acted the same way toward her appointment because she was a woman.[36]

The women felt so strong a hostility from their colleagues that neither of them ever attended a faculty meeting. "Certainly we could have gone," Lucy explained many years later, "but I know that it would have prejudiced the men against us, and we already had enough to live down."[37]

The attitudes of the male faculty came as a shock to Lucy. As dean of women, she was concerned with creating a more viable, active presence for women students at a campus that feared and scorned them. As a faculty member, confronting masculine professional hostility for the first time, she discovered that male antagonism to educated women was not merely an adolescent phenomenon. "In the course of my work," she wrote,

I came to realize the standards that our culture of that day held for women in education and in the general management of their own lives. I had long been kicking against these standards in my personal life but with no clear analysis of what so frustrated me. It came as a shock when I realized that most of the faculty thought of women frankly as inferior beings. The older men were solidly opposed to having any women on the faculty. Any woman who, intellectually, could hold such a position must be a freak and "unwomanly." To be sure, most of the Harvard faculty held the same opinion, and Radcliffe's creed concerning teachers was "no women" because Harvard had none. . . .

I applied all these arguments to myself. If, at twenty-five, I were still untrained, still shy in the presence of those who were trained, it had not been my woman's intellect that had made me so. It had been two powerful older men who had undertaken to run my life for me. I was humiliated by my lack of training: Now I had my chance—a chance for which I had had no adequate preparation but one I must take, nevertheless. I felt it was not only an opportunity for me personally, but somehow it also seemed a significant step ahead for women as a sex. I was very far from an aggressive "feminist." I simply felt I must do my job extremely well.[38]

Lucy was not an aggressive feminist, to be sure. Like Alice Palmer, she favored suffrage but her support was not vigorous. In an interview given to The New York Times in October 1911, while she was attending a meeting of deans of women in New York, Lucy explained her position. "There

are many persons who, believing in equal suffrage, think it would be better if it had not come just at this time," she observed. "We are trying so
many new things at once that if there is trouble we cannot tell what is
making the rumpus."[39] Yet the nominating committee of the Berkeley
branch of the Association of Collegiate Alumnae, of which she was a
member, sent a strong pro-suffrage slate to the state federation meeting.
On October 13, the voters of California passed the suffrage amendment,
making the women of the state eligible to vote in all state and federal
elections. In Berkeley, the amendment won by 650 votes, twice the expected majority.[40]

Lucy's cautious position with regard to suffrage reflected the view of
most women educators, who believed that if the vote came too soon it
might jeopardize the newly won gains of women within higher education. Though Lucy had begun to understand the workings of patriarchal
culture at the University of California, she had not yet made the leap
of identifying the slights of educated women with those of all women.
That would not come until the dimensions of her own experience had
broadened.

The failure of male faculty to support the teaching appointments of
Jessica Piexotto and Lucy Sprague undoubtedly contributed to Lucy's uncertainty about her own work and status at the university. She doubted
her own intelligence, her achievements, even her femininity—for most
women of her class and background did not work—but at the same time,
the excitement, difficulty, and satisfactions of her job nurtured her self-
esteem. She knew she was a competent, efficient, and "pioneering"
dean. In 1911, about to leave Berkeley, she gave this assessment of her
performance to Wesley Mitchell:

I feel superior to my kind, I feel I am abler in an executive way and that I touch
life through more sympathies than those with whom I am thrown. I have known
deans who excel me in any single qualification but none who have as high an average in the multifold desirable characteristics; I have felt that strongly these
last days. Potentially I rank myself with the best educational administrators
except—and this exception disqualifies me for any great education post—in intellectual training. . . . I have not had sufficient intellectual training along any
line to give me real standards or judgements.[41]

Many years later Lucy Sprague's successor, Lucy Stebbins, told Lucy:

You laid the foundation at the University of California for a rewarding life for
me. You had already rescued the conception of a Dean of Women from the bog

of discipline and decorum into which so many deans fall and you had given to
the office vision and breadth of service such as few deans or their constituents,
then or now, have ever had.[42]

Other deans also recognized her creativity and competence. Though
she was younger than most deans (she writes that several had opposed
her appointment at Berkeley because of her youth), they acknowledged
her, she recounted, as the "dean of deans." She recalled that one much
older dean once told her, "You have come to be a mother to us all."
There is no reason to doubt these recollections of honor from her peers,
but Lucy's emphasis on them suggests the insecurity she was contending
with at the time. Furthermore, while the creative aspect of Lucy's work
as dean is not to be minimized, much of her time was necessarily spent on
routine matters of student social life, especially housing. This was itself a
source of dissatisfaction.

Lucy's perception that most women deans, even her good friend
Evelyn Allen at Stanford (dubbed "The Lady" by students), were of the
motherly, protective "warden" type, was probably accurate. Ada Comstock of Minnesota (later president of Radcliffe), whom Lucy often
roomed with at deans' conferences, was one who did not fit this mold.
With Comstock, she used to discuss substantive concerns about the
higher education of women, not merely questions about dormitory rules,
financial aid, student dances, and the like. Even for the more traditional
deans, there were few guidelines. Official appointments of deans of
women were made at most coeducational universities only in the decade
after 1900.[43] Every dean, especially if her goals related to curricular
rather than purely administrative matters, had to devise her own approaches. Only in 1911, by which time Lucy had already determined to
leave the deanship, did women deans across the country begin gathering
on a regular basis. Not until 1918 did the deans organize their National
Association and become a department of the National Educational Association, a sign of the growing professionalization of their work.[44]

Lucy Sprague's innovations as dean had been colored by her own perspectives, biases, intuitions. Her approach to the problems of curricula
and social life followed two main lines. The first, as we have seen, was to
build the self-esteem of women students by encouraging self-government,
unifying women's activities, fostering relationships among students, im-
proving housing facilities, developing new clubs and all-women programs. In most of these efforts, she played a facilitating rather than
directing role, relying on her staff, faculty wives, upperclasswomen,

women benefactors of the university, and students themselves wherever possible. Until women had developed their own political and social life, they would continue to be passive spectators at the university's banquet; they would control neither how the table was set nor what nourishment would be available. An important part of her contribution at Berkeley was to enable women students to gain access to whatever a university experience might offer.

Her second approach employed her pedagogical impulses more directly. As we also have seen, she came to disparage the narrow vocational objectives of most female students. Part of the problem lay in the limited range of vocationally relevant courses offered to university women—an inadequacy she would eventually address. Now her solution was to enhance the education of women students by providing them with opportunities to discover at first hand the world outside.

Lucy's "curriculum of experience" was an innovative pedagogical approach to college education in the early twentieth century, one that she would later apply to the education of young children. It worked, as she recognized, because of two characteristics: students were directly exposed to sources of stimulation from real life, and the professor learned alongside the students. For Lucy, this was instinctive rather than acquired pedagogy. It was the way she had always learned, whether she was exploring the cosmopolitan environment of the World's Fair or sampling Chicago's diverse religious establishments. As a Dean she could create a context in which to share the learning style that had been effective in her own past, with a content designed to compensate for the deficiencies in a curriculum which, like Radcliffe's, she felt was too academic and remote.

From the perspective of most of the students and of the administration, she was doing a splendid job. If her recollections and those of Lucy Stebbins are correct, she also received considerable recognition outside Berkeley for her work. But Lucy was dissatisfied on several levels. Unable to conceive of her role in professional terms, she grew to like administrative work less and less. Despite the improvements she had promoted and the success of her own "heart culture," she continued to feel that women students were poorly trained at the university and given few options. Then, too, she felt intellectually inferior to other members of Berkeley's faculty, including Jessica Peixotto. She confided to Wesley Mitchell:

As a mere force in the world, if I could ever find a notch that fitted me as well as hers fits her, I think I could be her equal if not superior. But intellectually I humble myself before her . . . my training is so superficial—and must always be now—that my mind as an *intellectual instrument* must always be in a different class from hers.[45]

Finally, and perhaps most important, as she began to approach the limits of what she could accomplish in the role of Dean of Women, she had come to harbor grave doubts about the direction her life was taking, and she began to question her ambitions and her achievements so far.

The years at Berkeley had shown her that she could make good her desire to live as a working citizen rather than as an eligible Chicago heiress; more, she had found work that allowed her to feel part of the tradition of service and education that she admired in Jane Addams and Alice Freeman Palmer. Even less to be taken for granted, on the stage of the Story Book House she had been able to deploy not only her intelligence but her femininity, her taste, and her ardent engagement with poetry and the arts, all as part of her job. But in time, out of that very expansion of personal opportunity and the admiration that came with it, grew new claims for herself as a woman.

Lucia Sprague (*top*). Courtesy of Andrew and Paul Mitchell. Otho S. A. Sprague (*bottom*). From *The Encyclopedia of Biography of Illinois*, vol. 2 (Chicago: The Century Publishing and Engraving Co., 1894), facing p. 86. Courtesy of the Chicago Historical Society.

Lucy Sprague at age seven (*top*). Lucy as a bridesmaid at her sister Mary's wedding (1895) (*bottom*). Lucy Sprague Mitchell Papers, Rare Book and Manuscript Library, Columbia University.

The Sprague family in their library at 2710 Prairie Avenue, Chicago; Lucy is second from the right. Lucy Sprague Mitchell Papers, Rare Book and Manuscript Library, Columbia University.

Alice Freeman Palmer and George Herbert Palmer in the library of their home at 11 Quincy Street, Cambridge (*top*). Courtesy of the Wellesley College Archives. The Class of 1900, Radcliffe College (*bottom*). Lucy is fifth from right, third row. Courtesy of the Radcliffe College Archives.

Lucy's favorite picture of Robin, on the slope of Mt. Tamalpais, California (*top*). Courtesy of Andrew and Paul Mitchell. Lucy Sprague, Dean of Women, University of California (ca. 1906) (*bottom*). Courtesy of the Bancroft Library, University of California, Berkeley.

Costume sketches for the 1912 Masque of Maidenhood (Partheneia) at the University of California. Courtesy of the Bancroft Library, University of California, Berkeley.

Lillian Wald (*top left*). The Bettmann Archive.
Florence Kelley (*top right*). The Schlesinger Library, Radcliffe College.
Pauline Goldmark (*bottom left*). The Schlesinger Library, Radcliffe College.
Jane Addams (*bottom right*). The Schlesinger Library, Radcliffe College.

Lucy Sprague and Wesley Clair Mitchell on their wedding day, May 8, 1912. Lucy Sprague Mitchell Papers, Rare Book and Manuscript Library, Columbia University.

7

Sierra Visions

Lucy had reached a transition point in the development of her professional life. She had successfully established new roles for herself within teaching and academic administration, but having rejected the standard scenario of middle- and upper-class womanhood, she was uncertain how to come to terms with her sexuality, her desire for intimacy and for family life. In her autobiography she admitted, "I know now how the fear of being *only* a professional woman had clutched me all through the Berkeley years when I was living a truly exciting work life."[1]

In her first year as dean of women, she wrote a poem called "Symbol of a New Career." Addressed to a vanished lover, it speaks of her personal loneliness, despite her professional achievement:

And now I have reached the utmost crest
Below is the intimate world I have left
But the other side of the hill is bare
I wanted to come—but I grope for your hand
What do I want: I don't understand.[2]

At the time, Lucy masked her doubts about her personal life by viewing her poems as experiments in verse form, exercises undertaken in connection with her new course on versification. As in childhood, writing sublimated emotions and fears she could not acknowledge, even to herself.

Like most young women of her time, Lucy had highly ambivalent attitudes about sex. In her autobiography, she portrays herself as sexually ignorant until her college years. It was not until she went to Radcliffe, she says, that she learned where babies came from or that menstruation was

related to reproduction. By the time Lucy came to Berkeley, she was not
very much more knowledgeable. But it turned out that her duties as
Dean of Women required her to become actively involved with issues of
sexuality. It was to President Wheeler, not to female relatives or college
friends, that she turned. Wheeler was a "tolerant man-of-the-world" and
gave her discreet, helpful advice.[3]

On one occasion, when a student became pregnant and Lucy sought
Wheeler's opinion, he insisted that the young man responsible must
marry the girl. The boy complied but ran off soon after the baby was
born. Lucy found work for the girl, giving her sewing and other odd jobs,
and encouraged her to complete her degree. Another student induced an
abortion while at a YWCA meeting and tried to flush the fetus down the
water closet. Although Lucy is matter-of-fact in relating these incidents
in her memoirs, we can imagine with what dismay she greeted them at
the time. Premarital sex, abortion, venereal disease—what she called
the "seamy" side of sex—had never been forced upon her attention until
now.

Towards the end of her deanship, however, a wave of education in sex
hygiene swept the country. Under the leadership of reform-minded
doctors and women's rights advocates, a "social purity" campaign was
launched to end the double standard of conduct and the evils of prostitution and venereal disease.[4]

As a consequence, open and frank discussion of sexual matters became
fashionable: in order to be modern, noted Lucy's sister Mary, you had to
say "syphilis" at least once a day. These trends "stormed" the campus
with "hysterical intensity," Lucy recalled. The five women connected
with the university—Lucy, Jessica Peixotto, May Cheney, Dr. Mary Ritter (now in charge of the new women's gymnasium), and Dr. Eleanor
Bancroft, the women's physician—met to form a plan of action. They
decided that Dean Sprague and Dr. Bancroft should inform all women
students about matters of normal physiology and sex disease.

Lucy and Dr. Bancroft tried to take a positive approach; several male
students reportedly had fainted during lectures on the terrifying aspects
of venereal disease. Dr. Bancroft lectured on menstruation, pregnancy,
and childbirth. Though Lucy recalled that she had scarcely heard of gon-
orrhea or syphilis and had to read up on them, she held discussions on
sexual diseases with small groups until all of Berkeley's nearly twelve
hundred women students had been reached. "Becoming a specialist on
sex diseases" was the "queerest" of all the queer things she had done in
her twenty-seven years, Lucy felt.[5]

The question of intimate relationships was not so easily dealt with in Lucy's own life. Her close friends and surrogate families in Berkeley were important to her, providing affection, approval, and warm contacts. But none of these replaced the deep relationship she had established in adolescence with Marion Jones, who still wrote to Lucy of her love and attachment; nor did they compensate for her loss of Joe, the one man she felt she had loved. Of the men who called upon her at the Story Book House, most were "sedate" professors, of whom she speaks with no great fondness. One caller was so boring, and she so weary, that she fell asleep during his visit, and awakened only as he tiptoed out. The two men she liked best were Rudolph Schevill, a professor of Spanish with a great interest in music, and Wesley Mitchell. Yet at least during her first few years at Berkeley, there is no sense that she had a romantic interest in either.[6]

Perhaps the deepest attachment she formed at Berkeley was to her niece Polly. Lucy took complete charge of Polly during the few months she stayed with the Millers, and played with her regularly thereafter. She found her young niece to be "eager, intense, full of curiosities." Lucy was especially enchanted with Polly's use of language. A favorite anecdote, which Lucy recalled throughout her later life, told how Lucy and Polly had gone exploring up the hill near Polly's garden. When Lucy tried later to get Polly to remember their climb, Polly responded blankly as Lucy described the sights they had seen, until suddenly she piped up, "Why, Tante Lucy, you mean the place where the legs ache!"[7] Lucy had learned that a child's memories were dominated by sense and muscle perceptions, an insight that became a key element in her later thinking about children's language. She began to take notes on Polly's speech and thought. Already, Lucy's pleasure in the company of a child she loved was mixed with her own drive to learn, observe, and teach.

Suddenly, however, Polly, who had always been frail, became seriously ill. Within a few months she was dead, the victim of a rare blood disease, the doctors said. The Millers were never to have another child: there had been complications with Mary's first pregnancy, and later she had undergone gynecological surgery. The loss was devastating to the Millers and scarcely less so to Lucy. Once again, when she had loved someone fiercely, that person was snatched from her. "When will I believe it?" she asked in a poem she wrote after Polly's death. The giant redwood groves of Boulder Creek near the Millers' vineyards where Lucy and Polly used to play became a tragic reminder: "Two thousand years of life to a tree and only four to a little girl" seemed impossible to accept.[8]

The role of "tante" had been deeply rewarding to Lucy, and though there were still the Howard and Gregory children, they could not replace Polly.

Lucy's anxieties about her personal life—whether or not she would have children of her own, or marry, or experience love at all—could not be put to rest. The "academic" poems she wrote during these years expressed some of her feelings about these issues. Yet Lucy interpreted the poems as products of her conscious, rational, schoolteacher self rather than of her emotions.

It is thus startling to read the few Shakespearean and Petrarchan sonnets written during this period that remain among Lucy's papers. They were love sonnets, and each expresses a vibrant sexual passion. Love is evoked in sexual terms—touching, quivering, caressing, possessing—the "sudden flash," the "blinding glare" of union. Physical desire and intimacy are explicitly and lovingly portrayed.[9]

The poems seem to have been written several years after Joe had left her romantic life and before Wesley Clair Mitchell had effectively entered it. There is no reason to believe that there was sexual contact between Lucy and any of her suitors at Berkeley. Rather, these poems of passion reflect her desires: the desire for "quiet tenderness and love," for intimacy, for consummation. Though I believe they were poems of fantasy rather than experience, they reveal a passionate and yearning nature. They also reveal the "demon loneliness" at the core of this much admired, competent young woman.[10]

"Through the day," Lucy wrote, the thought of her lover lay like a "dear warm thing / just beneath the surface of my thought — / comforting, sustaining, encouraging." But "through the night" the thought of her lover "flames to open fire / it clutches at my throat / it lays intimate lips on mine / it strokes my body with a loving touch / consuming, vivifying, satisfying."[11] "Night" and "day" were both integral parts of the psyche of Lucy Sprague. So far, on her own at Berkeley, only the day had found expression.

Lucy first met Wesley Clair Mitchell when he was a graduate student at the University of Chicago, and she was eighteen, on vacation from Radcliffe. Mitchell attended a dinner party given by Lucy's sister Mary and her bridegroom Adolph Miller. Lucy remembered being overwhelmed by the brilliant older group Mary had assembled that eve-

ning.[12] Though she knew most of the guests well, they seemed "ter-
rifyingly" informal to her, and, as usual, she felt excruciatingly shy
and tongue-tied in their presence. Lucy was impressed by the fact that
Mitchell, slender, red-cheeked, and moustached, did not seem awed by
the company. At age twenty-two, he seemed quite mature to her, and
though he too was quiet, Lucy felt it was not out of shyness. Most of all,
she remembered that Mitchell tried to make her feel at ease among that
frightening group. And—that she didn't like his moustache. It was too
much like her father's conspicuous handlebars.[13]

Years later, Lucy met Mitchell again in Berkeley, where he had been
called to "Adolph's department." Lucy took one of Mitchell's courses at
the university and met him frequently at the Millers' home. Adolph liked
good listeners, and Mitchell was unfailingly courteous, although he did
not hesitate to voice his disagreement with Adolph's ideas. Indeed, he
was the first person to encourage Lucy to question Adolph's infallibility.

Rarely in her first few years at Berkeley did she and Wesley Mitchell
meet except as fellow guests. Still, Lucy claims that Mitchell was one of
the few people at the university who understood her real purpose there;
her arrangement with Wheeler to survey the general needs of women
students before becoming dean of women was not generally known.
Mitchell treated her work during those years, and the ambiguity of her
undeclared assignment, in a "simple but serious" manner.[14]

The Berkeley years were extremely important to Wesley Mitchell's
own professional development. The second of seven children of John
Wesley Mitchell, a New England born physician, and Lucy Medora
McClellan, daughter of a mid-Western farmer, Mitchell had spent his
childhood years in Illinois. John and Lucy were affectionate and sympathetic parents, but the family's recurrent economic crises, caused by his
father's frequent illnesses, had placed a great strain on the children, particularly Wesley, the oldest son. Through much scrimping and saving,
the family managed to send Wesley off to the new University of Chicago
in 1892; he became one of its first entrants—the "aborigines," as they
called themselves.[15]

In his freshman year, Mitchell had the good fortune to take a course in
the history of philosophy with thirty-two-year-old John Dewey—whose
brilliant first book, *Psychology*, had been published five years earlier—
and an introductory course in economics with Thorstein Veblen, "a
large-eyed, brown-bearded, slow-speaking quiet person in the mid-
thirties," who was assigned to a minor post in the department.[16] Both

men made a profound impression on the eighteen-year-old Mitchell. From them he learned the tools of critical thinking, which led him to eschew forever all preconceived theoretical systems. And from them, he also acquired an evolutionary, genetic approach to the study of behavior, an approach that highlighted process as the key to the analysis of past and contemporary cultures.

"Writhing under Veblen's scalpel," Mitchell found his intellectual complacency shattered. "To a well-brought-up scion of American culture, taking one of Veblen's courses meant undergoing vivisection without an anesthetic," Mitchell recalled. "Those who could stand the treatment, and not all could, came out with a much more critical attitude toward economic theory, and toward themselves. . . ." Veblen brought to economics "the detachment of a visitor from Mars": he developed a wholly new approach to understanding economic systems.[17] His distinction between the pecuniary and industrial aspects of economic institutions played a particularly important role in Mitchell's thinking.

Veblen took as his focus the whole of cultural history, integrating economics with ethnology, anthropology, and psychology; Dewey, whom Mitchell thought of as "the first behaviorist," took as his subject the human mind. Every one of Dewey's courses dealt with the same problem, Mitchell recalled, "how we think."[18] Under Dewey's tutelage as well as Veblen's, Mitchell abandoned the traditional framework of economic theory. Dewey was especially influential in convincing Mitchell that economics must become a science of human behavior, to be measured and analyzed empirically.

Other influences at the University of Chicago shaped Mitchell's early thinking. He encountered the brilliant physiologist Jacques Loeb, whose studies of organic behavior were models of scientific method. J. Laurence Laughlin, chairman of the economics department, was important in a different way, for his conservative views provoked Mitchell's dissent. In his money and banking course, Laughlin introduced Mitchell to the topic of business cycles, the subject of Mitchell's mature work. And it was he who suggested the topic of Mitchell's doctoral thesis—a statistical study of Civil War greenbacks—in the hope of counteracting the radical influences of Veblen and Dewey. Laughlin and Dewey provided graduate fellowships, which enabled Mitchell to complete his doctoral work in economics in 1899, summa cum laude, with a year of study in Halle and Vienna. After completing his doctoral work, Mitchell spent a year at the Bureau of the Census and two years at Chicago as Instructor in Economics, with Veblen and Laughlin as colleagues, and his expanded doctoral thesis was published as A *History of the Greenbacks*. [19]

It was in 1902 that Mitchell joined the department of economics at the University of California, chaired by his former teacher Adolph Miller. The younger man admired Miller's abilities as a lecturer. "He had the finest gift of exposition of any academician I have ever listened to at length," Mitchell recalled. "What was worse, he had excellent judgment, nicely attuned to the prevailing views of the times. As students we had merely to admire his artistry . . . and to welcome the confirmation of what we already believed." [20] As department chair at Berkeley, Miller gave Mitchell the opportunity to teach whatever he liked and the time to continue his research. This freedom soon led to new ideas. Mitchell completed a second volume on greenbacks and gave a series of new courses. The first, which Lucy attended, covered the Economic Origins of Primitive Cultures. Others dealt with the current organization of economic institutions—Principles of Economics, Money, Banking, and Problems of Labor. Beginning in 1905, Mitchell offered several courses on the relation between the money economy and business fluctuations— Economic Origins, The Theory of Banking, and Economic Crises and Depressions. Later, he added the History of Economic Thought and Economic Psychology. Increasingly he had widened his conception of what the new science of economics should be about, and now, under the influence of ethnology, psychology, and philosophy, he determined to explore the history of economic institutions and ideas systematically.

In 1907, Mitchell began a manuscript on the money economy. After a leave at Harvard in 1908–09, he returned to California as full professor. The following winter, having abandoned the money economy manuscript as too speculative, he began a draft of a new work on *Business Cycles*. This project called for a comprehensive examination of the "recurring readjustments of prices" in four countries in which the money economy had reached full expression—the United States, England, Germany and France. As part of the research for this, Mitchell found himself pioneering the development of a statistical index of commodity prices, wages, stock prices, bond prices, and the money supply.

Although Mitchell's basic interest at Berkeley was his work, his daily diaries, which he kept regularly from 1905, record an extraordinary number of social events—dinners, parties, dances, tennis games, nature walks, concerts, and meetings of scores of clubs and societies. There were talks until the small hours with Veblen, when he was teaching at Stanford, and visits with his many friends on the Berkeley faculty, among them the brilliant but temperamental Jacques Loeb, literary scholar Walter Hart, poet Arthur Ryder, mathematician John Hector McDonald, and economist Henry Hatfield.

Particularly important in Mitchell's social life at the time were the Riebers' regular Sunday dinner discussions, usually attended by the Hockings, Howisons, and Overstreets. The topics recorded in Mitchell's diary included philosophers and religion, the meaning of "absolute truth," the necessary and sufficient conditions of human happiness, psychology and metaphysics, the idea of the absolute, and socialism, the university, and military service.[21] Mitchell lunched or dined occasionally with a number of single women around Berkeley, as well as with his close friends Sadie Gregory, Jessica Peixotto, and Dorothea Moore. Lucy Sprague appeared on Mitchell's social calendar only occasionally during these years. In March of 1905, she invited him to dinner along with the Gregorys, Jessica Peixotto, and other guests. A month later, Mitchell notes an afternoon call on Lucy Sprague. After a dinner and dance some weeks later, he notes that he escorted Lucy to her carriage. Lucy is not mentioned again in Mitchell's diary until January 1906, when she attended a dinner given by the Millers to which he was also invited. "Miss Sprague was there looking even more charming than usual in a pearl-colored dress with a myriad of narrow pleats," he wrote in his diary. She was also present one evening at the Gregorys, when John Galen Howard talked about modern poetry, and again, at a dinner party at Jessica Peixotto's.[22]

In 1907, their contacts increased. In January, Lucy attended a dance at the Riebers. The following month, she gave an informal reception to which she invited the Gregorys, the Hockings, the Welleses, Jessica Peixotto, and Wesley Mitchell. In March, Lucy and Mitchell were present at a philosophical discussion at the Riebers; the following week Lucy invited Mitchell and the Millers to dinner. At the end of the month, Lucy attended a Bachelors dance at Wilkins Hall. She was one of eleven women, all duly listed in Mitchell's diary, with whom he danced.[23]

But there was no evidence of special interest on either side, until May 8, 1907. On that evening, the Howards gave a fancy dress ball. Many of Berkeley's most eminent professors and their wives joined the party. The host, John Galen Howard, persuaded Lucy to come as Cleopatra to his Anthony. She was shy but not unwilling to take on this regal and passionate role. Howard's long legs showed to advantage in Shakespearean "fleshings." Accompanying Lucy was her house guest, her dear friend Marion Jones Farquhar. A few days earlier, Marion and Lucy had soundly defeated Mitchell and his partner at tennis. Mitchell too was at the costume ball, though we do not know in what guise. In his diary, however, he noted his dancing partners; Sadie Gregory led the list, with three dances; next came Lucy Sprague with two.[24]

The ball took place in the huge high-raftered lanai or porch that stretched across the front of the Howards' beautiful home on Ridge Road. Filled with flowers and climbing vines, it was a brilliant, dramatic setting. Toward the end of the evening, Lucy and Marion slipped away to Lucy's house next door and reappeared in gypsy costume: long colorful skirts, gay blouses and shawls. Marion, as she walked, played the guitar and sang songs by Debussy—a decidedly avant-garde choice at the time. The entrance of the gypsies was perhaps more dramatically effective than they had expected; it caught the attention of the whole company, and suddenly Lucy felt with embarrassment that "thousands of pairs of eyes" were staring at her. Her reaction was not to efface herself but to earn her share of attention; she threw herself into an improvised wild dance to Marion's music. Marion, startled but delighted, played on, performing a repertoire of gypsy and Russian folk music. Lucy did not stop, could not stop, until Marion put away the guitar. She danced for hours, it seemed, though it was near midnight when she began. Later, her brother-in-law Adolph reproved her for forgetting her "dignity" and her "position" in such a way. But it was this moment of feminine self-assertion and abandon that captivated Wesley Clair Mitchell and won for Lucy the full life that she had hoped for. In his diary he wrote only that "Mrs. Farquhar and Miss Sprague gave Russian folk song and dance" at the ball, but he added that, staying overnight with the Gregorys, he sat up till four. Lucy had moved him as no woman had before. He lay awake thinking of her.[25]

(On one other occasion in Berkeley, Lucy had danced with abandon. But there had been no spectators that moonlit night when she climbed onto the stage of Berkeley's outdoor Greek Theater. In her long accordion-pleated dress with yards of soft gray silk, Lucy danced and danced, until "satisfied," she "crept" home.[26])

Two days later Wesley Mitchell sent Lucy a poem, "The Dancer."

A lute, a voice, weird cries, strange words
A wraith which danced like flame. . . .

With rhythm wild our hearts beguiled
[Bringing] bliss without alloy.

"Where'ere I turn my face," he wrote, "still I see . . . the dancer's charms, her waving arms, her love-compelling grace."[27]

Three weeks later he noted in his diary that he had finished "*the* letter," in which he asked Lucy to marry him. On June 2, he received her response. Neither of the letters survives, but Lucy wrote in *Two Lives* that she responded firmly and coldly, refusing him outright, because she was emotionally involved with another man at the time. (Her correspondence with Mitchell a few years later does not confirm this involvement.) "The letter has come," he wrote to Sadie Gregory the next day. "She does not love me and is positive she never can." Mitchell noted that the letter had a "deathly kindness," but admired the "wonderful" frankness Lucy had shown. Mitchell told Sadie that he was still hopeful for the future. But when he called on Lucy a few weeks later, she responded so decisively that Mitchell gave up his campaign. After the summer they continued to meet at the Riebers' Sunday dinner discussions (Lucy seems to have joined this group as a regular member for the first time in September), at the Riebers' dances and other Berkeley social events. She invited him to a dinner party the next February along with the Millers, Jessica Peixotto, and other common friends; and then again in March to two more dinner parties, with the Gregorys, Howards and Wellses also present. But there were no more words about love or marriage.[28]

Wesley Clair Mitchell left Berkeley in September of 1908 to spend the academic year at Harvard. Though he had long dreamed of teaching there, he found the experience disappointing, mainly because lectures to large classes left him little time for his own research. At the end of the year, he declined an offer from Edwin Gay, chairman of the economics department, to stay on at Harvard to develop a joint statistical laboratory for the economics department and business school.[29]

Despite a busy social schedule, Mitchell was lonely at Harvard. Occasionally he visited the Hockings in New Haven, where Ernest had accepted a position with Yale's department of philosophy. His Harvard colleagues entertained him frequently, and he joined a basketball group, since tennis had a limited season in the Boston climate. Mitchell's calendar is also dotted with dinner engagements with single women to whom his friends were always introducing him, including Wellesley economist

Emily Greene Balch, and Maude Radford Warren, a writer who had attended the University of Chicago with him and who now came to Harvard to visit on several occasions. There was no communication between Mitchell and Lucy Sprague.[30]

On the day after his return to Berkeley in August, 1909, Mitchell met Lucy at the Millers. She invited him to lunch a few days later, along with the Gregorys. He called upon Lucy the next week, but did not find her in. In fact, she was preparing to leave for Europe with Benjamin Ide Wheeler and his family, accompanying them on Wheeler's sabbatical in Germany. Lucy scribbled a brief courtesy note to Wesley on the train that took her east. That would be their only communication for another year. Not until Lucy arrived back in Berkeley in early 1910 did she and Mitchell meet again.[31]

Although Lucy Sprague was developing an independent professional life at Berkeley, in many respects she remained as dutiful a daughter as she had always been. Nearly every other weekend she visited her father in Pasadena, a journey of more than five hundred miles each way that probably took about ten hours by train. She recalls her visits to Pasadena as being more frequent and lengthy than they actually were, but she did give up summer camping and hiking trips with Berkeley friends, as well as many weekends during the school year, to be with Otho. Mary, too, came regularly from Berkeley; usually, the two sisters arranged to alternate their visits.

Still devotedly cared for by Cousin Eleanor Atwood, Otho grew progressively weaker during Lucy's years at Berkeley. By early 1908, even breathing was a strenuous effort, and the visits from friends which he used to enjoy were now too exhausting. Soon, he also began to experience recurrent "head attacks" that caused him momentarily to lose consciousness. He wrote to Nan and Albert that he feared he would lose his mind completely. Eleanor added that he was so miserable all the time, day and night, that his doctors were giving him codeine to help him rest. Once resistant to any medication, Otho now meekly complied.[32]

Eleanor, at last worn down by her constant attendance on Otho, left in June to visit her own family in the midwest. Lucy came that summer to take her place, but this time a trained nurse was also hired. Otho wrote to his brother that he was delighted to have Lucy's company and that he thought her own health improved considerably during her stay.

Lucy perhaps thought otherwise, for she spent a few weeks recuperating from the visit at a resort at Carmel-by-the-Sea.[33]

Otho slipped steadily downward over the next few months. In February, Eleanor urged Albert and Nan to visit him once more, for she wasn't sure how long he would last. Otho was overcome with emotion when they arrived at his home on February 18. "My brother, my brother, I am so glad to see you," he whispered. He lost consciousness at eleven at night on February 19, awakening only once. Lucy and Eleanor spent the long night with him. By the next morning, he was gone. Eleanor had been like a daughter to him, Otho had often told his friends; now she was overcome by grief, while Lucy soberly helped arrange the funeral and the closing of Otho's affairs. Despite Lucy's quiet thoroughness, everyone noticed that she seemed weak, trembling, and distraught. With Otho's death, a long chapter in Lucy Sprague's life had come to a close. Otho's pedagogy would remain with her in important ways, but his ever-present, powerful claims, which had exerted a steady influence upon her conscience, will, and morals, even in his declining years, would be no more.[34]

The first effect of her father's death was to allow Lucy to face more clearly the question of what she wanted to do next. The dissatisfaction she had previously felt at the University of California now crystallized; she recognized that she did not want to continue in her present job. In May, Lucy was asked by president Nicholas Murray Butler of Columbia University to consider becoming dean of Barnard College.[35] Her reputation as an energetic and creative administrator was by now well established. Butler inquired whether he might raise her name with the trustees as a serious candidate for the job.

With this option in mind, Lucy began to consider alternatives. According to her memoirs, that summer she told President Wheeler of her intention to leave the deanship when a successor could be found and when she had made more progress in rationalizing the functions of the office. Her communications with President Butler were important in leading her to this step. In the fall of 1909, on her way to Europe with the Wheelers, she stopped to visit the Barnard-Columbia campus and to chat with Butler. President Wheeler thought her unwise to consider the proposition at all, she recalled, since it meant greater administrative responsibilities, and Lucy was already chafing under her office routine at Berkeley. Nevertheless, it was only early the next summer that she decided not to put her name forward for the job.[36] In December 1910, President Butler announced that Barnard's new dean would be Virginia Gildersleeve, Barnard class of 1899, who held a Ph.D. from Columbia. Gildersleeve was to serve with distinction in the position for thirty-six years.

Lucy's decision to leave Berkeley had as much to do with her father's death as with the Barnard invitation. "I couldn't have left California while he lived," she wrote. Otho had taken a kind of pride in her university position, although he felt "humiliated that a daughter of his should receive a salary."[37] The job at Berkeley had represented a compromise between the needs of father and daughter; it provided meaningful work for Lucy, yet kept her close enough to maintain contact with Otho.

With Otho's passing came a new consciousness of choice: although all her life her career decisions would respond flexibly to opportunities, she would no longer go fatalistically where others claimed her; she would consult her own interests. Now she made no immediate decision, but nonetheless, in beginning to weigh her choices more actively, she made an important break with the past. Not insignificant was the fact that Lucy had been well provided for in her father's will. Otho had set up a trust fund of $500,000 each for Albert, Mary, and Lucy. Separate provision was made for Nannie.[38] The income would allow Lucy to live comfortably for the rest of her life, while still managing to give away considerable amounts.

After her decision to quit her job, Lucy felt "rootless" and detached. It was now that President Wheeler, who was appointed Roosevelt Exchange Professor at the University of Berlin, invited her to accompany his family and spend the winter of 1909–10 in Germany.[39] The distance from Berkeley and her own problems would enable her to gain a fresh perspective on her life, she thought. Wheeler had been an important father-figure to her; just as she had turned to the Palmers after her mother's death, accompanying them to Europe as a surrogate daughter, so Lucy reached out to the Wheelers in this time of bereavement and uncertainty. Despite her steps toward self-reliance, the conflict between dependency and independence in her life had not yet been resolved.

Lucy viewed her stay in Berlin as an "incredible, even bizarre" experience, a "strange Hollywood episode." The University of Berlin, where Wheeler was lecturing, was dominated by the Kaiser and his court in a manner totally at odds with the assumptions of American higher education. The Wheelers and Lucy were guests of honor at many state dinners

where they met distinguished military and public officials—among them
Admiral Von Tirpitz, Chancellor von Bethmann–Hollweg, Air Minister
Geheimrat Lewald, and Count Zeppelin. The attitudes of the German
aristocracy and the social etiquette of Kaiser Wilhelm's court, along with
the treatment that she herself received as the Amerikanische "Fräulein
Dekanin," were the most baffling aspects of the visit.[40]

In the old Hotel de Rome (where the Kaiser came to take baths, since
he had no plumbing in his own magnificent quarters), she was comfortable and at ease with the Wheelers. The Wheelers had a big living room
at the front of the apartment, and Lucy had an adjoining room which
could be thrown open into the living room when they entertained, as
they often did. Lucy rented a baby grand piano and spent many happy
hours playing scores of the concerts she attended. Together, they were a
family, she recalled—Mr. and Mrs. Wheeler, "sweet, intellectual"
sixteen-year-old Benjamin, and herself. One American newspaper, reporting the Wheeler's European trip, described Lucy as their "niece."

Air Minister Lewald became Lucy's "devoted admirer." He followed
her everywhere, "oozing German compliments." At one dinner that
Lewald held for Graf Zeppelin, whose airships were in the early stages of
development, Lewald embarrassed Lucy by sentimentally toasting the
lovely "Fräulein Spraagooa." He followed Lucy to San Moritz, where she
spent the Christmas holiday with the Wheelers and the Millers, who had
come to Europe for a winter vacation. When Lucy finally left Germany,
Lewald told her with great emotion that "I loose you very sadly."[41]

Lucy was simultaneously dazzled and repelled by German high society
and her glimpses of diplomatic life. The conspicuous display of wealth
and privilege bothered her, here as in Chicago. After one dinner at the
home of the American ambassador, she wrote in her diary: "Whole thing
is formal, impressive, and farcical. . . . Feel out of place classed with a lot
of rich Americans who are tying to buy their way into social Berlin. Furious that I have got myself into this position. . . . I'm going to do something *real* after this. Half a mind to leave Berlin and all social glitter. I'm
really not the kind to make it work."[42]

Yet she stayed, greatly enjoying some of the formal social events she
attended in spite of her distaste for their ostentatiousness. The highlight
of the year was her formal presentation to the Kaiser and Kaiserin—an
event for which she was duly coached by the ambassador's wife. The
evening was splendid, with guests of every nationality in brilliant costumes—the men (except the Americans) in officers' uniforms, knicker-

bockers with gold embroidery, the women in long trains and veils. Lucy
wore a salmon pink dress with long train and gold trim. When it was her
turn to approach the Kaiser and Kaiserin, sitting at the end of a magnificent hall under a huge canopy, one of the ladies-in-waiting scooped up
her train with a silver baton and threw it out so that it trailed far behind
her. Lucy's name was called out and, trembling, she made the required
two bows.

At dinners, guests were always seated in accordance with their rank,
with the highest in the middle. She always found herself in the very middle, flanked by "overwhelmingly distinguished *Geheimrater* with tremendous titles." Everyone greeted her with respect and great curiosity, since
a dean represented high status, and a woman dean was without prece-
dent. Yet Lucy felt that she didn't look very learned, since she was not.
She felt like a "fake"—she hadn't earned her title and had no special
training. Still, she "tried to live up to my popularity based on false
assumptions."[43]

In years to come, her most vivid memories of her life in Berlin were often of ridiculous situations—incidents heightened by the stiff formality
of most social events. On one occasion Lucy sat next to a "large uphol-
stered lady in deep crimson velvet with a raw oyster poised on one end of
her fork." Jostled by a waiter, the oyster fell and disappeared into the
lady's ample bosom. "Her face shows horror and indecision," Lucy wrote
in her diary: "Shall she go after it, or shall she warm it up? She decides to
warm it but her wriggles show it takes a long time!"[44]

Lucy was determined that her stay in Germany not be entirely occupied with social diversions. After a struggle to get herself admitted to the
University of Berlin as a student, Lucy, who spoke fluent but somewhat
inaccurate German, registered for a course on Goethe with Dr. Erich
Schmidt and for an economics course with Professor Bernard, described
in *Two Lives* only as a "radical young Jew" whose lectures were evidently
incendiary, for people "raised their eyebrows" when they learned she was
attending them.[45] She also visited museums regularly, making sketches
of Greek vases for Wheeler, as she had sketched for George Palmer on
her earlier trip abroad. Lucy also enjoyed her excursions to German theater and concerts and to the homes of university professors; she developed a great liking for German food and beer. Later, however, she felt
that Benjamin Wheeler and the rest of the party, "flattered" by the Kaiser's attentions, had ignored the signs of impending war. Basking in the
"artificial" atmosphere of German court society, they "failed utterly to

grasp the deep social psychology of the Germans"—a psychology which in hindsight she knew was "sinister."[46] Wheeler's outspoken admiration for the Germans during these prewar years would lead to controversy at the University of California after the outbreak of World War I.

After the conclusion of the academic year in Germany, Lucy spent the summer in Italy with Adolph and Mary Miller, Mrs. Wheeler, and young Benjamin. By fall, she was back in California, certain now that she wished to be dean neither at Barnard nor at Berkeley. In October 1910, at Lucy's request, Lucy Ward Stebbins, whom she had known at Radcliffe, was appointed assistant dean of women and lecturer in Charities. (Lucy herself anonymously provided the funds for Stebbins' salary.) Stebbins' help in investigating boarding houses and managing other housing problems allowed Lucy to give her attention to curriculum questions related to the well-being of Berkeley's women students. Lucy hoped Stebbins would be her successor. As yet, however, she had not given a definite date when she would leave the university. Before tendering her formal resignation, Lucy recalled:

I wanted to do something more definite, more constructive about the kind of opportunities the University offered its women students. My early protest against the narrowness of professional training offered had increased rather than decreased. The more I saw of these vigorous western girls, the more preposterous it seemed that they should have no choice except to become teachers—preposterous for them and certainly not desirable for children. For what other professions could the University prepare them? To find an answer to that question became an obsession.[47]

In pursuit of this "obsession," she evolved a plan to take a three-month leave of absence in New York, timed to coincide with a meeting of Deans of Women at the annual convention of the Association of Collegiate Alumnae (ACA), October 22–29, 1911. The issue of vocational education for college women was in fact very new. At the 1908 annual meeting of the ACA, held in San Francisco, Lucy had presided at a session in which President Wheeler warned of the dangers of "unripe specialization" and argued that since the "bacteria of vocation" had infected most colleges, careful planning was necessary to ensure proper integration of vocationally oriented courses into the curriculum. The ACA formed a Standing Committee on Vocational Opportunities for College Women, whose members included Berkeley's May Cheney and Radcliffe's Mary Coes. In its report to the 1910 ACA meeting in Denver, which Lucy attended, the committee urged educators to acquire "concrete facts about the actual fields of occupation for college women" in fields other than teaching. Lucy's planned trip to New York responded to this injunction.[48]

Lucy hoped to learn about nonteaching professions for women by apprenticing herself to some of the leading pioneers of women's work in New York City. The plan took shape during a visit from John Graham Brooks, a Unitarian minister who had resigned his parishes in Roxbury and Brockton, Massachusetts, to spend full time studying social questions. He had taught at Harvard and Chicago, and in 1909, lectured on Social Economics at Berkeley. Adolph Miller found him to be a "charming guest with a great variety of interests and experiences" who knew "all sorts of people and the 'insides' of many things." With Brooks' help, Lucy hatched her scheme to "shadow" some leading women reformers of New York as they went about their work. Brooks was acquainted with all the leading reformers in New York. He outfitted Lucy with a "suitcaseful of letters of introduction" to women ranging from heiress Anne Morgan to social settlement leaders Lillian Wald and Florence Kelley. "As soon as it could be arranged," Lucy recalled, "off I went to New York."[49]

According to Two Lives, the trip was a simple outcome of Lucy's dissatisfaction with the narrow vocational training offered to women students at the University of California. Since there were few vocationally relevant curricula for women college students in areas other than teaching, Lucy's field trip made good sense in terms of her concerns as Dean. In fact, although she did not acknowledge it, the idea for the New York trip grew not only out of her concerns about Berkeley's curriculum, but also out of her desire to develop new vocational possibilities for herself. By studying nonteaching vocational opportunities in New York, she could explore her own goals and alternatives as well as those that could be of use to her students.

The trip to New York had a second personal motive, which was even less openly confronted. In the summer of 1911, the friendship of Lucy Sprague and Wesley Clair Mitchell had revived and blossomed into a deep romance. During the previous academic year they had met at the usual events—Poetry Circle dinners, philosophy discussions at the Riebers', evenings at the Millers'. However, they went their "separate ways," "friendly," Lucy recalled, but a "bit self-conscious."[50] Mitchell had been involved with Maude Radford Warren most of this time, and in fact they had been planning to marry. But on May 8, 1911, just four years after Mitchell had fallen in love with her at the Howards' costume ball, Lucy took a party of guests, including Wesley Mitchell, to see Sarah Bernhardt at a theater in San Francisco. Several days later, Mitchell took Lucy, Lucy Stebbins, and Winifred Rieber, along with his friends Noyes and Ryder, on a hiking expedition to Redwood Park. Several more walking tours, always with other friends present, followed in May and June—most of them, Lucy thought, planned by Wesley. This renewal of interest seemed to her as inexplicable as Wesley's "sudden proposal followed by his long indifference."[51]

However, relations between the two remained awkward. When Lucy heard that Mitchell would be joining a camping party to the Sierra that summer, organized by Walter Hart, she wrote to him to ask whether if she joined the party he would be unwilling to go along. A few days later, Mitchell wrote to Sadie Gregory that Lucy might be joining the party ("she walks very well and seems to have the necessary enthusiasm," he commented, though he questioned whether the Harts would trust any but "seasoned veterans"). But he confided:

I should like the prospect better if I could learn to talk with her freely. For some reason we seem always at cross-purposes. I can never think of anything not utterly commonplace to say to her, and she is one of the people with whom one feels under obligation to talk.[52]

As it turned out, there were five campers and a cook and a packer, six riding horses, eight pack horses, and a mule, on the six-week trip that July and August. Day by day, the awkwardness between Lucy and Mitchell diminished. Exhilarated by walking and by the beauty of the mountains, Lucy became serene and confident. She grew to know the "complete" Mitchell—she nicknamed him "Robin." No one who had not seen Robin in the great outdoors ever really knew him, she later said.

Robin was not only a good camper—practical, ingenious and seemingly tireless; he was an incomparable companion. He was positively exuberant—so full of gaiety that it was contagious, yet so sensitive that he never put over his mood if it were not mine—so eager in his vitality, yet so considerate and courteous that I, who was not a "veteran," never felt inferior.[53]

The trip was a wonderful experience for Lucy. First, there was the satisfaction of proving herself to be a "good camper," though not quite of the class of Mitchell. Lucy and Mitchell walked ahead, sometimes joined by Walter Hart. Behind the walkers came Agnes Hart and the fifth member

of the party, Stanley Yarnell, on horseback. Mitchell's record was a hike
of forty-eight miles in one day; Lucy managed only twenty-nine miles at
most. But she was proud of the fact that she did not have to use the horse
that the apprehensive Harts insisted be brought for her. She "kept up
with the men."

Secondly, there was the thrill of the mountain wilderness itself, the
daily excursions into remote sections of the upper ranges of the high Sierra Nevadas. Each day she and Mitchell would walk twenty miles or
more, finding a meadow where they could camp and where the horses
and mules could feed. The climbs were steep and rugged, but the sheer
beauty of the ranges "where the incredible was almost the usual" energized and inspired them. "Every day brought me more under the spell of
the hard, free life in the mountains:"

the physical well-being of working my body hard as I walked the dusty trail, the
luncheon pause by some stream followed by reading aloud from the *Odyssey*, the
glow after a dip in a cold mountain stream at the end of a day's walk, the nights
looking up at the stars—for summer rain is so rare in the Sierra that we carried
no tent, the excitement of the vast mountain tops seen from a peak, stretching
to the world's end, the almost mystic sense of identity with this wild, wonderful
wilderness of rock, so beautiful in color and shape, so untameable![54]

As the tensions of ordinary life shrank away, Lucy became more spontaneous. "I seemed to drop a set of inhibitions with each thousand feet
we rose," she recalled. On one bitterly cold and windy night, when it was
her turn to stoke the fire, she was suddenly overcome by one of her "crazy
dramatic inspirations." She became Brunhilde. Covered in a blanket, she
broke into Wagner's Fire Music. In the "wild" light of the Sierra night,
she sang herself out, then crawled back, exhausted, between Mitchell
and Hart, bundling together to keep warm.[55] Of course Mitchell had
fallen in love with her on the Howards' porch after just such an outpouring. Now Mitchell forgot his "cross-purposes" with Lucy and his self-
consciousness in her company; his earlier feeling for her revived and
strengthened.

In the mountain vastnesses and the quiet of its meadows and forests,
"primary values became clear, and secondary values, so demanding in the
valley, shrank to their proper place." The anecdotes she tells about their
Sierra trips reveal her sense of his courage and bravery, his mastery of the
wilderness, his reliability, his tenderness. Once he came back to rescue
her when a sudden thunder and lightning storm struck Mount Whitney

when she was trailing far behind. On another morning, after they had
failed to find their camp the previous night, Wesley arose early, before
the other sleepers had awakened, to walk the twenty miles back to the
camp to bring Lucy and Hart a breakfast of coffee and biscuits. And once
Mitchell turned a stream from its course to provide a campsite conven-
iently near an expanse of orange lilies blooming under a grove of evergreen trees.[56]

Robin and she were "deeply in love" when they returned from their
long camping trip at the end of August. He urged marriage, but she was
hesitant.

I had come to love the Sierra "Robin," as I had begun to call him, and he
had come to love the Sierra "Alta," as he then called me. But what of the
valley Robin and the valley me? Did either of our valley selves know the other's
inner drives, the other's essential values well enough to be sure of a genuine
acceptance?[57]

In fact, she never allowed herself time to get to know his "valley self"
before she left for New York in October. Lucy had been tempted to cancel her New York visit after her summer in the Sierras; she dreaded going
to New York, she admitted to him. But for the sake of her "larger plans,"
she went through with the trip. Mitchell was proud of the "strength and
character" that carried her off, even if he also recognized in her flight to
New York an expression of her ambivalence about him.[58] She was not
exactly running away from Mitchell and the intimate companionship he
offered, but neither was she sure that she should give up her plans and
ambitions for the sake of marriage, although she had found a love that
satisfied, even dazzled her. And then, what sort of career was best suited
to her developing goals, skills and experience? Her trip to New York became a quest for self-knowledge, for a resolution of her personal conflicts.

New York Apprenticeships: Exploring the Professions for Women

The question of marriage and career was much on the minds of educated women as the twentieth century opened. In an article in *Harper's Bazaar* in 1906 on "The Passing of Matrimony," feminist writer Charlotte Perkins Gilman set out to explain why unmarried women, primarily from the middle and upper classes, had become a prominent feature of America's social landscape. The tendency of highly educated women to decline even "good matches" and to criticize the state of matrimony itself was a new thing, Gilman observed. While spinsters of earlier generations had been objects of scornful pity, convicted of a deep and shameful inadequacy, the self-confident "bachelor maids" of the present refused the marital yoke by their own deliberate choice. Marriage had grown distinctly out of fashion.[1]

For a decade or more, Gilman had been writing about the artificial limitations of marriage and particularly about the way in which marriage dehumanized women by denying their need for relationships that extended beyond the household into the larger world. For Gilman, the solution was simple: women, like men, needed to express their humanity by working outside the home, not only prior to marriage but throughout their lives. Gilman argued that the high price of the "maternal sacrifice"—the renunciation of the "dream of self-realization for the great duties of motherhood"—was causing women increasingly to prefer the single state.[2] Only if the forced choice between marriage and work was removed would educated women again choose to marry and, once married, remain so.

Even the staunchest advocates of women's higher education were nonplussed when evidence concerning the marital and childbirth rates of college women first became available. By the first decade of the twentieth century, it seemed clear that the marriage rates of women graduates were considerably lower than those of college men and especially of women as a whole. Even worse was their rate of reproduction: "From the available data," summarized psychologist G. Stanley Hall, "it seems that the more scholastic the education of women, the fewer children, and the harder and more dreaded is parturition, and the less the ability to nurse children." Hall's concern was echoed by President Roosevelt, who made well known his disgust for childless marriages and small families among the better classes. A nation that did not reproduce its best equipped citizens could not expect to meet the strenuous challenges that faced it.[3]

While feminists disputed the contention that educated women were responsible for the low matrimonial rate (why not indict college men, asked M. Carey Thomas, president of Bryn Mawr, for it was they who found college women less desirable as wives), it was undeniable that female attitudes toward marriage had undergone a remarkable change within a generation.[4] For both young girls and older women, since marriage was incompatible with a planned, full-time, lifelong commitment to work, spinsterhood had become a respectable choice.[5]

As she began her journey to New York in 1911, the dilemma of marriage and career was very much on Lucy Sprague's mind. Only slowly during her seven years at Berkeley had she come to define herself as a professional woman; her ideas about future work had remained inchoate. Indeed, the very notion of "career" was foreign to most women at that time; it was a masculine concept. Now, however, she prepared to make more considered choices. In a letter to Wesley Mitchell written aboard the Overland Limited from San Francisco to Chicago, where she stopped to see her Aunt Nan and Uncle Albert, Lucy expressed great enthusiasm about her emerging plans. "I am still seething with ideas over the projects I have left behind," she wrote, "and my talks with Mr. Wheeler have started a ferment over the problems I am about to plunge into. . . . The world begins to seem a diverting place full of things . . . to conquer and once more I begin to feel myself capable of bearing arms and conquering through them." Mitchell's proposal of marriage—the option of escape from her fears of being "*only* a professional woman"—may have helped to release this sense of empowerment. Lucy announced her intention not to think very "consecutively" about romantic questions, although she would carry with her wherever she went "the consciousness of possibilities." "I'm ready for an experiment in a new world," she wrote.[6]

In a letter to the "Robins," the members of her Radcliffe Round Robin correspondence club, Lucy wrote: "My present trip is [a] sort of wild experiment, and I may get nothing out of it except the exhilaration of novelty. I expect to be in New York for two and a half months trying to get a bird's-eye view of social conditions and the modern methods of tackling those conditions." At Berkeley, the details of practical, problem-solving work had allowed her little time to view issues in any broad "program perspective." Now, however,

I have got a vague idea that to do *any* work, educational or otherwise, in a large way—in a way that lifts it out of routine [into] a constructive plane—one must know human psychology as it works under various kinds of economic pressure. . . . So I am going to try to see a city from the factory-inspectors', from the settlements', from the Associate Charity's, from the Socialists' points of view. I expect to return bewildered and depressed but eventually I think it may help me to see more of what lies behind the eyes of my 1200 girls. I also want to form an estimate—and for me that always means to see at first-hand—of the value of some of the modern philanthropic methods, and above all, of the value of the modern woman who is constructing these methods.[7]

The thrust of Lucy's experiment—to get a "bird's-eye" view of social conditions, and to explore how economic pressures affected human psychology—was an extension of her "curriculum of experience" as Dean; it also clearly reflected Wesley Mitchell's "ethnological" perspective. She was excited about her plan, yet simultaneously she deprecated it, calling it a "wild" idea based on an "absurdly grandiloquent" view of behavior. For the benefit of her Radcliffe peers at any rate, she was "quite aghast" about the grandiosity of her intentions: "little Western me alone in great New York asking to know its city-sorrows and its city-wisdom!"

But her trip had other purposes as well. Above all, she had written to her club friends, she wanted to see "the modern woman" working in philanthropy and social reform—to understand the nature of such work and perhaps also to measure herself against the achievements and visions of others. Was she like these new careerists who had dedicated their lives to community service? Could she realistically include herself in the ranks of the pioneer women, all of them unmarried, who were "bearing arms" and "conquering" as she hoped to do? And in order to join them, would she also need to renounce marriage?

Lucy told the "Robins" of her trip to the Sierras that summer (although not of the proposal of marriage that was its outcome) and of her discovery there of beauty, inner peace, and contentment. "I was made over, body and soul," she wrote. "For the first time in my life, I saw sharply— though I never *consciously* thought of it—the essential difference between primary and secondary things. . . . Most of us waste our precious, precious lives over secondary things and let the primary slide."

What *are* the essentials, anyway—what the significant, what the sacred? Most of us would instinctively say "babies" and yet can anything *tangible* be an essential? Must it not rather be an attitude? For most of us would agree that one had no right to marry for babies—though some of us may be tempted—and that really means that we think something is *more* primary than even children, does it not?[8]

The question she was asking had immediate personal meaning. The off-handed closing of Lucy's letter—"Love to the babies. I have a sneaking belief they *are* the primaries even if metaphysics doesn't admit of it"—recalls her dissatisfaction with the remoteness of Harvard philosophy and confirms that there was more at stake in her apprenticeships in New York than decisions about Berkeley's curriculum. The real agenda was to discover what was "primary" and what "secondary" in her own life—to explore the nature of her emotions and ambitions, to examine the key question of intimacy versus independence, to hold up to the cold winter light of New York her Sierra visions.

Just before Lucy left California, her former teacher George Santayana delivered an address at Berkeley's Philosophical Union that contrasted a mode of "primary" experience like Lucy's in the Sierras with what he called, in a phrase that was to become famous, "the genteel tradition."[9] Santayana attacked American academic philosophy as rooted in the Calvinist tradition, and praised in its stead the vitality and spontaneity of William James's new pragmatism. The older tradition—Calvinism, transcendentalism, and the abstractions of academic idealism—was dry, tepid, pedantic, and moralistic. It was "American intellect," the sphere "predominantly of the American woman," as opposed to "American will," the "sphere of the American man." The genteel tradition inhabited the colonial mansion; masculine will inhabited the sky-scraper. The Sierra came into Santayana's scheme in its identification with this untrammeled masculine will. In the towering giant forests of California, Santayana located a force that could "lift the yoke of the genteel tradition"; the "wild, indifferent . . . infinity of nature" allowed human imagination to make its own meanings. The beauty of the Sierras thus was equated with the true "life of the mind," with meanings that were made by the individual, not received as rigid rules of morality and thought. Will and action could be grounded in beauty and feeling.

Santayana's Berkeley address was his farewell to academic life; in 1912 he resigned from Harvard and exiled himself abroad. Lucy surely concurred in his indictment of academic sterility; but his vision, though it touched on themes that stirred her deeply, was a vision of unification within masculinity, and it could solve no problems for Lucy. For Santayana, the wilderness was a source of unity because its beauty was rugged and indifferent—it did not prejudice the masculinity of those who loved it. For Lucy, New York's "city-sorrows and city-wisdom," the economic realities to which her intelligence and her conscience drew her, threatened the womanly fulfillment that had opened before her in the Sierras. As she set off for New York, struggling to give due weight both to her own will to action and to her Sierra "primaries" of beauty and love, she still saw them as conflicting, not only in practice but in principle.

As Lucy plunged into New York's vigorous world of social reform, she met women whose forcefulness and dynamism astounded her, and gradually she began to gather materials for a different mapping of women's possibilities, a different view of the relations between intellect, feeling and action. From this distance, even her Sierra Robin seemed an academic removed from the field of action; the man she loved loved passionately in California she now suspected—for a time—of lacking masculinity. When she came to New York, she had not resolved the question of what was "primary" for her; and her experiences during her stay seemed only to make the question more difficult.

Lucy's apprenticeship in New York acquainted her with five of the most exciting women in the city—Lillian Wald, director and founder of the Henry Street settlement; Florence Kelley, national secretary of the Consumers' League; Mary Richmond, head of the Charity Organization Society of the Russell Sage Foundation; Pauline Goldmark, research analyst for the Russell Sage Foundation; and Julia Richman, a district superintendent in the New York public schools. Richman worked in the public schools to help children from needy families; all the others were working in female-oriented reform occupations—nursing, organized charity, social research, lobbying, policy-making. Together, they represented the entire spectrum of modern social welfare methods.

Lucy's attraction to the world of social reform was shared by many well-educated upper-class women in the Progressive Era who joined settlement houses. They found a sense of purpose for their own lives in teaching, organizing, and sometimes preaching to the poor and working-class residents of settlement neighborhoods. As Jane Addams wrote in her autobiography, for many women like herself, reform was a "subjective necessity."[10]

Lucy, of course, knew Addams and the outlines of settlement work from her Chicago days. But she had never immersed herself in the squalor of slum neighborhoods and the problems their residents faced. She did not join a settlement after college as many alumnae of women's colleges did, although she was one of sixty Radcliffe alumnae listed as sponsors of the College Settlement Association in 1908. Not until her last years at Berkeley, when she began to take her students on field trips to San Francisco, did she seem especially cognizant of the problems of immigrants and poor people. Her awakening came belatedly, after she was thirty, and may have been associated with her father's death.

Otho might well have been displeased by Lucy's association with John Graham Brooks, whose views on the labor question made many of his contemporaries consider him a dangerous radical. As a lecturer on industrial subjects at Harvard, the University of Chicago, and in 1909 at the University of California, Brooks played a leading role in agitating for an American system of social insurance. He established the National Consumers' League, hoping that the power of consumers could be brought to bear upon management to improve working conditions and to aid workers. His own publications on the plight of the American laborer were widely influential.[11]

After Otho's death, Lucy was free to respond to the impulses that Brooks's friendship had fostered.[12] As the Palmers and Wheelers had opened doors to the wider worlds of scholarship and culture, so Brooks held the key to the world of mass urban life. Lucy's wish to take part in this alien "real" world, or at least to observe it and know it, now became pressing.

First, urgent problems of the urban poor offered a ready outlet for the call to service and duty, to which Lucy, like so many well-educated middle-class women of her era, had been reared to respond. She was drawn to the polyglot, tumultuous environment of the urban working class because it offered an antidote to the money-snobbery she condemned in her father's circle and to the narrow scholasticism of university life.

Secondly, the social reform professions that beckoned to her in New York were women's professions. In her search for vocational alternatives to teaching for her students, she deliberately avoided the masculine-dominated professions—law, medicine, scientific research, business, and finance. Perhaps she believed that her students lacked the training or drive to succeed in these professions, all of which maintained substantial barriers against women. Perhaps, like many other women reformers of the time, she simply could not contemplate such nontraditional roles for women. In searching for role models for her students and herself, she chose the separatist path. Intuitively rather than explicitly, she concluded that women-centered, women-managed, women-initiated professions offered the greatest possibilities for female career development.

Lucy's apprenticeship with these five New York female activists thus indicated both the awakening of her reform impulses and her increasing identification with women professionals. Most dramatically, it marked a shift away from male guidance. Safely out of the reach of George Palmer, she now took steps to shed the influence of Benjamin Wheeler. In the company of Palmer, Wheeler, and Adolph Miller, she had found friendship, sponsorship, and valued connections. Yet at the same time, their support lessened her self-reliance, for they always treated her, if not as a daughter, then as a woman—differently, that is, and protectively. To discover what she could do on her own, she had to turn to women. Brooks played an important role in introducing her to these women, but he acted as a friend, perhaps as a mentor, not as a model for her own behavior.

Once, in Cambridge as a student, she had "tried out" an academic career by observing and then literally imitating her august professors of philosophy. In Berkeley, she had tried out a combined administrative-scholarly model, relying on Benjamin Wheeler as her guide. She had found no female role models at the university. Jessica Peixotto, learned and experienced as she was, was as low in status and seniority as herself. Most of the deans of women she met she regarded as too traditional and maternal. Now, in New York, she prepared to try out new behaviors again. She would "shadow" the five pioneer women she had selected in order to experience their reality. Through first-hand observation she would bring their worlds into herself.

In the company of women, then, Lucy began a fresh attempt to explore her ambitions and her developing identity as a professional woman. The only person who effectively stood in the way of her emerging professional identity was Wesley Clair Mitchell. He offered intimacy and companionship through marriage, but marriage stood in stark contrast to the committed work life of her new friends, the women pioneers, all of whom were single.

Lucy's first stop in New York was the Henry Street Settlement. Lillian Wald had been directing the settlement for sixteen years when Lucy came to her in the fall of 1911. By this time, Wald had received considerable public acclaim for her work and, like Jane Addams, had become a popular heroine. Wald, daughter of a prosperous German-Jewish family which had settled in Rochester, New York, after the revolution of 1848, had graduated from the New York Hospital school for nurses in 1891; she had chosen this career because it was "serious" work, yet feminine.[13] For a short time afterwards, she enrolled in the Women's Medical College in New York, to train as a doctor, but she spent much of her time as a volunteer with a Jewish charity organization, teaching hygiene and nursing to immigrant women. A harrowing experience attending a sick woman in a dilapidated tenement convinced her that she should devote her life to alleviating human suffering in the slums. She concluded that no medical degree was needed in order to bring desperately needed help to women. With a nursing colleague and the support of philanthropists Mrs. Solomon Loeb and Jacob Schiff, she joined a settlement on the Lower East Side, working as a nurse. In 1895, she established the "Nurses' Settlement" at 265 Henry Street. Gradually her concept of settlement work broadened, much as had Jane Addams' at Hull House. She came to see nursing care as the organizing principle around which a full panoply of social services—among them preventive health services, recreation, education, and employment—could be provided, helping neighborhood residents to resist illness, stress, and dislocation. Poverty, she now understood, was a consequence not of individual disease or moral weakness but of systemic social problems, which could be fought by community action as well as by legislative reform.

At Henry Street, Lucy Sprague became Lillian Wald's "big-eyed shadow" for several weeks.[14] Arriving in October, in the midst of a garbage strike, Lucy's first glimpse of the Lower East Side was of hordes of children playing on huge mounds of uncollected garbage, a sight that she learned only later was not quite typical. Soon she was accompanying a Henry Street visiting nurse as her assistant on calls to patients. Lucy's knowledge of German allowed her some understanding of Yiddish, the language spoken by most of Henry Street's clients. On several occasions, Lucy took over a class of boys which met at the settlement house. She wound up taking them to the Brooklyn Bridge, where they all became absorbed watching ship traffic at the nearby docks. It was the same kind of excursion on which she had ventured alone in her Chicago girlhood, on which she had taken Berkeley women, and on which she would regularly bring Bank Street children and teachers twenty years later. Lucy also listened in on discussions of social, economic, and particularly labor problems at Henry Street, stirred at this chance to understand the "real," not just the "theoretical," aspects of poverty. "For the first time I have seen life at the other end of the scale," she wrote to Wesley Mitchell.

It isn't so much the injustice—hideous and haunting as that is—as the incomprehensibility of it all. How did it come about? How has it lasted? What are these creatures? Are they like you and me? If so, why do they endure it? Why don't they rebel or die? I have no *real* desire to live among them. That seems, for me at least, artificial and petty. But I have a great and overwhelming desire to have my life count towards the bettering of the hideous conditions which surround other lives. For the first time, my money rejoices me. I *must* learn to use it wisely and effectively and must also make what mind I have and what talents I possess help to straighten out this human mess. *I must do it.*[15]

Though she could not see herself as a permanent settlement resident, Lucy was filled with the "new ideas, new impressions, new points of view, and new personalities" she had discovered at Henry Street. She grew to admire Lillian Wald, not only for her work, but for "the spiritual equipment" that fit her for it. In Wald's "constructive ability, administrative skill, wide human sympathies, aesthetic insight, and clear sane thinking" she seemed to find the role model for which she was searching.[16]

Florence Kelley became another role model, of a different kind. Kelley grew to adulthood in Philadelphia, influenced by the Quaker beliefs of her mother's family and by her Congressman father's staunch abolitionism, devotion to the welfare of children, and early support of women's suffrage.[17] At the age of sixteen, she entered Cornell University, which had opened its doors to women just two years earlier. She received her bachelor's degree in 1882, after completing a thesis on the legal status of children. Because of her sex she was not admitted to study law at the University of Pennsylvania graduate school. Instead she started an evening school for working girls in Philadelphia; but at the suggestion of M. Carey Thomas, she soon began advanced studies at the University of Zurich. There she came in contact with socialist theory, and became an eager member of the Socialist Party. She began a correspondence with Friedrich Engels that lasted for a decade, visited him in London, and completed a translation of his *Condition of the Working Class in England in 1844*. Her translation of an address on free trade by Karl Marx at this time provoked controversy in the United States, not least because she was the daughter of "Pig Iron" Kelley, Congress' foremost defender of the protective tariff. Following her marriage in 1884 to Lazare Wischnewetzky, a Russian medical student and socialist whom she met in Zurich, and the birth of a son, Florence returned to the United States. Two more children were born in New York. Financial problems and her husband's emotional instability led to the breakup of the marriage, and in 1891, Florence Kelley-Wischnewetzky moved to Chicago, where, under Illinois' more permissive laws, she secured a divorce, with custody of the children.

Now Florence Kelley again, she became a resident of Hull House. Largely in response to her influence, the Hull House women began to collect and systematically tabulate information about problems affecting their working-class neighbors, developing a broad reform program for industrial workers. Kelley became an investigator of the "sweating system" of home manufacturing for the Illinois Bureau of Labor. Responding to her efforts, the state passed a factory law limiting hours of work for women, prohibiting child labor under the age of fourteen, and controlling tenement sweatshops. Appointed Illinois' chief factory inspector, she took a law degree at Northwestern University to help her in getting cases prosecuted. In 1899, she moved to New York and became general secretary of the National Consumers' League: she was convinced that organized consumer pressure, which she did much to develop, was an alternate method of reforming capitalism and assuring that goods were manufactured and sold under proper working conditions. In this position, she continued her efforts on behalf of maximum hour and minimum wage legislation. The passage of minimum wage legislation in nine states was credited in substantial part to her tireless efforts. Kelley also helped organize the National Child Labor Committee in 1904 and later, with Lillian Wald, participated in the founding of the Children's Bureau.[18]

Kelley and Wald were close friends, but Kelley's politics, ideology, and mode of action moved her away from the more nurturing, feminine, "spiritual" model that Lucy had found in Wald. Lucy had mixed feelings about Kelley's style, though not about her work. Kelley was willing to have Lucy as an apprentice for several weeks; she was working on current labor legislation at the time. Lucy accompanied her to child labor committees and government hearings, and worked on one piece of labor legislation in Kelley's office, where she listened to labor discussions and "tirades against capitalists and politicians." She found Kelley incredible. "Never before or since," Lucy asserted, "have I met such a single-minded human dynamo. . . . I can still feel my terror," she recalled, "at crossing through the traffic of New York streets with her. She behaved like the Red Sea. It simply dammed up on both sides while Florence Kelley and I walked through an empty lane."[19]

Lucy roomed with Kelley on the parlor floor at Henry Street, and was struck by the fact that Kelley had only two dresses, which were identical. Each had a dickey that could be "yanked out, and suddenly her work dress was transformed into her evening dress." All Kelley's possessions were equally pruned, Lucy noted, and all her energies were concentrated on her work drive.

While she was still living at Henry Street, Lucy's working period with Kelley ended, and she apprenticed herself next to Mary Richmond, director of the Charity Organization Department of the Russell Sage Foundation. Lucy joined the department responsible for placing homeless children, mostly babies. Kelley became "indignant" that Lucy was wasting her time on such "mawkish charity" and practically refused to speak to her. It was then that Lucy decided to go to a hotel. "Living at the Henry Street Settlement and rooming with Florence Kelley was more than I could take, physically and emotionally," she recalled. At a small hotel in the West Forties, she felt like a "pampered darling," but at least she could sleep again. Now she could manage the intensity of her apprenticeships.[20]

Mary Richmond was fifty years old when Lucy Sprague met her in 1911; she had spent more than two decades working in the charity organization movement. Reared in Baltimore by a grandmother and two maiden aunts, Richmond, who had only a high school education, began in 1889 as a clerk for the Baltimore Charity Organization, then became a volunteer "friendly visitor." She was appointed general secretary in 1891, a position previously held only by men with graduate training in political economy. In 1900, Richmond became general secretary of Philadelphia's Society for Organizing Charity, and in 1909, she became the director of the Charity Organization Department of the new Russell Sage Foundation. Once a firm believer in meting out charity to the deserving poor through the efforts of volunteer "visitors," she later took the position that social service was most effectively distributed to needy clients after a full investigation of social conditions had been undertaken by trained professional workers. A speech she delivered at the National Conference of Charities and Correction in Toronto in 1897, calling for a training school for professional social workers, had great influence. Employing the term "casework," first coined by the London Charity Organization Society, to describe her methods, Richmond pioneered in developing a theory of social work. [21]

At Russell Sage, Richmond directed research on many social problems, distributing the results of the foundation's investigations to charity organizations throughout the country. The study that was probably occupying her during the time Lucy Sprague apprenticed with her in 1911 concerned a survey of 985 widows with children who were "treated" by charity organization societies. In its conclusions, the report called for more systematic reviews of case records by member societies, better coordination of services, and the discouragement of widows from full-time work and a more careful scrutiny of their budgeting procedures to learn about family dietary and housekeeping habits. [22]

Florence Kelley abhorred such methods and their intervention into individual family lives, much preferring to attack the problems of dependent women and children through legislative means. Kelley was a strong supporter of widows' pensions; Richmond opposed this measure and other social insurance. Championing radical reform and "wholesale" social reconstruction, Kelley and other settlement leaders criticized the piecemeal, gradualist, "retail" approach of caseworkers like Richmond, concerned more with social amelioration than with social justice. In the weeks Lucy Sprague spent with each of these women, she witnessed at first hand the serious, sometimes bitter, divisions that split the ranks of social workers over the next half century.

Lucy's next apprenticeship was with Pauline Goldmark, whom she described as a "beautiful young research worker with eyes like moonstones."[23] Pauline was one of ten children of German-Austrian Jewish parents, who, like the family of Lillian Wald, had participated in the Revolution of 1848 in Europe. One of her sisters had married Boston lawyer Louis Dembitz Brandeis, who became a justice of the U.S. Supreme Court in 1916; another sister married Felix Adler, founder of the Ethical Culture Society. A third sister, Josephine, worked closely with Florence Kelley on labor legislation, helping Brandeis prepare the landmark brief in *Muller v. Oregon* in 1908.

Pauline Goldmark graduated from Bryn Mawr in 1896, and became executive secretary of the New York Consumers' League, where she met Florence Kelley. She was soon appointed supervisor of the Bureau of Social Research of the New York School of Philanthropy. Supported by funds from the Russell Sage Foundation, the Bureau employed fellows from the School of Philanthropy who conducted various social research projects. One of these, later published under the title *West Side Studies*, was ongoing when Lucy appeared for her apprenticeship.[24]

Like Wald, Kelley, and Richmond, Pauline Goldmark allowed Lucy to participate fully in the workings of her agency. As Lucy explained it, the women "not only gave me a small practical job to do, but they explained the relation of my small job to their total work." Lucy sat in on committee and staff meetings, and followed workers on their daily investigations or to meetings with clients. She learned "more in those few months than in any comparable period in my life." It was an educational adventure that taught her not only about the varied content of social reform and modern philanthropy but about the very process of learning itself.[25]

The West Side district that Goldmark and her researchers were investigating covered eighty blocks bordering the Hudson River between 34th and 54th Streets, a neighborhood different from the tenements of the Lower East Side in that it boasted a fairly stable, homogeneous population of long-time German-Irish residents. But, because it was thought that the most prosperous of these families had moved to other areas, leaving only the least ambitious—the "wrecks of the population"—Goldmark believed the district demonstrated one of the most acute, but least addressed, problems of modern urban life—the "discouragement and deterioration of an indigenous American community." The West

Side Studies conducted by Goldmark's bureau included investigations of juvenile delinquency ("Boyhood and Lawlessness" and "the Neglected Girl") and of economic pressures caused by underemployment ("Mothers Who Must Earn").[26]

Through Goldmark and her assistants, Lucy discovered "a new kind of intensity—the passion to gather accurate social facts and interpret them by logical, impersonal reasoning." Her apprenticeship with Goldmark was an "intellectual" rather than an "emotional" one. But though Lucy felt "blessed relief" that she was out of the turmoil of dealing with practical emergencies and into the discipline of thinking scientifically, still she wanted to go beyond the "detached, scientific" approach and view the problems of the West Side more concretely. So she enlisted in the Salvation Army. She began climbing tenement steps, as she had done with the Henry Street nurses, this time bringing spiritual aid along with practical necessities like food and clothing. She came to admire the religious fervor and humanitarianism of the Salvation Army, but concluded that it lacked "the constructive attack" on family problems that characterized Henry Street.[27]

One of Lucy's tasks as a Salvation Army worker was to escort clients to Bellevue Hospital, city clinics, and almshouses. On one occasion, an elderly lady she took to Welfare Island begged Lucy to tell the authorities that she was her cousin in the belief that she might then receive better treatment. "How she clung to me!" Lucy recalled more than fifty years later, still shocked by the old lady's terrible fear of the almshouse to which she was going.[28]

But encountering the district children jolted Lucy most of all. "Their condition almost killed me," she recalled. "They were a large influence in determining what I should do for my life's work."[29] She respected the intellectual brilliance and originality of Goldmark's surveys, but it was the concrete reality of the disadvantaged children of the neighborhood Goldmark was studying that touched her to the quick.

Lucy's last apprenticeship was with Julia Richman, a district superintendent of the New York City public school system. She was only an "observer" during her stay with Richman, since the school bureaucracy did not allow nonschool personnel to participate in daily work in any way. It was a concession, Lucy thought, to allow her to visit in the first place. Here too she became Richman's "shadow," spending much of her time in a vocational high school. In her recollections, Lucy asserts that "I was very impressed and decided then and there that working with children in the public schools was the work which I really wanted to do," yet she gives no further details.[30]

Richman was an unusual teacher whose educational vision had much in common with the ideas of the settlement leaders whom Lucy admired. Defying the wishes of her father, a status-conscious German-Jewish emigré, Richman had become a schoolteacher in 1872, at the age of seventeen, and rose quickly in the New York educational hierarchy. Within twelve years she was principal of a school and in 1903 she became a district superintendent of schools, supervising two Lower East Side districts; she was the first woman so appointed. Her policies over the next nine years, until her retirement and premature death in 1912, were considered bold and pathbreaking, though she had less personal success as an administrator because of her uncompromising style. Most troubling to some district residents was Richman's vigorous war against pushcart peddlers, whom she viewed as backward remnants of immigrant culture, to be eliminated in the interests of Americanization.[31]

Richman's contribution to public education covered two general areas.[32] First, she created special classes for children having serious difficulties in school, whether because they were truants, behaviorally disruptive "incorrigibles," or "mentally defective" children. When Richman arrived on the scene, she found that classes in her districts typically consisted of upwards of sixty children of widely different abilities. Within her first year as superintendent, she instituted "special" classes for homogeneous groups of children (three of these, designed for mentally deficient children, were ungraded). The immediate result was a dramatic improvement in the children's learning. Richman also promulgated standardized testing for school children to determine which youngsters had exceptional problems and required special classes. Homogeneous grouping and standardized testing of students became common approaches among reform-minded educators in the 1920s. Richman's adoption of these methods more than a decade earlier, in the interest of promoting a school experience more responsive to individual children, was truly pioneering.

Richman strongly believed that the school must be concerned with the "whole" child. Problems relating to the child's physical and emotional health or family life should be as important to the teacher as scholastic performance. By focusing only on the classroom, teachers, she felt, were not doing enough for children; she envied the accomplishments of settlement workers who, she believed, often did more for school children and their families than teachers did. In Richman's view, the school could be a legitimate social center of community life. Through the schools, forces and ideas for promoting the well-being of children and general social betterment could radiate.

Richman's Deweyite views were common enough among Progressive educators. Her primary innovation lay in the development of a new institutional means to translate these goals into concrete programs. In 1906, she created Teachers' House, a settlement-like residence on Montgomery Street in the Lower East Side, designed to bring teachers into direct contact with neighborhood life. Funded by Richman's friend Felix Warburg, Richman herself, and the contributions of residents, Teachers' House usually numbered about a dozen occupants, including not only teachers but social workers, who worked with the teachers providing support services to school children and their families. In addition to the permanent residents, it offered meals to principals, teachers, and social workers in the neighborhood and sponsored conferences, receptions, and special events.

Teachers' House closed in the spring of 1912, shortly after Richman's retirement from her district post. Although it was a new approach to Progressive efforts to merge education with social reform, it seems to have called forth few imitators and to have disappeared almost entirely from the historical record as well. It is likely that Lucy was aware of the experiment, however, which was Richman's pet project during her last years as district superintendent.

For Lucy Sprague, the placement with Julia Richman was of "tremendous significance." She recalled:

This is the work for me, I thought. Public education is the most constructive attack on social problems, for it deals with children and the future. It requires endless research concerning children and what they need to make them grow wholesomely. It requires experimentation in curriculum for children and in teacher education. It requires an understanding of our culture. It is the synthesis of all my interests, all my hopes for humanity. I returned to Berkeley with a clear focus in my own life from which I have never since deviated.[33]

But this account is to some extent a projection back from her career as it in fact developed; Lucy's "focus" at the end of her New York time was not as clear and explicit as it seemed in memory. In the story she shapes in her autobiography, Lucy emphasizes the way in which several early influences converged on her career in education and stresses her instinctive leanings toward teaching. It was at Berkeley, she wrote, that her interest in education and in children became sharply defined through three new kinds of experiences—her attachment to her niece, Polly Miller; her classroom teaching; and her work as dean in developing policies about women's higher education. In this perspective, the apprenticeship with Richman articulated her interest in children's education by demonstrating how effective, reform-minded teaching might be implemented at a public school.

This interpretation is significant in several respects. First of all, the choice of education for children as a profession marked a major shift in Lucy's vocational life. Her rejection of a high-status position as dean of women at Berkeley and a possible office as dean of Barnard College for a career in the less prestigious field of childhood education was a surprising move. Her colleagues at Berkeley undoubtedly saw her choice as a step down, rather than up, the career ladder.

Secondly, Lucy presents her decision to abandon higher education in favor of public education for children as her own deliberate initiative. For the first time in her life, she was no longer responding to the plans and pleas of others. Thirdly, Lucy's mission to discover vocational alternatives to teaching as a profession for women ended, in this account, with her own conversion to teaching as a career, a paradox of which she seems unaware. In this choice she was joining the majority of her college-educated contemporaries: in 1914, for example, 83.5 percent of all graduates from the Eastern women's schools who had been employed at any time had been teachers. Of her own Radcliffe class, 40 percent became and remained teachers, never marrying.[34]

The fact that Lucy failed to describe the substance of her learning from Julia Richman in any specific way—either in her letters to Wesley Mitchell at the time, or later in her autobiography and oral history— suggests that her retrospective account of the significance of her apprenticeship with Richman was overemphasized, even though Richman's ideas undoubtedly influenced her later work.

There is evidence that shortly before the conclusion of her apprenticeship, Lucy was still confused about the specific direction of her future. All she knew for certain was that the world of social reform, and not that of academia, now beckoned her. She recognized in herself some of the force and spirit of Lillian Wald, Florence Kelley, Pauline Goldmark, and Julia Richman, women who as practical workers and doers lacked the intellectual equipment of the trained scholar, but who had nonetheless attained power, influence, and recognition. "I do not think I am a Lillian Wald," Lucy wrote to Wesley Mitchell, "but I think I am of her tribe. Miss Wald and not Miss [M. Carey] Thomas is my logical leader. . . . Even as a novice and an outsider, as one who has lived in what they regard as a shadowy world, they [the reformers] welcome me and acknowledge a spiritual kinship."[35]

Lillian Wald had indeed taken Lucy Sprague to her heart. No doubt, Wald appreciated Lucy's generosity (on two occasions she impulsively sent checks to Henry Street), but she also respected Lucy's intense concern for the well-being of Lower East Side residents. Lucy had spoken with Wald about her most urgent social and personal ideals, and about the ambiguity of her future plans. As Lucy was preparing to leave New York, Wald wrote to thank her for her "generosity . . . confidence, and . . . affection." She added:

I have it in my heart to believe that you will know how truly I guard the trust and how earnestly I hope to be able to help you find your path. It may be that you are there and that distance from this busy part of the world may help you determine its values better than when you were in it. . . . Always know how gladly I welcome your fellowship."[36]

Wald's friendship and acceptance were important to Lucy. At the same time, Lucy knew she was an untried novice compared with Wald and the other women with whom she had apprenticed. She had been warmly welcomed into New York's elite cultural and social circles, but her very success alarmed her. Unlike the women reform leaders, she felt she had done little to merit the interest of anybody worthwhile. On one occasion she wrote impatiently to Mitchell:

The editors and the rich philanthropic set have discovered me. Do you know what my present despair is due to? It is because these New Yorkers, these men and women whom I have looked upon as leaders—as arrived—pay attention to me. I know what I am and if I'm worth their while, then the world hasn't got very far along—that's all I can say.[37]

Seeing herself still as an "outsider" to the real world, she wondered whether, despite her warm reception by the social reform women and the "kinship" they felt with her, she lacked the interior depth of a Wald or a Kelley. Perhaps the problem was her own social advantage and charming exterior. When, for example, the literary editor of Harpers' Magazine asked Lucy to write her impressions of "philanthropic New York," the request depressed rather than pleased her. "I'm a perfect fake," she told Wesley, "but I seem to be the only one entirely aware of it. . . . Do you know I think what people call my 'personality' will be the ruin of me?"[38] Such comments reveal Lucy's characteristic combination of pride and lack of self-esteem. "If I can do it," the classic female syndrome goes, "it is not worth doing."

After two months in New York, then, Lucy was uncertain of her future course. In her final few weeks there, however, an idea began to take shape in her mind; it was in some ways unanticipated, but it combined her New York experiences with her background and her own deepest instincts. It was not poverty, not the class struggle, and not the education of young children per se, she now decided, that ought to be the focus of her professional work. In an ebullient letter to Wesley Mitchell she described her emerging "vision":

The thing I am interested in and would like to help straighten out is the attitude of children and young people towards sex problems. I mean that in the broadest sense—to include ideals of marriage, attitudes towards having children as well as questions of decency and lovemaking. I have thought much and read a good [deal] on the subject these last years. The experience of these last weeks has intensified—or perhaps crystallized is a better word—an intangible idea which has been in my mind all my life. Contact with the immigrant girl, the prostitutes in the night courts, with the tough dancing-hall girl, with the shop girl in the settlement clubs and in the school recreation centers, has given me the feeling that unless tangible ideals, unless real education is given to girls *in the school*—the only place where we can be sure of touching all kinds—the sex problem will always continue to be twisted and abnormal. I would rather contribute my life towards making that problem normal and sane, towards making courtship clean and marriage holy and children welcome—for I am interested in the girls of Fifth Avenue as well as those of the East Side—than towards anything else.[39]

Among Lucy's miscellaneous papers is a document, written two days after this letter, that spells out this plan in detail, although it is not clear to whom she addressed it. Her aim, she explained, was "to stimulate, crystallize, explain and justify the ideals which have to do with all sex relationships which manifest themselves in the civilized world in conventions (manners founded upon sense of privacy and responsibility) and the institution of the family (including courtship, marriage, childbearing and child rearing)." The issues she saw as problematic included:

general slackening in sense of personal dignity (kissing, etc.); general cheapening of courtship; secret marriages among students; lack of normal response among "elite wives"; lack of desire for children; easy divorce standards; lack of knowledge about sex matters; prevalence of venereal disease; fear of frankness between parents and children; general sophistry in regard to sex emotions; immorality among all classes; prostitution; perverted sexual desires (women's colleges . . . etc.).[40]

As Lucy saw it, at the bottom rung of society were individuals whose ideals had been "twisted because of economic pressure"—girls driven to immorality because they could find no other way to remain alive; boys postponing marriage for economic reasons, turning elsewhere to satisfy their sexual needs. They knew little about the physiological basis of sex and they had no good role models for sexual feeling and conduct.

Upper-class men and women also grew up without understanding the physiological basis of sexuality. Women were repelled by sex, "even with their husbands." Often they regarded marriage as only a "worldly partnership" since their parents and other exemplars had lacked healthy sexual ideals in their own marriages. Many women never developed instincts for either "wifehood" or motherhood, neither of which roles she claims was "acknowledged" or "glorified" by society. Some women wanted children but did not know that sterility might be due to remediable physical causes. Finally, there were women who were "strongly sexed" but had no outlets permitted by society.

Lucy proposed a multifaceted educational plan to alleviate some of these problems. Though she recognized that it did not directly attack the economic conditions that promoted sexual unhappiness and deviance, she felt that by working with children in schools and by coordinating education programs with work with immigration bureaus, vocational and home-visiting agencies, hospitals and clinics, playgrounds, and dancehalls, it might be possible to influence the institutions that shaped sexual ideals. With the schools as leverage, young people could be educated about the "physical necessity for some kind of expression, the need for clear understanding, for the *why* of the sacredness of sex."

The schools were particularly important, Lucy felt, since they could reach boys and girls from kindergarten age or younger through adolescence. Instruction should be given in the classroom in physiology, hygiene, venereal disease, and other aspects of sexuality. In order to make such courses meaningful and to avoid an overbearing didacticism which students would resist, Lucy suggested two approaches, both reminiscent of her successes at Berkeley. First, she felt that students (and she was particularly interested in women students) would be more likely to accept instruction if the "intangible ideals" of sexuality that they were taught were embodied in a school official with whom they had frequent personal contact. Such an individual, who ought to be of "radiant personality" so that she might serve as a role model, working individually and collectively with students, would in fact be a "Dean of Women in the High School." Secondly, she suggested that self-government be introduced— she would have older girls talk with younger ones about sexual problems. Such a system would provide girls with the means for judging their own behavior as they judged others; would train them for "intelligent trade unionism and labor legislation" after school, and would reduce the need for supervisory authority. With the "dean of women," the self-governing discussion groups, and courses in sex education as a core, a system of collateral services would be provided to ensure the "consolidation" of sexual ideals outside the classroom. These could include programs in recreation centers (to provide "controlled and healthful outlets for excess physical and emotional energy"); medical inspection with home visiting to help school authorities understand and alleviate economic pressures on families; employment bureaus to find jobs for graduating students and help them resist the unhealthful pressures of the industrial world, and a loan fund to help make graduates self-supporting.

Both in its focus on the "social evil" and in its suggestion that a carefully coordinated approach to the educational and social environment could lead the way to a broad-based social reconstruction, Lucy Sprague's plan for sex education is a characteristic Progressive document. Linking together the sexual sphere, economic and social conditions, and a systematic, progressive program of sex education in the schools, Lucy was suggesting that a single remedy—the establishment of appropriate sexual ideals—might alleviate a wide range of social ills. Implicit in her plan was the belief that issues of private morality and lifestyle could be conditioned by public policy in ways that were more forward-looking and beneficial than in the past. Like other Progressives, Lucy assumed that providing information or practical supports would enable individuals to make choices that accorded with her own standards. She frowned upon premarital and extramarital contacts. But, from women's standpoint, she saw the sexual side of marriage as riddled with disappointment, apprehension, even loathing. Lucy thought the answer lay in education. If women were taught about sexuality at an early age, they would grow up knowing that sexual expression was normal and necessary—within the proper context of marriage.

In many respects, then, Lucy's plan reflects typical Progressive concerns about private and public morality, as well as an overriding faith in education as the lever of broad social reform. When, shortly after formulating her plan, she read the report of the Chicago Vice Commission, a prime example of Progressive thinking about social purity, she was struck by the fact that all the educational suggestions the Commission had made—and many more—were embodied somewhere in her scheme.[41] Still, Lucy's plan was distinctive in its linkage of lower-class immorality with the sexual disaffection of upper-class women. Her community-oriented, experimental plan for sex education in the schools was also novel.

Many elements of Lucy's later involvement in education are incipient in this early project: instruction in sex hygiene in the public school; the importance of early schooling, even at kindergarten and pre-kindergarten levels; the need to create what she later called "intentional" school settings; self-government, or what might today be called self-help, or consciousness-raising groups, as mechanisms for effective learning; the linkage between personality and environment; and the school as an agency for broader social change, involving health, vocational counselling, labor legislation, and trade unionism. These would be the trademarks of her later work in progressive education.

On December 24, stopping in Chicago to visit her family on her return to California, Lucy went to see Jane Addams to discuss her plan for sex education. The talk with Addams made a deep impression on her. "She is the one person in the world for whom I have almost boundless admiration," Lucy wrote to Wesley Mitchell.

She was very gracious and tolerant with me, seemed interested in me and my plan, and left me with the feeling that the world was great and I was unequal to it. I like to feel I have touched a soul incomparably greater than mine, wiser, more balanced, more controlled and sweeter. I'd like to serve my apprenticeship under Miss Addams—only I couldn't in Chicago. I could [never] be treated quite seriously [here].[42]

She found in Chicago that Aunt Nan and Uncle Albert and her brother still wanted to treat her as a young girl. "I feel so misplaced in Chicago at the hands of my family," she admitted to Mitchell. "I get so tired of fencing and bartering. And yet I love them all and they do me. But our pri-

maries are different." The Chicago visit reawakened her adolescent conflict between the privileged world of the Spragues and the noble one of
Jane Addams. But now, though she felt "unequal" to the "large-minded"
qualities of Jane Addams—"that sanest and wisest and most lovable of
women"—there was no question on which side her future lay. She came
away from her "long talk" with Addams inspired to carry forward her new
project. "I feel a vital and interesting piece of work gradually shaping itself in my mind, a work which frightens me by its importance and its bigness," she wrote to Mitchell. "And this is what I like work to do."[43]

The plan Lucy envisioned had its origins in the teachings of Wald,
Kelley, Richmond, and Goldmark as well as Richman. The community
ideal she learned from them strongly influenced her ideas about sexual
education for adolescents, and indeed, much of the entire set of educational concepts she evolved over the next decade. Like Richman, Lucy
envisaged the school, rather than the settlement house, legislature, or
charitable agency, as the source of social reform energies. Yet in her later
plans, as we shall see, the school itself became a miniature settlement,
coordinating and initiating social services for children and their families.
Though Lucy rejected the settlement house lifestyle—she was a "pampered darling," as she admitted, and one who had not ruled out marriage,
as had many settlement women—she absorbed the greatest part of the
vision and commitment of Wald, Kelley, Richmond, Goldmark, Richman, and, indeed, of Jane Addams as well.

In the world of social reform to which these women had introduced
her, she could find a place for her own aspirations to be socially useful
and professionally productive. They had shown her that the realm of female action could be as broad and visionary as she wished to make it, and
thus confirmed her break with the powerful men who had guided her education in the past. From each mentor she learned significant lessons. In
Lillian Wald, she found a model of an intelligent, competent, yet highly
nurturant and deeply spiritual reformer. Florence Kelley demonstrated
the techniques and persona of the single-minded political organizer and
lobbyist. From Mary Richmond, Lucy gained a sense of the possibilities
of efficiently administered yet charitable bureaucracy, while Pauline
Goldmark showed her a more intellectual, research-oriented approach to
poverty. Julia Richman's teaching centered on schooling as the key to
community reform. She showed Lucy that an executive program-ori-
ented administrative style need not be rigid or sterile.

Underlying all was the influence of Jane Addams. Since adolescence

Lucy had seen Jane Addams as representative of goals of service and mission that contrasted with her father's materialism. Perhaps, indeed, Addams represented an amalgam of all the professional and personal attributes Lucy found in her other mentors. Lucy's ties to these women were strengthened after she returned to New York a year later. She would continue to learn from them even as she forged her own model.

In her plan for sex education, Lucy had fastened on a problem of the deepest personal, as well as social, urgency. Sexuality and marriage were issues very much on her mind as she corresponded almost daily with Wesley Mitchell during her stay in New York. In placing sex at the center of her program of social, economic, and cultural change, she was bringing into focus not only the experiences of the last months in New York and the views she had developed during her years at Berkeley but the immediate dilemmas of her personal life.[44] Her plan for sex education and her notion of a Dean of Women in a high school—in effect, a Dean of Women for Sex—indicates that even as she had begun to make decisions about her professional future, the issue of sexuality in her own life loomed large. For a further understanding of the context of her concerns, we must now examine the nature of her courtship correspondence with Wesley Clair Mitchell.

9

A Passionate Woman

Wesley Mitchell's love for Lucy was unequivocal. During their Sierra summer, he had found her even more irresistible than the "dream woman" of four years earlier. "Life is infused with you now," he wrote to her in New York. "You have made life so much more intense, so much more real, so much more deep and holy for me. . . . You have life itself to give me."[1]

Lucy Sprague was much less sure of her own feeling. She loved Wesley but was quite uncertain that she wanted to marry him. She had doubts about his strength of character, even about his love for her, because he had so readily accepted her rejection of him after the night of her gypsy dance. Just as important was her ambivalence about marriage itself. The marriage she knew best—her mother's—had meant subordination, loss of autonomy, and emotional constraint. And in New York, as she became acquainted with professional opportunities open to women, she was increasingly attracted to the "alternative" single life and less convinced that marriage could absorb her interests.

Lucy's three-month absence from California gave both her and Wesley the occasion to explore their ideas about marriage. Their correspondence ruthlessly examined the compatibility of their temperaments, personalities, ambitions, and ideals. Betweeen the lines lay an equally significant set of issues involving trust, intimacy, mutuality. Through the letters, the lovers came to understand each other's thoughts and feelings, to know each other's "real self"—a phrase that appeared repeatedly. This exchange became a crucial part of the couple's experience.[2]

When Lucy arrived in New York, there was a letter waiting for her from Wesley. Before she left Berkeley, she had asked him to describe himself, so that she could know him better. Though he was not in the habit of self-examination, he did as she asked, and wrote at length about his family background, schooling, early career, and intellectual and professional aspirations. With convincing insight into his own temperament and a clear vision of his role as a researcher and economic theorist, he presented a self-portrait of a dedicated, visionary, active scholar committed to a significant agenda of public work. In the pursuit of his goals, he was determined, vigorous, urgent. "I have deliberately chosen the life in which a certain kind of thing was likely to happen," he wrote. "My character has determined my life much more than my life has moulded my character."[3]

Though Wesley acknowledged that economic theory and scientific research did not readily attract public sympathy, he felt that his work as an economist, pioneering new ways of thinking, was vastly more important to "social reconstruction" than the limited contributions of piecemeal reformers. "Puttering" with philanthropy and "coquetting" with reform only "alleviates at retail the suffering and deprivation which our social organization creates at wholesale," he declared. What was needed to bring about social justice on a broader scale was "sure knowledge of the causal interconnections between social phenomena." To discover this knowledge, to "recast inherited ways of thinking," was his deepest innermost urge. He portrayed himself to Lucy as a prospector, a pioneer, an adventurer.

My world is the world of thought; but the world of thought has a realm of action and I live there. It is a place where one has to depend upon himself—his own initiative, his own sustaining faith. My danger in this realm is not from lack of vigor, but from lack of caution.[4]

Lucy was excited by Wesley's economic vision; the need to collect and correlate partial truths in order to plan wisely for social change had been in her own mind for several years, though "vague and unformed," she told him.[5] She did not acknowledge, however, that his justification of the significance of scientific research and critical theory over and beyond piecemeal social reform challenged the very fabric of her own incipient social vision. The purpose of her apprenticeships, after all, had been to observe reformers who were involved in precisely that tinkering with the social fabric that Wesley Mitchell scorned. Later in her letters she was to reveal how unfavorably she regarded her own efforts as contrasted to his confident scientific rationalism, a comparison that increased her apprehension about marriage.

Now, however, in the first of her letters from New York, she told Mitchell that although she felt his letter had revealed his maturity as a scholar, she was not convinced that he was as forceful and aggressive in a personal relationship as she would like. His life had been guided by a consistent purpose, she admitted; he had made "things" conform to his will. But she asked why, when courting her four years earlier, he had allowed one written appeal to her to be his only effort, and one written objection from her to stand as final. "The lack of knowledge of human, not to say feminine, psychology was 'academic,'" she insisted; "the ready submission was 'unaggressive.'" She argued that a man of "more 'force'—not intellectual or even emotional, but mere force in meeting the world and whipping it into line—would have persisted and insisted."[6]

Wesley tried to explain his behavior. Having fallen "violently" in love with Lucy on the night of her gypsy dance, he was bewildered and angry when she told him later that he loved an "imaginary" woman. In confusion, he accepted her answer and left her alone; he became involved with other women, and almost married Maude Radford Warren, until he realized he did not love her. His "absurd misunderstanding" of himself, as well as of Lucy, was what had made him appear unaggressive. His lack of vigor in pursuing her was a result of his "self-delusions", not a lack of passion or forcefulness.[7]

Lucy declared herself relieved to understand the past history of Wesley's feeling for her. She had felt "very little" and "very humble" because of his former conduct, she admitted. The thought of his "disapproval" and "intentional aloofness" had made her feel "helpless, hopeless."[8] In asking him to reaffirm his love, as she was to do many times during the next few months, she was asking for reassurance that if she herself risked loving him fully and freely, his love would be steady. The memory of his past retreat fed her already substantial fear of intimacy. Scarred by childhood guilt, a natural reticence, and the loss—by death or betrayal—of those she had loved most openly, she could not easily trust the promise of a new and deeply felt relationship. The negative aspects of marriage for women, apparent from the personal lives of those who had been close to her, also made her wary. If Wesley wanted her as a wife, his love and his persistence had to be tested.

While Lucy's challenges to Wesley's manliness, her shifts in mood, and her raising of ever new objections might well have tried his patience, Wesley Mitchell responded each time with courteousness, grace, and sympathy. He understood her bouts of moodiness and her need to intellectualize her feelings. His own earlier uncertainty about marriage also made him understand her hesitancy about commitment. Then, too, he clearly enjoyed matching wits with such a formidable mind. Her probing nature was one of the qualities that attracted him to Lucy in the first place. Now he had before him a dramatic challenge to his powers of persuasion, affection, and empathy, one upon which the future course of his personal life would depend. Could he convince Lucy, persuade her rational self as well as her equally resistant emotional self, that marriage to him would be the most rewarding of the possibilities before her?

Having dealt with the question of their earlier relationship and Wesley's goals and ambitions, the problem Lucy next raised was whether her own career aspirations, deeply influenced by Wald and the other women reformers she was meeting, were compatible with his. First, was the type of work represented by Wald and her group compatible with Wesley's scientific scholarship—that is, would she and he be "intellectually appropriate" to each other? Secondly, would he whole-heartedly accept Lucy's passionate involvement in *any* full-time work should she marry him?

Lucy carefully discussed with her suitor the professional choices open to her. Each of the three roles she mentioned—administrator, scholar, and reformer—required distinct abilities. As a dean, she admitted that her work had been "constructive in high degree." Yet she saw these talents as inferior to those of the scholar. Lucy viewed women like Jessica Peixotto and Sadie Gregory, who were trained in economics, as having greater intellectual capacities than she did. When she wrote to Wesley that intellectually she "humbled" herself before Peixotto, the message was apparent: Wesley Mitchell, with his similar training, was also Lucy's superior.

Lillian Wald, however, personified a third kind of career: that of reformer. It was not even Wald's work so much "as the spiritual equipment which makes her fit for her work" that stirred Lucy and set Wald and her like apart from the administrators and intellectuals. While Lucy was persuaded that Wesley's views about economics were practical, innovative, and visionary, he still was part of the academic world that she felt was not her own. "The intellectual job you are at I approve of and sympathize with," she wrote, "but I could never be a part of it. . . . I don't mean to say that I could not marry a man in whose job I could not share," she continued. "To share would be a tremendous bond which would make for mental stability and practical happiness. But of course it is not a necessity, though it is more nearly a necessity for me than for most women." What was essential was that "I have an outlet, a use for my own constructive force—and I think, though I am not certain, that that would have to be wider, though not deeper, than my home. This theoretically you would approve of," she told Wesley, "But practically, would you? Could you? Could I?"[9]

Lucy's desire for a constructive outlet—for work—and her fear that a lifestyle including professional work would be impossible for a married woman to maintain now became the "real point" of her objections to marrying Wesley. "Would this side of me make marriage with you more or less worthwhile, both for you and for me?" she asked. "Would it need to be suppressed, if not ignored? If it hindered, it would have to be squelched. If I marry you, your work and your standards shall prevail." Lucy was caught in a dilemma between a nineteenth-century view of marriage, and a strong but still tentative twentieth-century sense of her own potential. She was strongly attached to the idea of work of her own, and almost ready to make it a condition of their marriage. But she assumed, and insisted, that in case of conflict she would not enforce her own claims—because of her sense of Wesley's superiority of intellect and training, because she had no model of a marriage in which the husband's work and standards did not prevail, and perhaps out of fear of the strength of her own personality. The only way out of her dilemma would be an equitable relationship in which the work of each would have equal claims; but she had no confidence that such a marriage was a real possibility. Her insistence that she would not compete with Wesley was an appeal to him to guarantee that she would not need to.

I don't mean, of course, that I would become a mere Haus-frau. But I do mean that unless I consider what things I gain myself and the things I could gain without you, I shall not marry you. For example, I want to live in New York. I see a line of thought which I want to follow and which New York would help me to follow. But if we are married, I shall not consider that unless it is equally good for your work. Our life will be planned for the most important, and if your work is not more important than mine (leaving aside the most important of all which is *our* work, our home, and our possible children), why, then, I do not wish to marry you.[10]

Wesley did not vacillate in his response. Marriage would not threaten Lucy's desire for "constructive action," he insisted; he welcomed her de-

sire for work outside the home. His vision of a successful marriage centered on two people directing their energies along the lines of their own
work interests, supporting each other's ambitions and projects wholeheartedly. As he outlined it:

Your need of work is to me one of your most splendid qualities. I not only admire
but also sympathize keenly with it, because it answers my corresponding need.
To stifle it would be to cut off the direct source of happiness to you and helpful-
ness to others. If marriage threatened such a result you certainly ought not to
marry.

Furthermore, I agree most heartily that the home in and of itself would not give
adequate scope to your constructive energies. You have proved your fitness to
serve a larger circle, and you ought not wilfully to make it narrow. How an intelligent woman, with trained capacity, and the just self-confidence won by successful work can subside into a merely domestic and social life and remain content with herself I have never been able to understand. Even children need not
be a bar to much vigorous effort outside the home, if the mother retains the
strength and if the family has sufficient means to get other hands to do the routine work.

My idea of a home has always been that of a household of busy effective people—parents and children, whose relationship is founded on love for each other
but guarded by genuine interest in objective tasks. Most of the [ones] which I
know fall short of what you and I want for ourselves and for each other. [They]
fail largely because the wife lives too narrow a life. . . .[11]

Wesley went on to discuss the ideal he and Lucy shared and how, because of their individual interests, he thought this ideal could be made
"practicable." Taking up the issue that had loomed so large for Lucy—
their differences in training—he converted a supposed drawback into an
advantage. Their separate experiences and abilities would be comple-
mentary, he suggested, rather than divisive.

But you and I have certain qualities and certain circumstances in our favor. As for
the qualities, we respect each other as well as love each other. Neither wishes to
throw the whole burden of managing our common life upon the other, and neither wishes to absorb the other's whole life. You can be a better help-meet to me
for the very reason that you bring in so much experience that I do not have and
because you are trained in ways that I am not. And just so I can make life more
worthwhile for you by being different from what you are in various ways—each
of us can feel a just pride in what the other accomplishes. And this feeling will
enable us to make what for others might be a bar separating them in sympathy a

bond uniting us—a bond re-enforcing our love and steadying the life we build up together.[12]

Wesley attacked Lucy's notion that economic theory, his "large task"— an intellectual, academic one—was fundamentally different from and superior to Lucy's vision—the "spiritual" realm of philanthropy.

The chief circumstance in our favor is that while our specific tasks are different on the surface, they have a common basis. If you wanted to decorate china and I wanted to make money in steel we might find a chasm difficult to bridge between our interests as they developed. But the further you can develop your philanthropic plans, and the more I can make of economic theory, the nearer we shall come together.[13]

There was no reason, in fact, why Lucy could not share in his work. He felt that he would benefit greatly from "close and sympathetic contact" with philanthropy, obtaining important information and, even more significant, a sense of the "vividness" and "reality" of the conditions his research addressed. His analysis of the processes that brought about these conditions could in turn assist Lucy's work, giving her reform plans a "wider sweep" and making them less vague. "Surely, dear one," he concluded

your work would supplement and aid mine and mine would supplement and aid yours. You would not have to give up your plans; on the contrary you would realize them more effectively by marrying me. And you would have the pleasure of knowing that instead of hampering you were stimulating and helping me.[14]

Lucy was impressed by these arguments. Several days later, she interrupted their discussion to tell Wesley for the first time of her deep longing for him. "Today I am swept by an emotion which brooks no reserve," she began.

I want you dear, as never before. I want you with all the quivering longing of a passionate woman. I want the sound of your voice, the touch of your hand, of your lips, of the whole of you. If I were with you I would put my arms around you and come close. I want you with all the intensity of a lonely child—I want you to talk to, to share with, to do with. I want to feel protected in your arms. I want you with all the tenderness of a brooding mother. I want to comfort you, to praise you, to love you. I want you as the one person who loves me for what I really am, who is not afraid of my faults and not ashamed of my virtues. I want you as the one person whom I absolutely respect and honor without any reserves, as the one person whose real self calls to my real self and to whom my real self answers with a leap of gratitude and joy. Oh, my dear one, the one-I-love-best-in-the-world, I want you, I want you.[15]

Yet Lucy's admission of her passion for Wesley was not quite without "reserve." Her desire for him, as she told him, was counter-balanced by an even greater ardor: the "passionate intensity" of her desire to help those less fortunate than she. Though it was mingled with "the cry for little children" of her own, and for a "companion" to "share the fight," the urge to devote herself to a cause that was social rather than personal seemed primary.

These "lurking doubts" did not trouble Wesley. He was certain that a "great epoch" had arrived. At last *the letter* has come, he noted in his diary. Henceforth, he told Lucy, he would address her in his letters as "dearest Lucy," the term of intimacy he had reserved for her in his thoughts.[16]

There was no disparity between Lucy's philanthropic ideals and the passion she felt for him, he insisted.

The cry in this letter, the intense need to help those who are less fortunate, is not your cry alone. It is ours. . . .I would not surrender an atom of my passion for you, the thrilling in my blood, the choking in my throat, the desperate need to press you tight against my heart—but the passion itself could not be so intense if I did not believe so wholly in your ideals and did not share them without reservation.[17]

In turn, Lucy admitted the force of Wesley's arguments about the congruence of their physical passions and social commitments. But she remained ambivalent about her own intense sexuality and bewildered by the conflicting feelings that possessed her. When he closed his letter by telling her that he adored her and was "humbled" by her, yet was determined to prove himself "worthy," her resistance stiffened; his humility was not what she wanted.

Again, Wesley responded tenderly and with understanding. He understood her moods, he assured her, "in which spectres come from the hinterland of the spirit to confuse and sometimes to affright you." He tried to bolster her confidence, reproaching himself for bringing the struggle upon her. But he insisted that they grapple openly with any demons that threatened them. "For you and me the great 'specific' for all ills, even the ills that come of frankness itself, is to be more frank still."[18]

On November 20, when they had written about half of the thirty-two letters each would send during Lucy's three-month absence, Lucy admitted: "I have thought all the time that my *only* resistance was intellectual. But it is not so." Though there was "still struggle, still denial within me somewhere," a real turning point had been reached.[19] "Don't let's *discuss* any more," she repeated in her next letter. "I think and think to no avail. It must be left ultimately to feeling."[20]

This retreat from "discussion" heralded a new chapter in their correspondence. The first had been occupied with Wesley's explanations of his aspirations and his earlier courtship behavior; the second, with the gradual clarification and resolution of the issue of marriage versus career; and the third, following the dissolution of Lucy's "intellectual" resistance, focused on the two correspondents' deepest emotional concerns about dependency and love. What remained were questions of personal psychology, the nature of feminine and masculine identity, and sexuality.

Wesley asserted that there need not be an antithesis between intellect and feeling.

To me one of the most wonderful things about loving you is to find no conflict between the desires of my eyes and the voice of my judgment. I have had my touches of passion for other beautiful women, I have liked others, I have admired them. But always there has been something wanting. Where my judgment has approved, my blood has been cool: where my blood has been hot my judgment has said no. With you there is none of this discord.

I want you as the companion of my days, as my counsellor and critic, as my fellow worker. It is all crystal clear that life with you would be better than any other life I could imagine—not only because it would turn the desires which trouble me now into sources of ecstasy, but because it would bring days of serene happiness and a sense of heightened efficiency.

Their sexual union would enhance everything else they desired to accomplish. "We have the power of such white heat that it will forge us fast together into one bond which will have the strength of us both."[21] Wesley felt that Lucy's mind, now convinced, would not remain a "neutral spectator" in the struggle that still went on in her feelings. So vastly important was the first struggle they had overcome—the understanding that in marriage, they could supply "mutual support" to one another's work—that he was sure the "mysterious force" still holding out within her would now inevitably succumb.

Wesley was sympathetic to Lucy's continuing resistance. He recognized that for a woman, sexuality could not be considered apart from the issue of independence and autonomy generally. "Ah, well!" he wrote,

It must be so different with a girl. You have lived splendidly proudly alone, as much as a man lives alone. You have been independent. You have cultivated a sense of privacy. A man may do as much and set store by all these things, yet marry without great reluctance at giving them up in a measure. But a girl? Don't these things, when she has them at all, become more part of her fibre? Does not she become a bit of an Amazon in soul? Is it not hard to yield, even to one beloved, an intimacy such as she has never known save with her own soul? Must not the mere shadow of a bond seem like fetters? And while she longs to be captured, must she not flee? And can she even understand what *wild*, shy thing of *forest freedom* it is within her which holds out—which bids her struggle against her judgment and her passion?[22]

He hit a responsive chord when he spoke of Lucy as a "wild" independent thing, an "Amazon" who was also "sweet" and "shy." In her next letter, she admitted that she was indeed "an Amazon," but because "the world demanded it," not because her own heart wanted to live in isolation. Beneath her free-spirited, unconventional exterior, lay a softer, more vulnerable self, fearful of the very independence she desperately sought. For the first time Lucy revealed that among the emotional resistances she harbored were doubts about herself, about her own courage. It now became clear that the alternative life in New York attracted her not only as an arena for the fulfillment of her social obligations but also because it would ensure that she did not fall back upon the more passive, dependent life of a wife. The strong pull of this traditional role, and her own urgent longing for children, made her mistrust her personal feeling for her lover.

"It is the fear that I should be marrying *for the sake of bonds* that keeps me undecided," she told Wesley. "It is the lurking fear that I am cowardly about my great freedom. The fear that I am running to shelter not because I feel the shelter is my proper abiding place but because I am weary with the storm."[23] That same night, in "white heat," she wrote and sent to him a poem about her desire for children, telling him that in addition to the many gifts the world had given her ("music, color, poetry, work, friends"), she prayed for still another: "that I may feel beneath my heart / the sacred pressure of an unborn child / the gift of him I love."[24] Later she told Wesley the poem was written in an "impersonal frenzy as all my poems are. Very likely my love for you produced it indirectly. But I had no thought of you or any man when I wrote. . . . It was the mere cry of the . . . woman to conceive and to create."[25] Wesley was nevertheless delighted with the poem and her letter. He felt that none of her "infinitely changing moods" was so expressive of her soul as the one in which she acknowledged her desire to bear his children.[26]

While admitting her own insecurities about dependency and her yearnings for children, Lucy continued to dwell on Wesley's limitations. None of his arguments, it seemed, had yet convinced Lucy of his manliness. Following along the line of her previous attacks on his "force" and the quality of his "aggressiveness," Lucy now set forth a new anxiety— "personality"—which was to occupy their attentions for several letters. She agreed that the logic of their work seemed satisfactory and that their "minds fit." Thus, she no longer refused marriage on the basis of incompatibility of interests or ambitions. But, she admitted, "the old objection" was still there.

I fear to marry you lest I find that dread of an unshared life and the longing for physical children has led me to mate with a man whose personality is less than mine and whose conquest of me was due not to dominance of his soul over mine but to the cowardice of my own soul. . . .

As I told you on Alta, your character, your loveableness and your intelligence appeal to me convincingly. In those three great essentials I acknowledge you my superior and I find yielding easy. But there is a subtle something which I have which you lack—a something which kept me from considering the possibility of marrying you for many years, a something which would make my friends (those I inherited) feel I was making a mistake in giving myself to you—a something which you feel when you say you are unworthy of me. It is called—when we force ourselves to name it—"personality."

She went on to tell Wesley that this thing called "personality" (by which she seemed to mean compelling vitality, charm, and sociability) was her own great gift as well as menace, the only thing that raised her above "the common level." But she thought that her personality needed to be guided, lest it "run riot." Could Wesley be the one to guide it that without breaking its spirit? Lucy doubted whether anything but "personality" could control "personality," whether "intelligence" or "character" could really curb "the impetuous rush without bruising or mutilating the wild thing." Though she now understood that she loved Mitchell both as an intellectual companion and as a passionate human being, she wondered if he could be the one to share her "inmost soul"—whether, indeed, this last "ultimate sharing" were possible. "You do not compel my world," she confessed. "The people you draw to you are not *my* people. You need to be interpreted to be understood by those who instinctively choose me as their own." Though she longed to yield, to be bound to Wesley by the bonds of "mutual love and service," she could only do so with "one whose spirit commands mine." Thus, she concluded, "I have no choice. I cannot surrender."[27]

"We are going to have a hard time together," Wesley responded when he received this letter. Finally provoked to strike back, he answered in careful detail the new challenge she had flung at him. Lucy had raised a critical issue, but he felt that her discussion of it merely skimmed the surface. They needed to go beneath the superficialities and examine, point by point, the true measure of their differences.

"You say there is something which I lack—personality—and that it is this lack which I feel when I say I am unworthy of you. Oh, my dear, don't you know men are better than that?" he wrote.

Do you suppose that any decent man ever asked a woman whom he loved to marry him without saying exactly that to her? Why, it's as much a part of the old, old story as kisses, and it means, if you must be told, it means that every decent man reverences the maiden fineness of his beloved and feels conscience smitten about his own male coarseness. Perhaps the feeling is often a mistake—it's not with reference to you—but it is just part of being in love and wanting the woman in your arms—the contest between the spiritual and the sensual in your attitude. You endow her in your imagination with superfine sensibilities and want to kiss the hem of her garment and aver that you are unworthy to be blessed by being on the same planet with so eternal a creature. But you also want to rip that garment off! To feast your eyes on her naked loveliness! The first feeling you express since it is decorous—the second you try to keep to yourself in fear of frightening her.[28]

Lucy had simply misunderstood the male psyche. More to the point was Lucy's literal reading of the romantic convention Wesley had innocently used, a product of her inexperience, perhaps, but also of her inveterate overintellectualization.

Wesley next turned to probe the differences in personality that supposedly set them apart. The term was a psychologically vague one, he asserted, accusing Lucy of hiding behind it. If they were to examine each other's true assets, they would find that despite Lucy's superiority in aesthetic training, quickness of mind, social accomplishments, directness and honesty, it was Wesley who had the greater "inner strength."

A few days earlier, as part of their ongoing effort to assess the compatibility of their interests and temperaments, Wesley had told her that she was "self-centered in an unusual degree" and at the same time "particularly subject to suggestion." Whenever she was with anyone doing anything of interest, she responded intensely, but soon the interest became transferred to her own "self-centered system of schemes." "Like everyone who is largely the spectator of his own mental processes," she often became weary of this kind of "subjective life" and took easily to self-denunciation. "Life becomes a series of episodes, and one becomes a creature of chance instead of the guide of his own life."[29]

That Lucy overvalued the judgments of her social circle was an indication of her impressionability. Wesley readily admitted that he did not "compel" her world, but argued that her social world was not the world of her own real self or her ideals. He went on to compare his own steadiness of purpose to Lucy's.

Have you found yourself as I have found myself? Have you my purposeful continuity of interest? Have you my firmness of purpose? Which of us is the more moulded by the influences of environment? Which of us can stand the more firmly in the face of misunderstanding and disapproval? Which of us is freer from the domination of conventional values which we have not made our own? Which of us has the bigger vision to express his soul and to guide his life?

"You are the one of us two who most needs help," Mitchell told her, "the one. . . . whose fluttering spirit is more likely to fail amidst the storm of life."[30]

Wesley's most telling criticism of Lucy's "true self" came indirectly when he wrote about the strength of his enduring vision compared to her emerging one. Throughout Lucy's apprenticeship, she had written about her new commitment to social reform, admitting, however, that her "vision" was in a formative stage. Wesley's, on the contrary, was steadfast. "I shall cling [to it] even if it should mean the sacrifice of you whom I hold so dear. If ever anything should arise to make a choice necessary between following this gleam of mine and holding your love, understand well beloved, that I should be loyal to the vision." As Lucy commented years later, this was certainly a strange promise for her ardent lover to make, pressing all the advantages of his courtship he could muster.

Wesley's honesty may have displaced his strategy on this point. Lucy reacted by feeling all the more insecure and unequal to him, and all the
more uncertain about marriage. In any case, the message was clear: nothing was as important to this Wesley as his work. "If your vision is not as
bright as mine," he concluded, "if it does not command your energies as
steadily, if it is more personal, then dear one, learn to make my vision
yours."[31]

Lucy felt the sting of these words. At the same time, the eloquence of
Wesley's argument about marriage as freedom, with which he closed his
letter, moved her profoundly. They both knew that the decision to marry
was the opposite of the one many educated women were making. "Would
you not be exercising freedom—making a splendid effort of your very
own will against the pressure of environment," Wesley reasoned, "by
deciding that you want to marry me?"

You would not be running to a shelter in which you would be free from the pressure of duties. I'd guard and cherish you certainly, but one of the things against
which I'd protect you—if that ever became necessary (wild thought!) would be
the feeling that you could shift the burdens of life upon the soul of anyone else.
. . . You will find life not less full of opportunity for choosing, not less heavy
with responsibilities as a wife than as a spinster. It's not a refuge that I offer but a
fighting mate.[32]

Wesley's assertions about the strength of his vision caused Lucy to retreat, at least on this front. "The whole question of this 'personality' is
unimportant, anyway," she now declared, "compared to the question of
character." They had already agreed, of course, that there was little question about the firmness of his "character." Now Lucy took the defensive.
"You must know that mine is not a 'fluttering spirit,'" she protested.
"You must know that I have courage to defy everyone and everything for
the sake of my vision." But though Lucy admitted that "character" was
more important than "personality," she was not entirely willing to relinquish her advantage. However insignificant was "personality," she still
had more of it than he. "Remember I love you," she wrote, "though I do
not think you have a compelling personality."[33]

In his response Wesley tried again to minimize their differences in
"personality," considering them to be as insignificant as any difference in
their "objective tasks" or social visions. All that mattered, he felt, was
that there was a "considerable force" within him which neither feared
Lucy's strength nor acknowledged "inferiority."[34]

It was no longer Wesley's personality that troubled Lucy in her next letter. She now understood that the real issue was "masculinity." She explained to Wesley the "woman's side" of the "old, old story":

A woman always feels a rush of gratitude, founded on humility, that she is given to serve a man. She bows with proud humbleness before the masculine creature she acknowledges as her lord, her leader. This is only a part of her devotion—*but it is a part.* It is that that I have been trying to say when I first called you "unaggressive" and academic and then said you lacked personality and when I told you in the mountains that you could not "carry me to the heights." Define it as you will or leave it undefined. The fact remains that your masculinity does not compel me.

It was not a thing to be reasoned about, Lucy told him, but one that was instinctively felt. Lucy's "world" intuitively knew that Wesley lacked this quality. She was too much the "primitive woman" to be satisfied without his mastery over her.

Character you have and I honor you, intellect you have and I love you: but leadership, mastery, personality you have not and you do not compel me. You ask me, would I have everything? And I answer "yes." You ask me can I give everything? And in humility and shame I answer "No." I cannot give in character, intelligence or sweetness in the same measure that you can. I know I am asking an unfair bargain of the world. But unless I can get all, I cannot give even what I have.[35]

Though they could be happy together, nonetheless, in her soul she would not feel "humbled." She would not feel "the best" had come to her.

This new argument revealed much about Lucy's ideas of both femininity and masculinity. Though she insisted that her notion of masculinity did not "contradict a companionable equality," it was clear that Lucy believed that to be a woman at the deepest level meant to be dominated by a man—or at any rate that she turned to this model, more deeply rooted in her experience than any other, as a way of expressing her reservations about her suitor. Aggressiveness, mastery, and leadership were qualities she thought she could not do without in a husband; the rationality, tenderness, and willingness to compromise that Wesley had demonstrated so consistently were not enough. On a "primitive" level, she continued to see marriage as a relationship between unequals, with the husband dominating, the wife proudly humbled. Ironically, she felt the lack in Wesley of the very qualities she had hated in her father.

These "primitive" feelings about the way a woman ought to feel toward a "masculine" man did not fit the model of marriage that Lucy and Wesley had bandied about for several months. On one level, she was telling him that she could not marry him because marriage signified the loss of a woman's freedom and independence; on another, she argued that he was unsuitable as a mate because he did not assert his mastery over her. The contradiction was in part between her rational and her emotional self, the same confusing polarities she had recognized earlier. Yet her conception of marriage had in fact held steady throughout. Marriage, as she viewed it, implied dominance and loss of self for at least one partner. Normally, the male prevailed. When he did not, when the woman had more power, the situation was less acceptable (perhaps here she had in mind the model of "executive" Aunt Nan and "gentle" Uncle Albert). If Lucy feared this reversal of roles, perhaps she feared her own domination over Wesley, her own "executive" traits, her power and force, qualities that struck her as unfeminine and unnatural. She had yet to be persuaded that his power was a match for hers. She now had another word for the mysterious, vital quality evidently missing in Mitchell: masculinity.

Wesley went over this newest charge three times to make sure he understood it. He told Lucy he was touched by the obvious pain she felt writing this letter, by the "honesty of soul" and the "kindness" that breathed through its every line. Otherwise, he was not "greatly moved." In rebutting her argument, he ignored almost entirely her claim that truly masculine men dominated their wives. Instead, he shifted to the theme of "leadership," which she had incautiously mentioned as an expression of masculinity. He wrote again of his scientific work in the field of theory and research. Using the metaphor of exploration, he stressed his separation from, and superiority to, men and women who were "captains" in the "world of today," doing their work in the "well-settled busy land of the present." He had long ago left that world to blaze trails into the future. "Such an explorer is no leader," he acknowledged, because he did his best work alone and did not seek to raise bands of followers. "How can a man who has no company of followers be a leader?"[36]

He admitted that many other people shared Lucy's view of him and his kind, not recognizing the "courage required to stand at odds with the conventional scale of values." The "captains," in contrast, were publicly honored, since the world easily understood their achievements. But Wesley felt that these so-called leaders were in fact quite "limited" people, lacking vision, insight and courage. They were "half-blind leaders of the wholly blind."

Lucy Sprague, who had grown up among these captains, felt some loyalty to their strengths and virtues. But Wesley believed she did not really belong to this world. She was capable of much better things.

When you come with me and climb the high ridges which our leaders are content to look on from a distance you will find that your world—your real world— is a bigger place than the neighborhood in which you grew up. And while you may not feel called to give constantly to the work of exploration, you will do your work as a leader in the land of the present with an explorer's vision of the land of the future. And you won't think your companion, the one who loves you best of all the world—lacks virility.[37]

Only when they met again in the Sierras upon her return from New York would the issue of mastery be decided—"whether your feeling that I cannot dominate you or my feeling that you belong to me" would conquer.

As Wesley mailed this letter, Lucy was already on her way home. First, however, she stopped in Boston for a day to meet with the Board of the Women's Educational and Industrial Union, which was considering her for the job of president. Then she went to Pittsburgh to attend a conference for deans of women at state universities, at which she led a discussion on vocational work for women within the university.[38] She reached Chicago on December 23, where she found Wesley's latest letter waiting for her. "That is *more* what I meant," she wrote him in response. But she added cautiously, "perhaps only spoken words can really make us understand: perhaps we can never quite bridge the unintelligible chasm between soul and soul except by love."[39]

The following day Lucy met with Jane Addams to discuss her plan for sex education. Addams' enthusiasm for her ideas assured Lucy of their importance. "I find myself unconsciously thinking of this work as my next step in life . . . not marriage with you!" she told Wesley. But recognizing on some level that helping other women to understand their sexual needs was no substitute for an intimate relationship of her own, she remained indecisive. "Help me to decide as I should!" she implored him. "Why isn't it 'clear as crystal' to me as you? . . . I who usually know my mind in a minute have questioned myself for half a year in vain."[40]

The next day she sent Wesley a poem setting forth the alternatives offered her—first, the attractions of her wealthy, cultured background (the "easy comforts" of "lavish" society, which she readily dispensed with, and the "subtle balanced blandishments of art"); second, and "more precious," the desire to serve the needy (especially the "stumbling

women hardened to defeat" and their "stunted children"); lastly, marriage and motherhood, which she still saw as contradictory to her sense
of social obligation and professional ambition. She had come to suspect
that her fear of independence might be driving her into marriage; and
this mistrust of her own motives became a new and formidable barrier.

Free, for I'm neither daughter, mother, wife
(But oh, this treasured freedom costs me dear)
And I who've feared no other burden, fear
To bear the burden of this unbound life
Beloved of my heart, and can it be
You've come to free me from my liberty?[41]

Their planned reunion in the Sierras was itself a matter of increasing
concern. They felt they could not spend two weeks together, unchaperoned, in the mountains. Their friend Mary Howard was ready to accompany them but it appeared that she could not join them immediately
upon Lucy's arrival. "Would you think it unwisely unconventional for me
to meet you at Mercid and take you into the valley?" Wesley wrote to
Lucy. "Mrs. Howard seems to think that arrangement sufficiently proper.
Please let me know whether it would embarrass you. We should have to
stay overnight, of course at the Del Portal Hotel. You know I have no
great respect for conventions that do not recommend themselves to my
mind as sensible. But I am most strongly set against doing anything
which might make you feel uncomfortable."[42]

As it turned out, Mrs. Howard changed her plans, and the two lovers
did not need to trouble themselves about the propriety of spending a
night alone at a hotel. According to the new plans, Lucy would arrive in
Los Angeles on January 3, met by Marion Farquhar, "to be whirled away,
as you love to be," wrote Wesley, "in the torrent of her intensity." Wesley understood Marion's deep affection for Lucy, and wanted Lucy to accommodate it. "Make Mrs. Farquhar happy, by giving her all of yourself,"
he urged.[43] But Lucy would spend only one night with her friend. On
the fourth, she would take the Southern Pacific Valley Express out of Los
Angeles, arriving at Mercid at 1:45 P.M. on the fifth. Mrs. Howard,
leaving Berkeley that same morning, would arrive fifty minutes after
Lucy. Wesley Mitchell would take the train the day before, so as to be
able to meet Lucy's train. For their first fifty minutes together, they
would be unchaperoned.

As the day of their meeting drew nearer, Wesley reiterated his passion and devotion:

I don't think there has been a half hour for a month when you have not come into my conscious mind. . . . I see you . . . in the corduroy dress you wore in the mountains, with roses in your hair as you were when the Millers gave their din- ner to the Lanes, with your blue Chinese coat on, in the filmsy [sic] dresses you wear at home. . . . Oh my beloved, you don't know how much I have made you a part of myself. . . . Let [me] give you the gift of my love . . . cherish it, make the most of it for both our sakes.[44]

Lucy, meantime, became increasingly anxious. "My heart grows heavy. . . . with dread," she wrote to Wesley, a strange sentiment with which to anticipate a reunion with a loved one, but one that reflected the anxiety of her continuing indecision and her feeling that her entire future rested on the outcome of that unpredictable encounter.[45] Lucy did not like to leave so much to emotion, although she had often admitted that this was perhaps the only way to resolve her dilemma.

How far apart Lucy Sprague and Wesley Mitchell remained is reflected in the last of the letters she sent to him, written on the eve of their meeting.

I *do* believe you are an explorer, moreover I believe you will blaze pathways into unknown and fertile valleys for I feel the promised land lies just over the hills which you are even now at the foot of. It is just this belief which has made me love you. And yet there is something which keeps me from putting on my moun- tain clothes to follow you into your mountains—no, *our* mountains. I cannot explain: but I can feel. It may be that I enjoy the altitude only as a tonic, as an escape, it may be that I am too much of an explorer by temperament to follow *any one's* trail, even yours, or it may be that I do not feel you are a surefooted guide, that I have not found *my* leader. I do not know. But something there is that rises in inexplicable pride and refuses to let me make the last surrender. Dear, dear, explorer, may I pack the Rucksack even though I have not the strength nor the steadiness of head or of purpose, to follow you along the trail? I should like to share the journey as far as I can in my valley home and to go for occasional "ausfluge" with you if you will let me.[46]

It seemed that Wesley's patient persistence had not been rewarded. Lucy's resistance no longer had the flamboyance, exaggeration, or confidence of earlier accusations. But while she now admitted that the barrier to marriage lay in her own deficiencies as well as his, the result was the same: the "last surrender" was impossible, albeit inexplicably. It was with a "no" on her lips that Lucy Sprague went to meet Wesley Clair Mitchell at Yosemite.

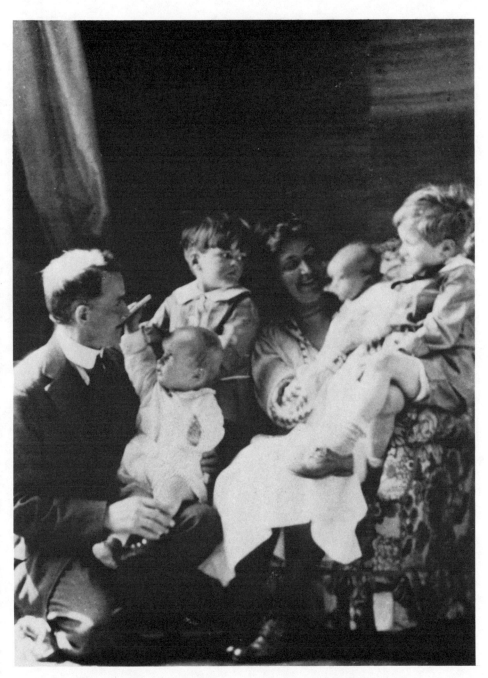
The Mitchells and their children (1918). Lucy Sprague Mitchell Papers, Rare Book and Manuscript Library, Columbia University.

Lucy and Marian (Marni) Mitchell. Lucy Sprague Mitchell Papers, Rare Book and Manuscript Library, Columbia University.

Lucy and Wesley (ca. 1915). Lucy Sprague Mitchell Papers, Rare Book and Manuscript Library, Columbia University.

The Mitchells' brownstones on West 13th Street, Greenwich Village. Courtesy of the Bank Street College of Education, Office of Public Information.

Harriet Johnson (*top*). Lucy Sprague Mitchell Papers, Rare Book and Manuscript Library, Columbia University. Barbara Biber (*bottom*). Courtesy of Barbara Biber.

Lucy Sprague Mitchell teaching a class at the Bank Street College of Education. Courtesy of Barbara Biber.

The Mitchell compound at Greensboro, Vermont (*top*). Photograph by Stephen Antler.
Lucy and Wesley at Greensboro (ca. 1945) (*bottom*). Courtesy of Dr. John Coolidge.

Lucy Sprague Mitchell. Courtesy of the Bank Street College of Education. Photo by Hank Kranzler.

A Masque
of Maidenhood

Lucy, Wesley Mitchell and Mary Howard journeyed together to the southern Sierras at the beginning of January, 1912. With clouds sweeping across the face of the cliffs, brilliant skies, snow falling heavily, peacefully, "nothing could have been more beautiful," Mary Howard wrote to her husband, "there was nothing left to be desired." Tamaya Canyon, the object of their pilgrimage, was "alluring and . . . forbidding, . . . a fairy land . . . a holy place, wondrously enchanting and stupendously awful, both at the same instance."[1] In these mountains, where "Robin" and "Alta" had discovered their love for each other six months earlier, Lucy found her way back to the immediacy of her feelings, without the screens of analysis, self-doubt and self-assertion that she had deployed in her letters from New York.

On January 29, two weeks after they had returned to Berkeley, Lucy at last told Wesley that she would marry him. Although the explanation she provides in *Two Lives* reveals little ("I finally achieved faith in myself which gave me faith in *us*—faith that through carrying a common load each would build a life richer and more joyous than either could build alone"), undoubtedly the romantic interlude in the mountains had allowed her to overcome her doubts.[2]

Together with her decision to marry came the definite resolve to leave the West. Early in her correspondence with Wesley, she had told him that she wanted to move to New York because it was there that she could best pursue her work; and he had agreed to this without difficulty. Though he knew of no specific academic opening in New York, Wesley felt that the economic processes he wished to study were better represented there than "anywhere else in the world."³ He gave in his resignation from the University of California in March.

Lucy told President Wheeler she would leave Berkeley after the spring term and move to New York with Wesley once they were married. She submitted a report to Wheeler proposing new courses and field work to be given at the university, which presumably incorporated her experiences in New York. The report has not survived, but it is likely that Lucy Stebbins' early measures reflected her predecessor's concerns. After Lucy Sprague's departure, Stebbins surveyed thirty-seven campus departments regarding instruction for women that could relate to fields other than teaching. She took the leading role in establishing a department of Home Economics at Berkeley, which she believed could help make college more "relevant" to women and "dissipate the intellectual haze between the college woman and her probable life in the world."⁴

Now Lucy began to reveal her engagement to family and friends. On February 4, she went south to tell her news to Aunt Nan and Uncle Albert, who were spending the winter in Pasadena. Lucy acknowledged to them that neither Adolph nor Mary was "cordial" or "sympathetic" to the engagement; they felt that Wesley was not her equal.⁵ Nan and Albert met Wesley a week later when he accompanied Lucy on another visit to Pasadena. "We are all very pleased with Mr. Mitchell," Nan jotted in her diary, "though we all feel Lucy is his superior. She seems very happy [and] assures us she knows her man, that he is *all right*. God grant it may be so!"⁶

Cousin Elizabeth, responding to Lucy's news, wrote of the rewards of marriage, although her husband's now chronic tuberculosis had made her own a perpetual struggle. "I know that you are one of those superb women who make the normal lot the most glorious one," she wrote. "The one thing I am questioning is whether 'Clair' is good enough for you. If he is, he must be almost the only one of his kind."⁷

Lucy's brother Albert immediately contacted acquaintances at the universities of Chicago, Berkeley, and Harvard to find out what he could about "this Mitchell." A letter from Harvard reported that he was regarded as "one of the most brilliant of the younger economists." He had given "great satisfaction" as a visiting professor a few years earlier, showing himself to be an unusually agreeable man who took a keen interest in students. Indeed, he had been offered, but rejected, a permanent position at Harvard.⁸ Other reports were consistently favorable, though Wesley's former teachers and colleagues at Chicago implied that he had not yet made as much of a mark as they had expected. Albert concluded that Adolph Miller's negative feelings about his sister's fiancé had been inspired by "professional jealousy."[9]

Albert wrote to Lucy that he was delighted at her decision, and hoped she would consent to be married at his home in Lake Forest. "As a matter of fact," he indicated jauntily, "I think you are just coming to your senses which I feared you never would do, so deeply immersed have you appeared to be in your work of spanking and directing all the little coeds."[10] As far as Lucy was concerned, Albert remained the incorrigible older brother who never missed a chance to tease his little sister. But he warned her in all seriousness to keep her inheritance under her own control. Though unstated, the class difference between Wesley and the Spragues was undoubtedly a major element in the family's misgivings.

Once the engagement was announced, Adolph and Mary adopted a neutral attitude, but Lucy and her aunt and uncle were well aware of their lack of enthusiasm. Nan Sprague knew that Adolph complained of Mitchell's "drawing room manner"—he was not as urbane or polished as Miller would have liked—but this was a failing Nan did not take seriously.[11] Years later, another family member suggested that Miller's jealousy might have been personal as well as professional.

President Wheeler and his wife were also unenthusiastic, as Nan readily detected when she and Albert visited Berkeley in April. The Wheelers did not dislike Wesley but believed Lucy to be so exceptional that her lover did not seem worthy of her. Wheeler at any rate respected Wesley's abilities, for he had once asked him to become dean of Berkeley's graduate school.[12] Wesley for his part was not fond of President Wheeler, whom he thought "opportunistic."

Only months later, after Lucy's wedding, did Nan learn another source of Wheeler's reservations. Visiting Chicago in June to attend the Republican Party convention Wheeler admitted to Nan that Wesley was "bright and good." The question was, "will he be equal to living his own life and *growing*, rather than settling down comfortably with a rich wife?"[13] In fact, it seems to have been Adolph Miller who had settled down comfortably with a Sprague heiress and failed as yet to fulfill his intellectual promise.

Lucy and Wesley had anticipated the response of Lucy's family and their friends to their intended marriage. But Wesley had persuaded her that they were not the "world" that mattered most. Now Lucy held fast to her choice. She was eager to have Nan and Albert get to know the "real Clair Mitchell. . . . I know that would mean to love him," she wrote. "His unswerving idealism with his sane judgment and keen intelligence makes that a foregone conclusion in my mind." But, she admitted, "he is not readily known."[14]

At the end of February, Lucy sent notes to about forty friends telling them about her forthcoming marriage.[15] Almost all the people who had been important in her early life—other than the family members and the Wheelers—responded with enthusiasm.

Mrs. Caswell, still at the Marlborough School, warmly approved of Wesley Mitchell, whom she had met on several occasions. "I am old fashioned enough to believe in marriage with all my heart," she wrote, "and to feel that the woman who has the love of a man like Mr. Mitchell is to be literally congratulated."[16]

From Marion Jones Farquhar, preparing for the birth of her second child, came an emotional letter. "I can't tell you with what ardor I long for your happiness, my dear one," she scribbled. "Not ordinary happiness, but happiness in scale with your generousness and bigness and tenderness. Oh, how I love you Lucy! I don't believe any one will ever love you any more than I do—at least in proportion to the capacity for loving." Marion was sending her a copy of a pearl pendant of hers which Lucy had admired. "I wanted you for a twin," she wrote, hoping that the identical brooches would always remind them of each other. "Oh, my darling," she added, "it is hard to let you go even though I am so happy for you. I think people's mothers must feel like that. . . . I put my arms about you, my beloved, and kiss you and love you. Remember that very little time ever passes without your being in my thoughts, without my wishing good for you and loving you all. I know how to love."[17]

Lucy had never doubted this. She and Marion had established the kind of intimate, emotional friendship that was common among this generation of women, though Marion was the more openly demonstrative. Now, as Marion prepared for her baby's birth, Lucy took her friend's seven-year-old son, David, with her to Berkeley, where she cared for him for five weeks. Her willingness to have David live with her at this difficult time in her own life, when he might have stayed with his extended family at Santa Monica, testified to the closeness of her friendship with Marion, and to the importance of mothering in her sense of herself.

George Palmer, who had been disconsolate when Lucy did not visit him in Boxford the previous year, also sent word of his pleasure at the proposed marriage. Since Lucy's rejection of his proposal, George had let her know of his abiding attachment in many ways. He wrote her eloquent, subtly manipulative letters deploring her absence from Cambridge, and detailing her unique virtues. Now he maintained that, "inheriting you from Alice, I have always thought of you as a creature apart, queenly or semi-sacred." Marriage was the proper destiny for such a creature. If it were not to be himself, he was at least glad that she had chosen someone as suitable as Wesley. "You are to have not merely marriage," Palmer declared, "but a great marriage, such as I had . . . with one . . . whose tastes and mind are so like your own that neither of you in coming to the other need turn away from anything. It is glorious and worth waiting for."[18]

Biologist Jacques Loeb, who had known Mitchell at Chicago and Berkeley, wrote that he was a man "of the highest character as well as of the highest intelligence and initiative, and the interests of both of you are so closely related that we feel that it is almost a case of predestination." In her letter to him announcing their news, Lucy had asked Loeb to recommend a reading list for her as he had done in the past. Loeb complied, suggesting Wilde's *Soul of Man under Socialism*, among other books, but asked if she really cared to "read much just now," considering the nearness of the wedding. But Lucy and her fiancé always had time for the books and poetry they both loved. It was one of the joint interests that in fact "predestined" them.[19]

From Agnes Boyle O'Reilly Hocking, at Yale with her husband, came a typically effervescent letter:

I have never been happier at the thought of a marriage, dear Lucy, I fairly love Mr. Mitchell, you know (I don't feel about many men as I do about him) and to think of his having beautiful you in his life from now on warms me to the center. You will be a beautiful pair of beings. Lucy . . . I could bless you for it![20]

Jessica Peixotto also felt the match was "perfect." But her feelings were tinged with regret. "Most heartily . . ." she wrote to Lucy, "do I rejoice in your joy. Mine would be quite as real as yours had you not also driven home so tersely the news that you go 'never to return to Berkeley.' To lose either of you is hard; to lose you both makes a very painful gap in the circle of friends nearest my heart. I mourn for the University and [myself]"[21]

Florence Kelley's response was vintage Kelley. After abrupt good wishes—"I wish you a sunny wedding day (I suppose that is assured in California!), a fortunate voyage [Lucy had announced that they would honeymoon in Europe] and 'living happily ever after'"—she got down to the point.[22] She urged Lucy to use her travels abroad to gather information on European practices with regard to protective legislation for women and children, interviewing English and French authorities.

From Pasadena, finally, came a heartfelt letter from Dr. Henry Stehman, physician to Lucy's father and mother for many years, who had treated Lucy as well. "Confidentially, I have sometimes felt anxious about your health," Stehman admitted, "but with a husband who loves you and understands you, my fears are relieved, for I feel sure that it [is] the medicine you need." "If it is not too early," he wrote, "you may congratulate Mr. Mitchell. . . . For the life of me, I am at a loss to know how he caught the gazelle."[23]

The gazelle was caught, but before she finally renounced her singlehood, she was to celebrate its passing in a unique way. Before Lucy left for New York, she had originated a plan that had little to do with curricular issues directly. Out of the poetry readings at her house and her knowledge of festivals at the Eastern women's colleges had come the idea of a Woman's Festival or Women's Day. As we have seen, she had been dissatisfied with women's participation in campus activities. "Wherever there are men, women's interests shrink . . . particularly in the eyes of the women themselves," she remarked.[24] Now she wanted to remedy that problem by providing a single experience for college women that could stand as an expression of their power, resourcefulness, and creativity, a "unified expression of women's personality" through a unique kind of festival, pageant, masque, or ceremony. It would increase the self-possession, self-reliance and responsibility of women students and, well after college had ended, would stand in their memories as an expression of its best ideals of culture, beauty, and learning. Such a festival could involve all women on campus, even the isolated, detached students who had long been a concern of Lucy's, and could bring together women's groups that usually had little to do with each other. The Associated Women Students had previously run various outdoor dances, but students' energies had been dissipated among these and other scattered activities. Most importantly, the pageant, or masque, would be written and performed by women.

The idea as it emerged after one of Lucy's at home poetry readings was "like a match put under dry evergreen boughs which turned into a sizzling roaring flame shooting sparks into the air." Lucy called a meeting for interested students and faculty to discuss the notion further. Many came, intrigued with the idea of developing a woman-oriented dramatic ceremony. "How could it be done? What kind of thing should they write? Who would choose from the manuscripts? Questions. Excitement. Suggestions."[25]

The Dean tried to express her own vision to the students. "You remember the Spring Festival? It'll be something like that—a kind of play—dancing, something beautiful at any rate, something that every single woman in the University can take part in—something that will make the University mean Beauty as well as Truth, and that we can do ourselves over and over every year, our gift to the University."[26] She described the rituals of Tree Day and Daisy Chain at the Eastern women's colleges, and read some of the folk poems recited at Rumanian harvest dances. Elements in each of these could be used as models, she suggested. Porter Garnett, who had directed Berkeley's popular Bohemian Grove plays, suggested that a minimum of words be used for the pageant, whatever its theme, and that, since only male actors took part in the Grove Plays, this Woman's Pageant should certainly not employ men as actors. Both suggestions met with general agreement. Chauncey Wells of the English department spoke of Ben Jonson's masques for the Elizabethan and Jacobean courts as another type of model. John Galen Howard recalled the noble simplicity of Hellenic pageants, and Ivan Linforth of the Greek department told of the Panathenic festival where virgins brought Athena her new robes.

A mass meeting was held at Hearst Hall to discuss the plan with more women students. Lucy announced the theme that had finally been selected—the development of a girl into a woman. Through the use of ritualistic elements, she hoped that the masque could transform the particular, subjective aspects of this life transition into a drama of universality. A competition would be held for the best script written by a woman for an outdoors dramatic performance on this theme. The only proviso was that the primary aim should be "beauty." Lucy chaired the selection committee, whose other members included Winifred Rieber, Ivan Linforth, John Galen Howard, Porter Garnett, and several women students. The Associated Women Students enthusiastically endorsed the competition, giving it much publicity.[27]

Twenty-three scripts were submitted. John Galen Howard even submitted an entry, to make sure that his friend Lucy was not left without any script at all! The winner was a senior, Anna (Nan) Rearden, daughter of California man of letters Judge Timothy H. Rearden, friend and comrade of Bret Harte and Ambrose Bierce. Nan Rearden, a classics major and an aspiring writer, had been influenced by Linforth's description of the Panathenic Festival. She titled her script "Partheneia: A Masque of Maidenhood" in reference to the songs sung by virgins as they brought their offerings of new robes to Athena.

Lucy did not write the masque, but there is little doubt that she inspired it. Rearden recalled Lucy as a "warmspirited Dean whose very essence seemed to stir a new kind of electric vibration." As, in her poetry readings, Lucy had opened doors to the worlds of beauty and culture, so her spirit made the masque come alive. The masque was Lucy Sprague's "intimate production," Rearden testified.[28] Lucy was "a glowing sentient figure to whom always, life and living [were] so intimately commingled that dreams themselves (by most of us never realized) [took] on for her the matter-of-factness of richly endowed reality."[29] The women students of Berkeley officially dedicated the Partheneia to Lucy Sprague, "whose dauntless faith in undergraduate ideals and tireless energy in their realization have given the women of the University of California a new tradition of sweeter and fuller life."[30]

As soon as the script was selected, Lucy threw herself into its realization with total commitment. She directed and more or less produced the drama, providing most of the funds to support the huge undertaking. Tryouts for the choruses and dancing parts were held in the gardens and lawn of Lucy's house. A rented piano sat on her closed porch for rehearsals. No woman who wanted to participate in the pageant was turned away. Though less than a dozen had speaking parts, 470 acted in the chorus and dances. The leading role, the Spirit of Maidenhood, was played by Radiana Pazman, who later went on to a career in opera.

Lucy had the help of many people in putting on the pageant. Porter Garnett was responsible for staging the performance, to take place at the Le Conte Oak, near the west entrance of the campus. The plot was plowed and sowed, so that by April 6, when the performance took place, the grass was green. Thirty different varieties of costumes for the hundreds of women who took part were designed by Adelle Barnes. Women students from the California School of Design submitted entries to a competition for posters and programs. The score of the pageant was taken from the compositions of Edward MacDowell, orchestrated especially for the pageant by composer Edward C. Stricklen. Conductor Paul Steindorff and twenty-two members of the San Francisco orchestra crossed the bay on the day of the performance for their one and only rehearsal, two hours before the show, to avoid the great expense of a second trip.

Initially, the dancers were coached by a dance instructor, but by the end of February she had given up. Lucy and Porter Garnett had insisted that the dances of the hundreds of sprites, spirits, and maidens be done in a fresh, unconventional way rather than through used routines from formal ballet. But it proved impossible to find dancing coaches willing to improvise so many dances for such a large cast. At the beginning of March, Lucy took over the task herself. She seemed to thoroughly enjoy the choreography, rehearsals, and actual dancing she did over the next six weeks. On one occasion, Lucy was rehearsing the girls who represented "spirits of the ocean fog" in the Le Conte glade. At the performance, the fog-spirits were to be encased in swirling, billowing gray veils which they would lift at the precise moment when the script called for the sun to shine through, revealing plates of gold on their breasts. Now, rehearsing them, Lucy crouched low in the glen, waving her arms with the swirling Liberty scarves she had brought with her, swaying in every direction as she gradually rose to her full height, ready to toss back the scarves at the precise dramatic moment. Imagine her surprise when she emerged, tousled and frenzied, to find an amused President Wheeler with an eminent visiting savant from Berlin beside him, waiting to greet her. All her German fled from her, as she imagined what the dignified professor must have thought of the wild American *Dekanin!*[31]

Lucy's spirits seemed to thrive on the logistical, creative, and technical problems posed by the pageant. The students who worked with her recalled her untiring enthusiasm and vivacity, which regenerated their own. Freed at last from agonizing decision-making about marriage versus career, she poured all her energies into the masque. The Partheneia proved to be a fitting project for her final days as Dean. This masque of maidenhood became, symbolically, Lucy's own rite of passage.

On April 6, in the green of the Le Conte Oak, nearly five hundred women students created in visible form the enchanted "fairyland" inspired by Lucy. The three San Francisco papers—the *Examiner*, the *Call*, and the *Chronicle*—each gave the masque a full-page review, with pictures, on the Sunday following the pageant. "*Partheneia*'s Beauty is beyond Words," noted the *Examiner*. "Masque Is Masterpiece. Defies All Comparison." No California stage had ever known a play of such light, shade, and color. Its appeal to the eye was irresistible: for two hours picture flowed into picture, each one more vividly beautiful than the last. There was an "iridescent lacery of color . . . a rainbow shattering itself to fragments against the sturdy Le Conte oak could not have drenched the glade in more glowing hues."[32]

The appeal of the masque was not merely visual, wrote the *Examiner*'s critic. "Its aim was leveled higher. . . . Through it the women of the university gave expression to their philosophy of life, a high philosophy erected on high ideals." Commenting on the theme of the play, the critic wrote that "seldom has symbolism with its evanescent beauty been able to endure the sneering scrutiny of logic and realism as serenely as this quiet little masque," with its "delicate grace" and "intellectual fitness."[33]

"One feels quite powerless to praise it sufficiently," he concluded. "When compared with some of the trivial and senseless concoctions of claptrap encountered on the stage in the way of moralities, it shines like a work of art. So great a sense of refinement, delicacy and high intelligence seemed to permeate the *Partheneia* that it would be unjust to compare it with anything that has been done, especially on the stage. Here in California, which is the nursery of what is best in the outdoor play, it stands alone."[34] "As an art form it is unique," added another critic. "It verges on the highest ideals of poetry."[35] All proclaimed the masque a wonderful tribute to the glory and beauty of womanhood.

Five thousand spectators evidently concurred. Sitting on overcrowded bleachers and in the fragile limbs of old oak trees, they cheered the performance heartily. Interest in the masque had been so great that thirty-one ushers and several uniformed policemen could not control the crowds. They rushed in before the gates to the grove were opened, making it impossible for reserved ticket holders to take their seats.

Nan and Albert, who had come from Pasadena for the spectacle, were not disappointed. Sitting with the Millers, the Wheelers and Mitchell himself, they found the performance "beautiful and very unique." They were "more than proud of Lucy," recognizing, as did most spectators, that "she is the real *creator* of the show." Proudly they watched their niece honored when the masque ended.[36]

From the perspective of the 1980s, this spectacle of beauty performed by 470 maidens seems remote and ingenuous, with its laughing and

leaping nature spirits—Eucalyptus dryads, sea sprites, spirits of the California woods, fog, rain, earth, leaves and flowers—and its historical and
allegorical figures: Antigone, Una, Beatrice, Saint Elizabeth, Joan of Arc
(riding on a white stallion), the spirits of Endeavor and Achievement,
and the Ideals of Nobility (representing "purity and virginity"), Joy-In-
Life (representing "family happiness"), and Service. Yet the play spoke
powerfully to the sensibilities of the period. Its appeal lay not only in its
visual and musical qualities and its poetry but in the representation of
what critics agreed were the finest ideals of American culture. Lucy had
at last achieved the goal she formulated early in her stay at Berkeley: to
create a potent presence for women on the masculine-dominated campus
that would symbolize the positive aspects of female culture. She had
successfully brought what she identified as the feminine tradition to
the parched and arid aesthetic landscape of the University of California. The festival (still called the Partheneia) remained an annual tradition at Berkeley until the early 1930s, although the masque changed
annually.[37]

On one level, the "Masque of Maidenhood" symbolized and celebrated
traditional feminine ideals of nurturance, sacrifice, grace, service, and
beauty. Yet it also celebrated the actual and potential contributions of
women. Women had a significant past and a future, the 1912 masque declared. The past was filled with real achievements—illustrated by the
symbolic crowning of women students who had made notable contributions to university life. The future, too, would be shaped by women's
power. In the last image of the masque, almost five hundred women link
arms and, with torches lit, encircle the Spirit of Maidenhood, now become a Woman, cloaked in vivid shades of red and violet. Armed only
with her own power, the company of other maidens, and the spirit of
light, or life, she goes forth into the world.

While the masque reflected a romantic view of women's role and potential, the idyll was not all sweetness. As the pageant opens, bands of
young girls, dressed in pure white, are mournful and weeping, singing
songs of sorrow, for they have learned that the first lessons of the world
and of experience are tragic ones. They seek consolation from women's
past and the ideals of womanhood. Much later, Rearden was to describe
the theme of her pageant compared to later ones at Berkeley. "From sorrow," she noted about her own script, "the woman's soul is brought to
flower."[38] Women, as Rearden saw it, ultimately come to understand
that this is not the best of all possible worlds, yet they realize that though

sorrow must be encountered, life can be lived wisely, full of all that one had hoped. The gaining of this wisdom was reflected in the final rite of passage from girlhood to womanhood.

And so it had been in Lucy Sprague's own life. She had begun to learn at last that the lessons of sorrow, pain, conflict, tragedy—the lesson of "yielding," as she had expressed it in her philosophy papers at Radcliffe and in her letters to Wesley Clair Mitchell—were not the only ones. Beyond sorrow and conflict lay choice, autonomy, and selfhood, if one were willing to risk the struggle to attain them. Life could offer hope as well as despair, intimacy and love as well as discord.

In the congruence of Lucy's own life with the theme of the pageant, the masque revealed another irony. Designed to mark the passage from adolescence to adulthood, the masque was nevertheless true to the experience of an older woman. Constrained by powerful family claims, and limited by lack of opportunities, prejudice, discrimination and their own inchoate ideals, women of Lucy Sprague's generation who sought independence often struggled for many years to achieve autonomy and adult status. Lucy Sprague stepped into womanhood on the brink of her thirty-fourth birthday, having made the choices that could lead her to a more fully realized life. "Grant thy light to these my maidens that they may at last pass forth with glory into womanhood!" Athena asks the Spirit of Light as the Partheneia concludes. And so, with her Berkeley maidens, Lucy, too, became ready to pass into womanhood.

Though the next year's masque, The Awakening of Everymaid, introduced motherhood as a basic motif, a theme that remained popular in the eighteen pageants that followed, the first Partheneia made no specific reference to marriage.[39] For Rearden, to be a student and to be carried away by love was a "contradiction."[40] Berkeley students were to look to womanhood and adult status as a function of their own maturation and their own initiatives.

But marriage was an integral part of Lucy Sprague's maturation into womanhood: it was the key to the reconciliation of her passion and her intellect. For Lucy, womanhood meant an acceptance of her sexuality and the release of sexual and creative energies. With hundreds of women students performing under her inspiration and coaching, Lucy Sprague crowned her first career as Dean of Women and at the same time symbolically became the Dancer with whom Wesley had fallen in love years before. The masque for her was an unmasking; her power of expression, of self-display, had outgrown its guilt and won her a double triumph. "Now at last I can put my mind on getting married," she sighed when it was all over. "I thought the day would never come."[41]

Lucy was profoundly exhausted after the masque, physically and emotionally. On campus, the seniors gave a loving reception for her, though she could barely drag herself to it. She complained of terrible headaches and dizziness, but could get very little rest. Just then Millicent Todd, a friend visiting from Amherst, Massachusetts, was suddenly struck down with a serious, though undiagnosed, illness (possibly a heart ailment). Lucy thought Millicent was too ill to be moved to a sanatorium or hospital and insisted on caring for her herself.[42] When her family complained that tending to Millicent's needs was overtaxing her own strength, Lucy overruled them, arguing that it was of "such supreme importance to her that the utmost I can do is not too much." Invalided Millicent remained with Lucy for seven weeks.[43]

Wesley thought the entire year had been grueling for Lucy, beginning with her apprenticeship in New York and the worries over the marriage question, in addition to her supervision of the pageant and her dedication to the care of David Farquhar and Millicent Todd. Lucy went through great anxiety over the impending wedding. After the Partheneia, her aunt and uncle had returned to Chicago with the understanding that Lucy would be married in their home in May. Lucy was grateful for their solicitude and love. She wanted her uncle to give her away in marriage, and she knew that a California wedding, for which Nan and Albert could not return, would be a crushing disappointment to them. On the other hand, she felt that her real home and friends were in California and that it would be simpler to be married there.

The date of the ceremony was also problematic. If it were too early in May, neither Adolph Miller nor President Wheeler would be able to attend. But a later date in Chicago was equally unsatisfactory. Lucy confided to her aunt that she expected to be "unwell" on May 27, and thus did not want to be married later than the twentieth. Nor did she want to postpone the couple's planned departure for Europe on May 29 for a long honeymoon.[44] As her health continued to slip downward after the Partheneia, Lucy agonized over the wedding decision. Finally she decided on Chicago. Still, she wanted everything to be as simple and informal as possible, she told her aunt, from the invitations to the music, ceremony, and reception. No Wagner or Mendelssohn, please; she requested Beethoven—a quartet, if there were to be strings; a sonata, if only an organ. She also asked Nan not to arrange the parlor too grandly for the reception. Couldn't she just push the piano back in the corner and lift the rug? The wedding breakfast, too, should not be lavish. And finally, the ceremony: Dr. McClure, the eminent Presbyterian minister, would be fine, but nothing too expansive. "I would feel like a fake with a formal ceremony," she warned Nan. [45]

Nan's preparations were interrupted, however, by a telegram from Wesley informing her that Lucy's health had worsened under the strain of finishing the Berkeley semester, planning the wedding and caring for an invalid, while packing the contents of her house for a move to New York and preparing for a seven-month honeymoon abroad. [46] At his insistence, she had finally agreed to two weeks' enforced rest "away from the telephone bell" at Carmel-by-the-Sea, accompanied by Winifred Rieber. Wesley told Nan that after Lucy's return, they would cancel the Chicago wedding only if it seemed necessary to "prevent a relapse into nervous strain." Nan and Albert wired back their agreement. [47]

As it turned out, the doctor who examined Lucy after she left Carmel felt that she was not in such critical condition that the wedding could not take place, but, as Mary reported to her aunt, believed that she was "so worn out after the long strain of *everything*" that the least possible effort now was desirable. [48] By April 30, the matter was settled. [49] Lucy and Wesley would be married in a small church in San Francisco the following week. Nan was terribly disappointed not to be with her niece upon the "day of all days," but accepted the decision. She would give the couple a proper reception later when they passed through Chicago on their way to New York. [50] Only Lucy's brother would come from Chicago, joining Adolph and Mary as representatives of the family. Eleanor, who had remained in the Spragues' Pasadena home, would attend if her health allowed (it did not). She wrote to Nan how sad she was that Lucy would be without most of the family at the wedding, "especially those who sympathize most with her." [51] Marion Farquhar, under doctor's orders to remain in bed following the birth of her son, also would be unable to attend. In spite of the absences of Nan and Albert and Marion, Lucy was relieved to return to her original wish to be married in California.

On May 8, 1912, five years to the day since Mitchell had first fallen in love with Lucy Sprague, the couple was wed in a simple Swedenborgian meetinghouse in San Francisco. A warm fire glowed on the hearth, the tiny, homelike space smelled of roses and eucalyptus and a Beethoven sonata replaced the Wedding March. A friend of both Lucy and Mitchell, the Reverend Worcester, a white-haired Swedenborgian minister with a wavering but expressive voice, performed a short and simple ceremony. Along with Lucy's brother Albert, Adolph and Mary Miller, and the couple's good friends from Berkeley, student Nan Rearden attended the wedding, which she was to recall forever after. In the "earthly paradise" of Worcester's church, Lucy Sprague, demure, feminine, and alluring in a long gown of white taffeta, made "real—actually visible and even material," Rearden thought, the dreams and ideals she had inspired in her students. There was something "mysteriously lovely and divine" about the way in which her wedding so perfectly expressed the ideals of all women. It was a "fitting climax," Rearden believed, to the history of the "fairy princess."[52]

The wedding had turned out much as Lucy as wished. Back in Chicago, Albert told his aunt and uncle that he thought the affair much too informal and unconventional. (Lucy suspected that he was upset by the fact there was no special role for him in the ceremony. Since she could not be given away by Uncle Albert, she chose not to be given away at all.) Albert reported his impression of Wesley Mitchell, whom he had met for the first time; he was another who felt that Mitchell was in no way Lucy's equal. Nan wondered again if Lucy had made a mistake, yet she assured herself that happiness in marriage did not depend on the "brilliancy of manners" which Mitchell lacked.[53] Albert had to admit that Lucy looked radiantly happy. "I am married. Love to all," she cabled to her aunt and uncle shortly after the ceremony.[54] The simple message said all there was to say.

Mary Miller gave a luncheon for sixteen guests immediately after the wedding. Adolph, who certainly had not promoted the match, toasted Lucy's health, and Benjamin Wheeler responded affectionately on her behalf. He then toasted Wesley, and Sadie Gregory, Wesley's closest friend, responded.[55] With that, the newlyweds were off for a quiet week at Shasta Springs, north of San Francisco, in a cottage overlooking the Sacramento River. In the distance lay Mount Shasta, which Lucy thought was "the most beautiful mountain in all of America."[56]

After Shasta, they returned to Berkeley to make final plans for their trip abroad. On Friday, May 24, they arrived in Chicago, stopping first at Sprague, Warner & Co., and then at the bank where Lucy arranged financing for their long stay in Europe. Saturday, the day of Nan's "proper" reception for Lucy, dawned bright and beautiful. Seventy guests came to lunch on lobster newburg, chicken cutlet, punch, sandwiches, salad, and cakes and to hear a performance of lieder, folksongs, and love ballads by George Hamlin. "Lucy wore a white taffeta, looked pretty and was admired," Nan noted. Wesley made a "favorable" impression.[57] Two days later, the couple left for New York. Nan, saddened at the parting, wondered if she would see them again.[58] A letter from Mitchell, written as they were about to sail on the Hamburg-America's *Moltke*, told Nan and Albert that Lucy was "still vigorous and happy," though slightly weary. After they had dined with their friends the Jacques Loebs, now resident in New York, and Jessica Peixotto, who was visiting, they both felt that "New York is at least a possible place for friendships to flourish in, whether a home can grow there or not." But Mitchell's real reason for writing was to give the Spragues "one more assurance" of his intention "to make Lucy happy now and always, and of my faith in success." He felt that now the family ought to accept and share her belief in Mitchell and the couple's future. "I wish you might feel a little confidence," he wrote.[59]

The Mitchells sailed from New York on May 29, 1912. They went first to Sicily, then north to Italy where they explored the hill towns up from Paestum and the central ridge of the Apennines. At Todi, they stopped to see an altarpiece by Lo Spagna. On her trip to Paris with the Palmers years before, Lucy had purchased three small figurines of saints supposedly taken from the frame of that altarpiece, which had been among the Italian art treasures stolen by Napoleon. Then Lucy and Robin, as she would always call him after their marriage, went on to Turin, Perugia, and Florence, where they visited churches and galleries with something "approaching ecstasy," as Lucy wrote Aunt Nan.[60] In Ravenna, the fifth- and sixth-century mosaics surpassed her "wildest dreams" of beauty. In Bologna, Lucy was stricken with a stomach upset, at first misdiagnosed by a local doctor as appendicitis. She recovered and, feeling almost "vulgarly well," took her first bicycle ride in twelve years, pedalling for ten miles. "It's all such fun, such unbelievable fun," she wrote. Crossing over to Milan, where the Mitchells spent a few days walking, reading, and visiting galleries, Lucy again "lost [her] head completely" over the old pictures. "We seem a tame generation in comparison," she observed to Aunt Nan.[61]

Leaving Italy, the Mitchells went to Salzburg, then on to Berchtesgaden, "the loveliest spot on earth," Lucy felt.[62] There they spent three weeks, proofreading portions of Robin's manuscript of *Business Cycles*. When the work was finished, they took a long hike with their rucksacks from Berchtesgaden to Innsbruck, through the Hohe Tauern Alps, seeing the glaciers and the Gross Glockner on the way. After their beloved Sierra Nevadas, the Glockner, at 12,000 feet, hardly seemed challenging. The days in the Tirol were "simply magic," Lucy wrote to her family. Though it often rained, the colors of the velvet fields and forests and the granite peaks delighted her, even on the worst of days. "I never knew such a place," she exulted.

After Germany, the Mitchells were off to London, where they stayed for three months at Mrs. Garlant's hotel behind the Haymarket Theater, which Lucy had visited with the Palmers ten years earlier. They saw Sarah Bernhardt in "Lucretia Borgia" and plays by Pinero and Shaw, attended a Post-Impressionist Exhibit, heard concerts by Mischa Elman and Pablo Casals. They visited the Elgin Marbles at the British Museum, saw Madame Tussaud's Waxworks, Westminster Abbey, and the National Galleries, where Lucy once more received permission to sketch.

Their stay in London was not without professional activity. Eager to learn more about education at the lower levels, Lucy visited neighborhood schools and attended weekly meetings of the Education Committee of the London County Council. She also stopped in at the National Child Association and at a children's employment office, perhaps in response to Florence Kelley's request that she look into European child labor legislation. With Wesley, she attended meetings of the Fabian Society, heard a lecture series given by Beatrice and Sidney Webb, whom they visited on several occasions, and met a number of British economists, among them William Beveridge, Arthur Bowley, James Muirhead, and Graham Wallas. Among the most memorable events of their London stay was an Albert Hall demonstration against poverty in October, on a night when the fog was so thick that it penetrated the interior, hiding the speakers, one of whom was George Bernard Shaw. Out of the mist she recalled his booming voice, crying "I *hate* a poor man."[63] Ten days later, the Mitchells heard Mrs. Emmeline Pankhurst at a suffrage meeting, an equally memorable event. Lucy recalled that a cockney voice kept interrupting Pankhurst's impassioned remarks, crying "It's a brutal shime!" The Mitchells attended several other suffrage meetings at Hyde Park and Trafalgar Square. Perhaps this encounter with militant British suffrage leaders helped to persuade Lucy of the need for more active support of suffrage at home.

The Mitchells felt carefree and unhurried in Europe. Neither was troubled by the lack of specific work to return to; both were confident that they would find interesting employment in New York. In August, in fact, Alvin Johnson, then teaching economics at Cornell, had cabled Wesley Mitchell on behalf of President Jacob Schurman, offering him a position at the university. There was universal agreement in the economics department, Johnson wrote, that "no other man in the country could even be considered a reasonably close second." If Wesley would come to Cornell, then the difficulty of securing other "first-class men" would be greatly reduced. "Everything depends on you," he emphasized.[64] But Wesley's decision to delay any decision about future work until they returned from their honeymoon remained unchanged. "The past was cut off by our resignations," Lucy observed. "The future [was] a glowing question mark." For Lucy, this suspension between a "closed past" and an unknown future heightened the present. "It released us to play."[65]

During these months abroad, Lucy learned much about the man she had married. "You were the Robin I had loved before marrying you," she wrote many years later, "only more so. More tender, more gay, more kindling to the imagination, more intelligent, more honest." Yet there were minor conflicts, as Lucy learned that Wesley was "no mush of concessions." At every hotel, Lucy always wanted the room with the view, while he wanted the one with plumbing—preferences that expressed the differences in their personalities. They worked out a compromise, alternating scenery and convenience. Wesley also overtipped absurdly by Lucy's standards. He couldn't help it, she recognized, and she submitted, but with "suppressed irritation."[66] Lucy loved his warmth, his sharpness of mind, and his quick sense of humor. Once she asked him the meaning of the letter "H" that appeared at intervals on London sidewalks. He replied that he thought they were the H's the cockneys had dropped.

On December 7, the Mitchells sailed from Liverpool on the *Mauritania*. At first the weather was rough, with gale winds and high seas. Characteristically, Wesley was cheerful and healthy, while Lucy suffered miserably. When the skies finally cleared, so did her health. She joined Wesley in reading the remaining proofs of *Business Cycles* and also read the new teachings of Maria Montessori, the Italian physician, which had stirred great interest in the educational world. On the thirteenth, they landed in New York. They had planned to spend Christmas in Chicago with the Spragues, but their funds were exhausted. So they went to the Hotel Seville in the West Thirties, where Lucy had stayed during her apprenticeships. There, in bed in their cold hotel room, they took turns reading aloud from John Masefield's recently published *Widow in the By-Street*, each reciting until too choked to go on. Thus they began married life in the metropolis.

PART
THREE
DEFINING
THE
CENTER

11

Getting Started

From the very beginning, it was apparent that marriage had brought Lucy fulfillment and well-being. "Their happiness is *so* evident," wrote Mary Howard to her husband after a visit to the Mitchells in New York in May 1913. Lucy looked "blooming . . . very lovely . . . and very happy." Wesley Mitchell too showed "the joy they have found in living together. . . . If ever anything in this world has turned out right," Mary proclaimed, "it is this marriage."[1]

That month Lucy wrote to her Radcliffe correspondence club that although a "bit embarrassed either to defend my conduct this last year"— her defection from the single state, that is—"or to ignore the blight that has been cast with Cassandra-like cheer upon my future," marriage had only positive effects. "I feel very much myself, only a bit enlarged and emancipated" with "fewer inhibitions."[2]

Marriage released rather than stifled Lucy's personal and professional aspirations. Now that she knew she would not be "only a professional woman," she could focus with far less anxiety on her "vision." She found in marriage the emotional and sexual intimacy she had hoped for, and now she devoted herself fully and enthusiastically to developing her professional identity. Her writings about her experiences in New York during the long middle period of her life reflect this shift from emotional to professional preoccupations, and the character of this biography shifts accordingly.

Lucy found New York, as she had expected, full of vocational opportunities and committed, experimental people.

New York seemed to me . . . the perfect place for people who love jobs and I am one of them. In California, I worked alone. I had many friends but most of them thought me slightly crazy to care so much about my work. In New York, I found a group of people as crazy as I was and about the same things.[3]

Many of this supportive group lived in Greenwich Village, and it was there that the Mitchells took up residence after four months in a rented house on East Thirty-sixth Street—a "hideous" place with purple walls and mountings of stuffed moose heads and sheep. In May 1913, they purchased a brick-front four-story brownstone at 37 West Tenth Street, off Fifth Avenue. The house was bright and sunny, only two rooms deep, and its back windows overlooked a row of well-kept gardens. Greenwich Village was to remain the Mitchells' permanent neighborhood for more than three decades.

A flood of cultural experiment characterized the Village in the prewar years. There was a "kind of magic in the air" wrote one historian, as in 1912 "Greenwich Village stood ready to assume its destiny as the Left Bank of New York—or America."[4] Drawn by the Village's inexpensive, picturesque quarters, artists, writers, and political radicals descended on the tangled streets of this comfortable, residential neighborhood.[5] Seldom mixing with the working-class Italian and Irish families who had preceded them, these new immigrants became a community unto themselves—often shocking older residents with their unconventional morality. Especially before the opening of the West Side Subway in 1917 made the area more accessible to outsiders, the Village was an enclave of bohemian lifestyles and artistic modernism. Even in the 1920s and 1930s, the Village continued to attract intellectual and political rebels.

The explosion of bohemianism in Greenwich Village was part of a larger rebellion against tradition which characterized American intellectual life in the prewar years. The opening of the International Art Exhibition at the 69th Regiment Armory on February 17, 1913, which the Mitchells attended, stands as the landmark event of this revolt.[6]

New currents of music, dance, theater, and poetry also fascinated the Mitchells. "At first," Lucy recalled, "we felt the impact of New York almost as tourists do. We were afraid of missing something!"[7] Lucy attended concerts regularly, often with her cousin Elizabeth Sprague Coolidge, who by the end of the 1910s had become a notable patron of chamber music and sponsor of new compositions, and had established the South Mountain (later Berkshire) Chamber Music Festivals near her estate in Pittsfield, Massachusetts. Lucy was particularly responsive to modern dance, and she eagerly attended performances by Isadora Duncan, whom she had long admired, Ruth St. Denis, and Pavlova. She and Wesley held season tickets for the Theater Guild and the experimental Provincetown Playhouse and went regularly to the Princess Theater, the Belasco, the Comedy Theater, and the Yiddish Theater.

In New York, the windows of the Mitchells' life opened onto a thoroughfare teeming with every variety of modernist expression in social, political, and cultural life. Dogmas of religion, politics, science and art were challenged by the men and women they began to meet through their associations in the worlds of education, social reform, journalism, and the arts.

Through novelist Ernest Poole, whom they met at Lillian Wald's settlement and who quickly became a friend, they were introduced to Max Eastman, editor of *The Masses*, the socialist literary and political magazine which led Greenwich Village's revolt against conformity and became a national touchstone of intellectual innovation. The Mitchells dined with the handsome, exuberant Eastman and his wife Ida Rauh, and sometimes accompanied them to Mabel Dodge's white-walled Fifth Avenue salon to talk about psychoanalysis.[8] Both Lucy and Wesley shared the intense excitement of New York intellectuals about Freud's work, just then becoming widely known in the United States. The Mitchells also read *The Masses*, agreeing with its views on many subjects, especially feminism and birth control. In 1915, Lucy was one of a dozen people who signed a call for the formation of a Birth Control League to promote the work of Margaret Sanger.[9]

But neither Lucy nor Wesley endorsed free love or political revolution, as did many of the *Masses* radicals.[10] While Lucy championed efforts to make full information about sexuality and contraception widely available, her ideal of open, honest love did not include multiple sexual relations, however freely chosen. She believed that legally sanctioned marriage offered the best basis for a new mutuality between men and women. Drawing on her own experience, she was optimistic that other women, too, could find fulfillment within marriage, provided that they found husbands willing to share with them not only thoughts and feelings, but power as heads of households.

Although, to a greater degree than Wesley, Lucy joined the Village radicals in their denunciation of capitalism, she did not become a follower of any political movement. She was sympathetic to the goals of Marxism, anarchism and syndicalism, but she believed in the power of education, rather than political revolution, to end exploitation. The

Mitchells' own beliefs accorded more with what Wesley termed the "respectable fringe" of intellectual radicalism than with its left wing. Their favorite journal was not *The Masses,* but the left-of-liberal *New Republic,* whose first issue of November 1, 1914 they exitedly read aloud together. Economist Walter Weyl, one of the *New Republic*'s editors, was a close friend of Wesley Mitchell. Another editor, Walter Lippman, dropped by for tea "to discuss psychoanalysis" on occasion; the Mitchells read his *Preface to Politics* and *Drift and Mastery* avidly, impressed with his extraordinary ability to combine the new politics with modern currents in psychology and aesthetics. Like Lippman, who by 1914 had foresworn both anarchism and revolution, the Mitchells kept their faith with the "respectable" progressives and planned social change.[11]

While the Mitchells were inspired by modernism, in many respects they remained comfortable with the culture of the previous generation. Their own walls were lined with the lyric Sierra-like landscapes of Arthur Davies, the Symbolist painter who had organized the Armory show.[12] They admired the dramas of O'Neill, Ibsen, Pirandello, and occasionally Strindberg, but never abandoned their devotion to Shakespeare. And despite their keen appreciation of the works of new poets like Amy Lowell and Edna St. Vincent Millay, it was Coventry Patmore, Wordsworth, and especially Browning, to which they always returned.

Just as the Mitchells' aesthetic tastes had been formed in the late nineteenth century, so had their moral values and political beliefs. Wesley Mitchell's convictions had largely been shaped in the 1890s at the University of Chicago, where, through Dewey and Veblen, he was exposed to new currents of cultural relativism. Like Dewey and like Mitchell's good friend, Jacques Loeb, now at the Rockefeller Institute for Medical Research, Wesley Mitchell emerged as a sober, meticulous scientist-scholar committed to the careful research that could guide social planning and pave the way to a progressive society. While he believed that the government and the economic system needed radical overhauling, he shared the belief of these fellow progressives in evolutionary rather than revolutionary change and in the leadership of intellectuals in public life.

Lucy's college and sporadic postgraduate training had not given her a firm identification with scientific professionalism. What she took from Radcliffe, and applied and fine-tuned at Berkeley, were the critical reasoning skills with which to approach not only philosophical problems but their practical applications. She had acquired a fund of diverse knowledge that combined metaphysics, idealism, and the emerging tenets of pragmatism. Resolving difficulties of interpretation, questioning meanings and consequences, and especially, implementing ideas would remain among her deepest sources of pleasure. Eclectic and tolerant of ambiguity, she did not give her allegiance to any single ideology. During their courtship correspondence, Wesley had worried about Lucy's impressionability, but because of her susceptibility to imaginative suggestion and innovation, she would never be rigid or dogmatic. In New York, she would be open to many different kinds of ideas and people—reformers, radicals, married professional women, lesbian couples, artists, musicians. [13]

Wesley Mitchell's diary records a steady stream of company and such constant attendance at dinner parties and informal get-togethers and receptions that Lucy, reminiscing in her seventies, found herself shocked at how busy they had been. Occasionally they held parties for fifty guests or more, though they favored smaller, informal gatherings at which guests were mixed to make "jolly dinner parties": the Deweys, Loebs, and Eastmans; the Deweys, Lillian Wald, Florence Kelley, and economists E. R. A. Seligman and Joseph Schumpeter; the Ernest Pooles, Walter Weyls, Pauline Goldmark; Marion Jones Farquhar, Pablo Casals, economist Vladimir Simkhovitch, Wesley's friend from student days in Europe, and his wife, Mary, director of the Greenwich House settlement. Mitchell's diary recorded the topics, though not the details, of discussions on these evenings, among them Freud and psychoanalysis, technocracy, education, women's suffrage, Cubism, the mayoralty campaign, the situation in Russia, poetry, astrology, socialism, syndicalism. [14]

A small party at the Mitchells was likely to end with either Lucy or Wesley reading poetry—sometimes Browning or selections from Lucy's favorite The Bard of the Dimbovitza, or the new poets anthologized in Miss Rittenhouse's Little Book of Modern Verse. When the company consisted of one or two close friends, the Mitchells read aloud from other contemporary works. Like their social life, their reading was eclectic. In 1913, for example, the Mitchells read Veblen's The Place of Science in Modern Civilization and The Theory of Business Enterprise; Thorndike's Original Notion of Man; Poincaré's Foundations of Science; Whitehead's Introduction to Mathematics; Fabre's Social Life Among the Insects; as well as works by Dewey, Lippman, Montessori, Jane Addams, Mary Antin, Robert Herrick, Maeterlinck, Fraser, Shaw, Ibsen, H.G. Wells, Rebecca West, Galsworthy, Turgenev, Plato, George Herbert, Swinburne, Poe, Emily Dickinson, Lewis Carroll, and the Brothers Grimm. [15]

Neither Lucy nor Wesley moved immediately into a professional commitment. Wesley Mitchell's reputation as a leading exponent of the new school of institutional economics was well established by the time he and Lucy came to New York. By the spring of 1913, he had turned down half-a-dozen teaching positions, including those from Harvard and Yale. In the fall of 1913, he joined Columbia's Faculty of Political Science as a lecturer in economics, then a small distinguished department consisting of E.R.A. Seligman, Harry Seager, Vladimir Simkhovitch, and J.M. Clark. Promoted to full professor the following year, Wesley would remain at Columbia until his retirement in 1944, except for a three-year hiatus in the early 1920s and various short-term visiting professorships. He was a highly articulate speaker whose lectures were models of clarity and grace, and attracted graduate students from all over the world. It was said that the best, as well as the worst, of students often took his courses twice, just for the pleasure of hearing Mitchell. In the late teens, his courses on "Business Cycles" and "Types of Economic Theory"—the latter treating students to an unusual exposition of intellectual biography placed within a broad social context—were among the university's most popular offerings.[16]

Mitchell's massive work on business cycles was published in the summer of 1913. It was the first extensive treatment of these movements, and quickly established him as the authority on the subject. The comprehensive statistical evidence it provided showed convincingly that business cycles were an inevitable—not an occasional—effect of the money economy. In Mitchell's view, the recurring shift from prosperity to crisis to depression to recovery was the normal state of affairs, a never-ending process.

While the book was widely regarded as a tour de force in the use of quantitative data, its equally important theoretical implications became apparent only later. To Mitchell, the subordination of industrial and commercial processes to that of moneymaking was the key feature of economic life. But Mitchell disagreed with classical theorists who assumed that the pursuit of pecuniary profits employed a rational calculus. Following the lead of Dewey and social psychologists William McDougall and Edward Thorndike, Mitchell acknowledged that human nature was a complex amalgam of irrational, instinctive, and instrumental motives. He believed that through detailed, statistical analyses of observed behavior, economists could contribute firm knowledge that could lead to intelligent control of the institutions which shaped human nature and all cultural life. *Business Cycles* was a landmark work in the history of quantitative science; at the same time it revealed the progressive faith that was fundamental to its author's beliefs. An enlightened populace and its leaders, guided by the findings of social scientists, would be able to mold public policy and improve human welfare.[17]

For Lucy Mitchell, the development of a career was a more difficult matter. She had come to New York to work, but she had not settled what her role within the broad field of education ought to be. She began exploring her professional future almost immediately. A few weeks after arriving in the city, she went to see John Dewey and Edward Thorndike at Teachers College, Columbia University, for advice about an educational career. With their concurrence, she attended Dewey's lectures on the philosophy of education and Thorndike's on educational psychology. Studies with these men, who led the two main wings of the progressive education movement—Dewey, its thrust toward social reform, and Thorndike, its adoption of the statistical methods of science—deepened her knowledge of experimental education and established the two poles of her own future work in the field.

During the two terms Lucy Mitchell attended Dewey's lectures, she was exposed to the key ideas of his great work, *Democracy in Education*, published in 1916. Education as growth, a continuous "reconstruction or reorganization of experience"; an emphasis on "continuity" rather than the traditional "dualisms" between subject matter and method, intellect and emotion, theory and practice; and the principle of education as a "social function," promoting the ideal of a "truly shared or associated life," were notions which were to have a lasting influence on Lucy Mitchell's educational practice.[18]

Dewey's influence on Lucy Mitchell in the prewar years came as much from social contacts as from his writings and teaching. The Mitchells dined frequently with the Deweys during the years 1913–17, and occasionally visited them at their Greenlawn farm. Lucy found Dewey a wonderful listener, completely lacking in self-consciousness and able to respond enthusiastically to views presented by others. Whether they were discussing education, politics, and war, or Duchamp's provocative "Nude Descending a Staircase," which the Deweys and Mitchells had seen together at the Armory exhibit, Lucy found that Dewey always called forth new ideas. (It was after talking with Dewey one afternoon in March 1913 about the social aspects of education that Lucy developed a new scheme for using schools as community centers, an idea that became central to her first views about educating young children.) In later years, she asserted that Dewey's greatest contribution was to "stimulate others to think for themselves. Each of us has his *own John Dewey* formed by what John Dewey made each of us think." Lucy's John Dewey was a scientist who aproached the study of human behavior experimentally.[19]

Edward Thorndike influenced Lucy's developing ideas in a different way. Thorndike's three-volume work, *Educational Psychology*, published in 1913–14, revolutionized American pedagogy with its brilliant demonstration of the application of science and statistics to education.[20] At Teachers College during these years, Thorndike transmitted his views about mental testing, educational measurement, and child study to a corps of eager graduate students. More conservative than Dewey in his social beliefs—he insisted that heredity was a much greater influence on human behavior than environment—Thorndike nevertheless gave great impetus to progressive educators with his contributions to the psychology of individual differences, which, he argued, implied the necessity for specialization based on the different abilities of students. From Thorndike's as well as Dewey's classroom, Lucy emerged with a greater sense of the need to adjust old-style schooling to the distinct, individualized needs of the child.

Lucy also solicited the advice of Lillian Wald about working in education. Wald suggested that she start a school as part of Henry Street. Lucy rejected the idea, fearing that she would get "swamped" in settlement life. She also felt that there was "much to *learn* before I could *do*," and wondered whether a settlement would be the best place to learn about experimental eduction.[21]

Lucy's decision not to link herself directly with settlement life was significant, for it meant that her reform work within education would take place outside the arena chosen by most educated women of her generation. Instead, she plunged directly into work in public schooling as a volunteer, rather than as a paid worker. Perhaps on Dewey's or Wald's suggestion or because of her prior experience with Julia Richman, Lucy volunteered her services as a visiting teacher to the Public Education Association (PEA). Organized in 1895 by a group of urban Progressive clubwomen, the PEA believed that urban problems should be addressed by making schools more relevant to the needs of individual children. It promoted compulsory education, vocational education, and experimental programs like sex education, school lunches, and programming for "special children."[22]

The Visiting Teachers project was the most successful of PEA activities around this time. The project had its origins in 1906 at the Greenwich House and Hartley settlements, each of which assigned one resident to work with settlement children in several public schools on the Lower East Side. The following year, the PEA took over the project at the request of Julia Richman. In 1913, half a year after Julia Richman's sudden death, there were ten visiting teachers (called "Home and School Visitors") in the public schools.

The job of the visiting teacher was to work with children who were presumed to be "normal," yet who had significant difficulties at school. In Julia Richman's words, the visiting teacher "individualized" the child, got to know him or her "whole," and then tried to "adjust" the child's home and school environments to "smooth out" rough places.[23] Ultimately, visiting teachers paved the way for the schools' focus on personal adjustment, but initially they brought the social, rather than the psychological, point of view from the settlements to the schools.[24] For Lucy, the project was an ideal place to begin her educational work: as a connecting link between the public schools and the wider concerns of settlement life, it gave direct expression to her developing philosophy that, like settlement houses, schools could become neighborhood centers that instilled community ideals.

Early in 1913, Lucy began work as a visiting teacher in a downtown public school. As she worked with municipal agencies and volunteer organizations to improve the home environments of troubled children and to help their school performance, she rapidly developed a new understanding of the possibilities of schools as agencies of social reform. "My convictions have grown into real passions," she wrote her Radcliffe "Robins" in May that year.[25]

The director of the Visiting Teachers project was Harriet Merrill Johnson, and a good part of Lucy's learning came from her. Born in Portland, Maine in 1867, Johnson had taught at public and private schools in Bangor and then trained as a nurse at Massachusetts Homeopathic Hospital. She took further graduate training in nursing and health at Teachers College in 1902, which led her to district nursing at Hartley House under the auspices of the Henry Street Settlement. She became interested in the problems of maladjusted children in public schools, and in 1905 she helped to organize the PEA's visiting teacher program. A member of the Women's Trade Union League, she was concerned about opportunities for working-class as well as professional women.

Johnson shared her personal life with Harriet Forbes, a nurse active in settlement work. In 1916, the "Harriets," as the Mitchells called them, together adopted a baby girl; Harriet Johnson was officially the adoptive parent, since New York State did not permit adoption by two women living as a couple. Harriet Johnson became Lucy's closest personal friend and the deepest influence on her professional work. "It was luck that brought me into contact with her," Lucy later wrote, "but it is to my credit that I immediately recognized her as a wise and great person."[26]

Lucy was involved in other educational work during her first year in New York. She pursued her original interest in the use of the schools for sex education. In the fall of 1913, she delivered a paper on sex hygiene to the annual meeting of the Social Prophylaxis Society. Later that year, she met with a group of public school teachers to discuss her ideas about bringing sex hygiene directly into the schools. Here she encountered Laura Garrett, a worker at the Henry Street Settlement whose interests paralleled Lucy's own. Garrett was trying to bring a program of nature study involving live animals into the public schools as a method for discussing normal sexuality. Lucy warmed to this controversial project immediately. She consulted with Garrett on teaching methods, exhibits, and school and funding possibilities, acting as an ally, goad, and moral and financial suport and speaking to philanthropists on Garrett's behalf.[27]

In May 1913, Mitchell described her developing ideals about education to her Radcliffe correspondents. Sex education and the role of schools as agencies of larger community reform remain predominant, though as yet undeveloped, themes. As she explained it:

I want to help evolve a method for making the schools effective in stimulating community ideals—particularly the ideas of self-direction and of sex. I want the schools to face these problems positively, not as they always have, negatively. I want to work with some subnormal children to try to evolve methods of instilling a healthy sex idealism: I want to work with some portion of the really twisted, to try to understand causes of these twists: and I want to work with social workers in general to feel sure of what the "community ideals" really are which the school should try to inculcate. I feel the school must undertake to train the whole child—mind, body, and ideals—asking for supplemental aid when it needs it, but always supervising and directing.[28]

She elaborated these ideas in an unpublished piece written in the spring of 1913: "The Public's Schools and the Public's Ideals." Lucy was concerned with efficiency, coordination, and the avoidance of waste. In her view, children's potential could be maximized by making the school the "central guiding intelligence" which coordinated separate aspects of child development. To work on behalf of the "whole child," three changes in traditional school functions would be necessary. First, the school had to make direct contact with the child's home environment and provide a link to the modern industrial world he or she would enter. Secondly, the school had to develop appropriate pedagogical techniques to foster the child's growth in both the home and the world. Thirdly, the school needed to coordinate the resurces of other agencies that benefited children.

This prescription was influenced not only by Lucy's experience as a visiting teacher but also by her observations of the London school system's "after-care committees" and municipal juvenile labor exchange, which linked schools to industrial society. During the Mitchells' three-month stay in London, Lucy had seen vigorous experimentation with educational techniques; British schools were reaching out to accept new responsibilities for children's lives outside the classroom. She had been especially interested in the arrangements British schools had made with neighboring clinics, public baths, and lunchrooms, and with the after-hours use of schoolhouses for community functions.

Lucy was also impressed with the experimental programs she had seen in New York that attempted to individualize children according to their special needs. In the standard vocabulary of progressive scientists and educators of the time, she approved of programs that separated the "feeble-minded," "imbeciles," "border-line defectives," and "syphilitics" from each other and from "normal" children. But she added that in designing new programs based on children's individual needs, attention should be directed to the training of character and ideals as well as intellect, particularly the ideals of "self-guidance" and of a "healthy sex-attitude." She felt that the "philosophy of self-direction" was responsible for the growing interest in socialism, anarchism, and trade-unionism, and for the new modernism in the arts. Experience in self-government during the school years would foster self-reliance and self-dependence, the basis, she believed, of socially responsible movements for progressive change. School children should be given opportunities to choose certain aspects of their curriculum, an experience that would stretch their ability to think for themselves. "Our industrial world would be safer in the hands of men and women thus disciplined," she argued.

The classroom was also the place to inculcate sex ideals. If nature-study were begun early and linked with hygiene, then sex physiology, sex hygiene, and the dangers of venereal disease could be taught "without any shock or embarrassment to either the child or the teacher." Older children would learn about normal sexual matters dealing with courtship, marriage, and child-bearing. "Housewifery centers," like those she had seen in London, could be used for further instruction, and eventually, lessons could be given in connection with *crèches* where older girls could care for "real babies" and come to feel both the "privileges" and the "dangers" of sex relations. Only frankness in sex instruction could combat prostitution, illegitimacy, homosexuality, and venereal disease, she asserted. Regulation could not be "constructive," she emphasized; "education can."

Even in this early paper Lucy recognized that the progressive framework for schooling which she wanted to develop required a new pedagogy that would give teachers "a broader conception of life and of social responsibility." Teachers would have to deal with "ignorant or antagonistic" families, broad urban-industrial problems, and the difficulties of revamping traditional modes of instruction and developing new curricula in sex education and community life. "If the colleges, particularly the women's colleges, were to turn their serious attention to the problem," she asserted, "they might, perhaps, make greater contributions to the world and to themselves than they do at present." There was "no harder task in the world and none more worthwhile" than the education of teachers."[29]

The essay, which in later years Lucy would recall as a statement about "the whole child," is noteworthy too for its anticipation of Lucy's mature work in child development and teacher training, linking individual learning to the social uses of education, the child and family to the community and world. In her first outline for a "community ideal" in schooling, what Lucy had learned in her New York apprenticeships was now expressed in Deweyan terms.

A further reflection of these views appeared in an article Lucy wrote for *Survey* magazine the following year on "School Children and Sex Idealism." Lucy noted that the discussion of sex had made its way from drama, fiction, and medicine into the public schools—to the "accompaniment of hysteria." Part of the reason for the strenuous opposition to sex education was that "when we talk about sex, we pluck it out from its surroundings, isolate it, throw the limelight on it, and then wonder that it is difficult to explain to children."

Almost everything we give to children has had sex cut out of it. . . . History has become motiveless, poetry passionless, art prudish, anatomy fragmentary, civics and ethics pedantic and psychology and sociology and economics have been avoided or so transformed that their anaemic figures are hardly recognized as humans.

The solution was not to insert sex into the curriculum as a separate subject but to regard it as an aspect "of a hundred subjects." Educators should show children "how sex is interwoven through all of life."

Give whatever sex instruction the subjects taught to children naturally include, choosing the suitable subjects on general, not on sex, grounds; give it frankly, whenever the occasion arises and with whomsoever it arises; approach it from every angle, science, art and ethics.

Lucy recognized that the job of sex education did not belong to the schools alone—"everyone who touches life touches sex." But the inadequacy of schools in sex instruction seemed a glaring example of a more fundamental problem. If education meant "only facts with the breath of human passion squeezed out of them," it became "meaningless."[30] She had begun to relate the truth of her earlier experiences at Radcliffe and Berkeley to a program for children.

Yet Lucy felt that she had accomplished little after her first winter in the city. Perhaps it was because she couldn't shake loose the severe grippe that plagued her. Or perhaps, she joked to the Radcliffe Robins, "it's because I'm married!"[31] In fact, Lucy's marriage did little to slow her pace. In addition to her writing and her volunteer work in the public schools, she joined a variety of community-sponsored education groups— the Public Education Association, the School and Civic League, the Teachers League, the Scholarship Committee of the Henry Street Settlement, and the education committees of the Women's City Club and the Association of Collegiate Alumnae. But the lack of a clear focus troubled her. To sort out the opportunities before her, she went to see Dr. Henry Suzzallo, some of whose lectures on educational sociology she had attended at Teachers College. "Get off all those committees," he told her. "Get into some direct work with ordinary children but don't get swamped in it. Your real job is to write epoch-making books."[32]

Lucy remembered that at first she laughed at this "utterly fantastic" advice. Writing, for her, had always been precious, but private: she thought of it as a cherished self-indulgence, and as an indispensable instrument—"my gyroscope"—for maintaining her stability and checking on her course in life. But Suzzallo's forceful recommendation allowed her for the first time to try on, in imagination, the authoritative public role of author. She protested that she was not ready: "I would be a writer," she declared—"But first I needed to know more . . . where and how I could best learn to understand children?"[33] It would be seven years before Lucy committed herself to the writing of a book, but the thought had been planted. Even in retrospect, in her memoirs, Lucy invoked an external authority as a way of constructing her identity as a writer. The shift that brought her secret childhood passion into the center of her working life, and brought her work onto the public stage, was more than she could handle alone.

Only gradually did Lucy's work in education become more sharply defined. By 1914, two new projects had taken priority in her interests, each representing a different pole of the progressive education movement. In March, the PEA sent Lucy and Harriet Johnson to Gary, Indiana, to observe the innovative school plan instituted there by Superintendent of Schools William Wirt in 1907. Gary, the home of the U.S. Steel Corporation, had experienced enormous growth in the early twentieth century.[34] Under Wirt's leadership, a "platoon" school system was developed which allowed greater use of the existing school buildings without increasing construction expenditures. Students were divided into different groups, or platoons, which either attended class or participated in activities such as industrial workshops, music, art, and laboratory work outside the classroom. This flexibility in scheduling and efficient use of the school plant greatly appealed to Progressives. The construction of the school environment so as to match the adult world, bringing together work and study, also fulfilled a basic progressive goal.

When New York City Mayor John Purroy Mitchel assumed office on January 1, 1914, reform of the overcrowded school bureaucracy was one of his first priorities. At the same time that Lucy Mitchell and Harriet Johnson were visiting Gary, the mayor sent his own observers to examine Wirt's school plan, and later travelled there himself. Impressed with the experiment, he hired Wirt as a part-time consultant, to install the Gary Plan on an experimental basis in selected New York City schools. In the next two years, Wirt's controversial work in the city schools pitted parents against progressive educators, city officials against each other, and even children against teachers, administrators, and police. After a series of violent children's riots at the end of October 1917, shortly before the mayoral election, Mitchel lost soundly to a mediocre Democratic candidate, his defeat in part caused by reactions against the Gary project.[35] Lucy Mitchell and Harriet Johnson took up arms in defense of the Gary Plan. Johnson wrote a favorable report on the Plan for the PEA, which was widely disseminated; Lucy spoke on behalf of the Plan to the PEA, to the independent Gary School League, and at public hearings.[36]

The second project that came to occupy Lucy Mitchell's attention in 1914—the psychological testing of school children—had a greater long-term influence on the course of her educational career than the Gary controversy. The development of special, or "ungraded," classes for so-called mentally defective children had been a major concern of the PEA since 1910, when it established a committee to stimulate public schools to devise instruction for these children.[37] Mental testing, which had begun in 1905 when French psychologist Alfred Binet constructed a scale to evaluate children's intelligence levels, allowed the separation of "subnormal" from "normal" children.[38] For progressive educators, the great promise of psychological testing was that children could be classified by mental rather than chronological age, and educated accordingly. However naively, they believed that mental testing would permit the individualization of education, bringing scientific technique to the task of making education fit the child.

Early in 1914, Lucy Mitchell became a volunteer at the Board of Education's Department of Mentally Retarded Children, working under Elizabeth Farrell. She attended hearings on legislation for the education of defective children, visited the Carnegie Institute of Experimental Psychology and Eugenics at Cold Spring Harbor, Long Island, and became acquainted with the work of Frederick Ellis, director of the Neurological Institute in New York. By May, she had a proposal for the establishment of a psychological clinic to test children at neighborhood schools, and developed it in consultation with John Dewey, Frederick Ellis, Harriet Johnson, Eleanor Johnson, Elizabeth Farrell, and Lillian Wald. Late in May she visited Helen Thompson Woolley, director of the Vocational Bureau for the Cincinnati public schools, to observe Woolley's pioneer work in psychological testing of school children.[39]

In October, Lucy began working with Elizabeth Irwin at P.S. 15 in New York, observing the use of Binet mental tests on students. Like Harriet Johnson, Irwin would become a mentor to Lucy and exert a formidable influence on her ideas. Born in Brooklyn, New York, in 1880,

Irwin graduated from Smith College, then became a free-lance journalist and a social worker at a New York City playground and at the College Settlement. In 1911 she joined the staff of the Public Education Association, where she developed programs for backward children. Irwin lived with Katharine Anthony, a writer of women's biographies who had formerly taught at Wellesley College. Irwin and Anthony were an acknowledged lesbian couple in the Heterodoxy Club, a group of radical feminists who met in Greenwich Village from 1912 through the 1930s. Lucy and Wesley visited Irwin and her circle of "bachelor women" on numerous occasions.[40]

Lucy's experience working with Irwin on intelligence testing deepened her resolve to establish a clinic which would perfect testing instruments and develop an age-graded evaluation scale. First, however, she had to obtain the suport of the New York Board of Education. She repeatedly visited the Superintendent of Schools and members of the Board of Education to explain the project. After many delays, the Board responded favorably to her proposal, and the Psychological Clinic, or Survey, as Lucy called it, was established in January 1915 with partial funding from the city. Its long-range goal was to establish mental and motor performance norms for children aged eight through thirteen, following the same lines of research as Helen Woolley's Cincinnati work on older children, and adding certain other tests.[41]

At the beginning of January, Helen Woolley came to New York for a two-day conference about the clinic, attended by John Dewey, Frederick Ellis, Elisabeth Irwin, and two school principals. Woolley returned later that month to stay with the Mitchells and take charge of the clinic. The Mitchells' home on West Tenth Street became the scene of frequent all-day conferences about psychological testing. At night, the Mitchells invited many of their friends—Vladimir and Mary Simkhovitch, Pauline Goldmark, the Deweys, and the Jacques Loebs—to meet Woolley and learn about the Survey's work. After Woolley left at the end of February, the staff of the Psychological Clinic worked under the direction of psychologist Joseph Hayes. Lucy Mitchell herself began working as a trainee at the Psychological Survey in the fall of 1915. Eventually she tested children at the four public schools in which the Survey administered tests, each school enrolling children of different economic and ethnic backgrounds.[42]

Wesley Mitchell and John Dewey were greatly interested in this experimental project. Once they came to school to take the same tests given the children. Dewey's daughter, Evelyn, his co-author on the book *Schools of Tomorrow*, a description and analysis of experimental schools, also participated in the clinic's testing projects along with Harriet Johnson and her housemate, Harriet Forbes, who were released by the PEA for this work, and Eleanor Johnson, who joined the staff in 1916. When more space was needed, Lucy offered the Survey the roomy attic of the new home to which she and Mitchell were moving at 15 Washington Square North. The Survey was now in full operation, and expanding.[43]

The establishment of the Psychological Survey provided Lucy Mitchell with a new focus for her varied educational activities. Working with the Survey, she rapidly gained expertise as a tester as well as new knowledge about children's abilities and the learning process. Though Lucy did not direct the project, she had been the catalyst that brought the clinic into existence and she remained the driving force behind it. Within two years of her arrival in the city, her work in setting up the Survey and her material support of the project assured her a place in New York's community of experimental educators.

Although she was fascinated by the work of mental testing and convinced of its social importance, Lucy was not committed to the psychological examination of school children as a permanent career. She had not yet found her particular place within the public school system or among the varied experimental possibilities outside, a "work niche" that could channel her interests and compel her to form a new "vision."

12

A Cooperative
Career

In the early morning hours of March 25, 1916, Lucy received a distraught telephone call from her brother Albert in Chicago.[1] Aunt Nan had died unexpectedly the night before in her hotel in Lakewood, Illinois. Lucy went immediately to join the grieving family at Lakewood, and then went on with them to Chicago in the two private railroad cars Albert had secured. On a chilly morning late in March, Nan was buried in the city that had been her home for more than fifty years, alongside her husband who had died the previous year.

Nan had been the center of Sprague family life; for Lucy, the loss was great. Though Lucy had parted company with Nan's social world, her aunt's maternal warmth and unstinting affection had always been a source of emotional support. For Elizabeth Sprague Coolidge, the tragedy of her parent's death was compounded by the recent death of her husband Fred, a long-time sufferer from tuberculosis. She had inherited from her father almost half of an estate of more than two million dollars, to be kept in trust, in addition to a personal fund of two hundred thousand dollars to be used at her discretion. She determined to use her inheritance to honor the memories of her family.

Two weeks after Nan's death, Elizabeth had dinner with Lucy and Wesley to discuss her plans. She had already used a part of her inheritance in gifts to the Chicago Symphony Orchestra for a musicians' fund, to Yale University—her father's cherished alma mater—for a permanent music building, and to the Anti-Tuberculosis Association of Pittsfield, Massachusetts, to build a tuberculosis hospital.[2] According to

Lucy's recollection of the visit, Elizabeth told her, "My real interest in life is music. But I don't think music is going to get me into heaven. I have a feeling that my best chance of heaven is to do something for education."[3] Lucy told her about plans for a Bureau of School Information, which had been drawn up not long before by the Mitchells and a group of friends—Caroline Pratt, Helen Marot, Harriet Johnson, Harriet Forbes, Evelyn Dewey, Elisabeth Irwin, Eleanor Johnson, and Jean Lee Hunt. The Bureau, which the group proposed to run cooperatively, would collect and disseminate information about various experiments in education throughout the country. Elizabeth had great confidence in her "little cousin": on the basis of Lucy's sketchy outline she offered to provide ten thousand dollars to support the establishment of the Bureau.[4]

In the coming weeks, Lucy remodelled her scheme, acknowledging that she had not been thinking in terms of as large an organization as Elizabeth's offer would allow. Now, in response to Elizabeth's generosity, Lucy suggested a Bureau of Educational Experiments, which would coordinate and sponsor experiments rather than merely acting as a clearinghouse. Such a plan had "enormous scope," Mitchell assured her cousin. She singled out four kinds of practical educational experiments worthy of support: a laboratory school to work with children who were potentially normal but handicapped by "mental peculiarities"; psychological analyses of normal children; sex education through nature study (based on Laura Garrett's scheme); and an innovative "Play School" recently started by Caroline Pratt in Greenwich Village. The experimental Bureau to be established would not only support such new work, but would attempt to bring the staffs of the various projects into a "joint faculty."[5]

Elizabeth was enthusiastic. On May 6, she came to dinner with her son Sprague, a Harvard student, and offered Lucy fifty thousand dollars a year for ten years for her "school experiment."[6] Her only conditions were that Sprague serve on the new organization's board, and that Lucy promise not to make her try to understand or become interested in the group's work![7] Later she clarified and limited her offer. She would give the annual dividends she received from Sprague Warner and Company stock, whatever that might amount to, up to fifty thousand dollars per year, to the new Bureau.

Elizabeth's generous gift gave life to the Bureau of Educational Experiments (BEE). In May, shortly after Lucy's meeting with Elizabeth, the ten original members of the previously planned Bureau of School Information, plus two new members, Laura Garrett and Frederick Ellis, organized themselves into a temporary governing committee, called the Working Council. The two Mitchells and Elisabeth Sprague Coolidge and her son became the organization's first board of trustees, with Lucy as its chair.

By the fall of 1916, the Working Council established the organization's by-laws. There would be no director or other executive officer: instead, the Council would formulate and implement policy collectively, though it selected a chairman (Lucy Mitchell) and a five-member Executive Committee, headed by Evelyn Dewey.[8] John Dewey turned down Lucy's request to serve as the Bureau's unofficial adviser, but was made an honorary Working Council member along with William Wirt and Elizabeth Sprague Coolidge.[9] When the Bureau applied for a New York State charter "to collect and disseminate information concerning progressive education" and "to promote and conduct educational experiments," it was refused on the grounds that New York did not recognize "untried experiments." For the next fifteen years, the Bureau operated under a District of Columbia charter.[10]

Initially, the Bureau surveyed and prepared bibliographies of schooling experiments in the region, assembled materials on the Gary Plan, and conducted studies of such topics as rural schools, dramatic literature for young children, record-keeping, civics teaching, nature study through animals, and psychological testing.[11] At first, it funded only two programs. One, a Laboratory School for "difficult and nervous" children, began operations in October 1916 under the supervision of Eleanor Johnson and Frederick Ellis. Lucy had hoped that the Laboratory School would complete a "chain" of experimental schools—including a school for normal children and a proposed school for precocious children to be established by Leta Hollingworth, the new chief of psychology at Bellevue Hospital. However, the Laboratory School failed to meet BEE objectives, and support for it was not renewed after its first six months.[12] The other "field" experiment the Bureau supported during its first year was Pine Ridge, a one-room school in Kirksville, a poor rural district of Missouri, run according to imaginative, experimental ideas. Its director, Marie Turner Harvey, became the first nonresident member of the BEE.

In 1917, the Bureau originated some projects of its own. In response to a request from Mary Simkhovitch of Greenwich House to try some experimental work in connection with the settlement, Laura Garrett, accompanied by her animals, began a project of nature and reproductive studies at P.S. 195 in Greenwich Village. With help from Leta Hollingworth, Elisabeth Irwin produced an exhibit on psychological testing, which was shown at the meetings of the National Psychological Association and the American Association for the Advancement of Science. The Bureau also prepared an exhibit on the Gary Plan. A third exhibit of materials for young school children was shown at the National Kindergarten Association and the National Educational Association.[13]

During this period of organization, the Bureau began the process of defining the goals of experimentation which it hoped to foster. At the outset, "experimental" applied to the exploration of any new procedure, rather than the scientific testing of hypotheses with laboratory controls. Lucy's "ideal inclusive plan of education," which served as a reference point for selecting projects, included for example thirty-one types of instructional experiments as well as health experiments (medical inspection, clinics, special education, exercise and play grounds); administrative experiments (local and district school boards, student self-government); and community experiments (visiting teachers, parent associations, contacts with welfare organizations).[14] Proposals from BEE members and interested experimenters outside the Bureau illustrated the wide range and eclectic nature of what was considered "experimental" at the time: plans for children with special defects; work in muscular coordination; a school for infants; welfare work; a Gary school project; coordination of vocational work; a nutrition study; the organization of household arts teaching; the administration of progress tests.[15]

Lucy's own proposal attacked the social problems of school children by coordinating school assistance with the welfare work of child-helping agencies, an approach she had suggested in her earlier paper on "The Public's Schools and the Public's Ideals." She argued that an attack on the "out-of-classroom" problems faced by large public schools was a more useful avenue of school experimentation than the testing of educational theory in small private school classes. She suggested that a BEE worker in each public school coordinate work with settlement houses, health department clinics, mental testing agencies, and child labor committees that affected school children. She also urged that each agency providing assistance to public schools—settlement houses, clinics, libraries, parks, zoos, and the like—develop a model plan to present its special services as they applied to school children.[16]

Lucy's plan was considerably more community-oriented than those of other BEE members, except Harriet Johnson's. Both their proposals anticipated the practices of modern social work. The plan that Johnson submitted to the Working Council called for the establishment of a So-

cial Service Department at each public school, to be supervised by a director and visiting teacher, so as to maximize positive results already obtained by small experiments at individual schools. The department
would concentrate on social activities outside the classroom—health,
families, after-school activities.[17]

Johnson's housemate Harriet Forbes proposed that the Bureau undertake a study in nutrition at a public school along the lines of nutrition
classes at the Massachusetts General Hospital in Boston. Lucy advocated
that this plan be undertaken in place of her own, with the understanding
that it would be the first step in the development of her larger scheme
to coordinate social and health services within a school setting. The
committee appropriated two thousand dollars to start the nutrition
experiment.[18]

After consultation with the PEA, the committee decided against implementing Harriet Johnson's administrative plan because of the uncertain
relations between the Board of Education and the Visiting Teachers
project. The committee did vote a small planning sum, however, for another proposal submitted by Johnson: a day nursery for "under school
age" children of working mothers, which could be the setting for research
into young children's mental and physical development. Alternatively,
she suggested a cooperative home for young children of working mothers
or for children for whom the BEE might serve as guardian. Allied with
these various nurseries would be a committee of mothers to prepare plans
for studying their children, making their observations available to the
Bureau.

Although the Bureau's research assistant began to gather information
about Johnson's nursery scheme and the possibility of linking it to a cooperative dwelling for professional women, nothing came of the attempt
to coordinate child care with the residential needs of working women.
However, within two years Johnson's interest in a nursery for young
children would become the center of Bureau attention: a small private
school setting, rather than the large public school environment that
Lucy had urged, would be the locus of the Bureau's major educational
experiment.[20]

America's entrance into World War I in April 1917 brought another
set of urgent issues to the attention of Working Council members. Lucy
opposed taking boys out of school for wartime vocational training as an
"uncourageous" attempt to "clip children until they fit into an industrial
system of which we disapprove." The relationship of industry to educa-

tion was a borderland which she called that "darkest of educational fields." She urged Council members to be alert to the need for solidarity between educational experimenters and industrial workers, especially women, and warned that they could not allow "capitalist industrial leaders" to set the tone of their response to the war.[21]

A special committee, headed by Helen Marot, was formed to consider the broad subject of vocational education in wartime conditions.[22] The committee proposed a survey of existing school practices as the first step in the development of a comprehensive, "scientific" scheme for vocational education. It also called for a "parallel experiment" to provide employment for the workers trained in school programs. Elizabeth Sprague Coolidge had suggested that the Bureau establish an experimental school on her property in Pittsfield, Massachusetts, to be located adjacent to a mill and a number of model homes for mill workers; the committee felt that this might provide the kind of "laboratory" that could connect the Bureau's studies with a program directly affecting industrial life.[23]

After the April declaration of war, however, vocational education programs were so transformed by emergency measures that a study of existing practices seemed futile. Instead, the Bureau undertook an examination of labor camps that enlisted city boys for wartime work on farms. During the summer of 1917, it cooperated with farmers in a community in upstate New York in establishing Camp Liberty, a farm labor experiment for twenty-five New York City teenage boys. When the city boys first came to camp, they did not know the difference between a "radish and a cabbage plant," as a local newspaper put it. Over the summer, they learned to weed carrot fields, hoe corn and beans, pitch hay, harvest wheat, cultivate and clear woodlands. Because the boys worked ten hours a day, in the fields of thirty-five farmers, the Bureau's hope of providing a coordinated educational curriculum had to be abandoned. Yet learning on the job and from talking with farmers proved rewarding, as did the experience of self-government promoted by the BEE. Bureau members concluded that such farm labor camps held significant educational promise.[24]

By the end of its first year in operation, the Bureau of Educational Experiments was thus involved in a wide variety of projects—the farm labor camp, public school nutrition, educational testing, rural schools, play materials, day nurseries, vocational education, and the Gary School idea. The "scattered experiments" to which members had to turn their attention, and the Bureau's admittedly "sketchy" cooperative central organization, made it difficult to develop a coherent point of view and to measure results. "Our vision has not been clear enough and our practical mechanism has not been definite enough to make a consistent program possible," Lucy admitted.[25] It had become clear that some consistent way of observing, recording, and analyzing the behavior of children participating in the Bureau's diverse experiments was necessary. The next phase of Bureau work would be devoted to making a "scientific study of children and the way they react to different environments in order to plan intelligently an appropriate environment."[26]

Despite its problems of focus, the Bureau had become a working experimental group. Its members shared the progressive conviction that with the benefit of enlightened schooling, children could be the harbingers of an improved society, and they hoped to act as a coordinating agency of educational renewal. Perhaps most important of all, the Mitchells and other Bureau members had succeeded, within the first year, in establishing the cooperative milieu they had wanted from the start. The Working Council met every two or three weeks to consider policies and programs, as did the score of special committees which were established. It was difficult for a dozen determined individualists to work cooperatively, but gradually a group consensus and joint working style had emerged. The Bureau had created a network of women experimenters in close contact with progressive school teachers and child development workers (also mostly women) throughout the city. Friendships that ripened during marathon Working Council sessions spanned both personal and professional lives. The "Harriets" and their daughter, Polly Forbes-Johnson, joined the Mitchells so often at lunches, dinners, on weekends, vacations, and holiday celebrations, that they became almost an extended Mitchell family. Evelyn Dewey and other Working Council members also remained close to the Mitchells.

Lucy Mitchell provided neither a systematic theory nor a concrete, defined plan of action to the dozen experimenters she assembled at the Bureau. The guiding principles of the group came not from her but from Dewey. But she contributed the inspiration and energy that organized its disparate experimenters; her role as chair of the Working Council was to guide the group's decision-making by drafting policy and acting as catalyst and spur. She seems to have done the job well: there is no record of any rancor on the part of other members towards her role as first among equals. Through the substantial gift of Elizabeth Sprague Coolidge and smaller subsidies provided by Lucy Sprague Mitchell herself, it was the Sprague family fortune which created and maintained the Bureau of Educational Experiments. This fact itself could have generated resentment, if Lucy had not been a genuinely enabling collaborator.

It was not unusual for wealthy women to endow educational enterprises. It had been Chicago philanthropist Anita McCormick Blaine, heir to the McCormick reaper fortune, who was responsible for publishing Dewey's influential "School and Society" lectures (first presented in her living room) and for underwriting the School of Education which opened at the University of Chicago in 1900, incorporating Dewey's laboratory school and Colonel Parker's Chicago Institute. For a few years, Mrs. Blaine served on the Chicago school board, but her active work in politics as well as in administration of educational institutions was brief. Blaine viewed herself as a patron rather than as a participant in the educational process.

Lucy Mitchell in contrast saw her role as going beyond philanthropy. The BEE embodied the diverse currents in Lucy's prior educational work in New York and her developing ideas about new directions for experimental education. She invested the full force of her idealism in the Bureau, serving its cause through active involvement as a worker, administrator, and leader. This was essentially a new model of participation in the traditional arena of female philanthropy.[27]

The Bureau began as an educational agency, not a scientific organization concerned with the collection, verification, and analysis of empirical data. Yet its wide umbrella provided room for research. Perhaps it was this opportunity that especially attracted Wesley Mitchell to the BEE. Wesley was a founding trustee and secretary of the board, member of the Working Council, chairman of the committees on Toys and on Research and Statistics, and participant in the many informal conferences, luncheons, and dinners the BEE held at the Mitchell home. Though he had had no previous special interest in children's education, he was drawn into the intellectual excitement of this new collective effort; Lucy's venture now became the shared project of the first years of their marriage.

The BEE focused Lucy's work energies as well as strengthened her marriage and friendships. Even more than the Psychological Survey, whose functions were gradually merged with those of the BEE, the Bureau provided channels for her strong executive talents. Most important, it offered a vehicle for the work in education to which Lucy had become committed. With its flexible structure, it allowed for continuous, open-ended experimentation and the constant reshaping of objectives. Nothing was set in advance except a general focus—education—and a broad goal—the enrichment of schooling as a lever to improve society. The methods of the Bureau ensured that it would function collegially as a kind of institute, or think-tank, but one designed to implement promising ideas in concrete form. Theory was tied to practice from the very beginning.

The Bureau in fact allowed Lucy to continue the process she had begun in her earlier apprenticeships with New York reform leaders, when she systematically tried out a variety of professional career models. It provided her with a network of valued friends and colleagues and a setting that allowed her continually to reappraise her educational and social objectives. The Bureau became the institutional context for the experiments in learning that would engage her over the next forty years. By her characteristic mixture of compelling purpose and flexible response, Lucy Sprague Mitchell had created for herself a professional home—one that she could integrate with her life as a wife and mother.

"A Kind of Miracle"

With the BEE well launched, this narrative backtracks to catch up with the other side of Lucy's life in New York. Lucy believed that her marriage to Wesley Clair Mitchell, more than any other factor, helped her to realize her professional and personal ambitions. His unswerving devotion, support, and acceptance of her "as a person in my own right" allowed her to shed her self-doubts and clarify her desires to be of use in the world. "When [he] first came into my life, I was an anguished, guilt-hounded soul," she admitted. Her "other self," watching over whatever she did, made her feel that whatever her achievements, she was a "fake" and fundamentally insincere."[1]

With her marriage, Lucy's self-esteem flowered. "In this new life with Robin, I became a new person. I became happy, satisfied, secure. I became relatively relaxed, unafraid to play in the broad sense. I began to use what powers, what talents, what abilities I had instead of trying to ignore or suppress then."[2] Her husband became a "best friend" to whom she could confess "every horrid thing" about herself. He "never tried to educate me, nor to reform me," she wrote. "He just accepted me . . . even the horrid parts of me. . . . And so I learned to accept all of myself."[3]

Wesley Clair Mitchell *was* an unusual man. His gentleness, his gaiety, his capacity for mutuality and friendship, and especially his sympathy with women's desire for autonomy would have made him exceptional in any era. Lucy wrote that before she met him, "the men I had known best had all been impressed with their own infallibility." Her discovery that Robin truly had "no taint of masculine superiority" was almost incredible to her.[4] "He respected both men and women as human beings who should be given equal opportunities to develop their potentialities" and saw the existing limits on women's opportunities not as a "woman's problem" but as the world's. Lucy proudly reported that when a younger male colleague irritably complained of a woman as "such a feminist," he had replied pointedly, "Well, I'm not a masculinist, are you?"[5]

His childhood heritage provided him with the "security of affection and approval" which fostered a sense of his own abilities and an appreciation for the humanity of others. Born in 1874, he spent most of his boyhood on a farm on the outskirts of Decatur, Illinois. The Mitchell family was not financially successful, but emotionally they seemed far richer than the Spragues. Lucy Sprague grew up in an atmosphere dominated by fear and guilt; the atmosphere in the Mitchell home was open and positive. As a consequence, Wesley was a "unified personality," Lucy thought, secure in his ambitions for work and personal life. "I think we had an ideal childhood," Wesley's sister Beulah told Lucy.[6]

Wesley derived his sympathy for women's rights and his strong belief in their natural abilities from his mother, Lucy McClellan Mitchell, known as Medora, who had studied at Oberlin College and taught music before her marriage.[7] Her beliefs were "liberal beyond those of her generation," Lucy wrote. Above all, she recalled, Medora said she wanted "to give all her children the chance to get trained to live the life each thought best; but if that were not possible, her girls should have the chance, because the world gave boys more opportunities than it did girls."[8] Lucy was equally fond of Wesley's father, "an impulsive, restless, adventurous spirit that welcomed rather than feared the unfamiliar."[9] It was from his father that Wesley derived a good part of his boldness, his readiness to innovate, his identity as an experimenter. Trained as a surgeon, John Mitchell transferred to the Colored Infantry during the Civil war when he learned that Negro troops did not have adequate medical care. A leg injured in boyhood, and crushed again during the war, intermittently restricted him to crutches, frequent bed-rest, and finally, a wheel chair. To keep up family income when his ability to practice medicine declined, Dr. Mitchell began a variety of business ventures in real estate, farming, and engineering.

Entering into this family, Lucy was struck by the admiration and devotion of the seven children for their parents. Wesley had grown up with a "sense of group living, an enjoyment of simple things, a taking for granted that work is a part of daily life, an uncomplicated recognition of primary values—human relations and education" that seemed to contrast markedly with her own "pampered" existence and the emotional strains of the invalidism that haunted the Sprague children's early years.[10] In the Mitchell family, "service to others" was based on "affection rather than on duty."[11] Once Lucy asked Wesley if they were just "born different" or if his childhood environment and experiences, so unlike hers, had given him the strength of character and "sustaining inner poise" that she did not possess. Laconically he replied, "both."[12]

And yet "with all his charm and his capacity to enlist friends for life, Wesley as I first knew him was a lonely man," recalled his friend Alvin Johnson, "a man who passed from the exhilaration of intellectual intercourse to the desert of isolated life. You came into his life," he told Lucy, "and he never again experienced the desolation of a lonely man."[13] Mitchell's friend Vladimir Simkhovitch believed that Lucy "broadened [Mitchell's] horizon greatly," stimulating his deep love of drama, painting, and music. Largely as a result of her influence, Wesley became not merely a scholar but a "many-sided cultivated gentleman."[14] Lucy played down her contributions to Wesley's professional work; in fact she read all his writings, making concrete suggestions for changes in content and style. In the last paragraph of his major work, the 1913 *Business Cycles*, Wesley noted that "more than all others, my wife has shared in making this book," an acknowledgment which his friend Walter Hart later observed could well have read: "more than all others, my wife has shared in making my career, my life."[15]

As Lucy and Wesley had agreed during their courtship, they had different traits and talents: she was the force, the strong power or personality, of passion and movement; he was the ballast, the steady, patient support. While in many respects Lucy was as cerebral a being as Wesley, in his company and with his encouragement, her emotional life flourished. Throughout their marriage, he would ignore the "horrid" aspects of Lucy's emotionalism—her egocentricity, volatility and imperiousness— while responding lovingly to her enthusiasms. In contrast with Otho Sprague, who stifled his wife's spontaneity, Wesley cherished Lucy's fervor. One of Lucy's children was to write her many years later that "Father told me it was your intense emotional life which made you different from other women for him."[16]

Lucy's verve was apparent to all who knew her. "How much energy, wit and vitality you carry about with you," Sadie Gregory once remarked to her. "Robin used to say you got your rest on the tail of a comet," her friend Elsa Ueland told her.[17] "She was the tornado, he was the calm," Wesley's colleague Arthur Burns agreed.[18] Wesley helped to channel Lucy's emotional impetuosity, and played a key part in her professional activities as well. "Always the wisdom of Robin was woven in and out of the background of anything we were doing," commented Ellen Reese, one of Lucy's colleagues."[19]

To his own co-workers as well as to Lucy and her friends, Wesley was a man of "unfailingly fine perceptions" whose judgment and fairness could always be relied on. "He had the great gift of always finding the important point in a confused situation," one of his faculty colleagues recalled.[20] "His friendly and sympathetic ways made him play another great role," Vladimir Simkhovitch observed. "People of different attitudes and temperament could always cooperate with Mitchell, though without him such cooperation could hardly be achieved. Hence he was very valuable in every scientific and scholarly cooperative enterprise."[21] In later years, President Hoover would call him the "great umpire."[22] Another friend commented that Mitchell's middle initial surely must have stood for "Compromise."[23] All of his colleagues found him to be "a great *encourager*": "he stood back of all those he thought were on the right track; gave generously of his time to guide and advise them; he criticized their work, but always constructively; he used his great influence to get them a hearing; he was so magnanimous that he forgave their often awkward convictions."[24] Perhaps the core of the humanity that so many noted in him was that "he understood what mixed creatures men and women are, forgot about their weaknesses . . . and gained joy from what good qualities they might have."[25]

Lucy asserted that "the 'modesty' and 'humility' others recognized in [Wesley was] in fact the negative way of describing his positive characteristic: he accepted people as they were." And so, she wrote, he accepted himself, wasting no time questioning his abilities or accomplishments. This Lucy felt was his "greatest power, both in [his] work and with people."[26]

Lucy had neither the self-confidence that supported her husband's "modesty," nor the effortless warmth and tolerance that characterized all his human relations. Yet as Lucy enlarged the emotional sphere of Wesley's world, so he brought to her a tranquillity which she had not attained without him. Marriage was a "long, satisfying, exciting period during which I finally grew up," she wrote. In marriage, they found a new wholeness that despite what Lucy called "minor irritations" would endure and grow deeper. [27]

Though marriage brought a new sense of ease and belonging, the larger family that Lucy Mitchell longed for had been slow to materialize. In 1913, Lucy at thirty-five and Wesley at thirty-nine were well past the age considered best for conceiving a first child, and it seems likely that they believed that Lucy could not conceive. Medora wrote Lucy that "if I had no children of my own, I should certainly adopt some. I would *never, never, never* undergo any surgical operations for the sake of physical motherhood." She reminded Lucy that her own mother had died at age 31 as a consequence of child-bearing. [28] By the end of 1913, the Mitchell's had begun to visit the New York State Charities Aid Association to talk about adoption; and on February 3, 1914, they brought home an eight-month-old, blonde, blue-eyed baby boy. They named the baby John McClellan Mitchell, after Wesley father, and called him Jack. Three weeks later, the Mitchells legally adopted the baby.

Friends and family were sympathetic. "Lucy adores the baby," Cousin Elizabeth wrote to her mother after a visit. "He is a darling, pretty and lovable, you will love him I know. . . . I am enthusiastic about him and about her." [29] Benjamin Wheeler wrote from California: "My dear and only Lucy, I am very glad you have assumed the care of little Jack. May he bless your life. He ought to grow up good, for your sake alone. You deserve a child and lots of them and I hope and pray you may yet have them and Jackie too. Your heart is big enough for a host." [30]

Evidently the adoption of abandoned children by wealthy families was not a common practice, for *The New York Times* reported the event on page 1 of its April 1st edition, under the headline "Rich Adopt Foundlings." [31] One of the reasons upper-middle-class families of this period rarely adopted may have stemmed from the widespread concern about the effect of hereditary determination of character. This was in the heyday of the eugenics movement, when, to prevent an increase of the "defective" or "degenerate" population, even progressives advocated such measures as registration, marriage restriction, forcible commitment, and sterilization. [32]

The Mitchells were well acquainted with eugenics ideology, but they believed much more strongly in the powers of environment. "Jack's heredity need not worry us much," Wesley wrote in March to Lucy, who was visiting Gary, Indiana, "for human nature is indefinitely modifiable. . . . If Jack does not form a good character, as disciples of Dewey we shall have to blame ourselves."[33]

In fact, Jack proved to be a happy, responsive baby. Both Lucy and Wesley noted every infection, fever, and teething crisis with the greatest attention. Lucy recorded most details of his development and his daily schedules in her notebooks. A baby nurse stayed for about a month, then Lucy relied on the household help of a number of Irish maids who lived with the family, especially Mary (called Mollie) Aloysius Cotter, who stayed with the Mitchells for many years.

Barely six months after Jack's adoption, Lucy and Wesley were expecting a child of their own. Though she was nearly thirty-seven, Lucy experienced an easy pregnancy. According to Aunt Nan, who came to spend several months with Elizabeth at her new Park Avenue apartment, Lucy had never looked prettier or seemed happier.[34]

Like many first children, the expected baby delayed its arrival. Medora wrote anxiously that Lucy should do nothing to hasten it, advising against long walks or undue exercise.[35] Nevertheless, on March 24 Lucy went to Sloane Hospital for a "cocktail" to induce labor. She slept at home that night and was admitted to the hospital the following day. Labor did not commence, however, until three days later. Finally, on Sunday, March 28, at 10:09 A.M., Sprague Mitchell was born.[36]

Wesley visited the hospital three times a day, reading Conrad's "Victory" and favorite poems to Lucy. To celebrate the birth, he bought her a glorious star sapphire. An anxious letter came from Medora, fearing that Lucy's "ever urgent ambitions" would tempt her to come home too soon and start work again too quickly.[37]

Lucy remained at Sloane, in fact, for three weeks. Although Sprague's arrival did not make the front page of The New York Times as his older brother's had, the Mitchells' friends greeted his homecoming with great fanfare. Streams of callers came, more than a dozen in the first two days alone. For the next few months, hardly a day passed when several visitors did not stop by to watch the babies being fed or bathed or to play with them.

In June of 1915, the Mitchells, their two children, and two maids traveled to Berkeley, where they spent the summer visiting old friends and family, especially Medora, and Wesley's sister, Beulah Clute, both recently widowed. There were luncheons and parties, evenings at the old

Berkeley poetry circle, and visits to campus where Lucy saw the new Partheneia and met with women students.

In mid-July, Wesley left for a three-week camping trip in Yosemite, leaving Lucy with the babies and his diary. Lucy entered comments about the family's activities and herself in his absence, though in a more abbreviated form than was Wesley's custom. This was the only occasion during the thirty-five years of their marriage when Lucy took over the diary—until the few days before Wesley's death—but it shows that like many of their undertakings, the diary could be a cooperative project.[38]

Lucy recorded the visitors who came to see the children and her visits to friends. But often she spoke of her own feelings, mentioning how tired and worried she was, the kind of details Wesley never noted. She was especially troubled that Sprague had not been gaining weight. A sample of her breast milk was analyzed as satisfactory; the problem, the doctor said, was simply her weariness. Then Sprague began to suffer from attacks of colic, crying often and lustily; and sometimes Jack joined in. During these weeks, Lucy was also writing a paper on sex education that she was scheduled to deliver to a conference on social hygiene in San Francisco in early August. That strain, plus the care of the boys and a troublesome knee, which she had injured again on the train, contributed to her exhaustion.

Lucy was cheered by Wesley's letters. Yosemite was as "beautiful and splendid as ever," he wrote. But he could not stop "wondering whether your bandage has slipped, whether Sprague has been sitting up, and whether Jack has wet himself this morning." Recalling their courtship on the Yosemite trail years before, he told her, "You mean so much more to me now than you did—sorely desired as you were—the heart's mother of Jack, the bodily mother of Sprague, the lovely companion of many varying days, the wife of all seasons."[39] "You are the center of the world to me and I feel wistfully lonely way off in this margin."[40]

Wesley returned at the beginning of the second week in August, just after Lucy had given her conference paper on "A Scheme for Presenting Social Hygiene to School Children."[41] Although still weary, she joined her husband for a week of camping at Lake Tahoe at the end of August. They enjoyed their hikes in the Sierras, but concern about the children made their vacation much less carefree than four years earlier. A stream of telegrams arrived in response to their queries, giving details of Sprague's weight and Jack's behavior. They were glad to return at the beginning of September. The camping trip was the last they spent together in their beloved Sierra mountains. Now they were a family, and a family required different arrangements.

In the spring of 1916, the Mitchells began to think of adopting another baby. Though there is no record of their reasons for this step, family members have suggested that it was their strong desire that Jack not feel in any way inferior to their naturalborn son, Sprague, that led them to take in a second adopted child.

From January through April, 1917, the Mitchells viewed two baby girls and one boy before deciding on a two-month old girl named Marian whom they had seen at Children's Hospital. On May 5, Marian came home with them, joining Jack, almost four, and Sprague, a few months past two. Marian kept her first name—though she was immediately nicknamed Marni—and it was assumed that Lucy had named the child for Marion Farquhar. Two months later, on a summer vacation, Lucy found herself nauseated much of the time, though she was strong and energetic, walking several miles a day. Perhaps this second pregnancy was as unforeseen as the first. Or perhaps the Mitchells wanted a second naturalborn child to "even out" their family. Again, Lucy seemed happier and prettier than ever to friends and family. Arnold Mitchell was born on February 18, 1918, a few months short of Lucy's fortieth birthday, during the hectic days of wartime, when Wesley was commuting back and forth to Washington, where he worked as Chief of the Price Section of the War Industries Board. Again Lucy remained in the hospital for three weeks, returning with a nurse who stayed on till the baby was two months old.

Now there were four little Mitchell, or two "teams" of children: Jack and Sprague, and Marni and Arnold (Little "Aa"). Between the oldest and youngest, there was only four and a half years' difference in age. Wesley Mitchell, increasingly involved in the wartime effort, spent more time in Washington than New York over the next two years. His job involved estimating war needs of various commodities, recommending import levels, and fixing prices. Though there were "uninteresting lulls" in the work, for the most part Wesley's life in Washington was heady with excitement. "I am ready to concoct a new plan for running the universe at any minute," he admitted to his wife.[42]

Yet Wesley worried about Lucy's health and overcommitted work schedule, urging her to follow a more "temperate course" and to hire a nurse for the children. He turned down a commission as major on "family grounds," assuring his mother that he would not have remained in Washington "if I did not feel it every man's duty to aid all he possibly can in getting the country organized."[43] Yet after the war ended, he requested that the Price Section be continued and enlarged so that the wartime statistical procedures he had developed could be incorporated into postwar planning. Wesley continued this work until 1920, though he repeatedly told Lucy how much he wanted to live at home again with her and the children. "They are so adorable these days that my heart aches over them," he wrote to her on Armistice Day. "And you are so dear that my eyes fill with tears when I let myself dwell on all you go through, on all you do, and on all you are."[44]

Despite her busy professional life, her separation from Wesley, and a number of serious illnesses which afflicted the children during the war years, Lucy carried on ably with the help of Mollie Cotter. "I was well and very happy," she recalled; she throve on the challenge of dealing with her family situation and her other interests. above all, she treasured the new life she and Wesley had made together. Older than most couples when they married, they had "almost given up the hope" of a shared home and children. "No one tried so hard to be happy without children," Lucy remarked to her cousin Elizabeth when she told her of her first pregnancy.[45] But in her late thirties and early forties, the family that Lucy had always desired became a reality. With four lovely children, a "full-to-overflowing" personal life, and "absorbing" professional work, a "kind of miracle" had come to her.[46]

Real Play
and Real Work

In the first five years of her marriage, Lucy Mitchell resolved many of the problems of vocational and personal identity that had beset her since college. Yet, according to her own retrospective account, she was not professionally content; she still felt that she was untrained and unspecialized, and, while she recognized that this very fact probably aided the collective functioning of the Bureau of Educational Experiments, she continued to feel that her professional life was "vicarious."[1]

After 1917, however, her absorption in learning about and teaching children led to contributions to education that she acknowledged were no longer second-hand. As a teacher and ultimately as a writer for children, she was to realize her full potential as a professional woman.

A vital element in this stage of Lucy's professional life was her association with educator Caroline Pratt. Pratt, a cultural and political radical, proposed a "revolution in education" remarkably congruent to Lucy Mitchell's emerging ideas about educational innovation. To Pratt, the "revolution" meant learning by experimenting and experiencing in group, rather than individual, settings. Traditional learning was a "by-product" of this real education, in which play—a reconstruction of the work relationships and processes of the real world—was the essential component. Behind Pratt's theory of education lay a radical vision of a new social order to which the individual child, taught to think properly, held the key.

As Pratt's collaborator, Lucy learned new methods of educating children through play and first-hand experience and expression. Ultimately

236

she was to reject significant aspects of Pratt's educational theory, and especially her working style. But Pratt's approach, combined with the ideas about school and society Lucy had absorbed from Dewey and from her earlier social settlement and school-visiting experiences, helped crystallize Lucy's views about the developmental functions of education. Her contact with children themselves at Pratt's "Play School" was particularly important.

Caroline Pratt was born in 1867 in Fayetteville, New York, a small farming village near Syracuse, and started teaching in a one-room schoolhouse not far from her home at the age of seventeen.[2] Eight years later, in 1892, she enrolled in Teachers College at Columbia. Later she taught manual training in the Normal School for Girls in Philadelphia, where she came to know Helen Marot, a thirty-two-year-old Quaker who had organized a library for those interested in social and economic problems.[3] While still teaching half-time, Pratt joined Marot in an investigation of the custom tailoring trades in Philadelphia, for the U.S. Industrial Commission.[4] Often, she and Marot talked about the futility of seeking to reform school teaching while, after leaving school, women still had to earn their living under horrible working conditions. Pratt resigned from the Normal School and she and Marot came to New York in 1901 to put into practice their evolving ideas about teaching and social change. Pratt and Marot lived together until Marot's death in 1940, sharing ideas, ideals, and friends. It was Marot's work on behalf of women and children that helped Pratt shape a new theory of learning.

Marot first worked for the Association of Neighborhood Workers of New York City, investigating child labor. The formation of the New York Child Labor Committee in the fall of 1902 and the enactment of New York's Compulsory Education Act were direct outcomes of her report. As executive secretary of the Women's Trade Union League of New York, she played an important role in the 1909 strike of women shirtwaist makers.[5] Marot resigned her office in 1913, in part as a protest against the fact that none of the WTUL's highest positions were occupied by working-class women. She then became a full-time writer, publicist and editor, devoted to the socialist reconstruction of society, and especially, to liberating women and children from the tyranny of the industrial machine.[6] She worked for protective labor legislation for women and the establishment of effective women's trade unions, compulsory school attendance, and abolition of child labor. Caroline Pratt's work in education—liberating children in the classroom so that they could change the world outside—became the reverse side of Marot's reform program.

In New York, Pratt taught manual training in two settlement schools and a private school, working part-time for the Women's Trade Union League. One day, as she watched the six-year-old son of a friend make his own railroad train with blocks, toys, and boxes, a revelation came to her. The boy, in his play, was thinking, learning, "setting down his understanding of the way things worked, the relationships of facts to each other. . . . This was the way a young child, if freed to do so, would go about educating himself on the subject which was of most immediate, intense interest to him—the world in which he lived."[7] All children had similar drives to learn, she thought, drives that were lost when teachers used methods that did not directly relate to children's lives. "If we could keep this desire alive through childhood and into adult life . . . we would release a precious powerful force," she concluded. "The child would learn in such a way that his knowledge would actually go with him from the schoolhouse into the world."[8]

Pratt decided that she had to work with very young children in order to begin to educate them effectively through play, and she began teaching five-year-olds at Hartley House, a West Side settlement. After a two-month trial financed by a WTUL colleague, Edna Smith, she set up her own school, the Play School, in a three-room apartment on the corner of West 4th and 12th Streets, again with the help of Smith. There were six five-year-olds in the first class, all from working-class families, who paid no tuition. When the school needed to expand, Pratt, Marot, and Smith rented a small house on West 13th Street, which they used for living quarters and classroom space. Pratt tried to develop an additional six-year-old class for the school but discovered that parents were generally reluctant to keep their children out of public school during the year when they would normally be taught to read and write. Only parents who were artists and writers seemed willing to take the opportunity of a "free" education for their children that would teach them not the three R's, but how to think.

One day at the end of November, 1913, shortly after Pratt's experimental school had its modest beginning, Harriet Johnson brought Lucy

Mitchell to meet Caroline Pratt. The two women were instantly taken with each other—Pratt, forty-six, short, sturdy, somewhat mannishly dressed; Mitchell, thirty-five, tall and elegant with her long bohemian skirt and colorful blouse, her crisp, polished, authoritative diction. It was this daughter of one of capitalism's favorite sons who would ultimately propel Pratt's theories about Socialist education into the progressive mainstream.

Lucy Mitchell described her first encounter with Pratt's work:

I had been trying for some years to get first-hand experience into the curriculum at the University of California. I had been taking the students on trips just as she took her school children. In the Partheneia, I had got the students started on translating their experiences into creative activity. . . . Indeed, it was just because Caroline Pratt's educational thinking was so consistent with what I had myself come through to that her experiment so excited me. She was in the early stage of working out experimentally a curriculum of experience for little children. The idea literally thrilled me. Here it seemed to me was a God-given opportunity to work with children along the very lines that I had come to believe were educational.[9]

Although Lucy was immediately impressed with Pratt's new school, it was not until November 1915, two years after their first meeting, that she came to Pratt with a plan that would link their futures. To meet the needs of their growing family, the Mitchells had bought a large brownstone at fifteen Washington Square North. Its old stable and backyard seemed a perfect place for Caroline's Play School, which two-and-a-half-year-old Jack Mitchell would soon be ready to enter. Would Caroline consider moving the school out of its cramped quarters on West 13th Street and into the mews of the Mitchell's new home?

In October 1916, after much discussion and planning, Pratt's Play School began operations in the Mitchells' converted stable on MacDougal Alley behind their home. As Pratt recalled in her memoirs: "Mrs. Mitchell brought with her a fresh tide of plans for expansion powered by her characteristic enthusiasm. She offered us financial support. She offered us a new home. . . . Best of all, she offered her own services as a teacher, and this was the beginning of a long and rich association."[10] Lucy became a teacher of the five-year-old group, and later Wesley began teaching carpentry at the school. The Mitchells' backyard became the school playground. When the Play School needed more room, the Mitchells gave up parts of their large house to accommodate it. And one by one, as the Mitchell children grew, they entered the school. For the next five years, a period of "intoxicating growth" for the school, the Play School remained on MacDougal Alley behind the Mitchells' house. When the Mitchells moved in 1921 to new quarters on West 12th and West 13th Streets, the Play School went with them. The symbiosis between Pratt's Play School and the Mitchell family could not have been more direct.

The Play School occupied a series of sunny interconnected rooms, decorated with the shapes of triangles and diamonds in bright primary colors. Hung above the wooden floors in most of the rooms were balconies where each child could play in his or her own floor space on a rug, with screens to separate the space from other children. Below, groups of children played together with large wooden blocks and flat wooden figures of men, women, children, farm animals, and wagons. Outside was an ample yard, equipped with see-saws, cross-bars, slides, climbing poles, carts, wheelbarrows, shovels, and dozens of large and small packing boxes. Here, too, the children played noisily together, building, carrying, climbing, working.[11]

Perhaps only experienced observers could recognize the revolutionary principles that lay behind the busy scene. For in fact all aspects of traditional pedagogy had been discarded. The Play School, whose title itself might be seen as a contradiction in terms, had no set curriculum or formal classroom goals. Even for older children, there were no periods devoted to reading, writing, or arithmetic. Instead, students played with toys and blocks, did shop work, painted, told stories, made music, did pantomime, or occupied themselves in other freely chosen ways. In later years, a "jobs" program for children aged seven to thirteen supplemented the original play program for children aged two to seven. In this program, traditional school work—history, geography, literature, etc.—was not taught as individual subjects, but stemmed from the central enterprise of a particular class—the printing of a newspaper, the buying and selling of school supplies, the selling of shop products—conducted throughout the school year.[12]

Pratt thought that the Play School differed from the usual experimental classrooms in which teachers were the experimenters, children the material. In the Play School, children worked in an open, free environment, and were themselves the experimenters. The school's guiding prin-

ciple was "self-education"; its primary goal to establish "the habit of being motivated from within; of having purposes and being able to stick to
them."[13] With teachers encouraging their efforts, children were free to
occupy themselves "according to their individual needs and desires." After their initial fears and self-consciousness were broken down, they
would develop imagination, initiative, "or whatever one may choose to
call this quality."[14]

In many respects, the Play School was typical of the progressive
schools that began to flower at about this time. Influenced by the educational philosophy of John Dewey and Francis Parker, the Play School ex-
hibited characteristics that became the hallmarks of the progressive tradition.[15] As pioneered by Parker at the Cook County Normal School in
Chicago and by Dewey at the Laboratory School at the University of
Chicago, the progressive school curriculum was child-centered rather
than adult- or school-centered. The purpose of the school was to promote the individual child's growth on all levels: mental, physical, social,
emotional. The production of "individuality, personality, and experience" thus became a key canon. Since the "whole child" was to be educated, the materials of education were as broad as life itself, to be found
outside as well as inside classrooms. Above all, children were to be active, not passive. They were to play and to work, not listen. Their self-
determined activities were the core of the curriculum.[16]

Although one of the key goals of the Play School was to liberate the
creative impulses of its students, the mainspring of its pedagogy was political. Pratt would have bridled at being called a "reformer," for she
identified herself firmly as a revolutionary Socialist, but in fact no more
complete representation of the Deweyite vision of the school as social reform agency could be found than in the new school on MacDougal Alley. It was this social, political, community-minded element in her work
that attracted many progressive educators, social workers, and other
reformers—including Lucy Mitchell—to her. Pratt's work exemplified a
synthesis of art and politics that was quite unusual in postwar American
culture.[17]

"A Socialist education," Pratt had written in an early position paper,

would first of all recognize that the method of gaining knowledge through the
medium of books exclusively is obsolete. Also, confining a child to expressing
himself through written language exclusively is obsolete. The Socialist would
throw down these methods as completely as he throws down the method of com-

petition in industry. . . . What is needed is revolution and the keynote is the application of a new method as fundamental as the one employed to bring about
the cooperative commonwealth.[18]

Pratt urged experimenters to change the school environment to give
children, first, "the freest possible scope for self-expression" and, second,
a method of learning which "regarded the community as the first and
most important field for the acumulation of related facts." Through play
combined with other firsthand experiences, children could discover for
themselves the facts of "industrial and distributive processes" and relate
them to their own lives and to the world. Until this was accomplished,
Pratt warned, "our schools will remain what they are—direct feeders to
the factory system."[19]

Like Pratt, Lucy Mitchell thought that through education, modes of
social thought and behavior might be fundamentally altered, leading to a
radical change in the "industrial system of which we so disapprove." As
she told her colleagues at the BEE:

We must find some way of joining forces with those workers who within their industrial world are striving for this educational opportunity for expression. Our
task, as educators, is to devise experiments that have both educational and industrial promise. This must be the combined work of educators who understand
industrial conditions and industrial workers who have the educational point of
view.[20]

Lucy Mitchell was not an avowed socialist like Pratt. Nevertheless,
schooled in progressive social theory by such teachers as John Dewey,
John Graham Brooks, Jane Addams, Florence Kelley, and Lillian Wald,
she believed in the need to reconstruct society, and like Pratt, she saw
the education of children as the pathway toward a more democratic, progressive, and cooperative world.

Essential to this vision of the good society was a new mutuality between men and women. Pratt believed that her school would radically re-
vise the traditional sexual division of labor and promote equality between
the sexes.[21] "In all activities boys and girls [must be] given equal opportunities," Pratt wrote.

Whatever her future is to be, we can see no reason why it is not as valuable for a
girl as for a boy to use materials which lead out into ever wider experiences instead of remaining centered in less acitve interests. . . . While we encourage
both boys and girls with suitable materials to carry out domestic experiences,
we also encourage girls as well as boys to follow and lead out into the bigger
world.[22]

Like Pratt, Lucy Mitchell assumed that changes in sex roles initiated in the experimental schoolroom would carry over to the larger society. Concentrating their attention on the classroom as both the microcosm and the nursery of a new egalitarian, progressive republic, neither of them gave priority to the political battles of feminism and socialism, though they agreed with the movement's ideals. For both women, as for Dewey, education at its best was identical with social change, with politics itself.

Although children were the leading actors, the Play School staff was vital to the school. Each group had a regular classroom teacher, whose job was "to enrich each individual child's performance; to help him adjust his social difficulties."[23] Pratt thought the best teachers were those who came from a social work background and therefore had greater "courage," "initiative," and "understanding" than traditionally trained teachers.[24] Many were political radicals.[25] Specialists like sculptor William Zorach taught art and Harriet Hubbell music. Instruction was also given in science, cooking, sewing, and carpentry.

Before World War I, few schools had systematically put such a child-centered, experience-oriented curriculum into practice.[26] Between 1912 and 1919, primarily at the urging of parents dissatisfied with traditional education, a number of "country day" or "park" schools opened which adopted elements of the progressive curriculum.[27] So rapidly did such schools multiply that in 1919 a group of educators founded the Progressive Education Association for mutual help and discussion. Pratt's school, with its innovative curriculum focusing on work-oriented play, made an important contribution to the unfolding of the progressive school movement, although later Pratt preferred the designation "experimental" rather than "progressive." Lucy, too, felt the term "progressive" was vague, "snooty," and "restrictive." Through the Bureau of Educational Experiments, which helped to disseminate its approach, the Play School's radical theory and practice became widely known and imitated.[28]

The Play School benefited in many ways from its association with the BEE. Lucy Mitchell provided a home, additional financial support, and, through the Bureau, a working base of operations. In return for being allowed to use the Play School as a laboratory to observe and record children in the classrooms and to carry out physical and mental tests, the Bureau conducted and financed the school's out-of-classroom work: its health program (physical examinations, procedures for contagious diseases, nutrition planning), social services, and registration and admission programs. BEE specialists like pediatrician Edith Lincoln and psychologist Buford Johnson, along with teachers and other Bureau researchers, diagnosed developmental patterns of pupils. The detailed factual records of Play School children amassed by the BEE's research staff helped to give the school the scientific legitimacy Pratt was convinced it deserved.[29]

As the Play School children grew older, they insisted that the name of their school be changed to connote what they considered more serious purposes. In 1921, the school became the City and Country School, in recognition of the summer farm program which Pratt and Lucy Mitchell had established at Hopewell Junction, New York. Nevertheless, Pratt always preferred the original name. She felt she could find no better definition of her intentions.[30] "Our opponents characterize opportunities provided by the school as opportunities 'to do as one pleases,'" Pratt once said, "but [we] think it is opportunity to produce, to produce not because one merely remembers, not because one is told to, but because all one's faculties are primed for work."[31] Through play, in fact, children become real workers, the highest attribute in the Play School vocabulary.

To become a "real worker" and simultaneously to release her instincts for play was a lifelong urge of Lucy Sprague Mitchell. In the Play School, she found an environment that answered her deepest feelings—that extended her commitment to experiential learning, and linked it with social change. Pratt's theory and practice influenced Lucy decisively, leading her away from the notion of the school as a community center or coordinating agency with which she had begun her work in New York.

Lucy and Caroline Pratt formed a close friendship which lasted many years. Pratt visited the Mitchells constantly, talking for hours with Lucy, dining with the family, visiting with the children, or playing softball in the school yard or poker with Wesley. Caroline and Lucy often went to the theater together and spent many weekends either at the Hopewell Junction farm or at the Mitchells' vacation cottages. Caroline and Helen Marot almost always spent Thanksgiving and Christmas with the Mitchells. Lucy took care of Caroline when she was ill. Sometimes Caroline moved into the Mitchells' house for short periods. But both Lucy Mitchell and Caroline Pratt were strong-willed. In spite of their shared ideals and mutual respect, friction began to grow. In her autobiography, Lucy recalled that working in the Play School—though inspiring—was never easy. Notwithstanding the school's participatory atmosphere and the focus on process, Pratt was clearly in charge, and this was hard for Lucy to accept.[32]

Caroline Pratt was a "kind of genius," Lucy conceded many years later, but she possessed the "flaws" as well as "virtues" of genius—flaws which Lucy prided herself on avoiding.

She was what one might call aggressively individualistic, too much so to be a genuine sharer. She had an intense childlike, even belligerent belief in her own thinking that made disciples rather than thinkers of those who worked with her. At the same time, she lacked confidence and was upset unless she received the unqualified approval of others. The result was a curious form of what she called "cooperation," in which no one was free to express an opinion differing from hers. We could not question: we could only support.[33]

By Lucy's account, she also had major differences with Pratt over the administration of the school. Pratt was uninterested in the daily details, and assumed that others would handle them. In Lucy's "first eagerness . . . enthusiasm and . . . humility," she had accepted the task of making the school run smoothly. For a number of years, she supervised the cleaning, bought the coal, planned and supervised repairs and remodelling.

More potentially disruptive were Pratt's attitudes about money. She thought Lucy "fuzzy and a bit sordid" to insist that the school have a budget. She refused to think about financial matters, even though tuition never even remotely covered expenditures. "She felt that the world owed her experiment its support and received all contributions, including my own, as a lucky break for the donors."[34] Lucy was shocked when Pratt wrote sharp letters to two benefactors, a private donor and a foundation, rebuking them for not automatically renewing their contributions to the next school year. Thereafter, Lucy refused to raise additional money for the school. Lucy's support of the school alleviated some of her "deep-seated sense of guilt in having money." "I was willing, though inwardly humiliated, to be a 'donor.' But I was not willing to be only a donor."[35]

However sincerely Lucy meant not to compete with Caroline Pratt, her generosity itself created a problem. She had opened up her family life and living space to the Play School, as well as her purse, and by doing so she had inevitably created a special role for herself: the school was part of her extended household. But the maternal role—central but not

directive—that had worked well for her at the BEE was not available to
Lucy as Pratt's collaborator.

This discomfort was alleviated for a time by a major development in
her own teaching. When Lucy began teaching at the school, she had
started to record the words and speech patterns children used in their everyday play, using these notes to create stories which she read and discussed with them. She used her home as a laboratory as well, observing
and recording her own children's speech. As her studies of children's language began to yield results, she could feel much more like an autonomous professional, a "real worker," less like an all-purpose benefactress.

After four years of this work, she made one of the "most exciting discoveries" of her life. "I shall never forget the day it suddenly burst over
me that rhythm and sound quality and patterns, which shot through all
little children's language, were the very elements that I had stressed in
teaching versification in the University."[36] With the insight that children used language as an "art medium" came Lucy's determination to
write an experimental book about the way in which the content and
forms of stories for children might be improved. She assembled many
children's stories, either ones she wrote herself or others she put together
from the language of Play School children, and tested them on students,
her children, and their friends. Her intention was to publish the best stories, grouped by age, along with a theoretical introduction. However,
while Caroline Pratt endorsed publication of the "here-and-now" stories,
she insisted that Lucy's introduction ought to be eliminated because it
was didactic, not child-centered. "Just words," Pratt said; "no one profits
by analysis by anyone else." Overriding Pratt, Lucy decided to publish
the book as it stood.[37]

Children and the
Here-and-Now

The *Here and Now Story Book* appeared in 1921, and was widely recognized as a radically new departure in writing for children. Henry Suzzallo's "fantastic" suggestion, made seven years earlier, that Lucy's "real job was to write epoch-making books," had not prepared her for the amount of critical attention and acclaim that greeted her first published work. The book was a mixture of argument and example. It was made up of forty-one stories and "jingles," for children aged two to seven, each with an explanatory note for parents or teachers, and all preceded by a long essay in which Lucy presented the working principles behind the unfamiliar form and content of the stories.

She argued that children's stories, like their play generally, should be based on material that offered children opportunities to explore their own immediate environments, and gradually widen those environments along the lines of their own inquiries. Anything to which children gave their spontaneous attention was appropriate content for stories, if it was presented in terms of relationships that were natural and intelligible at each age. Stories constructed in this way could help order the child's experiences, teaching not specific facts but how to think and understand the world. The place to begin, Lucy maintained, was the point at which the child had already arrived. With small children, this was the world of the familiar and the immediate—the child itself and its daily life. But, as education widened an individual's experience, so too, stories for children ought to widen their present worlds. "Here and now" stories meant stories that took the children's first-hand experiences as a starting point, not stories that were limited to these experiences.

This principle was based on Lucy's observations of children at home and in the Play School. She had watched children at each age to see what they "seized upon and made [their] own," what relationships were important to them. At ages two to three, children's own activities and body movements occupied their attention. They thought in terms of sense and motor experiences—"through their muscles." Stories for children of this age should follow these experiences. With the child as protagonist, each episode should be put together not as an "organic whole" but like a "string of beads," without climax or completion. Almost any section of a child's own experience—such as getting out of bed and dressing in the morning—retold in a simple chronological sequence made a satisfactory story.

At ages four and five, children were less egocentric and did not have to occupy the center of attention in every story. Yet until the age of six, they still thought in terms of sense and motor experiences and were most interested in engines, boats, wagons, animals and their own moving bodies. This is the age when constructive anthropomorphism flourishes. If personifications were built on relations that children understood and that had objective validity—like the new locomotive engine in one of the stories, who wants to learn to run—they could endow the imaginative world of the child with vitality.

At ages seven to eight, children went through a transition period, becoming more aware of the world outside their immediate physical and social experiences. To help them acquire social values and a sense of workmanship, information outside their own persons and familiar environments was needed. Stories for children in this group ought to open relationships in larger and more unfamiliar environments, leading back into familiar worlds. An example was the story about the diverse skills and distant raw materials that came together in the building of a skyscraper—a familiar but potentially exciting landmark in the life of a city child. Personification remained a useful device, helping to unify the child's multifaceted experiences or to elucidate scientific principles. But each process, product, or industry introduced into the stories—the city subway system or the use of a milking machine—was employed as a dramatic setting to provide adventure and mystery—the "thrill" of elemental contact with powerful forces. Stories for children were not encyclopedias; they should not be overloaded with facts and information.

Lucy had adapted the experiential play approach of Pratt's school to her study of children's language. In turn, her analysis of children's stories from the point of view of the here-and-now world helped Play School teachers to integrate reading and story-telling into the school's direct approach to learning. The Play School reading program had lagged behind its work in arithmetic, geography, and history, precisely because the connection between first-hand experience and literature had not been made.

It was not only Lucy's practical recommendations for helping children gain mastery of language that were original: her analysis of the stages of comprehension, extracted from detailed observation of children's responses and their spontaneous language-play, was a substantial advance in the theory of child development. Only later in the 1920s were Piaget's observations about the stages of the child's cognitive development translated into English; it was another few decades before his theories became the basis of significant numbers of school programs for younger children.[1] Lucy Mitchell's work on the stages of children's language development was a precursor to his.

The introduction to the *Here and Now Story Book* also emphasized that the form of stories for children was just as important as their content. Just as young children thought through their muscles, so they expressed themselves verbally through play that was rhythmical, even physical. The stories and verses they most enjoyed, like "The Gingerbread Man," "Jack and Jill," or "The Three Little Pigs," gave them "vicarious motor pleasure." Simplicity, continuity, and the use of repetitive patterned flows of words characterized children's spontaneous language: and these elements should be employed in stories told, or read, to children.

Though children played spontaneously with words as they did with other play materials, adults usually "killed" their natural word play, "just as we kill their creative play with most things. . . . Most of us have forgotten how to play with anything, most of all with words," she declared. "We are hopelessly utilitarian, we are executive, we are didactic, we are earth-tied, we are hopelessly adult!"[2] Even the best existing literature for children sprang from adult standards. First-rate writers creating literature for children according to *children's* standards had yet to emerge.

Lucy labeled her own efforts at story-making for children "pitifully inadequate." So as not to slip back into adult habits, she had forced herself to be deliberative and conscious in a way that perhaps contradicted her own message of spontaneity. Her stories should be considered only as "experiments," she insisted, just as the theses which underlay them were in fact "questions" whose answers would come not from adults but children. Calling upon "mothers and teachers everywhere" to gather and record children's stories, she urged them to drop the "utilitarian" speech they used with children, and to listen and talk with them in the spontaneous patterns, rhythms, and sounds children themselves employed.[3] By studying the way children thought and talked, she hoped to assemble the elements of a real literature for children. The "Leaf Story," made up of phrases dictated by six- and seven-year-olds, and "The Many Horse Stable," developed from a three-year-old's material, exemplified this method.

Lucy's proposal for a new child-centered literature was accompanied by a sharp critique of traditional children's stories. She attacked adventure tales of hunting and war, ancient sagas and myths, and especially fairy tales, as unsuitable for small children. Though such stories were accepted by parents and educators as "imaginative," Lucy argued that they violated the processes of ordered thinking and confused young children who could not understand their symbolic meaning. "The ordinary fairy tale which is the chief story diet of the four- and five-year olds, I believe does confuse them; not because it does not stick to reality . . . but because it does not deal with the things with which they have first-hand experience."[4]

Lucy claimed, further, that many of these stories were "vicious" in content. Either they were filled with brutality and violence or they represented relationships of economic and sexual inequality that could damage the development of young children's thoughts and emotions. She called for a new literature that would be not only more scientific but also more humane. Literature that was educative must "further the growth of the sense of reality, must help the child to interpret the relationships in the world around him and help him develop a scientific process of thinking."[5] She argued that stories like "Jack and the Beanstalk" delayed the grasp of physical reality by presenting a distorted picture of causal relationships. "Cinderella" and "Little Red Riding-Hood" were harmful because the one sentimentalized poverty and women's subservient role while the other was brutal and misleading about animal life. "Cruelty, trickery, economic inequality—these are experiences which have shaped and shaken adults and alas! still continue to do so. But do we wish to build them into a four-year old's thinking?"[6]

Classical myths, too, were a way in which parents dealt evasively or negatively with sexuality, depicting women as dependents or subordinates, to be given or sold to the highest bidder, rather than in relations of mutuality. Adults, "afraid of a reproducing world," fell back on such fables and on epics of sagas from remote cultures. "We grasp at them for our children," she wrote, because they

deal with great elemental human facts, life and death, love, sexual passion and its consequences, marriage, motherhood, fatherhood . . . the very things we are afraid of unless they come to us concealed in strange clothing. But what kind of a foundation for interpreting these great elemental facts will the stories of Achilles and Briseus [sic], of Jason and Medea, Pluto and Proserpina, of Guinevere and Lancelot make? What do we expect a child to get from these pictures of sexual passion on the part of the man—even though a god—and of social dependence of woman? Do Greek draperies make prostitution suitable for children? Does the glamour of chivalry explain illicit love? . . . Can we really wish to avoid a frank statement of the *positive* in sex relations, of the facts of parenthood, of the institution of marriage, of the mutual companionship between man and woman, and give the *negative*, the unfulfilled, the distorted?[7]

The war against sexual distortion, naivete, and injustice that Lucy had been waging since her Berkeley years found a new target in traditional children's literature.

Though Lucy wrote the *Here and Now Story Book* "chiefly as a protest against this confusing presentation of unreality, this substitution of excitement for legitimate interest," she did not call for rejection of fairy tales "en masse."[8] She felt that each should be judged on its own merits. Certain stories, like "The Gingerbread Man" and "The Old Woman and Her Pig," were neither misleading nor harmful, and might be given to even very young children for their pleasing patterns of language. Furthermore, children older than seven could stand a good deal of "straight" fairy lore. Having by this age acquired a firm background in reality, they would be swept away harmlessly by the imaginative flights they discovered in fairy tales.

Lucy's suspicion of folk tales was emotional as well as intellectual. They often championed the pervasive cultural ideals against which she herself had struggled—the self-sacrifice of daughters to powerful parents; the subordination of women in marriage; the rewarding of female passivity and punishment of self-assertion. Her criticisms foreshadowed those of present-day feminists who contend that fairy tales reinforce women's subordination by presenting negative female stereotypes and promoting marriage as women's sole destiny.[9]

In another sense, however, Lucy's campaign against fairy tales was directed against fantasy itself. She was reading Freud's *Psychoanalysis* in October and November of 1920, during the very time when she was writing her introduction to the *Here and Now Story Book*, so that her avoidance of any psychoanalytic insights at all in her work on children's development is striking.[10] Her theory of education, like Caroline Pratt's, gave scant attention to children's unconscious motives. Both women believed that their experimental method of learning could reduce children's inhibitions and frustrations, fostering self-sustaining initiative and motivation; but this was a far cry from such psychoanalytically oriented school experiments as Margaret Naumburg's Walden in the same period, which emphasized as key goals the creation of integrated personalities and the sublimation of destructive ego drives. Perhaps psychoanalytic models were still too new for Lucy to integrate them into her conceptual framework. But her refusal to recognize the symbolic function of fantasy in children's stories suggests a personal reluctance to recognize her own subconscious drives.

There were also social and ideological sources for Lucy's disregard of psychoanalytic concepts. Her exclusive emphasis on the material and social rather than unconscious world reflects the fundamental Progressive purpose that informed her educational objectives. Having come to grips with the question not of how people *know*—the subject of her philosophy professors' inquiries—but with how children *learn*, Lucy hoped that here-and-now learning would foster a sense of empowerment and interdependence that could lead to the "associative life" that, like Dewey and Caroline Pratt, she saw as the goal of all education. But also she was working out a theory and a practice that could offer to children what she herself as a lonely, alienated child, had always wanted: a vital linkage to what she had called, even then, "the real world." Lucy's project was creatively rooted in her own fantasy: in providing a technique and an analysis of how children could be helped to develop autonomy as well as a connection to others, she was expressing the deepest wish of her own childhood.

The *Here and Now Story Book* attracted widespread comment, not only in the world of children's education. Lucy Mitchell's daring as a theorist and practitioner of children's literature was hailed, and her stories were welcomed as both as good literature and as "scientific" pedagogy. Adolph

Meyer, chief psychiatrist at Johns Hopkins Hospital, wrote that "the principle is excellent and the execution is a great success." "Today this book is considered remarkable; tomorrow it may be considered epoch-making," wrote Elizabeth Jenkins in *The Journal of Home Economics*. "Really, this book is quite revolutionary," agreed Harold Ordway Rugg, a leading progressive educator, in *The Journal of Educational Psychology*.[11] In the *New York Evening Post*, William Carson Ryan, professor of education at Swarthmore College, called the book "a gold mine of literature for young children . . . the stories are among the most genuine things that have ever been written." Reviewing the book in *The New York Post Literary Review*, Arnold Gesell, director of Yale's program of child development, and Beatrice Gesell compared the realistic qualities of its stories to "Whitman and some of the newer poetry." Even more important, its method would give "a new impetus to creative work and artistic expression with little children. . . . If the ability to handle words, to make them into patterns, to regard them as tools of expression can be awakened at an early age," wrote the Gesells, "the whole technique of language instruction in the schools will be altered."[12]

Almost all reviewers recognized that the book would be useful to parents as well as teachers. This is "the first book I have found that puts into print the sort of story that mothers make to beguile a restless dresser, or that grandmothers tell about a little boy just like you," wrote the Reader's Advisor of the Post's *Literary Review*. "If you want to learn the secret of successful domestic story-telling to very small children get Lucy Sprague Mitchell's *Here and Now Story Book*. I have so often advised this work that I haven't the face to say over and over again how much I like it."[13]

The book found an appreciative, loyal audience in the progressive education and child development movements; even avant-garde writer Floyd Dell was effusive in its praise.[14] Its most important influence, however, was in the homes of young children. A good number of American children growing up in the 1920s and 1930s were weaned on stories like that of "Marni Moo" learning to dress herself, with rhyming refrains ("Peek-a-boo, Marni Moo, / Marni's head is coming through") the "Frog Boat Story," ("toot, toot, I'm moving"), "How the Engine Learned the Knowing Song" and others.[15]

Today, many of the *Here and Now* stories seem dated, but motifs and techniques they introduced are taken for granted in present-day children's books. Margaret Wise Brown, who studied directly with Lucy, became one of a number of prominent "here and now" writers; her classic

Goodnight Moon elevated Lucy's principles into poetic art.[16] Lucy's characters and themes are familiar ones: household animals; elements of the natural environment (trees, wind, lakes) or the built environment (roads, skyscrapers, motor vehicles and airplanes); how things work (gasoline pumps, fog boats, engines of all kinds). In some of the best of the stories children are protagonists, learning about themselves in new and unfamiliar places. "Silly Will" dramatizes the stupidity of a boy who ignores the importance of animal and plant life to humans; "The Room with the Window Looking Out on the Playground" tells of the experiences of a new girl at school; and "The New Boy," one of the most appealing stories in the book, chronicles the adventures of Boris, a young Russian immigrant, as he explores the streets and subways of the new city, seeking to link the workings of the strange new urban world with his faraway home.[17] Almost all the stories for the youngest group of children particularly, where the sound element is most dramatic, remain vivid and full of charm. Lucy's focus on direct speech and the rhythmic, patterned quality of children's language as an element that should be reproduced in children's literature is probably the most enduring contribution of the "here and now" books.

It is noteworthy that in all the stories, the child's persona and beliefs are to be respected. The world can be controlled and shaped if the child learns about its resources and makes this information his or her own. Adults are relegated to the background, although when they do appear, it is often in standard roles. A harbor pilot, an engineer, and skyscraper builders are men; a mother orders groceries. But in one story, a subway train takes women as well as men to their factory jobs. (In a later version, mothers carrying briefcases and books ride buses to their offices.)

To Lucy, the ordinary world of the here and now was full of possibilities for adventures and learning. With her career as a teacher, writer, researcher and administrator now consolidated, and with a loving, successful husband and three healthy sons and a daughter, that is how the world looked to her in 1921.

Not everyone liked the book, of course. While its emphatically child-centered approach pleased experimental educators, child-study psychologists, and some modern writers, traditional teachers and librarians defended the values of classical tales. And some critics asked whether there ought not to be "a hint, a promise, now and again of a There and a

Beyond," a world of aimless dreams and fantasies, beyond the here and now.[18] Such a dream world, reflected in the "common myths, common fables, common fairy tales, and in later life, common novels and drama," made a "thick tissue of connection between the lives of extraordinarily different people," creating a "spiritual bond" as necessary to the good life as was a "realistic" grasp of the immediate environment.[19]

In later years, Lucy became more sensitive to the criticism that the *Story Book* neglected imagination. In her preface to the 1948 edition, she noted that she had always recognized that young children were not limited to the real world, and she had used children's fantasies in many of her own stories. Now ("perhaps tardily"), she conceded that certain types of fantasies, even adult-inspired ones, might have a symbolic value for children: they could help meet children's needs for affection and success and release "vicarious" protests against adult restrictions. She felt that stories told for such a "therapeutic" purpose must be used cautiously and on an individual, rather than group, basis.[20] She stuck to her basic point that "children's imagination can and does spring from real experience in the here and now world."

In fact, neither criticisms from what Lucy called the "extreme magic" school, nor the unwelcome praise of others who invoked her theory to produce grim, literal-minded informational stories (the "extreme spinach" school), ruffled her greatly.[21] She took pride in the protests the book engendered, for they signified that it had, indeed, broken new ground. Most importantly, Lucy felt that the book marked her entry into the professional world. She recognized that her coordinating functions at the Bureau of Educational Experiments were important, but she still found the work "vicarious" and "unsatisfying." The public response to the *Here and Now Story Book* established her as more than an administrator and more than a wealthy donor or philanthropist. It did not make her feel like a real writer ("Nothing has ever done that to me," she wrote many years later) but now, at least, she felt like a "real worker."

At last I was beginning to accept myself and to be unafraid to use what talents and powers I had. Living with Robin, who believed in me and my work, had given me some personal self-confidence. But this external product—a book that was received as a serious professional contribution—gave me a different kind of self-confidence. My fumbling years were over.

At 41, she had at last begun to "grow up professionally as well as personally."[22]

"Unity"

As she became increasingly absorbed in professional work, Lucy Mitchell sought ways to maintain "unity" between her family and her career. Feminists of an earlier generation, like Lucy's mentors Jane Addams and Lillian Wald, had renounced conventional marriage and family life for the sake of their careers, but Lucy belonged to a new group of "truly modern women" who asserted, as Dorothy Bromley wrote in *Harper's* in 1927, that a "full life calls for marriage and children as well as a career."[1] Just as suffrage had been the issue that suggested a redefinition of women's roles before 1920, so in the next decade the entry of married women into the paid labor force seemed a possible, if controversial, step.[2]

But combining paid employment with family life was not much easier than it had been decades earlier. For women who could not afford household help, working outside the home entailed great family sacrifice. Although Charlotte Perkins Gilman and other reformers had long advocated cooperative child care, dining, and laundry facilities, only a handful of such services existed.

By the 1920s, moreover, a growing number of feminists had begun to agree with traditionalists that the problem lay in the very nature of the mother-child relationship. Writer Ethel Puffer Howes, stressing the importance "of mother-love in presence," insisted that the "child whose mother is not *on call* is bound to lose."[3] Howes' conclusion—that "the requirements of successful work in a profession are just those which conflict with the deepest needs of children"—was echoed in the 1920s in a rash of journal articles by women who had abandoned their careers to return full-time to domestic life.[4] Of the first few generations of educated women Howes wrote in 1925: "The more sharply focused their intellectual aims, the more completely did these seem in marriage to come to a dead end. At the worst, the professional interest was either pursued ruthlessly, to the exclusion or the neglect of family life, or dropped completely for it."[5]

To find ways to integrate women's professional and intellectual aspirations with their desires for family life, Howes established the Institute for the Coordination of Women's Interests at Smith College in 1926. Under her direction, the Institute developed a number of experimental nursery school and cooperative housekeeping programs designed to allow mothers to pursue vocational interests. The Institute collapsed after six years when it could not raise further funds, but its nursery school survived.[6]

Most married women who did work outside the home had to develop individual solutions to the problem of combining career with family life.[7] An increasingly significant contribution to these solutions was the nursery school movement, a movement in which Lucy Sprague Mitchell and Harriet Johnson pioneered. Lucy pointed out that resolving the "economic situation of working or professional mothers" was not the primary reason she and Johnson had organized the nation's first "scientific" preschool at the BEE in 1919, although she admitted that "this situation is distinctly a part of our problem."[8] Lucy Mitchell and Harriet Johnson's writings and appearances, and the extensive experimental research of the school, supported the concept of an all-day nursery school designed both as a laboratory to study child development and as an experimental school which fostered children's total growth.

The growth of the nursery movement from one or two dozen schools in a handful of cities at the start of the 1920s to perhaps several hundred schools across the U.S. at the end of the decade allowed many married women with preschool children to contemplate careers for the first time. Just as "the industrial revolution threw most workmen out of the crafts," one observer commented, the rapid rise of the nursery school movement seemed to be "the first glimmering of an educational revolution which m[ight] ultimately take most women out of the home."[9]

In some respects, Lucy Mitchell's own experience was typical of the growing number of relatively affluent professional women with children who tried to combine marriage and career after 1910. While only 5 percent of Lucy's Radcliffe class of 1900 worked after marriage, nationally the numbers of married college alumnae who continued in the work force during the 1910s and 1920s—at least until the birth of their first child, and usually after the completion of child-rearing—is estimated at between 10 and 20 percent.[10] A good number of these women were secretaries and clerical workers, but many were professional women—particularly teachers who had benefited from the relaxation of school board regulations prohibiting the employment of married workers. Lucy answered "yes" to a survey question which Radcliffe asked its alumnae in the mid-1920s—"Can a woman successfully carry on a career and marriage simultaneously? Can she if she has children?"—provided, she stipulated, that the career was not "too arbitrary" in its demands so that the woman could "meet family emergencies." She added that it was easier and more practical if the woman's career was in education.[11]

In 1926, in the belief that professional women were the "advance guard" of a larger group trying to cope with the marriage/career dilemma, New York's Bureau of Vocational Information surveyed one hundred professional women, including Lucy Mitchell, who were also wives and mothers.[12] Most respondents were well-to-do college graduates who lived in Boston or New York. Most had supportive husbands as well as the advantage of flexible hours, though two-thirds of them worked full-time. Ninety percent used household help; almost half employed two or more servants. The largest group worked as teachers; others were employed in social work, research, journalism, selling, or the arts. Lucy, identified in the study as "the executive chairman of a bureau which concerns itself with educational experimentation" was grouped with ten women who pursued "miscellaneous" occupations. It was noted that like the head of the national association for the study of child nature [Sidonie Gruenberg], she had "reached her work through her interest and activity in behalf of her own children."[13] Three other women in the study had started schools when they could find none for their own young children. And fully seventy-five of the hundred believed that the value and content of their work had been enhanced by their experience as mothers.[14]

Even among this elite group, most of whom were working not because of financial need but because of the desire for creative outlets or to answer "the vocational call," balancing the conflicting demands of family life and career proved difficult, especially where children were concerned. Only fifty-five of the hundred worked immediately after marriage, and thirty-six felt that childbearing and child-rearing had interrupted their careers significantly. Yet despite career strains and the difficulties posed by family demands, the women pronounced themselves fulfilled in their professions and family lives.[15] For most of them, a husband with an "experimental, objective and sympathetic" point of view had been crucial. "This study of one hundred women has turned out to be the story of one hundred men as well," the author concluded.[16]

For Lucy, arranging her life to include time for her husband, her children, and her work was an arduous and continuous effort. Both she and Wesley needed to realize their "imperious work drives" without neglecting the children's needs—"emotional . . . quite as much as physical." "We tried to face the situation realistically," Lucy explained, "and to plan a practical pattern that would give us a genuine group life as a family and also give a good life to each individual member—child or grownup."[17]

Though she saw her life in New York as a "four-ring circus—family, teaching, writing, research and executive work"—she believed that these interests fused into an "extraordinary personal and professional unity."[18] The center ring was her family. Second was teaching, which she began when Jack, the oldest child, was a year old and cut back to half time when there was a new baby to nurse. The third ring was writing, which grew directly out of her teaching and her life with her children. The fourth ring was the Bureau of Educational Experiments, which used the City and Country School and its own nursery school, established in 1919, as laboratories to explore children's growth. Thus, in each of the four, Lucy "carried one line of thinking." "It was a highly focused life," she asserted, "with everything concentrated on children, each aspect of my work illuminating the others."[19]

The proximity of Lucy's work to her home was important. Lucy's fortune made it possible for her to combine family quarters with her two main work places. After establishing Caroline Pratt's school on her Washington Square property in 1916, she sent her children to the school and began to teach there herself. In 1921, she sold the Washington Square home and acquired six "less pretentious" buildings, three on West 12th and three on West 13th Streets, with adjoining backyards. One building housed the BEE, and the City and Country School occupied most of the rest. The Mitchells created a large apartment for themselves from the two upper floors of the West 12th Street houses. A door from the school opened onto each floor of the Mitchell apartment; school children and teachers wandered in at will.[20]

Jack and Sprague started at City and Country when they were three years old; Marni and Arnold, at ages two and one-half and one and one-half respectively, enrolled in the first class at the BEE nursery. Lucy taught at City and Country either in the mornings or full day, and attended a constant round of meetings at the BEE. When her children were young, she could nurse the babies, lunch with the older children at home and greet them after school, while working at the school and bureau. With Wesley also participating in BEE work and teaching carpentry at City and Country School, Lucy's work became in every sense a family affair.

Moreover, both schools actively involved parents in reviewing and evaluating their children's progress. The Mitchells responded with detailed reports on all aspects of their children's behavior which they exchanged monthly with teachers. The dialogue between the Mitchells and their children's teachers was all the more intense because they lived across a corridor and a backyard from the schools. Often City and Country or BEE teachers joined the Mitchells for holiday celebrations or vacations.

The schools' interest in parent participation encouraged Lucy's tendency to carefully observe all aspects of her children's behavior. For many years, Lucy faithfully attended the monthly parents' meetings at the Bureau Nursery School and City and Country, speaking sometimes as parent, sometimes as teacher and educational theorist.

Wesley Mitchell also wrote detailed reports about the children's progress at home. Lucy took great pride in his attention to the children. When he was travelling, his frequent letters showed how deeply he missed them. His diaries, which often recorded each child's daily activities, reveal intimate participation in the children's affairs.

But Wesley's work schedule, like Lucy's, left little time for unscheduled play. He did his writing at home and was never to be disturbed in his study except for emergencies. The children could visit precisely at half-past eleven when he ritually peeled his morning apple for them to share, a tradition he had learned from his own father. In the late afternoon or evenings, he helped the children with homework, particularly languages and mathematics. On weekends and vacations he spent hours doing carpentry in his shop where the children were welcome.

Yet many years later, Lucy admitted that Wesley's singleminded absorption in his work sometimes blinded him to the children's problems. In an emergency he would do a "superb job," but she felt that otherwise he took only a partial kind of responsibility. He always talked with the children when they came to him about a problem, but he left it up to them to come, or to Lucy to explain. If one of the children or Lucy herself was ill, Wesley attended to the patient faithfully, but remained completely involved in his work nonetheless. He also underestimated work that was not desk work, Lucy felt, not really understanding what was involved in preparing meals, arranging schedules, and the like.[21] Caring for the children cut into Lucy's work time more seriously than into Wesley's. Yet for Lucy, Wesley's inattentiveness, however irritating, was a minor flaw. Overall, she felt that he was a model husband and father, truly devoted to the well-being of the children.

Lucy learned to accommodate the children's many interruptions and concentrated on managing her schedule carefully. Her pride in her powers of organization is bound up in her reminiscences with a compulsive frugality, quite inappropriate to the family's resources.

I learned to keep my hands busy most of the time. I carried my sewing with me everywhere, for I made nearly all of the children's clothes . . . and darned all the stockings for four active children and Robin. . . . I sewed steadily through all committee meetings and even invented a bag with a big wooden hoop, inside of which I could darn stockings on the subway unseen . . . I learned to do my writing by snatches and to scribble every free moment. . . . As for years I was always up at six to nurse a baby or give a bottle of orange juice, I formed the habit of going to bed to write until the family breakfast at eight. And I planned my outside work so that much of it could be done at home, though I did manage somehow to keep a half-time teaching job going with only a few weeks off for a new baby.[22]

Lucy could not have carried on her career without Mollie Cotter, the housekeeper who came with the Mitchell's first rented home and stayed for several decades. When the children were small, one parent was almost always home to bathe and feed them. Lucy also felt it important to take them herself to doctors' appointments, music lessons, friends' parties.[23] But as they grew older, Mollie often substituted for Lucy. Mollie was a warm, witty, though uneducated woman, who had been barely out of her teens when she first came to the Mitchells. In 1923, she married Paddy Casey, a handsome Irishman who had been a great football player in the old country. Mollie and Paddy went off to a ranch in Colorado for a year, later returning to the Mitchells.

In the 1910s and early 1920s, when the children were young, Lucy hired Mollie's sisters and other Irish maids to help with the housekeeping, though she boasted that she never had a nurse (or nanny) until 1918, when doctors forbade her to take care of eight-month-old Arnold in addition to Marni and Sprague, who had been stricken with influenza.

Lucy's pursuit of her professional interests would not have been possible without this entourage, which occasionally, during the children's early years, mounted to five live-in helpers. Mollie, who stayed the longest, felt that the Mitchells treated her well, though many years later, after the children were grown, there would be friction between the Mitchell family and the Caseys. In spite of the real bond between Lucy and Mollie, the gap between mistress and maid remained substantial. In the grand suffrage parades that passed by the Mitchells' windows on Washington Square, both Lucy and the maids marched, but never together. Lucy went off with the College Women's Equal Suffrage League contingent; the maids marched with their peers.[24]

The Mitchells' watchful attitudes toward child-rearing were shaped by the Progressive optimism and environmentalism of their broader world view. Although children "react and behave organically," Lucy wrote years later, "what their bodies, minds, and emotions will be like as they are growing and when they are grown, depends to an appreciable extent on how they are exercised."[25]

The Mitchells believed that to make the most of each child's potential, parents needed to create environments suited to the child's particular needs. They viewed children not as "diminutive adults" but as people with distinct traits to be nurtured in every possible way.[26] Children were complex amalgams of emotional, social, and intellectual behaviors— "whole," not compartmentalized, beings. If parents were sensitive to the cues children provided, they could support their offspring's continuing growth. Thus a constant observation of the child's development was required.

These two strands of the Mitchells' child-rearing beliefs—environmentalism, with its thrust toward social engineering, and naturalism, the holistic, organicist conception of children's growth—occasionally pulled apart. If they were to provide the best possible conditions for development, parents had not only to guide but to discipline children. Only if the children adequately met what Lucy called the "standards of maturity" appropriate to their age levels could they grow up as self-directing, creative human beings, responsible to themselves and to society at large.[27] At the same time, since development was a natural process, parents, like teachers, had to guard against imposing adult standards.

The careful notes Lucy kept during the children's early years, as well as both parents' letters to the children's teachers, reveal the confluence of controlling and libertarian attitudes. The Mitchells were capable of drastic measures if they believed the situation warranted it. When, for example, 18-month-old Arnold started biting, hitting, and scratching two-and-one-half-year-old Marni, the Mitchells produced a dramatic reform by shutting him in a wood closet. At three and one-half years, Sprague was put to bed early and "pinned in" when he refused to take his bath. Lucy once threw cold water in five-year-old Jack's face to end a screaming fit during his bath, and later spanked him after an outburst at dinner. She also occasionally imposed fines for misbehavior, a surprising reminder of Otho Sprague's hated practice, but one that seemed more effective and less drastic than force or isolation.[28]

But generally—"if there [was] time and leeway"—the Mitchells preferred to correct the children through the use of discussion and logic rather than punishment. When four-year-old Jack, for example, had an emotional outbreak after some "cement" he had been making did not harden, Lucy calmed him by explaining that water and sand never cured into cement. Then she brought home some real cement, and let him make molds to find out how it worked. Some years later, exasperated at the older boys' deliberate unruliness, Lucy instituted a "silly time" during which the children could be as foolish as they wished. On occasion, she also permitted pillow throwing. Often the Mitchells used incentives to promote their goals. For example, each child would receive the princely reward of five dollars when he or she learned to swim.[29]

While the Mitchells experimented with various methods to discourage misbehavior, they also devoted considerable emphasis to developing the children's individuality. Each child was recognized and treated as a distinct personality. Jack, more interested in "processes than people," liked to be left alone and could play happily for hours without speaking to anyone. Sprague, "charming," "alert," and "masterful," was more "preoccupied with problems of personal relations" than any other child the Mitchells knew. Marni was a gregarious, "radiantly happy" young girl who loved the outdoors, but whose "extreme susceptibility to social surroundings" worried her mother. Arnold, wilful, daring, temperamental and independent, demonstrated "eagerness over every detail of living."[30] Differences were candidly addressed. Jack's and Marni's adoptions were not hidden from the children or their classmates: at age five, Jack was told of his adoption through a playful story Lucy invented.[31] Presumably Marni learned of hers at a similar age.

The Mitchells tempered the encouragement of individuality with their insistence on the importance of cooperative behavior. They felt that the family was a less reliable arena for instilling democratic tendencies than the classroom. Lucy and Wesley were much concerned about sibling rivalry. While Wesley noted that "such struggles are an important feature of all living together, even in a family, and perhaps that natures that are gifted in this direction are best allowed to develop their powers in a rough and tumble fight for mastery," he nevertheless sought to channel the energies Sprague devoted to his relentless rivalry with Jack to more social uses.[32] This required constant alertness and consultation with teachers to promote collaborative skills. The children were also expected to share in the work of the household: cleaning their rooms, making beds, sweeping the roof, running errands, feeding the turtles, fish, and parakeet.

Though the children spent much time together, often in the usual pairs, the Mitchells tried to make sure that each child also spent time alone with a parent. Wesley usually read to Sprague and Jack together at night, for example; but when he felt the stories were more geared to Jack's maturity level than to Sprague's, he decided to read for a half hour to each boy separately. Lucy usually read or told stories to the two younger children at supper. Either parent would often take one child on a special weekend expedition—perhaps over the Brooklyn Bridge—to give him or her an "adventure."[33]

Because of her own poor health as a child and the serious illnesses of her parents and siblings, Lucy was unusually alert to health problems. She nursed any sick child personally, caring for him or her round the clock and sleeping in the child's room. The most serious and long-lasting problem afflicted Sprague and Arnold, each of whom suffered some deafness. From an early age, they travelled to Baltimore for hearing consultations, accompanied by Lucy or Mollie. Lucy worked diligently with each to improve enunciation.[34]

Marni was also sickly as a young child, and later had several stomach operations. Jack had serious back and skeletal problems in early childhood. At three, his fears of strangers, animals, and new situations seemed abnormal. Lucy took him to see F. Matthias Alexander, a physical educator whose innovative ideas attracted the attention of experimental educators. Alexander believed Jack's difficulties resulted from poor muscular coordination, and prescribed a series of exercises to correct the problem. Lucy also worked with Sprague to strengthen his spine and did exercises with Marni several times daily.[35]

The Mitchells hoped to enhance their children's self-esteem by encouraging each child's special abilities—Jack's workmanship, Sprague's social skills, Marni's talents in sports, Arnold's language ability. Even in their earliest years, Lucy wanted to ensure that no child outshine another. When as a toddler Arnold couldn't handle his toys as well as Marni, Lucy devised objects simple enough to manage without Marni's help—for example, a cape for a doll that he could take on and off easily, a basket to carry his toys.[36]

Though later the older boys commented that Arnold—little Aa— had apparently been their mother's pet, neither recalled specific instances of favoritism. All four children, they said, were treated with perfect equality. This included attitudes about sex roles. All the Mitchell boys played with dolls—in the case of Sprague, the most typically masculine and aggressive of the three boys, at least through age seven. When the children played house, Marni was often the father, one of the boys the mother. And Marni's passion for football and baseball as well as horseback riding was strongly encouraged.[37]

The Mitchells' primary goal was to develop each child's capacity to function independently. Independence meant control over the intellectual tools of learning and the emotional tools of relationship. The parents followed each child's progress in cognitive and social areas intensely. When, for example, seven-year-old Jack, previously a timid, blinking, nervous boy, suddenly demonstrated more aggressive behavior, his mother welcomed the "amazing change." Each night Wesley read to Jack from the Book of Knowledge or the Encyclopedia, after which Jack would dictate abstracts to Lucy, who would type them and put them in a book. Lucy also kept an easel with paints ready in Jack's room "so that he could paint at any time without making preparations." Thus the Mitchells tried to enrich the children's vocabularies and capacity for verbal, written, artistic and emotional expression.[38]

Although in true progressive fashion the Mitchells cherished spontaneity as well as self-mastery, the high value which they placed on growth and development meant they never left the children completely to their own resources. The duality of the Mitchell's child-rearing objectives— control *and* freedom—often led to inconsistencies in practice. One family member recalled an occasion in Marni's early teenage years when

Lucy absolutely refused to respond to a request for advice on a choice of clothing for an athletic meet. Lucy insisted that this was a decision to be made by Marni alone. Marni, distraught and disappointed, ran to the relative for comfort and suggestions. But Lucy sometimes proffered gentle hints to Marni about matters she deemed more important than dress— for example, the choice of reading material, schools, and later colleges.[39] Generally she conveyed to the children a closer interest in cognitive than in social and emotional matters.

An early photograph of Lucy with Marni, who was then about four or five years old, both dressed in identical jewelry and the identical blue-bordered gypsy-style long white dress, illustrates the paradox inherent in Lucy's views. Through she wanted the children to develop the capacity to choose freely for themselves amongst the variety of life's offerings, she could not help hoping that they would choose the intellectual system, life style, manners, and interests of their parents.

The Mitchells were less concerned with instilling proper habits of decorum than were many parents strongly influenced by Watsonian behaviorism in the late 1910s and 1920s. John B. Watson, who emphasized the force of the environment to the complete exclusion of any genetic factors, warned parents against spoiling their children through overly affectionate relations. Mothers were cautioned against kissing their children or holding them in their laps and advised to act impersonally, as they trained their children to develop regular, responsible habits. Like Watson, the Mitchells believed that human nature was modifiable, though unlike him they did not discard heredity entirely. Neither, however, did they adopt the Freudian view that a child's instincts, more than his or her environment, determined personality. And unlike the Freudians, the Mitchells regarded human nature as fundamentally peaceful, stable, and cooperative rather than aggressive and hostile. They believed that with appropriate guidance, a child would flourish, and that if enough children were raised on enlightened principles, a better society would ensue. Their views of parenting, as of schooling, incorporated both an inner, private notion of growth characteristic of child developmentalists after 1920 and a public vision of childhood common to earlier Progressive reformers.[40]

With their view of child-rearing in many respects more liberal than was common during this period, the Mitchells romanticized their relationship as companions to their children. Yet family time often gave way before professional imperatives. (On one busy day, Wesley noted in his diary that "Jack's birthday we remembered and forgot by turns, finally putting over his 4-candle cake until breakfast next morning."[41]) While many friends and relatives viewed the Mitchells as devoted and loving parents, others found them remote and detached. They were not physically demonstrative parents, though not because of Watson's influence. To some, Wesley seemed "cozier," more able to relate to young children on an immediate physical level. One friend believed that Lucy was afraid of transmitting any residual tuberculosis or pulmonary weakness to the children through close physical contact. In any event, she rarely hugged or kissed them, especially as they grew older, except for an occasional "peck on the cheek."[42]

This physical distance might have resulted, too, from Lucy and Wesley's emphasis on autonomy. Dependence in the children was to be feared as much as passivity. One episode involving Sprague, then ten, suggests how deeply the Mitchell parents believed in this credo. On vacation one summer in northern Vermont, many hours from their New York home, Sprague almost lost a thumb and finger when he got his hand caught in his father's buzz saw. Lucy boarded a midnight train and rushed Sprague to a New York surgeon. The fingers were saved, but Sprague was made seriously ill by an inadvertent dose of tetanus vaccine. During his recovery, he became emotionally dependent on his mother, with repeated outbursts of crying. In order to wean Sprague from his dependency, Lucy moved to Cambridge, Massachusetts, for some months, putting Marni in the Shady Hill School where Lucy joined the staff as a visiting teacher. The measure proved effective. That summer, when Sprague grew homesick after a month's visit to the Texas ranch of a schoolmate's grandparents, Lucy responded to his letter of distress by taking a train to Houston to meet him. As a "treat," she took Sprague, his friend, and the friend's grandmother on a sailing voyage to Key West and Havana for ten days of touring.[43]

When the Mitchell children were young, they saw their family life much as their mother intended it to be: carefree and pleasurable. But in greater or lesser degree, as they matured, they found their parents emotionally as well as physically distant. The intensity of Lucy and Wesley's parental concerns was either forgotten, or resented. Lucy conceded in later years that her determined mothering had had its limitations; yet she took pride in her ideals:

I might have been a more spontaneous mother if I had not been working so hard to find out what children were like, and how to fill their needs. I might have been a less experimental mother if I had not been constantly trying not to dominate my children's lives as my father had dominated mine and trying to share with my children as mother had never shared with me.[44]

As Lucy's wealth facilitated her professional work, so it played a large part in shaping the environment in which her children grew up. In spite of her notorious frugality about everyday things, Lucy gave the children whatever money could buy, if she felt the purchase might serve their best interests. There were frequent outings for the children and the many friends that always surrounded the Mitchell brood. Polly Forbes-Johnson, the daughter of "the Harriets," spent so much time with the Mitchells that they regarded her almost as a fifth Mitchell child. The three sons of "Aunt Marion" Farquhar, who bought a house in Greenwich Village around the corner from Lucy's, were also constant companions.[45]

As the children reached school age, the inevitable restrictions of city life and the constant phone calls and visitors led Lucy to search for some nearby weekend place in addition to a summer home in Greensboro, Vermont (to be discussed in the next chapter) where the children could have "plenty of leg room without an elaborate set-up." She found some oceanfront land a mile beyond the boardwalk at Long Beach, which the Mitchells rented for a hundred dollars a year from a development company that planned to build there at some future date: tenants were required to agree to leave their property at a moment's notice. Willing to take the risk, the Mitchells and the families of economists Stuart Chase and Karl Karstens built rough cabins far down the deserted beach.

The Mitchells' tarpaper shack was ready in October 1923. Standing on stilts above the sand, it contained a living room, three closet-like bedrooms, a dining room with two beds and extra mattresses, and a small kitchen with a kerosene stove. Fresh water was pumped by hand through a pipe that led under the beach from a fresh water lake under the ocean. An outhouse completed the plumbing arrangements. Wesley built benches and Lucy sewed cushion covers and curtains of red oil-cloth, making the cottage comfortable if not grand. For the next five years, until the company gave them notice, the Mitchells spent many fall, winter and spring weekends in their cottage by the sea.

For the children, usually accompanied by Polly and the Farquhar boys, the Long Beach excursions were the highlight of the week. Whatever their professional commitments, Lucy and Wesley tried to come to Long Beach for at least one day each weekend. Football, hockey, swimming, bicycle and horseback-riding, clam-digging, and clambakes were favorite activities. Each young Mitchell customarily celebrated his or her birthday at Long Beach, bringing some seven to ten friends out for a day. The family also enjoyed Thanksgivings at the cottage. Often there would be twenty or more to dinner (precooked in the city and carted out to the beach) crowded into the little rooms: the Mitchells, the Harriets, Caroline Pratt, the groups of children, Mollie, and the Chases and Karstens. For Lucy, the free times at Long Beach were "almost a reincarnation of Sierra days on a maturer level" for now she and Wesley had not only each other but the children.[46]

In 1927, the Mitchells had to leave Long Beach; they purchased a seventy-acre farm on the Mianus River in Stamford, Connecticut, expecting that the children might build their own homes there when they were grown. For the Caseys, who moved into the farmhouse, they added a big rear room, kitchen, and bath. The Mitchells used the front portion of the house on weekends. Often ten or twelve extra children slept over as well, joining the Mitchell four in skiing down the farm's sloping hills in winter, or, in mild weather, playing football and baseball in the meadows or swimming in a nearby quarry. In 1929, the Harriets built a small house on an acre of land bought from the Mitchells and they became a regular part of the Mitchells' life in Stamford.

With their stables of tricycles and ponies, their power tools, chemistry sets, trips to Greensboro and the Long Island shore, and many other "extras," the Mitchell children seemed to lead magical lives, their friends thought. But one boyhood companion of Jack and Sprague remembered their mother's "imperious demands" for correct behavior—"orange juice, teeth brushing at bedtime, the right companions, sleeping in the open, neat clothes, perfect speech"—which seemed less enviable.[47] The Mitchell children learned to circumvent Lucy's watchful regime, and for a time, at least, two of the boys were members of a rambunctious gang which threw missives at cars and trucks and occasionally stole items from nearby stores. ("We stole and buried the neighbors outhouse in the Mitchell's backyard as a clubhouse. Neither the neighbor nor Lucy ever knew where it went!"[48])

In general, though, the children seemed to get along well with their parents and peers. Reports from teachers described them as alert, engaging, spontaneous, happy, considerate, and indeed, independent. In 1924, Lucy wrote of her growing "grand quartet"—Jack, then eleven and a half, Sprague nine and a half, Marni seven and a half, Arnold six and a half—to her Radcliffe classmates in a "Round Robin."

Jack has always kept the luminous quality in his mind and in his face. He is equally a scientist and an artist and above all a philosopher . . . the best worker of his age I ever knew, responsible but engrossed in things rather than people.

Sprague . . . big, bursting and beautiful . . . passionately fond of all living things from his 42 white rats to the casual visitor, drains the cup of life and enjoys even the dregs. A vivid, intense child in whom responsibility is just dawning. But still in the "motor" stage.

Marni has emerged from a wee, spindly delicate passive child to a regular chairman who calls all the family to order. . . . In school she was allowed to have her "big muscle play" stage prolonged late. . . . Now she has caught up all around. She is a primrose child . . . but a primrose in trousers and overalls. Her passion in life is horses. . . . She is, I think, the most modern member of the Mitchell family.

Arnold is in the terrible transition period. . . . He is huge and very skillful with handwork. But he frankly prefers to score by virtue of strength and bulk. . . . A child with such charm that the world finds discipline difficult and still suffering from being the youngest.[49]

In the children's early years Lucy had been fearful that she and Wesley were not making "large enough personal concessions to our joint life," but in the long run she believed that despite their intense absorption in work, they had not "subordinated human values" to their professions.[50] With the help of a sympathetic husband, wealth and servants, and a career in education that related to her children's development, she was able to realize her own vision of a wholesome and progressive family lifestyle.

Lucy believed that the inevitable conflicts involved in combining marriage and career had not affected the children adversely. Indeed, she thought that insights developed in her teaching assisted her greatly as a mother. "I made many mistakes with my children," Lucy admitted. "But I believe I would have made even more without my work."[51]

Greensboro

An important component in Lucy's vision of unity was the family's compound in Greensboro, an isolated farming community in the northeast corner of Vermont. "I was happier at Greensboro than I was anywhere else," Lucy wrote. Greensboro was the "perfect place for each member of our family to live the kind of life he wanted," yet for the family to live fully and richly as a whole. For four months every year, from June through September, Lucy and Wesley could work in seclusion on books and articles, and still find time to spend with their children and with friends: their lives "touched at every point." The Mitchells came back to Greensboro every summer from their second in 1916 until 1948: it became their "one continuous home," the "gyroscope" that kept the family together.[1]

The Mitchells were introduced to Greensboro by Ernest and Agnes Hocking in 1914. Entranced with its rough beauty, they decided to purchase lakefront land. Greensboro already had an established community of summer residents—almost equal in number to the permanent population, most of whom tended the ninety or so dairy farms nestled in the surrounding hills. Fiercely independent, tough, and honest, with the typical Vermonter's dry wit and flinty integrity, the farming families were a good part of Greensboro's attraction for the "flatlanders." But its main appeal was the crystal clear, mile-and-a-half-long lake, amply stocked with Vermont trout and ringed by mountains thick with forests of spruce, cedar, balsam, and pine.[2] At 1400 feet above sea level, the lake had the highest altitude of any in the state, making Greensboro's winters long, its summers cool and delightful.

Academics and school teachers in the 1890s were among the earliest summer residents.³ One of these, Shakespearean scholar Bliss Perry, seems to have told many of his Princeton colleagues about Greensboro, for President Hibben and several deans and department chairmen established summer homes there. When Bliss Perry left Princeton for Harvard, several members of the Harvard faculty soon joined the community. In 1898, Albert Stanborough Cook, chairman of Yale's Graduate College of English, became the first Yale man to settle in Greensboro. He was followed by his colleagues Clive Day, professor of economics, Robert Corwin, director of admissions, George Parmly Day, treasurer of the university and founder of the Yale University Press, and William Ernest Hocking, professor of philosophy. Wesley Mitchell became the first Columbia professor in the community. A directory of a hundred settlements around the lake in 1915 showed that one-quarter belonged to families of university professors or school teachers, seventeen to ministers, and a fair number of others to doctors and lawyers. Greensboro in summer still has more the character of a retreat than a resort—a place for personal work and family pleasures. The shelves of its library are stocked with books written by Greensboro authors, among them John Gunther, Wallace Stegner, and Lacey Baldwin Smith.⁴

For their permanent vacation settlement, the Mitchells chose a wooded tract on the north end of the lake. The owners, a dairy farmer named Frank Chase and his schoolteacher wife, Myra, had previously refused to sell the site, fearing the intrusion of "flatland" neighbors. Apparently Wesley Mitchell's friendliness and his familiarity with farming won them over. In August 1914, for two thousand dollars, the Chases sold Mitchell three lakefront acres including woods and hilly meadowland, a long stretch of sandy beach, and Huckleberry Rocks—a narrow peninsula of tall fir trees and huge speckled granite boulders that juts a hundred yards into Caspian Lake. Lucy and Wesley determined to build the family compound on a hill a hundred feet above the point where the rocks led to the water.

Lucy had once dreamed of becoming an architect, and never lost her interest in design; she took every opportunity she could to shape the spaces she lived in. Now she went on a joyous architectural spree, designing three houses for the family's different activities. The houses were built to splendid perfection by George Fowler, a Greensboro carpenter.

Lucy set the three small houses at different levels atop a steeply sloping hill where woods rising from the promontory meet a cleared hayfield. The houses formed an open court fronting on the lake. At the highest point, in the middle of the compound was the kitchen-dining house. The two other houses faced each other at opposite ends of the semicircular layout, three hundred feet apart. One was Wesley's study; the other was the nursery house, where all the family slept. They were connected with the kitchen house by covered brick walks, or breezeways, extending from the overhanging shingle roofs of each building, supported at intervals by roughbark cedar poles. Overall, the effect was charming and rustic, a sophisticated group of cottages well suited to their functions, harmonizing with the site and each other.

To preserve the natural beauty of the setting, each structure incorporated the hillside environment. All had been built like turtles, Lucy wrote, close to the ground. The houses were of identical plan size (25' x 17'), all of rough-hewn spruce timbers, smooth on the inside, overlapping horizontally like clapboards. Wesley's one-story study, constructed from weathered spruce, had a fireplace and bookcases along the back wall. Wide, sliding barn doors opened to the outdoors. Its high raftered ceilings, tawny wood walls, comfortable natural wood armchairs and couches, and the huge bouquets of wildflowers and dried leaves that Lucy placed liberally throughout the room enhanced the working space. On warm days, Wesley drew back the doors behind his desk; on chilly days, a fire made the room cheerful and cozy.[5]

The central dining-kitchen house had foldback doors which remained open except in the heaviest rains. The brick floor of the house led to a wide veranda, where the family often ate their breakfast. Upstairs, a narrow railed gallery gave access to three small rooms where the maids slept.

At least in the first few years, Lucy and Wesley slept on the broad covered porch of the nursery house, usually with the youngest child in a bassinet. The next youngest slept in an adjacent dressing room, while the two oldest, until they acquired tents of their own, slept upstairs in a big room with sliding windows at two ends and a sloping roof on two sides. On rainy days, this large room became the playroom. The nursery house contained the only bathroom. Here Lucy bathed the babies in a folding rubber tub in front of the fireplace, over which she painted tiny figures that illustrated the stories she or Wesley told the children.

As the family's needs grew, more buildings were added. There was a boat house, and also an ice house which stored ice cut in the winter from Caspian Lake: it served as the family refrigerator until electricity came to Greensboro in the late 1920s. One of the earliest additions was a playhouse, a sort of "glorified pen," for the small children, open on all four sides with balustrade, awnings, a big octagonal sandbox in the floor, and swings hanging from the rafters. When the children had outgrown these trappings, the playhouse was turned into a bedroom for the senior Mitchells, which also served as a study for Lucy, where she wrote and painted. This comfortable room, filled with lovingly crafted objects—her "outdoors with a roof on it"—seemed the "perfect place to work."[6]

When Lucy's study was still the children's playhouse, the Mitchells built a woodshop for Wesley adjacent to it. There he worked every afternoon doing precise and highly skilled carpentry and building the original furniture that was used throughout the compound. Usually he was joined by one or more of the children, each of whom had his or her own carpenter bench.

A little stable built by Jack and Sprague, and a big barn bought by the Mitchells from the Chases in 1928, also stood on the compound. In the early 1930s, when the children were adolescents, the Mitchells converted the barn into a club house and dance floor for them, with a stable for Marni's horses. They did much of the work themselves with help from the children. Lucy then organized an association of neighborhood mothers, with every mother responsible for chaperoning two dances each season. "The Barn" became a social center for the neighborhood, its doors always open to local teenagers and their friends. Often as many as forty to fifty couples came to dance to popular music played on a victrola.

The other side of the barn housed Marni's horses, including her first Morgan horse, Ukraine, and its colt. Marni started a riding school for children and adults and organized annual horse shows. Lucy painted horses on posters, bookends, and souvenir pencils and match boxes, which were sold to provide revenue for the struggling hospital just opened in Greensboro.

In 1939, tragedy struck when the barn burst into flames. Fire trucks arrived from Hardwick much too late to save the building. The fire cost the lives of two of Marni's horses, including her beloved Ukraine, though she managed to rescue seven others. The Mitchells rebuilt the barn almost immediately, turning it into a modern stable and an office for Marni, but without a dance hall.

There was also a two-story guest house on the lake which had come with the original purchase. The Harriets and Polly stayed here almost every summer, and Caroline Pratt was a frequent guest in the early 1920s, as were Jessie Stanton and Marion Farquhar and her children. For several summers, the Alfred North Whiteheads and their daughter,

Jessie, used the cottage, joining in picnics and roasts on Huckleberry Rocks and the charades the family played in the evenings.

The Mitchell's blend of family life and professional work at Greensboro, as in the city, depended upon several maids. When the children were all preschoolers, the Mitchells would sometimes bring up three or four maids from New York, usually young Irishwomen. Most of the other academic summer people also came to Greensboro with servants, although fewer than the Mitchells. In the days before electricity, refrigeration, or plumbing, and even later, when washing machines and electric or gas ranges were still rarities, well-to-do vacationers found servants a necessity. Thursday was designated the maids' night out. Soon a ritual developed as the maids, strolling around the edge of the lake, were courted on foot or in buggies by the local men. Lucy's maids always had Sundays off as well, when they would go to the Catholic Church in Greensboro Bend, picnic with friends, or sometimes attend "kitchen dances" in the homes of beaux. Then, Lucy and Wesley would "fetch" supper by themselves.

While the children played freely along the shore of the lake, Lucy and Wesley labored steadily. Lucy usually wrote from eight to five, with, as she recalled, time out for meals, play with the children, and interruptions occasioned by "hurt knees and hurt feelings."[7] Wesley's routine never varied: breakfast in the Kitchen House at eight; then, in his study, after selecting a pipe and donning a green eye shade, he entered the previous day's activities in his diary and then got down to work. At precisely 11:30 every day, he rose from his desk, walked to the Kitchen House, and, as he did in the city, ate his apple, ceremoniously shared with the children. He usually worked again after lunch until three, and then he spent some time in the shop.

While the children ate their supper on trays in the Kitchen House, Wesley often told them elaborate serialized stories, another custom he seems to have learned from his father. One favorite series concerned the adventures of a warm, humorous veterinarian, a character very much like Mitchell's father. Another was a who-done-it series, modelled after the mysteries Wesley read voraciously. Perhaps best of all was a series about a magic car named Karnak which roamed the world. Each child took turns choosing a favorite story. But the children laughed so hard when Wesley told his stories that he would often have to start again from the beginning.

There were of course a number of activities the children shared with their parents—especially swimming in the icy lake waters, usually in the early morning and late afternoon, or shop work with Wesley. Often Lucy joined the family there, sanding, polishing, oiling, painting, and decorating the objects made by the children and her husband. Sometimes she took the older children rowing or canoeing and the younger ones raspberry picking or to see new milk machines at a neighboring farm, while Wesley played baseball with the children or took them kite-flying. Sprague's interest in golf brought his father to Greensboro's Mountainview Club, where he joined the "brain trust" composed of Deans Luther Eisenhart and Christian Gauss of Princeton and Clive Day of Yale. Clearing old trees, sawing wood, and gathering brush were also family activities, led by Wesley. The rhythm of work was punctuated by family bonfires in the meadows and corn roasts and picnics on Huckleberry Rocks and by mountain walks. Wesley characteristically noted in his diary on one such trip that he had climbed the summit in thirty-two minutes; Jack, then ten years old, in one hour, twenty minutes; Lucy, one hour, thirty minutes, with "the Harriets" huffing along ten minutes later.[8]

Greensboro allowed the adult Mitchells to incorporate family activities with their writing routines. In the country, the children hardly needed supervision. They roamed freely down dirt roads, through meadows, fields, and wooden forests, even in the shallow waters of Caspian's North Shore. It was a complete contrast with their life in New York, where Lucy's attempts to give the children greater independence were not always successful. When Jack and Sprague were about seven and five years of age, for example, she had called off the experiment of letting them play in Washington Square Park, across the street from their home, because they fell into bad company there. In Greensboro, there were few dangers, only adventures. It was magical for children; revivifying for adults. Still, Lucy could not lose herself completely in the spontaneous pleasures of the lake community. Neighbors' children, now elderly adults, who played on Huckleberry Rocks recall that she berated them harshly for disturbing her work and sometimes chased them angrily off the premises. Wesley Mitchell's genial disposition made him less intimidating to local youngsters. Nevertheless, visitors and neighbors tiptoed gingerly past his study as well as Lucy's. The Mitchell children also obeyed the rules. "Even the youngest child knew that he must not go to the study when 'Father was working,'" as Lucy put it.[9] As they grew older they were also discouraged from unnecessary intrusions upon their mother's privacy. Although Greensboro allowed opportunities for work and play as the Mitchells had hoped, the two remained more separate than Lucy's idyllic description suggests. Only occasionally did she depart from her own rigid work schedule.

The Mitchells became part of a community of families with similar lifestyles and interests on the North Shore of the lake and nearby Black's Point. They visited regularly with the Hockings and their three children, a half mile down the lake, usually canoeing back and forth. Even closer at hand were the Frank Watsons and their four sons. Frank Watson taught sociology at Haverford College. His wife, Amey Eaton Watson, older sister of Lucy's Radcliffe friend Sally Eaton Mower, taught at the Pennsylvania School of Social Work. Just off the north end lived Clive Day, who had been a member of the American Commission that negotiated the Treaty of Versailles, with his wife, Elizabeth, headmistress of the Day Prospect School in New Haven, and their two daughters, Ellen and Margaret. These families occasionally met for simple dinners—at the Hockings, the fare was never more elaborate than canned peas and salmon—or for cookouts, picnics, and water sports. On one such occasion, Elizabeth Day, an athletic woman who would regularly swim the mile from her home at Black's Point to Greensboro village, rescued Wesley Mitchell, who was close to drowning.[10]

Lucy's oldest friend among the group was Agnes Hocking. Agnes was the principal of the Shady Hill School in Cambridge, Massachusetts, which she and her husband started on the porch of their home in 1915 when they could find no suitable instruction for their young children. The Cooperative Open Air School, as it was first known, soon acquired buildings of its own at Shady Hill, a Cambridge estate, but even there its windows were kept wide open, even in zero weather, for Mrs. Hocking believed that air nourished creativity and helped banish disease germs that sapped the intellect. Daughter of the Irish poet and revolutionary John Boyle O'Reilly, Agnes Hocking was "a primal force at work," recalled writer May Sarton, one of Shady Hill's first pupils; "we never knew what would happen next, but what did happen was always immensely interesting." The core of the school was poetry. Bursting into spontaneous prayer or "noble anger," her eyes twinkling, weeping, or burning with indignation, Agnes Hocking "did" poetry all day long in addition to holding formal meetings with classes. She was "poetry incarnate," teaching it "by osmosis," showing students how to "live its life."[11]

She was devoted to her quiet, professorial husband, whom she always referred to as "Ernest Hocking."[12] In some respects, Mrs. Hocking could be quite unyielding. Because she believed in fairies, recalled a former Shady Hill student, everyone had to believe in them. Once the Hockings went to see Maude Addams in Barrie's *Peter Pan*. When, to save Tinkerbelle, Addams enjoined the audience to wave or clap their hands if they believed in fairies, Agnes burst out crying because her husband remained quiet. "You didn't wave," she sobbed.[13] A number of Shady Hill students did not enjoy the exercises of imagination Agnes required of them but were afraid to arouse her passionate anger.

Although they disagreed about many aspects of the progressive education that both espoused, Lucy and Agnes Hocking were warm friends. On the question of fairies and fairy tales, they could not have been further apart. The women argued about this and other questions during the summer months, but always without rancor.

Agnes Hocking believed that with the introduction of modern amenities such as electricity and telephones, Greensboro lost its rustic charm. Ernest wanted to remain in the country Victorian house he had built on a huge promontory of boulders overlooking the lake, but he saw the look in Agnes' eyes and could not refuse her wish to leave. In 1926, when the Hockings moved to a mountain top in central New Hampshire, which Agnes found appropriately isolated, the Mitchells lost two treasured friends, the "phoenix" and her serene, Olympian philosopher husband.

More conventional in her beliefs and personality than Agnes Hocking was her old friend, Elizabeth Day, with whom Agnes had started a short-lived open-air school in New Haven. In 1916, overcoming her husband's objections to her full-time work, Elizabeth Day bought a private high school in New Haven and became its headmistress. Mrs. Day taught English and drama at the school—renamed the Day School—and remained as principal for 22 years, until 1938. She spent much of her summer vacations working on school matters, writing romantic stories, or teaching the local children nature and animal lore. Although Day loved teaching, she worried about her daughters' health: she found that the hectic pace of both home and school life made her always tired and frequently cross, and her own children were "pathetically appreciative" of the small amount of time she could give them outside of practical needs.[14]

For many years the Mitchells' nearest neighbors were the Watsons. Amey Watson, who held a doctorate in sociology from Bryn Mawr, spent her summer writing articles on marriage and family life with her husband and doing organizational and research work for the National Council on Household Employment, which she helped found to train domestic workers and help protect their interests.[15] Mrs. Watson also served as executive secretary of the Parents' Council of Philadelphia, organized to promote child study and effective parenting. She routinely observed and recorded the behavior of her own four children, as did the Mitchells. But Lucy did not particularly like Amey, whom she found too full of psychological theories. Against her better judgment, she accepted Mrs. Watson's suggestion that they promote wrestling matches between Marni and Polly Forbes-Johnson, on one side, and Mason Watson, a tough youth several years older than the girls, on the other. Marni and Polly hated Mason and together they could beat him soundly. As she watched the two girls angrily pummelling the hapless Mason on the floor of the makeshift wrestling ring in the Mitchells' playroom, their faces distorted with rage, Lucy doubted the efficacy of authorized violence to resolve childhood hostilities. She didn't agree with Amey, who murmured, "They are sublimating."[16]

Of these North Shore professional women, only Agnes Hocking expressed regret about not being a full-time wife and mother, yet in the next breath even she would acknowledge that she wished to maintain her career. Farm neighbors were surprised at the freedom these women and their husbands gave their children and at their apparent lack of social conventions. The short swimsuits Lucy sewed for her children were much commented upon, and later, when the family of Lucy's cousin Sprague Coolidge moved next door to the Mitchells, the Coolidge children's custom of swimming naked—at a time when other children were covered to mid-calf—attracted local attention.

There were few barriers, however, between the farm families and the summer boys and girls. All the children were made welcome in the homes of farm women like Myra Chase, where they were plied with homemade doughnuts, pickles, pies and fresh unpasteurized milk. In years to come, the children remembered the friendly kitchen and warmth of Mrs. Chase with great fondness. Mrs. Chase, head teacher at the village school, was a working woman who kept abreast of the latest educational and psychological theories and eagerly read the books with which the Mitchells supplied her. Small, wiry, "keen," and "spicy," Mrs. Chase reminded Lucy of her quick-witted Aunt Nan. She and her more slow-going country husband were like grandparents to the Mitchell children.

Marni, in particular, developed a strong attachment for Frank Chase. When once Lucy embroidered some flowers on a pair of her overalls, Marni protested, sobbing, "Now I won't look like Mr. Chase."[17]

Some of the Mitchell, Hocking, Day, and Watson children, looking back in later years at their own mothers, compared them unfavorably to Mrs. Chase or Peggy Coolidge, the warm, perceptive wife of Sprague Coolidge, to whom the Mitchells sold some land in 1928.[18] The Coolidges built a simple wooden house next door to the Mitchells with a magnificent view of the lake, where they would spend every summer with their four children. Sprague Coolidge, a chemistry professor at Harvard, delighted Greensboro children with his collection of model trains and the railroad he built on the boulders near the Coolidge yard. His elaborate fireworks displays and the trolley and roller coaster he built out onto the lake also entranced them.

Coolidge's presence enlivened the local political scene as well. Before the 1936 election, Bliss Perry and Louis Kesselman, a well-read Greensboro tailor, socialist and lone Jew, organized a political forum where representatives of the three parties debated.[19] It was easy to find Republican spokesmen in Greensboro, and Sprague Coolidge, an avid Socialist, did brilliantly for his cause, but Democrat Crane Brinton had to be imported from Peacham.[20]

To the Mitchells, the Coolidges were a welcome addition to Greensboro. Peggy Coolidge admired Lucy enormously, even though she sometimes felt that Lucy and Wesley, a generation older than the Coolidges, wanted them as their Greensboro neighbors in order to help care for their teen-age children. And, indeed, Peggy was often available to the Mitchell children when Lucy and Wesley were not. The children responded affectionately to Peggy's warmth and friendliness as they did to Mollie Cotter and to Lucy's friends Harriet Johnson and Jessie Stanton, who also spent a great deal of time with the family every summer. When the Mitchell children grew to adulthood, they would complain of their mother's absorption in work, her high standards, willfulness, and strong character, just as some of the children of her North Shore neighbors were similarly critical of their mothers.[21] Yet whatever their shortcomings, these mothers were universally praised for providing their children with the experience of Greensboro. Each thought that in Greensboro, as children, they had found a little bit of paradise.

A Scientist by
Conviction

For Lucy and Wesley Mitchell, the 1920s were a period of rapid professional growth and unremitting work toward their respective experimental
"visions." Wesley Mitchell had emerged from his wartime work more
convinced than ever of the need for rational economic planning. The
war had revealed the grave deficiency of the government's normal economic controls and had shown that an orderly and efficient economy
could be organized under emergency conditions.[1] Urging that the lessons
learned in war should be applied in peacetime, Wesley devoted his energies to three new organizations designed to foster cooperative research in
the social sciences and to lay the groundwork for national planning efforts. They were the New School for Social Research, the National Bureau of Economic Research (NBER), and the Social Science Research
Council (SSRC). He was the only person who served as a founding member of all three organizations.

The New School was originally organized by Mitchell's colleagues
James Harvey Robinson and Charles Beard, following the latter's resignation from Columbia University over the issue of free speech. Wesley was
asked to serve on the distinguished faculty, which eventually included
his old teacher Veblen.[2] He told Lucy that the "geniuses" on the faculty
(among whom he did not include himself) would be as "hard a team to
drive" as the BEE's Working Council, but he had high hopes that the
school's interdisciplinary research in the social sciences could be a potent
force in public policy.[3] He joined Beard, Robinson, Alvin Johnson,
Herbert Croly, and Emily James Putnam in planning the school as a re-

search institute and an experiment in teaching: serving a student body of
adult professionals, it had no formal requirements, curriculum, or degrees. Though Wesley taught at the New School for only three years before returning to Columbia (he preferred to teach graduate students who
could be expected to contribute to the theory of economics), he served as
treasurer and as a member of its Board of Directors for many years.

In 1919, Wesley and three colleagues launched the National Bureau of
Economic Research. The NBER was to be an "intelligence service" or
"fact-finding agency" which would collect and analyze comprehensive
data about income, prices, and labor. Wesley hoped that such an organization would provide voters with the knowledge needed to make intelligent decisions about complex problems. As the Bureau's director of research for over twenty-five years, he was responsible for establishing and
implementing basic policies. Under his leadership the NBER launched an
ambitious investigation into the amount and distribution of income in
the United States. Unanimously adopting the final report, the Bureau's
twenty directors—including a socialist, banker, labor leader, manufac-
turer, farm expert, and three economists—fulfilled Wesley's hope that
social science research could serve as a unifying force.[4]

In addition to income studies, the NBER undertook group research
projects on business cycles, labor markets, commodity prices, industrial
productivity, consumer spending, the finances of government, and international economic relations. Though Wesley continued his independent
investigation of the money economy—he published a monumental second volume on business cycles in 1927—in certain respects, the cooperative research of the NBER became his life work.[5] He was the formative
influence at the Bureau, responsible for selecting and coordinating staff
members and research projects. His scrupulous standards, coupled with
his unfailing courtesy, generosity, and sympathetic guidance provided inspiration to dozens of young colleagues. Not only Bureau members but all
manner of economists, social scientists, business and labor leaders, and
government officials eagerly awaited his annual report to NBER directors;
it was always an absorbing discourse on the major economic phenomena
of the times. By the end of the twenties, Wesley's work at the Bureau, so-
lidifying his continuing researches into business cycles, had made him
the foremost spokesmen of those who sought a realistic approach to economic life based on the systematic analysis of quantitative data.[6]

Wesley also played an active role in the Social Science Research

Council, founded in 1922–23. Devoted to promoting interdisciplinary researches in the social sciences, the SSRC established research projects and fellowships in such areas of study as agriculture, business, consumption, criminology, culture and personality, family life, interracial relations, and population. Every summer for a period of a week to a month Council members and invited guests attended its annual conference in Hanover, New Hampshire. Lucy Mitchell often accompanied her husband to this event.

Wesley served the SSRC in many capacities. In 1923 and 1926, he was a Council member representing the American Economic Association; from 1927 to 1931, he represented the American Statistical Association. Following the term of office of the Council's first Chairman and chief organizer, political scientist Charles Merriam, Wesley served as chief executive officer, from 1927 to 1931. He was also treasurer, and a member of the Executive Committee, the Committee on Problems and Policy, and the Advisory Committee on Population. For over a quarter of a century, he played a leading role in developing the intellectual bases of the Council's work and implementing its program of interdisciplinary cooperative analysis in the social sciences.[7]

Like Wesley, Lucy was full of hope about the potential of social science to promote social progress during the postwar period. Her interests and his were distinct, but she believed that they shared goals and scientific methods.

From the beginning, he and I had the same broad end in mind—the betterment of social organization. And we both believed in the same means of accomplishing that end—a scientific study of human beings and their behavior. His work and that of his coworkers was to try to change socially harmful cultural patterns within our money economy . . . in the light of new knowledge . . . that had come from scientific investigations. . . . I [was] a member of a widespread group of pioneers who were working on a scientific approach to social reorganization in the field of educational research.[8]

Though Lucy acknowledged that she was not a scientist by "training or temperament," as was her husband, in her work at the BEE she became a "scientist by conviction," supervising an elaborate research effort to collect data on children's growth. "I was a child of the times," Lucy recalled, "and joined the movement to make education of children a science of human behavior."[9]

The Bureau of Educational Experiments, the joint creation of the Mitchells and Harriet Johnson, reflected the buoyant hopes of its founders in the possibilities of social reconstruction. In his monumental study *The Transformation of the School: Progressivism in American Education, 1876–1957*, Lawrence Cremin suggests that after World War I the progressive education movement, increasingly cut off from its connection with social reform, branched out in two distinct directions: towards educational measurement and scientism, on the one hand, and toward expressionism or Freudianism on the other.[10] The BEE attempted to merge these currents in the tradition of what Joseph Featherstone has termed a "high romantic mediation."[11] In 1919, it launched a nursery school for children aged fifteen months to three years, joined it to Pratt's City and Country School for children aged three to seven, and added an eight-year-old class, taught directly by Bureau staff. This was the base for a comprehensive "experimental laboratory program": for the next decade, the BEE's research into quantitative indices of children's growth and behavior at these schools coexisted somewhat uneasily with Dewey-inspired reform goals and child-centered, expressive curricula.

The principles on which the BEE program operated were those to which most progressive schools subscribed.[12] Emphasis on growth and the developmental needs of the individual child was central. "We think of a school as a place planned from the point of view of the children's growth," Lucy wrote.

We should call a school environment "good" if it permitted a child to expand in accordance with what we know of the laws of growth, whether physical, mental, emotional or social. And we should call an environment "bad" if it did not give scope for such natural expansion. . . .[13]

The multiple aspects of children's growth—physical, mental, emotional, and social—were to be promoted by ample opportunities for experimentation. They would depend

upon full experiencing and free expression of that experience. What experiences will be given to them the children will in a large measure determine for themselves through their inquiries. . . .[14]

While many progressive schools shared the belief in childcentered, experiential learning, Lucy thought that few actually put it into practice.

What was to be different in the new BEE laboratory school would be the actual school set-up, the "intentional environment" planned by the school for its pupils.

The translation of experimental ideals into practice, even for children as young as fifteen months old, would be ensured by linking schooling directly to scientific research. "We sought to give our children from the youngest up, a full life of rich experiences and an opportunity to function in and through these experiences," Lucy recalled. The problem "was to find out what a full life is, physically, mentally and emotionally," all the way up the age scale. It was thus necessary "to make an unbiased, scientific study of children, their nature and their growth." Research findings would be used to construct a school environment responsive to children's needs, and hopefully these results would be implemented beyond the laboratory, in public education.

This, I take it, is what we mean by a laboratory school. Both the scientific data assembled through our research and the practical experience we gain through out experiments within the school we wish to make immediately available to other workers in the field and the general public. Furthermore, we think of all our work ultimately in its relation to public education. We wish to keep constantly in mind and to be ready to attack whenever there seems to be a real opening those unsolved social and administrative problems of the public schools which will need attacking before anything we may work out in our laboratory school can be made effective.[15]

Before BEE staff could establish interrelations between psychological, intellectual, and physical growth, data had to be assembled on each type of development, since with few exceptions, no norms had been established. Systematic measurements of various aspects of growth in a large number of children taken over a consecutive number of years could be used to establish age-graded norms of children's development and ultimately to modify classroom practice.

We were working on a curriculum, checking it by our growth records; and working on how to record growth, evaluating our records by the children's reactions to our planned environment. . . . We were perforce recording growth of parts of children; but we were living with whole children so that each half of our thinking constantly served as a check for the other half.[16]

As chairman of the BEE Working Council, Lucy coordinated the diverse aspects of the laboratory school program. Harriet Johnson, the director of the nursery school, led its efforts to work out an educational environment for infants and toddlers. Harriet and Lucy believed that the study of preschoolers would help provide answers to the larger questions of how children grow and would perhaps lead to changes in teaching involving older children.

Lucy always thought of Harriet Johnson—whom she and Wesley affectionately called "John," to distinguish her from Harriet Forbes—as her "closest friend" and "greatest teacher." Enthusiastic and intelligent, with a "rare imagination" that kindled the imagination of others, she was the "perfect co-worker."

To Harriet, you could talk half thoughts or crazy thoughts. . . . She would soar with you into the stratosphere, but when she came down from those breathless flights, she always landed on her feet. . . . "I've an idea!" she would say. "Time to talk?" We talked, always we talked, about everything, about job, our children, the world.[17]

Lucy felt that Harriet was especially suited by "training and temperament" to understand young children. "Keenly alive to their emotional needs," she constantly adjusted the nursery school environment to encourage their development.[18] Above all, she sought to foster the growth of healthy, creative, autonomous youngsters. "The nursery school is an attempt to scale civilization down to the child level in its behavior demands and to open up wider opportunities for active exploration than an adult world can afford," Johnson explained in her book *Children in "The Nursery School"*, published in 1928.[19] She believed that other institutions for preschool children had been organized as laboratories which dealt with "all manner of behavior problems from tantrums to stealing" rather than as schools where children initiated their own activities.[20] The uniqueness of the BEE nursery school lay in its emphasis on self-direction and the deliberate steps it took to keep adults in the background. It was a place where children could "go native."[21] Yet the teacher was not to be passive. Through her continuing observations of children, she developed a solid body of data to be used in constructing the school's learning environment. She provided materials (wagons, shovels, and blocks) and activities that actively facilitated children's experimentation and supported their social explorations. Johnson's special contribution came in the elaboration of the concept of play: whereas Pratt focused on plain wooden blocks as the basic units a child could use to imaginatively explore the world, Johnson explained that the child used blocks as an art form, mastering techniques in a developmental sequence.[22]

The skill of Harriet Johnson made possible the close integration of re-search and schooling at the nursery school. Johnson pioneered the devel-opment of sustained, observational studies of young children, though she did not conduct experiments with specific hypotheses to be tested or with matched control groups.[23] She was one of the first educators to write down the spontaneous remarks of children in a group and to analyze them as a basis for planning curriculum. Her staff "lived with pencil and pad in their pockets, prepared for running comments."[24] Teachers col-lected a daily record of each child's physical habits, emotional upsets and relations to other people; a diary of daily activities, and for each child, a record of one full day each month, including verbatim speech records and descriptions of all activities.

Detailed physiological records were also kept. Routine examinations, including measurements of height and weight, were administered to all nursery and City and Country children. Supplemental medical examina-tions, including annual stool and urine tests as well as eye tests, electro-cardiograms, chest X-rays, schematograms of posture, measurements of wrist spans, and studies of teeth, were also conducted. Edith Lincoln, the Bureau physician, hoped that she would be able to determine the physio-logical age of a given child by analyzing these records over a period of years.

Psychological testing and record keeping were elaborate. The chief Bureau psychologist, Johns Hopkins-trained Buford Johnson, and her as-sistant, Louise Schriefer, conducted personality tests on individual City and Country children, which included age-level tests, such as the Stan-ford revision of the Binet scale, and the Pintner-Patterson performance tests, as well as specific tests of motor coordination and associative pro-cesses. Special studies in such subjects as fears, fatigue, and the develop-ment of muscular coordination (through motion pictures, a pioneering approach) were also conducted. Lucy remarked that the Bureau's labora-tory findings "threw as much light upon the tests as they do upon the children."[25]

Social records that included information about each child's early de-velopmental history and present social and physical environment were gathered. Full family histories were also developed with those parents who were interested in cooperating. The aim was to secure a develop-mental history of each child (as well as its siblings) which would include hospital measurements at time of birth, an account of the child's summer and winter home environments, a personality study of parents (to include occupations, interests, and social affiliations), and records of grandparents' health and "racial-genetic" histories. At various times, specialists were called in to give advice about the technical aspects of research. From Columbia, there were Wesley Mitchell's colleagues Franz Boas and Robert Woodworth, whose works in anthropology and psychology the Mitchells read together with enthusiastic interest. Boas came as a consultant to interpret all physical measurements, while Woodworth advised the Bureau on the relationship of physical to psychological measurements. Dr. Milo Hellman was called in to help organize a report on the records of teeth.

Few other progressive schools organized such detailed record keeping and observational research, joining specialists in medicine, psychology, and social behavior with classroom teachers in an all-out data-gathering effort.[26] In the late 1890s, Dewey's Laboratory School at the University of Chicago had related curriculum practices to stages of children's growth, but at none of these schools was there a concentrated attempt to conduct active, ongoing research within the school setting, to measure stages of growth, both mental and physical, and to relate each aspect to the other and to school programs.[27]

The Bureau's study of children's growth paralleled university-sponsored child-development research in the 1920s more closely than it did progressive school programs. Even though Bureau members considered themselves more akin to the progressive education group than to child-study people like Arnold Gesell, the Bureau's emphasis on measurement recalls G. Stanley Hall and his disciples rather than Dewey. Gesell, a student of Hall, had begun his research at Yale into norms of development in children from one month to five years of age in 1918. Other child-research programs followed rapidly.[28] The movement received its greatest impetus in 1924 when the Laura Spelman Rockefeller Memorial established university-based research centers on children's growth at Teachers College at Columbia University, and at the universities of Berkeley, Toronto, and Minnesota.[29] The Memorial's purpose was to promote scientific research on child life, but an equally important aim was to train practitioners to disseminate this information to parents, particularly mothers.[30]

Yet there clearly was a difference between the Bureau's efforts and those of these research centers, a difference that went beyond the fact that many of these programs studied only the preschool period while the Bureau's research extended to school-age children. "We cover a field not touched by the other laboratories," Lucy Mitchell wrote in 1925 to the Laura Spelman Rockefeller Memorial Fund.

We differ from Gesell in that we are not primarily interested in testing children. We are primarily interested in observing natural behavior in situations planned for children's development. . . . Our situation for observation has been much less invaded than has Baldwin's [at the Iowa Child Welfare Research Station], that is, it is more adequately educational. . . . His school, as far as it has a consistent philosophy, stands for training. . . . The Detroit school is organized for the training of mothers and teachers; the study of growth is incidental. With us, the working out of a consistent environment giving children the fullest possible opportunities for development is paramount.[31]

Only the BEE aimed to study children's growth "scientifically" and to use the data collected to plan the school environment deliberately, not to train parents or children. Growth as the BEE defined it was not to be discovered solely by "testing," nor could it be correlated with "training." Rather, growth involved observing and fostering "natural behavior." An anecdote Lucy Mitchell was fond of telling indicated that hers was a more organic, qualitative conception than that of most child development research institutes.

The early institutes were organized to follow methods that had been used in the physical sciences, that is, to take exact measurements of children, and what could not be measured was simply left out. They began with physical measurements since these seemed the simplest to make. Even here they ran into difficulty. One instance was really very striking—when the research institute in Iowa wanted to measure children's physical growth, the children wiggled and they would appear to grow one day and shrink the next—so the research staff put the children into casts in order to measure them. They knew the children wiggled, but wiggling seemed unimportant because it couldn't be measured. And they knew that it was an emotional strain for the children, but you couldn't measure that, so that was disregarded. Science ought to be obeyed, and science has measurements. Now, we cared, really, more about the wiggle and the emotional strain than we cared about the physical growth.[32]

While Buford Johnson was inclined to observe "what was quantifiably measurable and let the rest go," Lucy believed that her own work and that of Harriet Johnson provided a counterbalance to the staff's anthropometric tendencies. Harriet was "thoroughly scientific, always pushing for evidence, always open-minded, experimental, always re-examining her practices in the light of new evidence," Lucy noted. "Yet she was humanly warm with children, full of delight at their ways, humorous and playful with them, a true companion as well as a profound student of little children."[33] In spite of their respect for scientific testing, both women believed that "it is more important to know if a child is growing than his exact measurements in body, I.Q. and social adjustments."[34]

The Bureau of Educational Experiments came to occupy a unique place at the intersection of the child development and progressive education movements, even though its primary identification lay with the latter. Drawing from both Dewey and Hall, as well as from the trends in anthropometric and psychological research of the 1920s, the Bureau had much in common with leading progressive schools and the main currents of child-development research. Yet in its entirety, it resembled neither.[35]

The eclectic mix of educational and research styles that characterized the Bureau in its first years reflected the drive for cultural synthesis that characterized Dewey's writings. Part of the explanation, however, surely comes from Harriet Johnson's special qualities as well as from Lucy Mitchell's combination of rationalism and feeling, her prior experiences in testing and teaching, and the practical and intellectual lessons she had learned from Wesley Mitchell over the years.

In 1925, Lucy Mitchell expressed for the first time her growing concern that perhaps research and educational functions should *not* occupy an equal place in the Bureau's concerns.

There has emerged . . . a sense that the Nursery School is primarily an educational endeavor, as the City and Country School has always frankly been and that a Nursery School run by the group which constitutes the present Working Council would always be. . . . Whether this educational setting of Nursery and City and Country School affords the research staff the best opportunity they can obtain for the study of growth which is the chief endeavor of every member of all the groups is a question which must be clearly and definitely answered. . . . If it is answered negatively, some new line-up of work may seem wiser, splitting off certain research aspects which might ally themselves with other and differently organized research.[36]

By this time, Bureau specialists had gathered massive amounts of material about the children in its two schools. For about sixty-five children, there were consecutive five-year records detailing social behavior, physical and psychological measurements, language usage, and so forth. In many instances, case studies of individual children ran to one thousand pages or more. It was not unreasonable to begin to reexamine the original premise of the BEE undertaking: Could specialists, working together in a systematic reappraisal of the varied aspects of children's growth, develop age-related norms that could be implemented in the educational environment?

The question was, in fact, whether relationships between physiological and mental data and behavioral material would emerge merely because experts from disparate disciplines were studying the same children. The Working Council directed psychologist Frederick Ellis to conduct a study of how the records collected over the course of the Bureau's first decade could best be integrated and used as a base for educational planning. The council also formulated a five-year research plan, three years of data collection and two of assessment, the goal of which was the formulation of a model of relationships between physiological age and behavior. Until a decision could be reached at the end of the five-year plan as to whether the Bureau school as it was provided the best opportunity for such research, or whether "some new line-up of work might seem wiser," data collection was to be continued on a diminished scale. Though annual reports of the Bureau for 1926 through 1930 are not available, Lucy indicated later that she believed the Bureau's long-term effort to establish norms of growth ended in failure. The Bureau did construct a developmental chart of the physical growth of children from fourteen months through eleven years, but she felt that the product was unsatisfactory. Physical growth, which had first seemed to be most measurable, proved in fact as unquantifiable as social and emotional behavior. Only bones and teeth yielded satisfactory growth sequences; the growth of organs and digestive and nervous sytems could not be subjected to even gross measurements. The Bureau's work seemed to support a theory of "segmental growth"—that the greatest growth impulse appeared successively in different parts of the body—but this hypothesis formed merely "a hazy background" to the Bureau's thinking. "It was a limited and unsatisfactory picture of physical growth that emerged as a background to relate to other kinds of growth," Lucy admitted.[37]

The construction of indices of psychological growth also suffered. Ellis' analysis of intelligence records over a span of years showed that IQ was a composite of different abilities affected in part by a child's home situation. Later Lucy observed that his findings "changed our attitudes toward learning. Growth in an individual became more important than his actual achievement." Yet Ellis abandoned the whole five-year project because certain tests were not given to every child during one school year, and no results were ever published.[38] Lucy and Harriet Johnson remained hopeful that Wesley Mitchell's techniques for studying cyclical economic behavior might be applied to the BEE's growth measurements, but such a direct application of Wesley's methods apparently failed.[39]

Lucy believed that it was not until a brilliant young woman named Barbara Biber came to the Bureau in 1929 to work under Ellis that progress was finally made in determining psychological relationships between age and behavior.[40] Biber worked on a study of children's drawings, while two other young psychologists made studies of block building and children's language. Biber's contribution was to group drawings in stages of development, with accompanying descriptive analyses. Her methods made it possible to handle materials that could not be translated into numerical terms, and allowed for more realistic depiction of maturity levels. "At last THE CHILD became a small person interacting with his environment," Lucy wrote years later, "a complex organism behaving in certain characteristic ways . . . as he passed through stages of his development." The Bureau now had a technique of studying growth as a series of progressive stages, or maturity levels, that could be described unambiguously in qualitative terms. Bureau psychologists were no longer simply measurement-minded but, as Lucy explained it, "used laboratory tests to illuminate and clarify the behavior which they had themselves observed and recorded in the classroom."[41]

By the end of the 1920s, the Bureau was ready to abandon its faith that anthropometric measurement and intelligence testing could provide functional indices of children's growth to guide educational planning. The correlation of physical with mental and emotional growth had turned out not to be amenable to statistical treatment. Moreover, Lucy Mitchell had come to fear that the formulation of exact standards of normal growth might in fact distort individual variations in development and lead to the promulgation of mechanistic, rigid norms, which could deaden rather than enhance children's impulses to learn. Such a set of norms, furthermore, was not essential, as she had once believed, to a creative educational environment. Ironically, just as the Bureau was rejecting a research model based on quantitative techniques, most of the new child-development institutes funded by the Rockefeller Memorial were organizing along these very lines. These researchers sought to distinguish their work from the "pseudo-scientific" techniques of Hall's earlier child-study movement through research based on precise observation, controlled evaluation, and careful quantitative techniques. By mid-century, however, many of these researchers were asking themselves the same question Lucy Mitchell was posing as the 1920s drew to a close: Was the tabulation of growth norms for children feasible, and more important, to what use should such norms be put?[42]

For Lucy Mitchell, the Bureau's movement away from narrowly quantitative research at the end of the 1920s was personally as well as professionally significant. Lucy's ideas of social research had been deeply influenced by her husband, who perhaps more than any one else had been responsible for moving economics onto the path of empirically verifiable, quantitative research. To some critics, indeed, the "high priest" of institutional economics—the "prophet of facts and figures"—seemed to go much too far in his emphasis on quantification.[43] While they recognized that he combined factual investigation with theoretical reasoning, they pointed out that Mitchell's assurance that quantitative research would lead the way to social progress rested on faith rather than science.

Wesley Mitchell was never to relinquish his progressive trust in the benevolent utility of social research. As he expressed it, the scientist "does not delude himself into believing that anyone's personal experience is an adequate basis for theorizing about how men behave." What was necessary to the firm foundation of knowledge and to social change was the subordination of theory and practice to facts derived from the systematic investigations of "history, statistics, ethnology, psychology," and other disciplines.[44]

Lucy Mitchell, who came to quantitative science by "conviction," not by training, observed in later years that "qualitative analysis of behavior is as scientific as quantitative measurement."[45] By the end of the 1920s, though she still considered the Bureau's work to be scientific, Lucy had formulated a new pedagogy founded on precisely that "personal experience" which had so often guided her in the past.

A World of
Relationships

While guiding the research policies of the BEE through the 1920s, Lucy Mitchell continued to produce innovative works for children, all of them linked to her teaching and all of them, like her first book, founded on "here and now" principles. Writing had always been part of her "proto-plasm," she once declared.[1] In her forties, in writing about children's development, she gained the creative satisfaction that had long eluded her. Lucy addressed some of her books to adults, but for the most part they were not scholarly or scientific. She much preferred writing for children to writing about them. Teaching children and writing for them had "always gone together" for Lucy, so that her writings invariably had a didactic purpose, grounded in the "here and now" principle of relating children to the world.[2] Paralleling the development of her own children as they grew out of the pre-school and primary years during the 1920s, her new writings entered "here and now" realms more appropriate to older children: especially history and geography, or what Lucy called "human geography."

After the publication of *The Here and Now Story Book* in 1921, Lucy suffered a severe bronchial illness. Worn down by her busy work schedule, she contracted what doctors diagnosed first as pleurisy, then as tuberculosis, and finally as pneumonia. Large scars were found in her lungs, indicating that at some point she had had undetected tuberculosis. Active TB—the dread of her childhood—became an immediate threat, forcing Lucy into a severely reduced work schedule. She spent the next few months resting in a glassed-in room specially built on the roof of the West Twelfth Street house, away from her family and active work. Cut off from her pupils, and fearful of too frequent contact with her own children, she turned to reading and thinking about geography, a subject that had long interested her. She began to develop an approach to "human geography"—the study of the effects of geographic forces on people's lives.[3]

Lucy's sense of the environment had been a potent factor in her learning since her childhood, when she wandered alone to the Chicago lakefront and explored neighborhood streets. At the University of California and at Pratt's school, trips around the city had been favorite learning activities for her students. Her strong sense of place underlay the theory of her "here and now" work as well. She was dismayed that most schools relied on rote memorization of facts, like the capitals of states and countries, to teach geography, while history called up a series of unrelated facts about past societies. While certain progressive schools dealt with history and geography more dynamically by providing historical source materials, Lucy felt that their curricula were still "vicarious." At the Shady Hill School in Cambridge, for example, the development of historical cultures was studied sequentially, beginning with "primitive" peoples: Eskimos, Indians, then nomads, Vikings, Greeks, and so on. With such a schedule, she noted, they would reach their own environment—Boston—only at age twelve.

Lucy believed it was wrong to begin with "the logically simplest civilization and the logically simplest geographic situation."[4] She urged teachers to help children understand relationships in their immediate environment before turning to remote cultures. "If children can glimpse the world around them as a stage in the world's history and geography," she wrote, "they become to that extent, geographers and historians. They have acquired a method which will give meaning to all facts, however far-away or long ago."[5] "Relationship thinking" was the key to her method—an awareness of the relation of the past to the present and of the interactions between people and animals, natural forces and processes. To foster such thinking in children, she developed two types of materials: specially constructed maps, and original stories which demonstrated the interaction between culture and ecological change.

In 1924, when tensions with Caroline Pratt were high, Lucy took a leave from the City and Country School to learn about map-making by participating in the surveys of the American Geographic Society. She spent months wandering the streets, meadows, and dumping grounds of Long Island City, charting buildings, stores, public utilities, and other structures. Then, to understand how these social constructions were dependent on the environment, she superimposed on them various transparencies of population settlement and natural geographic features. She claimed in *Two Lives* that this technique correctly predicted key patterns of future growth.[6]

Lucy brought a variation of this mapping approach back to the classroom, substituting "tool maps"—maps for "active use"—for standard demonstration school maps. Her first maps for children from eight to twelve were large graphic relief maps, painted in oils on oilcloth with pictorial symbols indicating land forms—mountains, hills, plains, rivers, harbors, etc. The children worked with these maps on the floor, travelling in imagination across the terrain, discovering relationships between the various "earth forces" and people's use of them, and adding painted imagery of their own to the oilcloth background. A typical assignment involved a group of nine-year-olds using tool maps and other primary source materials—pictures, old diaries, stories—to study westward migration in the nineteenth century. Given a starting point at Independence, Missouri, they were asked the "pioneers' problem"—to find the best route across the continent to Oregon or to California.

From photographs or pictures, from accounts of pioneers, the children worked out answers to these questions and inevitably in the same way that the pioneers worked them out. And as they worked out the answers, in show-card water colors, they painted the string of covered wagons following the Platte River, painted grass on the plains getting shorter and scarcer as the pioneers got nearer the mountains, painted buffalo, deer, wild birds for food, trees near the rivers, Indians in the offing. They lived the lives of those people in covered wagons on the plains, fording the rivers, leaving treasured furniture on the banks, camping with covered wagons in a ring as protection against the Indians. They went up through South Pass through the Rockies with pioneers. They hunted for water holes as they crossed the great high dry regions. Up again into the Sierra. Here they were caught in the snow. They chopped down trees. Their food gave out. They were rescued. They came down into the warm wonder valleys of California.[7]

Seeking relationships between different ecological and social elements, students learned by active engagement with primary materials.

The same pedagogical approach was used in a series of books for children and teachers published in the 1920s and 1930s. First came *Horses Now and Long Ago* (1926): nine stories, each followed by related poems and ballads, most of them Lucy's own, descriptions of geographic and historical settings, and maps and illustrations. The book reversed the usual presentation of historical material; it led from the known to the less familiar, from twentieth century farm and trail horses, to delivery horses in the 1890s, to pack horses making the westward journey in the 1840s, to Texas horses in 1800, to Spanish horses before colonization of the New World.

The entire family enjoyed this book, perhaps more than any of her others. Wesley had helped find resource material, read works in geography aloud with Lucy, and, as always, commented on the manuscript. Lucy had chosen horses because she felt that their development demonstrated the importance of environmental forces more clearly than did human culture, but also because most children seemed interested in horses. Her own children were all riders, particularly Marni, who at age three had become entranced with a neighborhood pony. For years, Marni pretended that she was a pony, imitating its sounds, behavior, and feelings. Lucy dedicated the book to her own "four horsemen" and included a picture of each child on horseback as its frontispiece.[8]

Mitchell's next work in human geography, *North America: The Land They Lived In for the Children Who Live There* (1931), was organized in the same way, from the immediate environment to more distant ones, and drew on Lucy's talents as storyteller, mapmaker, illustrator, and poet. The book introduced children to the environments of the North American continent through action-oriented stories, largely about work, but sometimes with animal characters. Information was subordinated to the appeal to "sense and motor" interests. In each, the geographic environment became the "dramatic control," determining plot and action elements. At the end of each series of stories came a theoretical chapter on the geographic element described in the stories.[9]

Mitchell used a similar organization in *Manhattan Now and Long Ago* (1934), written with Clara Lambert. Highlighting the work patterns of the borough as they had been conditioned by ecological forces, through a series of lively stories, photographs, maps, and a few poems, the authors started with modern Manhattan and worked backwards through time. The volume included a list of ten trips readers could take to places described in the book.[10]

Lucy's book *Young Geographers*, published in 1934, articulated her theory of "relationship thinking" and provided a practical account of how teachers could assist children to make their own geographic meanings through discovering relationships. In part II of the book Lucy gave detailed instructions for the preparation of flat, graphic relief maps as well as modelled, three-dimensional plastic maps, neither of which was then on the market.[11]

For Lucy, the essence of thinking meant seeing, understanding, and interpreting relationships—in this case between earth forces, social groups, cultural traditions, and work habits. Students could discover these interrelationships if they thought scientifically and experimentally, rather than vicariously. Content, "in the old sense," had not disappeared, but would be made more vital through imagination. Through the "laboratory method," students could become "explorers" and "geographers." Teachers, too, had to become geographers.

They must themselves be experimenters, they must hunt for sources and study the relationships, they must explore their environment, they must analyze the culture of which they are a part. . . . Each year is a new lap in their own education, a new creative experience. . . .[12]

As they expanded their own horizons, teachers could help students utilize a "curriculum of experience."

Lucy's relationship thinking presaged not only the contemporary human ecology movement with its concern for the conservation of human resources, but the theory and pedagogic techniques of developmentalists such as Jerome Bruner who emphasize cognitive growth based on unified structures of thought. From a curriculum perspective, relationship thinking foreshadowed the social studies movement that developed in the 1930s and 1940s, linking history to geography and later, to science. Relationship thinking also reflected Lucy's firm belief in the importance of subject matter—a value which many experimental educators did not share. She understood that a child's creativity incorporated an intellectual impulse, and devoted much of her energies as writer and teacher to providing factual content that could stimulate the child's own discoveries.[13]

During the 1920s, Lucy also refined her approach to teaching language. The keystone of her pedagogy was the notion that children's language patterns have intrinsic value and need not follow adult norms. Children's speech was creative and dynamic, employing direct, concrete sense and motor terms and rhythmic patterns. To describe the setting sun, for example, a child spoke of "the place where the big shadow is." Lucy stressed the way in which children's artistic and scientific sensitivities were linked. A child's description of a worm's way of moving was a favorite example: "First he wiggles into himself, then stretches out and flats himself along in a jiggering kind of way." This, Lucy thought, was both a marvelous scientific observation and a lovely poem.[14]

Lucy usually began her language classes at the City and Country School by asking the children to discuss an experience they had had as a group, encouraging them to describe the event in vivid, direct "motor" language. She would then read stories and verse aloud, showing the children how concrete language and imagery were used and helping them to gain discrimination in sounds and rhythms. Her chosen authors included Homer, de la Mare, Stevenson, Kipling, Rossetti, Lindsay, Herbert, Whitman, Sandburg, Yeats, and especially, the Roumanian peasants whose poems were collected by Helene Vacaresco in The Bard of the Dimbovitza, Lucy's favorite book for reading aloud.

When instructing teachers, she would give counter examples of prose that did not use vivid associations and imagery. Often she pointed out John Dewey's Democracy and Education and John Watson's Psychology as works that failed to stimulate because of their dry, dull language. While she believed that it was important to help children make their words fit their thoughts and stressed the importance of logical unity in speech and writing, she insisted that too great a focus on exactness would spoil the creative, play aspects of language. Children would become critics, not artists. "Over-intellectualization" could become as great a problem as underachievement. She urged teachers to pursue their own experimentation with language, or at least keep "hands off" in working with children.[15]

Lucy criticized a new book by Swiss psychologist Jean Piaget, The Language and Thought of the Child—then attracting much attention in experimental circles—for its assumption that the exclusive goal of language development in children was the expression of logical thought and communication and its failure to consider the development of children's language as an "art form." While she believed that rhythm and pattern in the language of prelogical children were stimuli to greater skills in thinking, she argued that the main function of children's language was pure pleasure, and that teachers should focus on the development of sensitivities that could lead to later creativity.[16]

In 1924, Lucy wrote a first reading book, The *Here and Now Primer: Home from the Country,* for six- and seven-year-olds. She argued that stories to help children learn to read should use their own vocabulary, not words assigned by adults. She thus included words that recalled activities of the senses and muscles ("tickle," "prickly," "bumble bees," "boom") and made-up syllables ("chooks"), and omitted relational and connecting words ("is," "he," "there," and "which") and words that "smeared" over a number of meanings (like "go," "eat," and "pretty") so that they failed to produce vivid, concrete recalls. The result was an exclamatory prose, full of active, concrete words, in the manner of small children's talk.

The subjects of the primer came from the familiar environment: nature, animals, city streets, country sights, transportation. But, as in the *Here and Now Story Book,* Lucy asserted that the content of any story in a children's book deserved only half the consideration, "perhaps not so much as that." She believed that reading primers even more than oral stories needed a form adjusted to children's needs, employing vivid language and repetition.

At the time, most progressive educators believed that children learned to read most rapidly when they read by the "eye-full," as large a unit as they could take in. Lucy argued that what she called a "thought unit" and a "visual unit" should match exactly and reinforce each other, and that the visual unit had to be short. She also provided spaces in her text where the voice would naturally pause. "If their reading *sounds* like talking, reading will at once enrich their language experience instead of interrupting it for several years, as is now generally the case." She omitted illustrations, which she felt sidetracked children from the text. More importantly, children liked to make their own drawings. She suggested that children be allowed to use the blank pages and margins of her book to do their own pictures.[17]

Though Lucy Mitchell's language pedagogy helped to shape reading and literature programs at City and Country, Caroline Pratt did not allow her to use the records of children's language she had made at the school for a proposed book of stories for older children. She was also unenthusiastic about Lucy's geography programs: block play to help younger children become spatially oriented; and for older children, the construction of tool maps, dramatizations, science experiments, and the

study of past cultures linked to the present. Pratt thought history was irrelevant to present-day concerns.[18]

Caroline Pratt's rejection of Lucy's proposed language and geography
books forced Lucy to a major decision. After years of being "pulled violently in opposite directions"—on the one hand her devotion to the
school, on the other the recognition that her work could not propser
there—Lucy decided to leave City and Country.

> I came to realize that my pattern of work did not fit hers nor hers fit me. She
> worked best in an atmosphere where her own thinking was not challenged or in-
> terrupted by ideas originated by others; I worked best where ideas from many
> sources were being pooled and evaluated jointly. . . . I could not have learned as
> thoroughly or rapidly with anyone except Caroline Pratt. But she clipped my
> wings. I think she could not help it. Caroline's way of thinking and working and
> my way of thinking and working were too different to make it profitable for us to
> work together any longer. . . .[19]

Lucy stopped teaching at City and Country in 1928, although the final
rupture came later, brought on by the "eternal money end of things." In
1930, Lucy spelled out to Pratt in a letter the fact that for the past five
years, her support of the school had been carried out "at great personal
sacrifice." Because of enormous increases in taxes and maintenance expenses since Lucy first began subsidizing the school in 1916, she had
found her own resources severely limited, especially with the onset of the
Depression.[20] While she had supported the school without complaint for
fifteen years, she felt that City and Country had by now received public
recognition and could raise its own funds, allowing her to concentrate on
supporting the BEE. She argued that exclusive reliance on a single con-
tributor would hamper the school's development.

Pratt agreed that Lucy ought to be released from her obligation, but
asked for a moratorium so that the school could raise funds. "What you
have given to us is unlimited in every direction," she acknowledged.[21]
In 1931 Lucy sold the three West Thirteenth Street buildings and two on
West Twelfth Street to City and Country at a sizable discount from the
market price, incurring a $100,000 loss. Lucy also gave the school a
$300,000 ten-year mortgage and allowed it a five-year interest-free pe-
riod. Later she claimed that she had lost about one-third of her capital
during the period of her association with the school.[22]

Lucy took care that her parting with Pratt not be abrupt. The Mitchell
family continued to live at 161 West Twelfth Street, next door to the

school, until 1938. But relations between Mitchell and Pratt deterio-
rated. In 1940, after an angry exchange about the amount of interest
owed, Lucy's loan to the school was retired when City and Country
refinanced the property with a New York bank. Lucy wrote to her lawyer,
when the last mortgage checks had been delivered. "I consider the matter
closed. . . . So as a six-year-old ended a train story, 'Ssssh, all out! bang!
Amen!'"[23] But bitter feelings lingered: Pratt came to believe that Lucy's
demand that the school purchase her buildings during the financially unstable Depression years had been unfair. On her part, Lucy felt that Pratt
had again exploited her generosity. Though the two women worked together on several projects in the 1930s and 1940s, the close association
of their first years was never recaptured.

About the time Lucy gave up teaching at City and Country, the occasion for a more productive collaboration came; Elisabeth Irwin invited
Lucy to join an experimental program she was about to launch at a public
school in Greenwich Village.[24] In February 1929, Lucy began a seven-
year association with Irwin's experimental program at P.S. 41 in Greenwich Village, called the Little Red School House. Sponsored by the Public Education Association, and staffed by Irwin, Lucy, and three other
teachers, the project aimed to bring the methods and perspectives of experimental education into a public school setting where students came
from diverse working-class backgrounds. Three goals were foremost: first,
the substitution of the ideal of cooperation for that of competition—
there would be no grades, marks, merits or demerits of any kind; second,
an emphasis on understanding the child's social and emotional as well as
intellectual needs; and lastly, a focus on learning by experience.[25]

Irwin had conducted a six-year experiment at P.S. 61 in Manhattan
before establishing Little Red. At P.S. 61, she had started with a class of
regular first-grade children, designing a curriculum of trips around the
city, block building, dramatic play, and the like, with no academic work
of any kind. Only in the latter half of the second grade did these students
begin to receive instruction in the three Rs, and then for only one and
one-half hours out of the five-hour day. By the sixth grade, instruction in
basic skills was increased to two hours daily. When the students were
tested and the results compared to the scores of a control group that had
been trained according to the regular curriculum, they fared as well or
better in all subjects except spelling.[26]

Now Irwin hoped to duplicate these results at Little Red. Her experimental staff would teach kindergarten and two first grade classes, and at the same time they would train and supervise regular teachers for the higher grades. Within three years, thirteen classes had become part of the Little Red School House system.

Since the beginning of her work with the BEE, Lucy Mitchell had been interested in developing opportunities to reform public education. As an example of the worst kind of pedagogy, she frequently cited the remark of a superintendent of a large city school system whose goal was "to be able to look at the clock and know that all 2B children were reading the same page in the same text book."[27] But teaching at P.S. 41 proved to be a vastly different experience from working at City and Country, where parents sympathized with instructors' experimental purposes. At the public school, children came to kindergarten as a convenience to working parents, not for purposes of enrichment. They were unaccustomed to playing with blocks and tools, (or getting their school clothes dirty), and often rebelled at the new teachers' methods. Lucy recalled the puzzled resistance of parents to her very first request: that all the children, including the girls, be sent to school in overalls, since the girls were to become sturdy "little workers" like the boys![28]

Keeping full records of the children's behavior, conversations, and stories, Lucy discovered that words had been substituted for experiences. When Lucy asked her kindergarten class where a farmer they had seen at the Gansvoort Market got his turnips, they replied "from the A & P."[29] She worked out a here-and-now learning program based on neighborhood work experiences, and helped Irwin develop a country program for younger children.

Each June, a group of six-year-olds would spend several weeks at a settlement camp. Invariably, there was culture shock for the children. "Do teachers *sleep?*" asked one bewildered little girl when Lucy put her own night clothes on the bed. Another child, afraid of the swaying trees, refused to be comforted by the fact that city trees had not harmed her. "There you have them one at a time!" she wailed. Another girl, seeing some minnows in a pond, cried out "Look at the live sardines!"[30]

Gradually, the experience away from New York City "took." In the fall, the children's play began to profit from their encounter with the country. But it was another matter to convince city officials that Little Red's experimental approach ought to be followed in other public schools. Lucy recounted the time when sixteen public school officials came to hear her lead a discussion with forty-three six-year-old children who had visited Borden's livery stable some days before. All went well until one child told about a horse being cleaned with a vacuum cleaner.

He rose and dramatically began moving the nozzle up and down an imaginary horse with very realistic noise. Suddenly forty-three vacuum cleaners began to buzz and move up and down forty-three imaginary horses. The noise completely drowned my voice. I was terribly scared and dared not look at my sixteen visitors. Then I had an inspiration. I walked around the group of children and with a click turned off the electricity at each vacuum cleaner. The day was saved, for how could the vacuum cleaner run without electricity? The children sat down quietly, and we finished our discussion.[31]

Ultimately, public school officials were not convinced of the project's value. In 1932, after the Public Education Association withdrew its support from the Little Red School House because of lack of funds, New York City's Board of Superintendents decided against continuing the experimental classes. Despite a positive evaluation from a committee headed by Dr. Paul Klapper, dean of the School of Education at City College, the Board appointed its own review committee, which concluded that the program's achievements had been minimal. The conventional public school point of view was reflected by Dr. Joseph Sheehan, Associate Superintendent of Schools in charge of the district in which Little Red was located, who asserted that the experimental school allowed children "too much freedom." Instead of providing organized instruction in reading and basic skills, the school started out "with the idea that a child should not read until he wants to. Each child is a law unto himself; his individual taste is what matters most to him." As a result, Sheehan thought, its students not only lacked a solid foundation in the three R's, but became "self-centered and selfish."[32]

With the help of parent support, however, Little Red re-opened as a private school in Greenwich Village in the fall of 1932. "Whereas [parents] formerly had to drive their children to school," an observer reported, "they cannot now coax them to stay away."[33] Irwin deliberately kept conditions in the new private school similar to those in the public system: classes of thirty to thirty-five children; tuition equalling the per capita cost to the city; students accepted in order of application.[34] Unlike Caroline Pratt, she came to believe that small groups made children "precious," whereas large classes toughened them and trained them to get along with others. Lucy agreed: she preferred teaching her classes at Little Red, sometimes with forty or more pupils, to teaching classes with only a dozen youngsters.[35]

Lucy continued to teach at the Little Red School House for four more years, expanding her work in human geography and language. At Little Red, she experienced the "most stimulating contacts with children" she had ever known. And working with Elisabeth Irwin was always exhilarating. Lucy could never think of her shrewd, sharp-tongued, witty friend without smiling. "She thought and lived with such gusto! And she was not thin-skinned. I can remember losing my temper with her and spitting out more violent criticism than I really felt." But there was no difficulty afterwards. Elisabeth acknowledged what was useful in the criticism and discounted the rest. "She demanded no special protection for herself," Lucy recalled.

In this way, she was one of the easiest persons to work with I have ever known. She was herself all the time and let me be myself, and when we didn't agree— well, what of it? A disagreement . . . stimulated us both to more careful thinking.[36]

Irwin never dictated to her teachers, always giving them the chance to develop their ideas. She offered Lucy the perfect setting in which to extend her experimental here-and-now approach to a more diverse public. Along with Caroline Pratt, who had been a formative influence on Lucy's thinking during her early years at City and Country, and Harriet Johnson, with whom Lucy shared all her ideas, Irwin fostered Lucy's continued learning.

As "relationship thinking" was the key to Lucy's formal pedagogy, so in her own life, the processes of experience—her attachments and connections to people and to the world—provided ways to know and to learn. Lucy did not make relationships easily. Intense, absorbed in her work, impatient at delay and interruption, she had little insight into the effect her competencies and her manner could have on others. Some of her closest associates—even Jessie Stanton, a City and Country teacher who became a close personal and family friend of the Mitchells—were intimidated by her sharp-edged brilliance.

Yet Stanton and other teachers who worked with Lucy also found her to be an extraordinarily collaborative colleague, always supportive of their work and ideas. Her dedication to experimental education inspired many others, even when her zeal and conscientiousness appeared forbidding. By the end of the 1920s, Lucy's experiences at Little Red, City and Country, and the BEE Nursery School had equipped her with a coherent body of teaching practice and theory which she refined and personalized in her books for children and teachers. She was now ready to make a shift of institutional level: she would launch a program to train teachers for creative, experimental work.

69 Bank Street

In October 1930, a year after the sudden collapse of the American stock market, Lucy Sprague Mitchell began a major new venture at the Bureau of Educational Experiments: a cooperative school for experimental teachers. During the Depression, the search for a redefinition of the relationship between individuals and society brought fresh support to progressive educators who believed that the classroom could become the model for a new collectivism, integrating self-expression with larger social goals.[1] Despite recurrent financial crises, Lucy Mitchell's school for teachers flourished during the Depression years, offering an innovative curriculum that showed teachers not so much how to teach as "how to live." Over the next decade and a half, it became an influential force within experimental education as well as in the wider arena of public schooling. In teaching teachers, Lucy discovered her greatest generativity.

The Cooperative School for Student Teachers (CSST) marked a radical shift in direction for the BEE, which moved at the same time to new and larger quarters at 69 Bank Street, a primarily residential street on the west side of Greenwich Village. Lucy had to deal with the anxieties and exhilaration of opening this new experiment without Wesley, who was spending the year as George Eastman Visiting Professor at Oxford University.

After its relocation, the Bureau was informally known as "Bank Street." Its new quarters occupied the site of a former Fleischmann's Yeast factory. With the help of a responsive contractor, Lucy redesigned the four-story building, incorporating features of the former tenant's plant wherever she could. The top two floors were converted for use as the nursery school, allowing enrollment to expand to sixty or seventy children, almost three times its former size. The roof became a playground. The bottom two floors housed the new school for teachers and Bank Street's research staff. The ground floor loading dock became an auditorium and dance studio, while the superintendent's quarters and Lucy's geography laboratory were located in the space where yeast had been brewed. The smiling face of the Fleischmann's Yeast girl which had decorated every wall was removed, but two sets of pipes that ran from the fourth floor to the basement—water and electrical conduits—remained in plain sight, painted red and blue, a symbol to visitors that in this unusual institution, the here-and-now physical world of work—even the functional components of steam and electricity—would be imaginatively celebrated.

Teacher education was "almost as much a pioneer front in 1930 as the study of children and experimental schools for them had been in 1916," Lucy recalled.[2] The impetus behind the training program had several sources. Lucy's experience at the Little Red School House had made her eager to work on the training of teachers. The limitations of the BEE's research approach also convinced her that teaching, rather than data-gathering, should become Bank Street's first concern.[3] The great proliferation of experimental schools in the 1920s had created a demand for experimental teachers that was not being met. Finally, having separated from City and Country School, the Bureau raised the upper age limit of its nursery school from three to five, providing expanded opportunities for teachers and student placements.

After a "whirlwind campaign"—months of discussion with leaders of experimental schools—the CSST was established as the joint creation of eight experimental schools: the Bureau nursery school and the Little Red School House, both in Manhattan; the Woodward School in Brooklyn; the Livingston School in Staten Island; Rosemary Junior School in Old Greenwich, and the Spring Hill School in Litchfield, Connecticut; Carson College in Flourtown, Pennsylvania; and Mount Kemble School in Morristown, New Jersey.[4] Lucy and her colleagues agreed that student teachers would benefit from placements in these varied urban, rural, and suburban schools, with different program emphases, teaching styles, and student bodies. Policy and curriculum decisions for the CSST were to be made jointly by directors and teaching staff at the eight schools. Lucy

Mitchell and Jessie Stanton served as educational advisors to all participating schools; Elizabeth Healy, a social worker from Philadelphia, was
hired as general secretary.

At the core of the cooperative program was a single idea: rather than
learning either teaching methods or specific bodies of subject matter, the
teacher-in-training needed most of all to experience the excitement of
learning as children could. Just as experimental children's schools tried
to stimulate the development of the "whole" child, so the CSST wanted to
create a "whole teacher" who would encounter the world as a unity and
act upon it as a growing, creative, expressive, experimental individual.
As Lucy put it: "We want each student to feel in herself, her work, her
play, her social relations, her whole life, a response to her total environment . . . the habits, culture, and institutions of her time."[5]

Lucy explained the school's goals in its first bulletin:

Our aim is to help students develop a scientific attitude towards their work and
toward life. To us this means an attitude of eager, alert observations; a constant
questioning of old procedure in the light of new observations; a use of the world
as well as of books as source material; an experimental open-mindedness; and an
effort to keep as reliable records as the situation permits in order to base the future upon actual knowledge of the experiences of the past.

Our aim is equally to help students develop and express the attitude of the artist
towards their work and towards life. To us this means an attitude of relish, of
emotional drive, a genuine participation in some creative phase of work, and a
sense that joy and beauty are legitimate possessions of all human beings, young
and old. We are not interested in perpetuating any special "school of thought."
Rather, we are interested in imbuing teachers with an experimental, critical and
ardent approach to their work. If we accomplish this, we are ready to leave the
future of education to them.[6]

Though the guiding ideas of the CSST were strongly influenced by
Dewey, he was not involved in its planning. At one point, however,
Dewey's colleague at Teachers College, William Heard Kilpatrick, creator of the "project method," served as an adviser to the CSST founders.[7]
The CSST shared Kilpatrick's child-centered goals, but it approached
teacher education from a new perspective: its students could best acquire
the child's vantage point by unlearning adult habits and adult patterns of
response in creative workshops and through other firsthand experiences.

In its first five years, the school trained nearly two hundred teachers,
three-quarters of them college graduates, many of them from the Ivy
League women's schools. There was a lack of "qualified" male applicants:

one class had three male students, but most had one or none. While some students had already had teaching experience, others had been dancers, sculptors, actors, writers, secretaries. "We seek students who are somewhat 'on' to themselves and the world in which they live," the school bulletin announced, "students whose standards are well-developed, non-crystallized and who dare try to learn for themselves." The best applicants would demonstrate "intellectual curiosity . . . emotional insight, a profound interest in children, sustained physical and mental vitality, and awareness of social problems." Those with such "obvious neurotic traits" as lack of humor or "foggy professional dreams" were to be avoided.[8]

The CSST set out to provide firsthand experiences outside and inside the classroom. Students were placed as teachers in participating schools from Monday through Thursday: practice-teaching was the "central integrating core" of the curriculum.[9] They came to Bank Street from Thursday afternoon through Saturday noon for an intensive series of seminars and workshops. No academic courses were given, though the resources of the New School for Social Research were available. In addition to the regular program, the CSST organized occasional seminars for staff at a wide group of experimental schools.

Lucy Mitchell's courses in language and environment were the most memorable of a memorable roster. Barbara Biber's course on child development focused on the diverse types of learning patterns and on individual differences in children's learning and maturation. Harriet Johnson's course on observation (until her sudden death from cancer in February 1934) helped students understand the difference between facts and interpretation as they observed, recorded, and analyzed children's classroom behavior as well as the appearance and behavior of people on streets, subways, and buses.[10] Elizabeth Healy's course on "the development of personality" helped students integrate material from their teaching and classroom experiences by focusing on personal growth. These core courses were rounded out by offerings from Jessie Stanton and Ellen Steele Reece on curriculum for experimental schools. There were no courses on pedagogical methods.[11]

The expressive or "outgo" portion of the curriculum consisted of courses which allowed students to experiment with color (painting), form (clay and drawing) and creative movement (dance and dramatics). Mitchell and her colleagues believed that teachers needed to paint, model, sing, write free language, act, and dance, not for the sake of achieving technical proficiency or creating a masterful work of art, but "to wake up atrophied senses," so as to be able to help their pupils become "creators," not "critics."[12] They learned painting and modelling from Ralph Pearson, drama from Charlotte Perry, dance from Polly Korchien. Pearson's design workshop was directed to releasing creative impulses and "stimulating feeling." In drama, they did individual exercises in "muscular pantomine," then exercises in pairs, then struggled to develop spontaneous dramatic episodes as a group. In dance, the class learned to understand dance "as an art and our bodies as a medium" as they created new dances "for ourselves."[13]

The Cooperative School for Student Teachers (its name was later changed to the Cooperative School for Teachers) also offered seminars from visiting lecturers and creative artists: New School faculty member Max Lerner taught a course with Lucy and Eleanor Bowman on the social and economic environment; psychoanalyst Otto Rank gave a series of talks on psychology and politics; Marion Farquhar brought in cellist Pablo Casals to talk about music; New School director Alvin Johnson lectured on social reconstruction. Anthropologist Ashley Montagu's course at the New School on development was also available to students.[14]

The city itself provided opportunities to learn. Much as Lucy had once taken her Berkeley students to visit characteristic institutions of San Francisco, she and other CSST staff took students to witness the urban institutions they discussed in class: slum tenements, subsidized housing, detention centers, clinics, magistrate's courts. There were visits to labor unions, political rallies, and even a Nazi meeting in Yorkville. CSST students were interested in everything, Elizabeth Healy once noted—"politics, . . . racial groups, labor organizations, religion, production for profit, education, sex, the press."[15] On one occasion, Eleanor Bowman, a student in the first CSST class who became one of the school's early teachers, brought her class to the Transport Workers Hall, where a strike vote was being taken. There she met the union's president, Austen Hogan, whom she married in 1938.[16] To clarify students' own social philosophies and stimulate their "readiness to engage actively . . . in social reconstruction," they spent one morning a week for one semester doing field work for social organizations. Placements included the left-wing League of Women Shoppers and the League for Industrial Democracy was well as such community groups as the Lower West Side Federation on Health, Housing and Employment.[17] Years later Lucy explained in a journal article that teachers had to become concerned with "national policies, conflicts in the world of industry, or international and global relations." She felt that the teacher's "social education" was "perhaps the most important" of all aspects of teacher training.[18]

The two courses Lucy Mitchell taught reflected her belief in the unity of the arts and sciences and the need for first-hand experience. In her language course, the aim was to re-educate students so that they could regain the simple, direct approach to language characteristic of children as opposed to adults. Students did exercises to learn "to let things describe themselves directly" rather than in abstract or interpretive terms. Reviewing the language and imagery of children or the work of Lucy's favorite poets, they became sensitive to rhythms, sound quality, pitch, and structure.[19]

In her course on environment Mitchell taught "human geography." Using her home-made "tool" maps, she showed students how to discover relationships between the earth's natural geographic features and patterns of food production, transportation, settlement, work, and politics.[20] The course was not geography in the strict sense but "ecology discovered," recalled one student.[21] In Lucy's "five-finger exercises," students were asked to stand for fifteen minutes on some street and record everything they observed. For the last five minutes, they were to keep their eyes shut, using their remaining senses. They were then to analyze their observations, constructing social meanings according to the data collected. One student remembers a brilliant class during which Lucy provided students with resource maps of Europe on various transparencies and a bunch of crayons, asking them to create an overview of modern European culture and politics based on the interrelations they saw between natural resources and industrial factors. Students fondly remember Lucy's trips to such sites as the Fulton Fish Market, an A & P warehouse, dress and candy factories, and the headquarters of the International Ladies Garment Workers Union.

By the mid 1930s, students were also asked to prepare comprehensive studies of the communities in which they had been teaching. The product of a year's field work was a complex annotated chart showing the work patterns by which the community met its needs, along with an analysis of how local work was related to other parts of the country and the larger world. This focus on "relationship thinking," which she had emphasized in her first here-and-now stories and her later geography work with children, became the key to her approach to teaching the social sciences to teachers. "Everything," she often reiterated, "is related to everything else."[22]

During the first years of the school, Lucy combined a heavy schedule at the CSST with teaching at the Little Red School House and her own writing. On Monday and Wednesday she worked at Little Red; on Tuesday and Thursday she visited the cooperating schools, attending classes or teaching them herself, meeting with individual teachers, attending faculty meetings, organizing curriculum. On Wednesday nights she taught a class for teachers at the schools. On Thursday she joined the students in dance class. On Friday afternoon and evening and Saturday morning, she taught seminars at Bank Street. "Life is hitting up a fast pace now," she wrote to Wesley in Oxford. "I seem to keep up but I have the sense of running hard."[23] The Bureau provided her with a secretary, but Lucy could not find time to use her. The worst of it was that her time with her own children became more pressed than ever. "I try hard to be leisurely with [them], she told Wesley, "both for [their] sake and mine, but it's a little like the possum when he is rigidly quiet with fear."[24]

At the same time, Lucy was deeply troubled by the effects of the Depression. "Life here has been tense beyond anything I ever experienced," she wrote to her son Jack, at Oxford with his father.[25] "Everybody is either committing suicide or in a state of exaltation—much the earthquake psychology," she told Wesley.[26] She worried constantly about the family's finances and its priorities, asking whether they were caught in "expenditures which are of secondary importance" and risked sacrificing primary interests—like keeping Bank Street going.[27] She wondered whether the family should move up to their property in Stamford and send the children to public schools. After visiting the Stamford schools, however, Lucy decided to keep the three youngest children where they were: Sprague at the Deerfield Academy; Marni at the French School in Cambridge; Arnold at the Lincoln School in New York. "I feel ready for any personal adaptation that I can think of," she told Wesley, "but I balk at the children."[28] She worried, however, about class attitudes Sprague might develop at "deluxe, isolated" Deerfield and tried to involve the children in her effort to cut family expenses.

Lucy's deep-seated frugality ran rampant during these years. In the city, subways had always been her mode of travel; taxis were only for medical emergencies. Her family had long been amused by the containers of leftovers she carried back and forth between the country and the city. At the end of each summer, she loaded the running boards of their

Cadillac with heavy paper sacks full of Greensboro-grown potatoes to take back to the city. And when Lucy dined out in a restaurant, she would not hesitate to stuff the leftover dinner rolls in her huge carryall.

A good portion of the "wholesale threatening" Lucy felt at this time was due to the fact that her own financial losses in the securities market jeopardized her support of the causes she cared most about, Bank Street first of all.[29] Everything she loved seemed doomed to extinction. "Educational research and the arts are dropped by capitalism first," she wrote to Jack."[30] Teachers were running the nursery school on a survival budget, with salaries at an irreducible minimum. Students planned to live in the building and do what work they could to cut costs. Not one of the eight CSST schools was sure of survival. The Little Red School House was going under, Manumit would probably collapse, City and Country was surviving only because teachers were not taking salaries. All the rest remained doubtful.[31]

In the face of such catastrophe, new forms of cooperative action were needed. "Most of us believe the old social order must be supplanted by a new kind," she wrote to Jack. "We ought to be more intelligent than we are about working out a coordinating plan where we know connections exist. We boom right ahead producing as individuals, distributing as individuals and consuming as individuals when any blooming idiot can see how interrelated we all are."[32] To Wesley, she cried out for help. "The feeling of a break-up of the old social order and the need for clarity in thinking and in experimenting for social reconstruction that will bring about sounder human values than the old is so intense that I am completely exhausted," she wrote.[33] "How I wish I could have a few hours' talk with you!"[34] Though Wesley doubted that "revolutionary alterations are just around the corner," in the presidential election that year he joined Lucy in voting for socialist candidate Norman Thomas.[35]

Lucy had spent part of the summer of 1931 in Europe with Jack, Arnold, and John Farquhar, and had reached Oxford ahead of Wesley's arrival there. When she returned home in September on the *Norddeutscher Lord Bremen*, travelling in tourist, she encountered John Dewey and Franz Boas, in first class. She visited Wesley again in January and February of 1932.

In contrast to Depression New York, Oxford seemed to Lucy like the "peaceful Middle Ages." Although she enjoyed her contact with the "mellowness" of Oxford culture, she found the whole experience at the university to be a "discipline in not being herself." Because proper wives of British professors did not work, she kept her professional projects to herself. She recognized that it was a help to Wesley to have her there, fulfilling her expected social role, but she was unwilling to take more time from work. "I hate leaving you in Oxford," she wrote as she sailed back to America in February. "Not that you need *me*. But I rather think you need a *wife!*"[36]

Back in New York, Lucy's mood continued to alternate between hope and frustration. The new cooperative organization at Bank Street was "interesting, exciting, fatiguing," she wired Wesley in April. But in the next letter, she conceded that she was "in danger of becoming 'panicky' and 'hysterical.'" She urged Wesley to come home as soon as possible. "America and I both need you," she pleaded.[37] They celebrated their twentieth anniversary on May 8, 1932, on different sides of the Atlantic.

Of the eight member schools on the csst, only the experimental Little Red School House at P.S. 41 run by Elisabeth Irwin actually closed, and that was because of political as well as financial problems. Little Red re-opened under private auspices a short time later. But the crisis was not over. In November 1934, Lucy announced that Bank Street would have to close or reorganize.[38] Yet with the sale of part of a small securities fund, continued support from Lucy's own purse, a sizable contribution from her sister Mary, and money raised at Bank Street benefits, the Bureau nursery school and the csst stayed open, although its dedicated teaching staff suffered still further pay cuts.[39]

Bank Street's brush with disaster reinforced the need for joint planning. In 1935, Lucy joined with leaders of five experimental schools to form a new organization, the Associated Experimental Schools. In addition to Bank Street, the association included the Little Red School House, City and Country, Walden, Hessian Hills, and Manumit, a much more varied group than the eight cooperating csst schools. Elisabeth Irwin was president, Elizabeth Healy vice-president, and Caroline Pratt secretary. Lucy chaired the Education Committee, charting a joint educational philosophy to ensure that the group would be more than a "trade association." She helped to prepare an exhibit produced at experimental schools, and a volume about member groups' programs.[40]

The aes hired a fund-raising consultant and began working on a number of joint projects. An exhibition of children's paintings produced at experimental schools was shown at Rockefeller Center with Eleanor Roosevelt presiding: Mrs. Roosevelt had agreed to become an aes sponsor. The exhibit traveled throughout the country and became the group's most successful venture. Lucy organized a cooperative buying plan for such supplies as coal, soap, and paper towels. Cooperative purchasing and fund-raising proved mildly successful, but the benefits were insufficient to hold the group together once the financial anxieties of the Depression were past. By the end of the 1930s, the organization was abandoned.[41]

———————————————————————————

Although the original focus of the BEE had been drastically revised with the advent of the CSST, its aim of enhancing educational experiments so as to foster children's total growth did not alter. To limit travel time and expense, the CSST decided to restrict placements to the Bank Street nursery school and Little Red; eventually it added City and Country and branched out again to many public and private schools, nursery schools, and day care centers within the city. Yet Bank Street maintained close working contacts with experimental leaders from the original cooperating schools and with AES members, ties which helped it to refine its own school practices. From 1934 to 1938, it published a mimeographed bulletin, 69 Bank Street, edited by Lucy, which contained articles about the CSST and pieces written by teachers at other experimental schools. The place of art and politics in experimental schools was a frequent topic.[42]

In spite of revisions in curriculum and structure, the fundamentals of the teacher training program remained as its first catalogue described them. The elimination of most of the original cooperating schools allowed the school for teachers to become a more integral part of Bank Street, working closely with the nursery school and research division. Jessie Stanton became director of the nursery school upon Harriet Johnson's death, with Louise Woodcock as co-director, but following Stanton's resignation in 1941, coordination of the school with Bank Street's other divisions became more difficult. After Eleanor Reich, formerly a parent at the school, assumed the directorship, the school became financially self-supporting, and increasingly acted as an independent unit. With the nursery school preferring an autonomous position, and the research and teaching divisions advocating cohesiveness among the departments, tensions arose. Though the unity of its first decades could not be reestablished, Bank Street continued to advocate "joint thinking and joint planning." Lucy felt deeply that the institution's collaborative structure was a premise of its experimental value and uniqueness. She resolved to maintain this tradition in the research and teaching divisions, and to avoid an open break with the nursery school. "Bank Street grew with the times," Lucy explained, but its values remained constant.[43]

In May 1934, Lucy was invited to dine at the Roosevelt White House, accompanying Adolph Miller, a Commissioner of the Federal Reserve Bank since 1914, and her sister Mary, who had become a good friend of Eleanor Roosevelt during World War I. Lucy met Mrs. Roosevelt again in November at a dinner with Elisabeth Irwin, John Dewey, and others preceding the opening of the AES exhibit of children's drawings. Some time later, Mrs. Roosevelt toured Bank Street, delighting its anxious staff by her marked enthusiasm for the red and blue pipes.[44]

In 1935, Mrs. Roosevelt appointed Lucy to the National Advisory Committee of an experimental school project in Arthurdale, West Virginia.[45] Lucy's trips to the Appalachian region on behalf of the committee made a great impression upon her, and she decided that Bank Street student teachers would benefit from a similar exposure to the pressing problems of "alien" cultures. As a result, Eleanor Bowman and Lucy planned the CSST's first "long trip," which became an annual staple of the curriculum.

The trip was an extended exploration of the environment, structured by Lucy's concept of human geography. On the first trip, in 1935, Lucy, two other teachers, and twenty-eight students made an eight-day journey by bus to Morgantown, West Virginia, and Washington, D.C. On the way, Lucy talked to them about the geography and geology of the regions they passed: the rock formations of the coastal plain of eastern New Jersey; the triassic lowlands centering in Newark; the industrial "fall line" cities of Trenton and Philadelphia; the rocks of the old Appalachian ridge and the eastern edge of the Piedmont; the long Great Valley with its fertile farms; the wooded ridges of the folded Appalachians; then the great plateaus of the Allegheny front; and, at last, the coal strata. Welcomed by union officials in Morgantown, the group donned miners' helmets and lanterns and descended into the mines, where they wore out their guides with persistent questions and explorations. Under the leadership of Alice Davis, county relief administrator, they spent several days visiting destitute miners in Scotts Run, each student going on rounds with case workers, visiting housekeepers, and nurses. At Arthurdale, they visited the new community school funded by the government's subsistence homestead program. Then they spent two days in Washington attending hearings of the Senate Finance Committee, and visiting the Natural Resources Board, the Geologic Survey, and the Treasury. Back at Bank Street, students reconstructed their experiences through paint-ing, dance, music, stories, and poetry and discussed how they might or-ganize to help alleviate the problems they had seen.[46]

Over the years the itinerary of the spring trip varied. Coal mining towns, the TVA, steel mills, and war industry towns like Waterbury, Conn., were typical destinations. On each excursion, the area was in-vestigated from its geological beginnings to its contemporary socio-economic structure. School programs, as reflections of the community, were always included.[47] Though the sites varied, the rationale of the trip remained constant: students learned by direct immersion in unfamiliar cultures, however briefly. When on one trip students confided that they felt uncomfortable "slumming" in a depressed mining town, Lucy's re-sponse came quickly: "This visit is people-to-people," she emphasized. It took place "on a human level."[48]

The long trip became an occasion of community as well as learning. "Each day we arose we loved our bus more," went a student jingle; they named it the "Lucy Sprague." On one trip, when the "Lucy" tipped over, the students—uninjured and joyful—danced in the middle of the road in the moonlight. When Southern motels refused to accommodate the black students in the party, the entire group searched for places where they could all stay. They came home to Bank Street feeling deeply about themselves as a community and about other people.[49]

In the classroom and on trips, Lucy Mitchell "was vital and vibrant and unique. She was a teacher every minute," wrote one former student. "When we went on a field trip to the coal region of Pennsylvania she talked about the geology, the economics, the politics and the environ-ment. . . . Back in New York, she was never satisfied until we under-stood all the layers of the city, the sewers, the phone cables, the subways, the electric and water systems, where the food came from and how it was raised and transplanted." "There was always an air of fresh discovery in her class," another student recalled.[50]

Lucy Mitchell could be impatient with those who did not share her cu-riosity and energy. Her exacting standards were described by a former stu-dent, herself a faculty member at a small progressive school on Long Island:

One day Mrs. Mitchell observed as I taught a social studies class. The subject was the Erie Canal. When the children left the room for recess, she made it quite clear that she had found my approach inadequate. . . .

When the children returned from the playground, the discussion of the Erie Canal was resumed, but this time, as we had agreed, Mrs. Mitchell was at the helm. Instead of listening to a textbook review of related facts, the children were questioned about the human needs and the natural conditions which lay behind the building of the canal. They were literally sitting on the edges of their chairs; they were completely absorbed. They were learning under ideal conditions . . . had it been practical, Mrs. Mitchell would have taken the class to see the Erie Canal.[51]

But if students showed special interest or talents, Lucy was generous in her response—some colleagues believed too much so. Especially when it came to student writing, they were dismayed that she would "accept so little from a student with so much gratitude."[52]

Many in Bank Street's early classes found their lives totally changed by their encounter with Lucy Mitchell. Eleanor Bowman, Claudia Lewis, and Irma Simonton Black stayed on to become staff members at the CSST; Mary Phelps, Edith Thatcher Hurd, Margaret Wise Brown, Elisabeth Helfman, and countless others became successful writers of children's books. Even CSST students who did not develop careers in experimental education look back with wonder at their Bank Street experience and especially at their contact with Lucy. Sally Morrison Kerlin, who worked closely with Lucy on social science mapping projects, and succeeded her as chairman of Bank Street's Board of Trustees in 1956, testified to the effect Lucy had on students. "She shook us out of our academic molds, quickened our sensibilities, and opened our eyes," Kerlin noted, "freeing us to respond and grow as individuals." She was "mesmerizing" and "extraordinary."[53] Charlotte Winsor, who joined Bank Street's School for Teachers after teaching at City and Country, put it more dramatically: "To be her student was like being born again."[54]

Wesley Mitchell returned from Oxford in the spring of 1932. While teaching at Columbia and directing the research efforts of the National Bureau, he resumed the role he had accepted in 1929 as chairman of President Hoover's Research Committee on Social Trends, supervising the work of a distinguished panel of social scientists. The committee prepared a one-volume general report, edited by Mitchell, and sixteen additional volumes of special studies. These elaborately detailed surveys, widely read and praised, marked a pathbreaking attempt of government to gather data that could serve as the basis for national policy.[55] In December 1934, Wesley Mitchell was honored at a dinner celebrating his sixtieth birthday, attended by 120 guests at Columbia's Faculty Club. He was presented with a volume of essays in his honor by seventeen former students. President Roosevelt and ex-President Hoover were among the many who sent congratulatory telegrams.[56]

National planning occupied Mitchell's attention throughout most of the decade. President Roosevelt appointed him to the National Planning Board in 1933 and to the National Resources Board in 1934.[57] For Mitchell, planning meant neither socialism nor right-wing state control but a concerted effort to apply technical expertise to pressing social and economic problems, like those identified by the Committee on Social Trends. He worried that, like early Depression measures and a good part of the New Deal, national planning tended to be "piecemeal and inspirational" rather than "systematic and technically thorough."[58]

Mitchell lectured on planning to Lucy's circle of experimental educators on several occasions.[59] CSST students and staff also attended suppers at the Mitchell home where Wesley talked informally on the subject. Although he did not participate actively in routine Bank Street work as he had in the early days of the BEE, he served as a trustee of Bank Street and of the Little Red School House during these years and his support and counsel were always available.

In addition to their separate and joint working lives, during the 1930s each Mitchell was involved in guiding the development of the children as they moved through high school and onto college. Wesley helped with academic work, drilling the boys and Marni in composition, mathematics, and German. But Lucy felt he was more distant from the children in their adolescence than when they were younger. If a child was ill or in trouble, it was Lucy who took time off from work. Lucy remained as committed to promoting the children's independence as she had always been. Yet she continued to sleep in the children's rooms, even into their late teens, if she was worried about an illness.

New family social activities also reflected the children's passage through the last years of adolescence: now Wesley or Lucy would take them to movies or plays, buy special books, play chess and golf with them. Lucy traveled to Bermuda with Arnold when he was recuperating from an illness. And she took Jack and Arnold to Europe to improve their German.[60]

By mid-decade, all of the children had left home for colleges which Lucy played a major role in selecting: Jack to Harvard, Sprague to Bowdoin, Arnold to Amherst, and Marni to the experimental Black Mountain College.[61] Only Marni, the athlete in a bookish family, did not graduate. Lucy paid tuition for Polly Forbes-Johnson at Bennington, advising a career in stage design. But Polly proved as strong-minded as Marni. She dropped out of Bennington, purchased a motorcycle, and rode it from New York to Guatemala![62]

With the children away from home, the Mitchells gave up the spacious West Twelfth Street home where they had lived for seventeen years. Lucy no longer needed convenient access to City and Country School, and her own work had been relocated to Bank Street and the Little Red School House. In 1938, they bought a four-room duplex penthouse on the eighteenth and nineteenth floors at Two Horatio Street, around the corner from 69 Bank Street. Wesley had a study and terrace to himself on the lower floor; Lucy had a larger study and wide terrace on the floor above. From here, she wrote, "one boxed the compass," looking out at the ferries and barges of Hudson River traffic and the magnificent city skyline and its blazing sunsets.[63] Here they would spend a decade which Lucy felt were among the richest of their years together, each of them fully occupied with work, perhaps now more than ever, and with each other's "visions" and problems.

As Lucy turned sixty in 1938, several new adventures occupied her. The first was a trip to the Dutch East Indies with the Society of Women Geographers and her friend Elsa Ueland. After the official tour ended, Lucy and Elsa traveled through Siam (now Thailand), French Indochina, Burma, and India. Deeply moved by the color, vitality, and spirituality of the East, she came back a "chastened member of our western culture." Her students remember her telling them that her whole attitude toward life had changed: unwholesome pressures of time and work needed to be overcome; composure and tranquility were all-important. Nevertheless, they recall, she berated a Bank Street custodian who confused the order of some slides of the trip she was showing to students.[64]

For many years after, the Asian trip called up deep responses. Once, on a long trip to the South with her students, Lucy learned that a minis-

ter with whom she was staying overnight had recently returned from the
Far East. Without a word, she jumped up on the table and performed a
Balinese dance for the startled clergyman.[65] Convinced that the lack of
understanding between advanced Western nations and others needed to
be bridged, in the 1940s she became an enthusiastic supporter of the
"One World" concept and later of the United Nations.[66]

In 1938, Lucy launched another new cooperative venture at Bank
Street, the Writers' Laboratory. Feeling that even the best children's authors had a limited understanding of children, Lucy set out to help them
understand children's growth. She hoped to influence the kind of juvenile books being published.

She invited a group of professional writers plus a few of the best students from her language class at the cooperative school—ten to fifteen
people in all. They met weekly at first, and biweekly in later years. This
was "no common garden variety course" in writing, recalled Edith
Thatcher (Posey) Hurd, a laboratory member. If you survived Lucy's
classes on language the laboratory was the "whipped cream," an intense
but richly rewarding experience.[67]

In the workshop room on the top floor of Bank Street students pulled
their chairs around Lucy, seated on a large down-at-the-heels green sofa
on which she would spread the contents of her bulging briefcase—notebooks full of stories, classroom observations, scraps of paper bearing comments from books and articles. Carried away with enthusiasm, Lucy often forgot that one hand held a lit cigarette and would light a second.
Gesturing excitedly with both hands, cigarettes dangling, she put the
students at ease with her stories and reflections. As they read their own
creations aloud, she often interrupted with delighted laughter. Her criticisms were not harsh, Posey Hurd recalled, but always direct, focusing on
both literary merit and suitability for children.[68]

Lucy's here and now approach, focusing on the ordinary, environmental world of children, provided an impetus, though not a formulized line
of work, for the writers who studied with her. ("I get so tired of all those
chickens!" she told an author who favored poultry as characters.) Several kinds of stories—humor and adventure, straight fact and make-
believe—were produced. Lucy's ability to become excited at an idea and
especially a turn of phrase, and her openness to all kinds of experience
which she stored to use at opportune moments, made her a spontaneous,

exciting writing teacher. Everything was grist for the Writers' Laboratory mill.[69]

Lucy continued her association with the Writers' Laboratory until she left Bank Street in the mid-1950s. In later years, after the laboratory had been taken over by Irma Simonton Black, Lucy sat in as a member of the group, sipping sherry along with the rest, providing intelligent, useful criticisms.[70] By this time, many invited guests came to join in manuscript criticism or to offer information about their specialty fields: editors from major publishing houses, children's librarians, artists like Maurice Sendak and Remy Charlip; and teachers from experimental or public schools.

The Writers' Laboratory spawned a number of Bank Street writing projects. In 1939, the group began a "here and now" social studies series for public school children from first through sixth grades. Lucy served as editor of the series, wrote several of the volumes, and co-authored others with Writers' Laboratory members. After five years of disagreements and "harrowing" compromises, three books for the first three grades were published: Farm and City (1944) and Animals, Plants and Machines (1944), by Lucy Mitchell and Margaret Wise Brown, and Our Country (1945), by Lucy Mitchell and Dorothy Stall of the Little Red School House.[71] Lucy withdrew the manuscripts she had prepared for the three older grades after refusing to make alterations demanded by the publisher: the elimination of "humorous, imaginative and rhythmic" writing, and of controversial "social" issues like the oppression of Negroes, the history of monopolies, the union movement, and evolution. The episode had wasted valuable years of her own writing time and absorbed the attention of the Writers' Laboratory to the exclusion of everything else.[72] One compensation had been the opportunity to work closely with Margaret Wise Brown, who helped prod the project along when Lucy was most discouraged.[73]

Another Writers' Laboratory project had its impetus in Bank Street's first "long trips." At the end of 1938, Lucy set out with Eleanor Bowman and Mary Phelps, a member of the writers' group, to explore the country's use of its material resources. In many respects, the project represented a culmination of Lucy's years of teaching "relationship thinking" and "human geography." The special stimulus of the trip, however, came from the Depression. At a time when artists, photographers, and writers as diverse as Erskine Caldwell, James Agee, Lorena Hickok, and Margaret Bourke-White were taking their cameras and notebooks to the highways of America, Lucy also set out across the country to study the texture of American life first-hand.[74] In an old model Ford, "with a rumble well stocked with geology maps and physiographic charts; with books, magazine and newspaper clippings on agriculture, farm economics and social conditions; with thermos bottle, raisins and crackers," Lucy and her two colleagues drove from the Rockies through the High Plains, the central lowlands, and from Texas through the Gulf of Mexico and up the Atlantic plain to the Alleghenies, studying farms, mines, and oilfields. In the south, they visited the shanties of sharecropping farmers. In coal lands, they crawled through tunnels and shot hundreds of feet down mine shafts. In the west, they visited oil boom-towns and the tents of migrant workers. Everywhere they interviewed workers and their families, community officials, merchants, and industrialists.

"The life-gripping experiences" they encountered reaffirmed Lucy's belief that to understand social situations it was necessary to experience them emotionally as well as intellectually. She created an "experimental" volume about the findings of the trip which juxtaposed "fact and image, intellectual and emotional appeal, sources and interpretations," providing detailed explanatory material as well as poems, charts, and maps, most of which she prepared herself.[75] The result was a three-hundred-page book, My Country 'Tis of Thee: The Use and Abuse of Natural Resources, published in 1940.[76]

The book included three sections on the uses of soil, coal, and oil, all of which pointed to the "spectacular waste" of the nation's physical resources and the appalling exploitation of workers. Each section began with present conditions, presenting dramatic material that the authors or Bank Street students had encountered in the field. A second, historical chapter explained the evolution of current problems within the context of social and ideological forces, while a third chapter in each section provided geological case histories. In a concluding chapter the authors called for a "collectivist" program for a planned society; "Let us not shrink from the word," they wrote: "Democratic collectivism does not mean socialism, communism, or any other ism defined by present political parties."[77] But there needed to be a recognition that big business could no longer be considered as a private concern divorced from public control. Their program included federal regulation and selective ownership of the coal industry and of oil-bearing fields and the expansion of soil conservation programs; the creation of a permanent planning board to regulate industrial conditions, develop price and wage policies, and oversee international trade and investments; the development of federal and local planning groups, composed of nonpolitical specialists, to carry on continuous economic and social research; the reconstitution of the public works program and the expansion of national insurance and social security.

Most of these conclusions were in accord with Wesley Mitchell's espousal of thorough, deliberate planning efforts rather than the "crazy quilt" pattern of the early New Deal, with its varied effects. Yet nothing could be further from Wesley's careful, single-minded, microscopic analysis of quantitative data than Lucy's broad and passionate portrait of America's abuse of its resources. The book was clear and well-documented, but it consciously went beyond the "limits of any factual sources," stating that a defined "social philosophy" must be a "preliminary to action."[78] *My Country 'Tis of Thee* does not have the formal power that would have made it survive as some of the other products of that time and spirit have survived; Lucy was a poetic teacher but not a poet, as she herself knew well. But the book did put into practice the holistic goals with which the Bank Street School was founded. "Thinking and feeling should not be mutually exclusive," Lucy wrote in the preface, for "human beings [are] wholes rather than . . . intellects or emotional machines."[79]

In 1941, the Regents of the State of New York granted Bank Street an Absolute Charter which authorized the operation of its nursery and primary school and its teacher training program as a "progressive experiment." It had received a provisional charter ten years before.[80]

But Lucy Mitchell still viewed Bank Street's work in experimental schools as an apprenticeship for the larger work she hoped it would do in the public schools. Though Bank Streeters occasionally talked to public school teacher organizations and participated in giving a course for a teachers' union, Lucy was disappointed that no direct relations with public schools had yet been established.

Only in 1943, twelve years after the establishment of the Cooperative School for Teachers, did the time seem propitious for actively seeking contacts with the public schools. Bank Street drew up a proposal for a workshop for public school teachers. "It was the hottest June that I remember," Barbara Biber recalled.

Lucy and I tramped the sweating streets of Brooklyn, talking to recommended principals, trying to find one who could see that his well-ordered, efficiently run school would benefit from letting us in, with our promise to dispel boredom and make children eager to learn. We would feel them weighing the loss of a neat universe. To Lucy this experience was stimulating. She came away spurred on to help these school people see that they really wanted what we had to give.[81]

The workshop, which began in P.S. 186, an elementary school in Harlem, occupied much of Lucy's time for the next three years. Though the project was exhilarating to Lucy and Bank Street staff, it was not an easy one. The teachers wanted to be shown immediate, cut-and-dried techniques that would enable them to put into practice the more flexible, new style curriculum the Board of Education had called for. Yet they were wary of Bank Street's plan to work directly in their classrooms and to offer after-school workshops at no cost to the school. When Lucy first came in to direct the workshops in her colorful "gypsy" clothes with a little velvet band around her neck, they were not reassured. But hesitation vanished when Lucy took over classrooms of Harlem youngsters.[82]

The teachers at P.S. 186 gradually became confident enough to begin to plan their own projects, gathering and sharing materials. Eventually they planned curricula and developed graded materials for their school and the entire New York public school system. Their interest in social and political issues outside the world of education seemed to broaden during the course of the workshop. When at the end of the three-year project the Board of Education decided to extend the Bank Street workshops to other public schools and to send its own staff to take part in them, Lucy was ecstatic. "I see her now," Barbara Biber recalled, "doing a little fancy polka step in the august halls of 110 Livingston Street and saying in a heady, dreamlike mood: 'If I could be the power behind the throne of the Board of Education, that's all I ask in this life.'"[83]

Against difficult odds, the Bank Street workshops succeeded in transmitting an ardent and inventive attitude toward teaching and toward children through the hierarchical structures of public education. During the span of the workshop, typical functionaries of the New York City public school system had metamorphosed into creative teachers of whom any experimental school could be proud. Lucy's dynamic teaching of children and adults at P.S. 186 played a key role in the success of the venture. One young Harlem pupil told a teacher: "That lady is a genius." Why? "Because she makes us know more than we thought we could."[84]

Lucy had reason to congratulate herself. In setting Bank Street's course in the direction of teacher education in 1930, she had developed an innovative pedagogy for training "experimental," "ardent," and "creative" teachers. The relationship she was now inaugurating with the New York City school system had a significant influence on the quality of New York's public education and served as a model for similar efforts elsewhere. She had successfully shown that the experimental vision had relevance not only to affluent middle-class pupils of private schools but to a much larger population.[85]

The Cooperative School for Teachers, the Associated Experimental Schools, the Writers' Laboratory, and the Public School Workshops were cooperative enterprises set in motion and guided by a group of dynamic professional women—among them Elizabeth Healy, Elisabeth Irwin, Ellen Steele, Elsa Ueland, and, above all, Lucy Mitchell, Harriet Johnson, Barbara Biber, and Jessie Stanton. Harriet Johnson had developed the principles and practices of the Bureau's pioneering nursing school: Lucy once called her the BEE's "foundation stone." Her vision of the "modern" teacher who would treat children as equals was central to the conception of the cooperative teacher-training school more than a decade later. She combined intellectual perspicacity with an emotional warmth that made her a favorite companion of children and adults. Lucy placed Harriet Johnson with Jane Addams and Alice Freeman Palmer as one of the three greatest women she had known. "Without ever crossing the line into sentimentality," Lucy wrote after Johnson's death, "she had a warm devotion to everything that was human."[86]

Barbara Biber did more than anyone else to strengthen the intellectual underpinnings of Bank Street's child development approach, making explicit the linkages between psychology and education that had always guided the institution. Biber pioneered its "developmental interaction theory," which focused on the dual importance of cognition and emotion in understanding the various stages of children's growth as they interacted with the environment, with adults, and with each other. Lucy never emphasized the role of "p-p-s-ychology," as she called it, in children's growth. For Lucy, what teachers had to deal with were the emotions, never the unconscious forces behind them, to which she gave little credence. Despite their different orientations, Lucy respected Biber's work enormously, perhaps too uncritically, Biber thought. For her part, Biber drew inspiration from Lucy, cherishing her "great mind" and dynamic personality. Lucy "embellished the ordinary interchange of life," Biber observed, with the power of her ideas.[87]

Jessie Stanton was another key figure at Bank Street. Jessie came to the BEE in 1929, after ten years at City and Country. She served as assistant director of the nursery school, and became its director after Harriet Johnson's death. Warm and spontaneous, always breaking into giggles, Stanton enjoyed the things that made "children childlike," Lucy observed. Lucy, who related to children on the level of learning rather than feelings, admired Stanton's abilities. "More than any grown-up I know," she once observed, "she is able to enter into a little child's world and see things through a child's eyes." In one of her later books, she thanked Stanton for long years of "letting me use her insight into the way young children think and feel as a testing ground for my own work and thinking."[88]

While Lucy incorporated the ideas and experiences of these and other people in her own work, she helped articulate her colleagues' thinking and developed practical applications for their ideas. Her ability to integrate and penetrate complex concepts made her enthusiastic about the work of others. Colleagues report that after struggling with a new idea they would call Lucy in, and she would immediately clarify the discussion. "She understood everything even before you said it," Barbara Biber noted.[89]

"We grew up together with Lucy beside us, or more accurately, ahead of us . . . far ahead," Biber recalled. She was "a rare, an original, a creative mind" who sparked her colleagues to "'dream' for Bank Street."[90]

She was the founder. . . . She monitored the budgets, she weathered the crises, and more than anyone else, as she often said, she did all the other nasty chores. . . . She was the thinker who constructed a philosophy and a program from an idea. She was the leader, who created a working group of teachers and investigators who could ultimately be described . . . as a "committed society."[91]

Despite Lucy's preeminent role, Bank Street was a pluralistic institution. Lucy consistently refused to become its president or director, and insisted that none of its divisions enthrone the policies of a single individual. She resisted naming programs after individuals: the only exception came after Harriet Johnson's death, when Lucy and her co-workers named the nursery school after the beloved colleague who had founded it.

Lucy eschewed administrative hierarchy of any sort. At Bank Street, all decisions were made by the elected Working Council, a large unwieldy staff body. Every Monday the Council would hold marathon meetings to discuss matters of budget and policy. To those outside the institution and even to some of its trustees, such cooperative decision-making seemed to waste massive amounts of time, but Lucy resisted a more centralized administration in the hands of a powerful director.

At Bank Street in the 1940s and 1950s, she played a central role only in the Division of Studies and Publications and its Writers' Laboratory. She taught courses in the teacher education program, but happily left the division's operation to Charlotte Winsor, Eleanor Bowman, Agnes Snyder and others. She supported the research division, chaired by Barbara Biber, but had relatively little contact with the nursery school after Jessie Stanton's departure. And though Lucy helped initiate Bank Street's Public School Workshop and served as co-worker in the program for three years, the program was administered by Charlotte Winsor.

Lucy's own professional style was a collaborative one. As a colleague, she was "incredible," recalled Irma Simonton Black, director of Bank Street's Publications Division. "She would accept criticism like nobody I knew." Catalyst and mentor, she sponsored the work of many younger women: "It is my job to protect your primary work," she often told them. She enjoyed the fact that Bank Street had become a cadre of people with ideas, energies, and interests of their own.[92]

The strength of Lucy's relationships was not mainly on the level of intuitive, personal interaction, for her empathy with co-workers, as with young children, was primarily intellectual. Yet her awareness of deep emotional processes was in fact greater than she usually allowed herself to express, perhaps because of her own shyness as a child and her anxious sense of individual boundaries. Though not many recognized this underlying sensitivity, Barbara Biber noted that with a few women to whom she was professionally close, "she penetrated to a level that most people never even knew existed."[93]

A final factor in Lucy's ability to inspire and lead Bank Street was her pragmatic, self-assured working style and her creation of a sense of possibilities. From the beginning, Lucy imbued her vision of experimental education with the power of reality. Fueled by a sense of the overriding importance of Bank Street's mission, she was relentless in promoting its cause in the outside world, acting with daring and boldness. Her colleagues saw that such a fearless and dynamic entrepreneurial style was necessary if the goals of a nonconformist, experimental school like Bank Street were to make headway in the professional world and the wider public. Lucy was not so much the patient "professional," Biber observed, as a leader who was "idea-, program-, and work-invested."[94] Bank Street's mission *had* to be accomplished.

Lucy's commitment to the institution, her position as its founder, major financial support, and programmatic leader, and her "mesmerizing" personal qualities made her an authoritative figure at Bank Street. Yet it was her insistence on collective governance and her collaborative working style that provided the mainsprings of Bank Street's supportive environment. There was an extraordinary number of people in whom Lucy could be interested, one former student recalled. Her confidence in them propelled them to be active, sometimes despite initial hesitations. "The extent to which we at Bank Street were able to enact new ideas goes back to Lucy," Biber observed. She was the "prime mover."[95]

PART
FOUR
ALONE

Separations

In the mid-1940s, shortly after her sixty-fifth birthday, Lucy was confronted by a number of major changes in the relationships that had sustained her middle years. With the creation of Bank Street's Public School Workshops in 1943, she had reached a milestone in her professional work. Further opportunities to spread Bank Street's influence came as a consequence of World War Two. Because so many physicians were in the armed forces, medical advice for civilians was in short supply. The Blue Network, the predecessor of the American Broadcasting System, asked Bank Street to present a daily half-hour radio program on medical and psychological issues relating to child development. Lucy Mitchell and Irma Black wrote the scripts for the show—named "The Baby Institute"—and Jessie Stanton served as its host, discussing problems with physicians (prominent among them the young pediatrician Benjamin Spock), child psychologists, and preschool educators.[1] During the war Bank Street also helped initiate nursery and day-care programs throughout the country and was able to expand its own teacher-training program. The success of these efforts, and a growing interest in personal writing projects, led Lucy to contemplate reducing her commitments at Bank Street.

With their children grown and forming families of their own, Wesley and Lucy decided to leave Greenwich Village, where they had lived for more than thirty years. In 1940, Marion Farquhar's architect son Colin designed an elegant, simple home for the Mitchells high on a hillside on their property in Stamford, with wide windows on every side, looking out on the surrounding woods. The plans for Wesley's study went through a hundred revisions, Lucy recalled, as she tried to find space for the ten thousand volumes he had collected. Many of the books related to his professional interests, but the collection also included scores of detective stories and a vast number of books of poetry. Wesley's devotion to poetry struck some of his colleagues as incongruous; what did Browning, page after page of whose work Wesley recited at faculty club luncheons, have to do with business cycles, one friend wondered. But for Wesley as for Lucy, poetry remained one of the "primaries" of life.[2]

Ultimately the Mitchells added an extension to their bedroom in Stamford to make space for all of Wesley's library. In his study, Wesley built a mantel with butternut brought from Greensboro. From the same wood, he fashioned a frame for the big oil painting of himself and one-year-old Sprague that Lucy's friend Winifred Rieber had painted many years before, and hung the portrait in front of the huge "George Washington" desk they had brought from the Village. Here in this comfortable room, away from the hectic life of New York, Wesley planned to write a number of long-postponed books.

For several years, the Mitchells used the new house only on weekends. For Lucy, the prospect of separation from her work life and her New York home proved unsettling. As so often before, she turned to her "incurable habit" of writing to express her conflicts. In the summer of 1945, in a document she titled "My Second Adolescence," she discussed her complex feelings as she entered this new stage of life. And once again, as she faced important decisions, she generalized her situation in order to understand her choices better.

"A woman approaching seventy (or younger or older) is called upon to give up the familiar and loved activities which have been her support through middle life," Lucy began her essay. She noted that like the adolescent whose absorbing questions are "What shall I do? What am I able to do?" the older woman enters a difficult emotional period. "The question is not whether a woman who is growing old can do what she did in the vigorous swing of youth or middle age," Lucy observed; "She cannot." Rather, "growth at either end of life means successfully adapting to new . . . conditions, fitting one's activities and responsibilities to the highest level of one's powers."[3]

In her own case, Lucy admitted that she was not performing professional tasks as efficiently as in the past. Moreover, she increasingly enjoyed time off from official Bank Street work, as she found in 1944–45 when, with no definite intentions of publication, she wrote the first version of her autobiography. Giving up administrative work as Bank

Street's "leader" would not be painful. She realized, too, that in order to avoid turning into a "quoter, a human victrola," she should start pulling back from teaching—the one activity she thought she really did well—to devote herself to writing; she needed to determine "which kind of writing is most intrinsically *mine*."[4] Gradually she reconciled herself to what would in effect be her retirement. But the scenario she and Wesley had designed for their old age did not unfold according to plan.

On Christmas Day 1945, Lucy noticed a "blankness" creeping over the vision of her right eye. On New Year's Day, she underwent a three-hour operation at the Eye Institute of Presbyterian Hospital to restore a detached retina. For two weeks she lay flat on her back, forbidden to turn her head, to open her mouth widely, to raise her eyebrows or smile. She concentrated all her attention on remaining still. "I was held unmoving as by a great weight of water which swayed slightly far overhead," she wrote in a long letter to "Bank Streeters" in March. "I was a flounder, pressed flat into the sandy bottom of the ocean." Kept in total darkness, she found herself subject to amazing visions—"some pure design, delicate or vividly bold in form and color." While these gorgeous images were exhilarating—almost as if she were on an LSD trip, recalled one of her sons—the practical Lucy tried to harness her visions more purposefully. "I experimented. I visualized the foot of my bed. Slowly, I made it go down as my head gradually rose until I had the illusion of sitting up in bed. It rested my back but I could not hold the image."[5] Compensating for the temporary loss of her sight, Lucy relished the intensification of her other senses; she listened intently to the sounds of hospital life and smelled the pungent odors of flowers and perfumes. Even so the three-week hospital stay was harrowing. Wesley visited her daily and showed his concern in many ways, but later she marvelled—not without some disappointment—that he had been able to work steadily throughout this trying period. "His habit of control never deserted him," she observed.[6]

Lucy's recovery was total. But a new crisis came in October 1946. The previous year, Wesley had resigned as director of research at the NBER, but remained a member of its research staff. Now, Lucy and Wesley decided to make the planned move to Stamford and offered the use of their Horatio Street duplex to Arnold and his wife. The Mitchells retained use of the penthouse floor at Horatio Street for an overnight stay on Mondays. The new schedule gave Wesley five days of uninterrupted writing time in the country, with Mondays and Tuesdays at the National Bureau. Lucy participated in the Public School Workshop and attended meetings at Bank Street on those two days.

Although it had been Lucy's own considered choice to cut back her Bank Street commitments and begin full-time writing, the actual separation from Bank Street came as a tremendous shock. After the move to Stamford, Lucy began to suffer frightening bouts of amnesia. While her physicians diagnosed a spasm in a cerebral blood vessel, Lucy believed the attacks were caused in good part by the emotional strain of leaving her work. In her later account of this experience, her anger at Wesley, though understated, is apparent. He noted her memory loss in his diary, she observed, but made no reference to the deep insecurities it caused her. Since he did not recognize her emotional trauma, she did not speak of it to him or any friends or family; she felt they would be distressed at her confusion and her terror that another "spasm" might overcome her when she was alone. She did not exactly blame Wesley for his insensitivity, but it was he who had initiated the move to Stamford, and during this time of severe stress, he had been all too easy to deceive.[7]

Fortunately, Lucy's memory lapse was short-lived. Soon she became involved in a new book about Bank Street's Public School Workshop experience and made her adjustment to the commuting routine. She had begun to accept the occasional frailties that came with growing old and to make her peace with them.

At seventy-three, Wesley enjoyed superb health. Though a childhood bout of rheumatic fever had left a residual heart murmur, he had never been ill throughout the five decades Lucy had known him. His heart attack on September 3, 1947, came "like a crash of thunder on a serene summer day."[8]

The attack was a mild one ("wakened many times gasping for breath," was the simple notation Wesley made in his diary) and the prognosis was encouraging. Wesley had to limit his physical activity only moderately. Stairs were forbidden, which meant that the Mitchells had to give up their overnights at the Horatio Street duplex. Instead, Lucy fixed up a small apartment for them in her office at Bank Street, where they continued to spend one night each week. Ordered to curtail other activities by 20 percent Wesley simply rearranged his statistics, claiming that this meant he could exercise just as hard if he restricted his hikes up the steep Stamford hills to eight days out of ten.[9]

Consumed with a new sense of urgency, he recorded in his diary the number of pages written each day, as if to prove to himself that his mental capacities were unimpaired. Despite her optimism about Wesley's strong recovery, Lucy was disconcerted by this indication of anxiety. She had never known him to feel sorry for himself, and he almost never expressed anger or stress. Once, years before, when the Mitchells were talking with the gay and delightful Harriet Forbes, Lucy exploded. "You two are the most hopelessly normal people I ever knew. You haven't a complex between you." "I have plenty of complexes," Wesley responded. Asked to name one, he answered unhesitatingly, "I don't like tripe!"[10]

Because of his sound constitution, Lucy felt, he never understood the effects of illness, treating her own as either irrelevant inconveniences or dreadful calamities. Once, when Lucy had come down with pneumonia, a terrified Wesley insisted: "Now Lucy, you simply *must not* think of getting up to get my supper."[11] With him, she thought, there was health or death, nothing in between.

In December 1947, Lucy and Jack accompanied Wesley to Chicago to attend the annual meeting of the American Economic Association, where he received the highest honor of his profession: the first Francis A. Walker Medal, to be awarded every five years to the American economist who had made "the most distinguished contribution to the main body of economic thought and knowledge."[12] Later, Alvin Johnson was to say of Wesley Mitchell that he "stood out as Dean of his profession, a title never conferred upon him by an official body but by the universal acclaim of all men and women deserving the title of economist. . . . Wesley Mitchell by his own modest self constituted a great epoch in the economic thinking of our times."[13]

With Wesley's continued recovery, the first six months of 1948 passed companionably, uneventfully. In June, Lucy was discovered to have a ruptured appendix, but she recovered full strength after an emergency appendectomy, and only at Marni's insistence accepted the help of an "old lady" to assist them at home. "I've never seen old people like you," their new housekeeper told them. "He sits on one side reading; you sit on the other reading. He says something and you smile; you say something and he smiles. You're just like two old fairies!"[14]

Three weeks after Lucy's surgery, the Mitchells travelled to Greensboro for their thirty-fourth summer there. There were long mornings of writing, carpentry or golf for Wesley in the afternoons, a late swim, and evenings of reading together, alone or aloud. But the pace of Wesley's work on his manuscripts had quickened. That summer he completed the next to the last chapter of the first book of a planned two-volume work which would be the culmination of his life-long study of business cycles. Out of the masses of quantitative data collected and analyzed by the National Bureau, he made explicit in this volume the economic theory that guided the Bureau's work. The proposed second volume of the set would focus specifically on his own economic theory. Another project he hoped to undertake would return to an unfinished manuscript begun in 1916 at Columbia, a history of the development of economic theory. All during the many years of his detailed data-gathering and analysis, Mitchell's deepest interest was in economic theory. But the requirements of his role as director of research at the National Bureau had kept him from the individual studies in theory which he felt would have rounded out his work.

That scholarly reward was not to be. In Greensboro, on August 28, 1948, Wesley was stricken again. At first, neither Lucy nor other family members were alarmed, for they expected that he would recover as quickly as he had from his first attack, nearly a year before. Wesley was less sanguine. On the morning of the attack, he insisted that Lucy telephone Arthur Burns, his successor as research director at the National Bureau, to tell him to cut off his pay check immediately as he could no longer be a productive worker.

Lucy and Wesley returned to Stamford, where after a while Wesley slept in a high hospital bed pulled near the window of his study. Every word and gesture during the three weeks in Stamford was etched in Lucy's memory: how he gripped her hand tightly as she sat beside him; his calls for her when she left the room; how he whispered "hold me tight, darling, hold me tight." It was as if he needed Lucy close by at every moment to reassure him that he was not losing his own "authentic self," Lucy thought, the self that she knew as no one else did. [15]

Though Wesley's doctor urged him to put work concerns out of his mind, he could not do it. In *Two Lives*, Lucy poignantly recalls two of the work-related dreams that came to him during these sad days: one, a dream about his struggle to lead a group of people building a medieval cathedral, each of whom wanted to be assigned the best portion of work (a square inch of the Christ Child), while nobody but Wesley himself considered the effort as a whole; another, a dream about discovering a set of community records in Athens which included complete income statistics dating back thousands of years, "the sweetest records any economist could imagine."[16] Lucy recognized in the first dream a reflection of Wesley's vision of his public work; the second seems a direct reference to his desire to work privately on economic history.

Often he was delirious, mixing reality with his vivid dreams. Occasionally he sang softly, a low, rhythmic meandering melody. This was so uncharacteristic of Wesley, who was tone deaf, that Lucy puzzled over it until Margaret Wise Brown suggested that it might have expressed the poet that had always lain at the core of his soul. At the end, as he sought his authentic self, he sang.[17]

Eventually Wesley resisted all treatment, refusing to take food, water, or medicine. The time came to take him to a hospital in New York. On that last day in Stamford, a Sunday, before the ambulance came, he gave Lucy a sign that she would never forget. It was, she believed, the final affirmation of his real self.

You had looked intently from side to side, at your books reaching everywhere to the ceiling, at your desk strangely empty of manuscript. . . . From side to side you looked saying, "I'm taking this in. I'm taking this in." Then loudly, "I get it, damn you!" Suddenly you had thrown your hands up over your head and cried out, "Why and wherefore do we hunt for beauty and happiness? The ground is rough, very rough, very rough." Then you turned to look from your bed out towards our woods. Your profile was sharp against the background of your books. It was severe but not bitter. It was full of power but not rebellion. It was controlled but not serene. It was as if I saw the essence of your spirit—transfigured. I knew—Oh Robin, I knew you were accepting that for you this was the end. You were alone. I sat close to your bed. But you were alone. If there were a God, I thought that is the way he would see you. Beautiful—incredibly beautiful. Good—incredibly good. Great—incredibly great. Then you turned and came back to me and I went to you.[18]

A few days later, on October 29, he died. Desolate, but as always efficient, Lucy instructed Arthur Burns to prepare an obituary for *The New York Times*.[19] All the world needed to know about Wesley Clair Mitchell. That would be the only way she could endure this final separation.

"Becoming More So"

Lucy lived for nineteen years after Wesley Clair Mitchell's death. During her seventies and eighties, without either the companionship or the work that had sustained her during her middle years, she waged a constant battle against despair. Her conflicts and triumphs—for there were both—emerge in her remarkable written record of this time. Even in the last years of her old age, her aspirations were mighty. She was determined to live not a "shrunken" life but a life of fullness, a life that expressed "all of me," as she had once written to Josiah Royce, her Harvard professor. She searched for the excitement and adventure of learning afresh, and found it in exploring the aging process as it affected her own emotional world. In her late eighties, she was still searching, easily discouraged but also heartened that every moment she seemed to be uncovering facets of her "real self."

After Wesley's death, Lucy was stunned by the immediate outpouring of praise not only for her husband's scholarly achievements but also for his personal qualities. These tributes contributed to her "scalding guilt" at having, as she thought, taken her husband's greatness for granted. Perhaps another source of guilt was unacknowledged envy: envy of Wesley's professional eminence and the admiration of his colleagues. Her discovery of Wesley's correspondence with his old friend Sadie Gregory, which suggested that for a time Sadie had played a more important role than Lucy as intellectual confidante and counselor, seems at first to have distressed her. Had she failed her husband in his deepest interests?[1]

Even more acute was her remorse at her own "ungentleness." She castigated herself repeatedly for the "crossgrained streak" that she felt he had understood and forgiven but which now stained her memories of their happy years. According to her sons, Lucy had indeed been especially querulous during their last years together. Now she suspected that Robin might have been lonely for outward tokens of her love.[2]

Grieving that she had forever lost the chance to be more loving and gentle, Lucy began to write to and about Robin, declaring her love. Three weeks after his death, she wrote a long letter reliving the time of his last illness at Stamford and calling up all the images of their long acquaintance: their first meeting in Chicago, Robin in Berkeley and the Sierras, Robin in their several Greenwich Village homes and in Greensboro.[3] Then she wrote shorter pieces, often every day, pouring forth her grief, remorse and love. She called these musings "sonnets" or "songs" and wrote them as rhymed or free verse. These "outpourings" expressed Lucy's conflicts, reflected her bewilderment, fears and hopes, and, in certain ways, allowed her to expiate her guilt. She was to write to her husband in this fashion for almost two decades.

Shortly after Wesley Mitchell's death, Arthur Burns asked Lucy to prepare a biographical sketch of him for a National Bureau memorial publication. At first, Lucy refused this and other requests for her personal reminiscences, needing to dwell on her memories privately. It was not long, however, before she decided to do a biography of Robin on her own. Yet after fifteen months, she felt that she had not succeeded in presenting her husband's work in a fashion that non-economists could understand. Even more important, she could not describe him without including herself and their marriage. She had borrowed heavily from the autobiography she had written in 1945 to tell Robin's story, and could no longer think of publishing that work separately. She also felt that an account of Bank Street's development would be timely, given the institution's growing prominence. After consultation with Arnold and his wife, she decided on a "double biography," which she thought would be a "new and interesting literary form to experiment with."[4] Thus, fashioned out of "Myself: An Autobiography in Changing Culture" and the biography of Robin in progress, was born "Two Lives: The Story of Wesley Clair Mitchell and Myself."

For a time, Lucy reproached herself for compulsively writing sonnets about her grief instead of making progress with the dual biography. By the summer of 1950, however, she was working eight or nine hours a day, rising at six in the morning to write, as had been her custom all through life. Her work unleashed searing memories of their last days together and a "never-ceasing ache" as she came to understand her own "immaturities," revealed in the records of their courtship and long years together. Lucy intended the book as a tribute to her marriage and to her husband, and as an atonement for her "forgetfulness and fretfulness" to him. But many worries disturbed her. Would the public be interested in "what manner of man [he was]? . . . what manner of husband and father?" Could she portray him not as a "saint" but as a complete human being? Could she subdue her own "tyrant ego" that wanted to proclaim throughout that she was the love of his life, and he of hers?[5]

With many misgivings, she sent the completed manuscript to Arnold in September, 1951. He responded positively, as her other children did later, though they asked her to make some deletions. She went through another episode of doubt when she brought the book before a "cold, commercial auction block," worrying whether the words she had written "because I could not help it" should in fact become a book for strangers.[6]

Two Lives was published in 1953 by Simon and Schuster to favorable reviews. Lucy had combined family anecdotes with background material that "set the stage" for the changing events of the Mitchells' two careers. There were also excerpts from letters and long portions of Wesley's speeches and writings. Lucy was praised by his colleagues for the skill with which she presented his work. Though it was non-traditional as biography and problematic in chronology and organization, the book was splendidly alive, vividly written and compelling. Despite its heterogeneous content, Lucy succeeded in bringing unity to the personal and professional portraits of each subject. It was her most experimental and least didactic book, her deepest, most colorful and natural piece of writing. Increasingly over the years the book found an enthusiastic, if small audience, interested not only in the substantial public achievements of the two Mitchells but in the couple's conscious attempt to combine professional concerns with full family life.

To her friends and colleagues, Lucy's readjustment seemed normal. She used the Stamford house only occasionally, and in January 1950, she moved out of the Bank Street apartment into a new "compromise" apartment (sunny, but in a "grubby environment") nearby on Greenwich Street.[7] Although she concluded her long teaching career at Bank Street in 1948, she remained chairman of its Working Council until 1950, when Bank Street received its certification as the Bank Street College of Education. Productive even in her grief, she completed, with the help of colleagues, the manuscript of *Our Children and Our Schools*, a detailed study of Bank Street's Public School Workshops, published in 1950 by Simon and Schuster, and participated in writing Bank Street's first series of Golden Books.[8]

Privately, she declared that the "hard-won surface control" evident in these projects was only a facade. She despaired that her activities at work and her relationships with colleagues and friends were "insignificant" and "trivial." Yet despite her continuing grief, she still assumed leadership in the face of complex and trying professional problems. When a major crisis developed at Bank Street in 1953, occasioned by a bitter feud between the nursery school and the other divisions of the college, she set out to mediate the disagreement, and finally took decisive action when the parties were unable to reach agreement. The research and teaching staff, led by Barbara Biber, and some trustees insisted that Bank Street break with the nursery school, since its leaders refused to work more closely with the college. Lucy sided with this group, for which she was severely attacked by partisans of the nursery school. The criticisms wounded her—it was probably the first time that she was not hailed and admired by all her Bank Street associates—but she stuck with her decision. Less involved colleagues noted that Lucy performed ably, efficiently, and fairly during the agonizing months of turmoil.[9]

Lucy had offered her resignation as Chairman of the Board of Trustees every year since 1950, but it had never been accepted. Now, in the face of the rupture that threatened Bank Street's cooperative ethos, she was needed more than ever. In the summer of 1953, as she was celebrating her seventy-fifth birthday, the Trustees asked her to become Acting President while continuing to serve as Chairman of the Board. She had previously refused the title of president, but this time she accepted in the hope that she might help heal hurt feelings and assure the outside world of Bank Street's continued health. She remained as Acting President for three years, resigning in June 1956, when John Niemeyer, headmaster of the Oak Lane Country Day School at Temple University in Philadelphia, assumed the office of president. Out of respect for Lucy and his awareness of the staff and alumnae's great admiration for her, Niemeyer always referred to her as Bank Street's "first president."[10]

Lucy remained a trustee of Bank Street until her death, becoming one of Niemeyer's strongest supporters as he led Bank Street into new ventures. While some of her long-time associates opposed the inauguration of a textbook project (the Bank Street Readers) on the ground that Bank Street had never used textbooks before, Lucy welcomed the series as a tool that could empower teachers and aid children's effective learning. Likewise, she supported Niemeyer's plan to relocate the college. 69 Bank Street had been outgrown several years earlier, forcing the Research Division to move to an annex on West Fourteenth Street. Now, when Columbia University and the Morningside Heights Neighborhood Association made Bank Street an attractive offer to bring the college to their neighborhood, the opportunity to relocate seemed right. Some friends of Bank Street questioned the move, for strong community ties to Greenwich Village had grown up over almost fifty years. How could an institution named after a street in the Village prosper in the alien regions of northern Manhattan?

Lucy was enthusiastic. The idea was "simply terrific," she wrote her friend Sally Kerlin, the new chairman of Bank Street's Board of Trustees. "Bank Street began like a fairy tale with Elizabeth Coolidge's gift for ten years. The move to Morningside Heights with an elementary school carries on the fairy tale—and all in my lifetime!"[11] But she urged trustees to ensure that Bank Street did not lose its cooperative ardor and nonconformity in the more establishment Heights.[12] As Bank Street continued to expand its scope and influence, extending its new School for Children through the eighth grade and undertaking new training and consultancy programs for teachers and children outside its own schools, Lucy cheered on its work. As long as Bank Street did not deviate from its traditional goals, she had no quarrel with modernization. "A transformed Bank Street," she wrote to Kerlin, "seems like another fortunate miracle."[13]

Lucy's contacts with her children and their families helped to heal a part of the loneliness she felt after Wesley's death. In 1941, Jack had married Basia Jarjambowska, a Polish student he had met at Columbia University where they both pursued graduate work in economics. Now, with three small sons, they returned from New Orleans, where Jack had been teaching at Tulane University, to Connecticut. Jack taught economics at the University of Connecticut, later becoming a consultant on economic development in Peru and Iran; he continued to work on his doctorate throughout these years.

Sprague was also married in 1941, to Marion Roberts, a charming, good-looking woman from Old Greenwich, Connecticut, and began a successful career in advertising at Condé Nast. Lucy's first grandchildren were their twin girls—Beverly and Joan—born the following year. "I rejoice in married children," she wrote to her cousin Elizabeth Sprague Coolidge, "and I love being a grandmother. . . . The twins . . . are beautiful babies . . . the best theater I know!"[14] Sprague and Marion delighted Lucy by naming their third daughter, born in 1947, after her.

A Phi Beta Kappa from Amherst College, Arnold did graduate work briefly and then began a career in publishing in New York. Lucy was probably proudest of Arnold, her youngest son, a gentle young man who loved poetry as much as his parents did. She was especially fond of his wife, Jean Wilder, formerly an editor at G.P. Putnam's: they were married in 1942. Arnold and Jean and their two young daughters moved to Palo Alto, California, in 1947, when Arnold began work at the Stanford Research Institute. Two more children, a daughter and a son, were born there. Lucy made several trips to California in the years after Robin's death to visit them.

Marni was a trim, vigorous, beautiful blonde; her friend and admirer Elizabeth Coolidge thought of her as a "mini Babe Diedrickson."[15] Marni immersed herself in the world of horses—riding, showing, jumping, and teaching the equestrian arts in Colorado. During World War II, she had lost her aviator fiancé during a training accident, and she showed no later romantic interests.

A number of family issues arose after Wesley's death that disturbed Lucy as much as the dissension at Bank Street. After his return from New Orleans, Jack and his family wanted to take over the old Stamford farmhouse, where the Caseys had been living since 1927, paying nominal rent to the Mitchells and performing some caretaking services. At Jack's insistence, Lucy wrote to Mollie, reminding her that the Mitchells had asked the Caseys to find new quarters as far back as 1935. Mollie conceded that Paddy was a "maladjusted person, afraid of new situations, afraid to take new jobs, lacking in initiative"—but she had clung silently to the hope that they would be able to stay on, doing some work for the family, even if the Stamford property were divided among the Mitchell children.

After further correspondence and the threat of eviction, the Caseys bought another piece of property in Stamford where they built their own home. Lucy wanted to give Jack what he asked, and she felt that her offer to the Caseys had been generous; conditional upon their move, she had set up a trust fund for their son's education and gave Mollie an additional sum in securities. But she was uncomfortable with the way things had gone; if Robin had lived, they might have found another, gentler way to resolve the problem.[16]

There was trouble, too, about the Greensboro property. The land bought from the Chases in 1914 had been deeded to Wesley Mitchell. In his will, he left this property to the children. After Wesley's death, Lucy followed his lead by deeding over to the children a second large piece of property which the Mitchells had purchased jointly from the Chases in 1928.

But after this she no longer felt that Greensboro was her home. With-out Robin, in any event, Greensboro could no longer be what it had been for her. When she came back one summer to put things in order, relatives found her snappy and churlish, scowling if as much as a vase had been rearranged in his study. She yelled at the Coolidges for being too noisy when using the boathouse on the Mitchell property and for other malfeasances, and almost caused a rift with these long-time friends. She seemed unready to accept the life and joy that continued in Greensboro in Robin's absence. She did not return.[17]

In August 1955, Lucy made a momentous move, leaving the East for California. Here, in the "magic land" where she had lived during her early adolescence and the first unmarried years of her professional life, she would spend what she often called the "second adolescence" of her seventies and eighties. She purchased a charming little house, complete with white picket fence and trellises of roses, in Palto Alto, three blocks from her son Arnold. She felt unable to settle there permanently as yet, for her sister Mary in Washington, now a widow, had become very de-pendent on her since Adolph's death four years earlier. As Lucy watched Mary's decline, she had become apprehensive about her own future. "Still afraid to be alone," Lucy wrote of Mary, "her world had shrunken through the years." She died in 1957 a "child-princess," never achieving "the stature of a queen."[18] In California, close to Arnold and his family, Lucy hoped to avoid the loneliness of Mary's last days and perhaps recap-ture something of the contentment she had once found near the great mountains where a half century earlier she had fallen in love with Robin.

She was not disappointed in her little house, with its great gnarled oak tree that towered over the mossy yard and the wild strawberries, violets, and bright California flowers that filled her garden. From her former homes, Lucy brought many of her best-loved possessions: Oriental rugs originally from her Story-Book house in Berkeley; the many-angled tables, benches, and lamps crafted by Robin at Greensboro; yellow chairs from the Horatio Street penthouse; the Arthur Davies landscapes they loved. Then she worked on the house herself, painting its picket fence, cabinets, and shelves, and redesigning a long narrow room to "let the outdoors in." The twenty-foot sheet of glass she installed became her "magic casement" through which she watched the unfolding of the geraniums, carnations, and poppies that filled her garden and the great oak that cast dappled shadows on the lawn.[19] No visitor ever left her house without getting a tour of the yard.

In the Palo Alto house Lucy found the serenity she had sought since Robin's death. Her garden became a "patch of the cosmos" that allowed her to feel at one with the earth forces she had always celebrated. With the living things around her, she was "alone but seldom lonely," for she had "companions," even "colleagues." Her joy in the changing world— "the unfolding of a fuchsia, each day revealing a new design, sometimes a startlingly new color . . . or the sky, never twice the same, or the great tree . . . the sun . . . or the wind"—left her imagination free to roam in unaccustomed ways. "The world holds such unending treasure," she wrote, "that I joy to sing."[20]

Her peace, however, was not uninterrupted. In November 1955, Lucy journeyed to Kansas City to be with Marni, who had to undergo a series of severe operations on her liver. Though Lucy never mentioned Marni's alcoholism, she must have been aware of it. Family and friends believe the habit developed after Marni joined a heavy-drinking, high-living riding circuit centered in Kansas City. Others note that she had always been lonely and unhappy, remaining an outsider in her family circle. Though her parents had encouraged her to make her own choices and supported her equestrian interests in every way, no doubt she had reason to feel that they were disappointed that she was not more intellectual. Guests remember that at family gatherings Marni was reclusive, her infrequent remarks ignored by other company. Her closest family relationship was with Sprague, whom she adored, and his three daughters. Close relatives also comment on Marni's nonconformity. In the 1950s, her casual manner, passionate interest in sports and her unvarying costume of jeans and tee-shirt set her apart from most female contemporaries. A friend who knew the adolescent Marni guessed that her affectionate physicality with girl friends during those years expressed an inherent, if never actualized, lesbianism.

From Lucy's perspective, Marni resisted any sign of pampering or dependency and never allowed her mother or others in the family to demonstrate their affection. Marni was the one who showered them all with gifts carefully selected for them through the year, though she did not like to receive gifts herself. But now, when she admitted her need of Lucy, Lucy stayed at her side during the months of her hospitalization and recovery.[21] Soon after this Marni fell from a horse and broke her collar bone. This painful accident and her second slow recuperation left her greatly saddened, aware that her riding days were probably at an end.

Lucy admitted to one of her Bank Street friends that she had gone through terrible "spasms of guilt" over Marni but had at last gotten over them. Though she knew that Marni was not yet well and would not be for a long time, she recognized that "she and she alone can decide what she can and cannot do."[22] "All is not guilt that jitters," she told herself. Characteristically, on her return to California she wrote a short essay with this title, sending it to Bank Street for possible publication.

But there was a special irony in this essay. She started from the observation that adults were often unable to outgrow the habit of guilt "put over" on them as children because they did not act exactly as their parents wanted. Rejecting Freud's notion that guilt came primarily "from a suppression of sex impulses," she argued on the basis of her experience that guilt was a direct product of Puritan pedagogy. To her father, and she assumed to many others, guilt had been a desirable end in itself. "If I *enjoyed* trying to express myself or to think for myself, I felt guilty for not feeling guilty."[23]

Yet Lucy apparently ignored the fact that her own progressive methods of child-rearing had produced a similar emotional pattern in Marni. Just as Lucy had felt that she was "the wrong kind of person" because she was "unlike her parents," so Marni, too, suffered a deep lack of self-esteem, at least in part for the same reason. The fact that this parallel escaped Lucy's attention is surely itself a clue to what Marni had had to deal with. Lucy would not face her relation with her daughter directly: she dealt with her guilt partly by generalizing, partly by focusing backward in time, on her own experience.

In the early 1950s, Marni had found a surrogate family in Greensboro—Bernie Atherton, a farmer who had once delivered milk to the Mitchell compound, and his schoolteacher wife, Lora. With no children

of their own, the Athertons—fifteen and ten years older than Marni—
welcomed her into their lives. They sold her a prime piece of land near
theirs, atop a long sloping hill, surrounded by meadows and overlooking
Caspian Lake. Here Marni planned to raise beef cattle and build a house
of her own, distant from the Mitchell family compound where Sprague
and Jack, who had purchased Marni and Arnold's shares of the Greensboro inheritance, regularly vacationed. Marni got along particularly well
with Bernie Atherton, whom she admired as she once had loved Farmer
Chase. The Athertons and Marni planned to retire together, travelling
some, but spending most of the time enjoying the four seasons in Greensboro.[24]

Marni did not have a chance to see her new house completed, though
she had proudly taken Lucy to visit it during its final stage of construction. Her plans were interrupted by a four-month hospital stay in New
York. Suffering by now from chronic cirrhosis of the liver, in the spring
of 1958 Marni required surgery again. Lucy was by her bedside in New
York all the time, returning to California in July only when Marni
seemed out of danger. Those months with Marni were the most dreadful
of Lucy's life. Marni hemorrhaged severely and required repeated blood
transfusions; she "had kissed death three times," the doctor told Lucy.
Her survival was a miracle. Yet Marni never complained of her terrible
pain. When Lucy had to leave her for the last time, Marni gave her an
orchid, ordered from her hospital bed, to match her travelling outfit. At
Christmas, which mother and daughter had spent together since Lucy
was widowed, there had always been orchids from Marni.[25]

Back in California, Lucy found herself "numb . . . passive—
battered—hurt—almost inert—unequal to life," her peace "shattered."[26] She had stopped writing her sonnets to Robin during Marni's
hospitalization; now she hoped to find solace in renewing them. In late
summer, however, she suffered a heart attack and was hospitalized briefly
in California. She had had several previous attacks, the most recent
nearly two-and-a-half years earlier. Now her doctors advised her to be
more cautious. She was forbidden even to walk the three blocks to
Arnold's house.

Marni, meantime, living in the Mitchells' Stamford house and cared
for by Mollie, made a good recovery. Toward the end of September, she
wrote to her mother that she was well enough to drive her prized car, a
black Plymouth. Still Lucy felt she could not be secure about Marni until
she remained without reversal for a much longer period.[27]

At about this time, Lucy received word from the University of California that on September 29 she was to be one of four recipients of an honorary doctor of laws degree on the occasion of Clark Kerr's inauguration as the university's twelfth president. Lucy's doctors allowed her to participate on condition that she would not walk in the procession or attend the luncheon honoring President Kerr.

Several days before the ceremony, tragic news came from Stamford. Marni, who had been enjoying the New England fall, had fallen sick late in the evening of September 25. Mollie was there throughout the long night, cradling Marni in her arms and soothing her fears. In the morning, the fatal hemorrhage came. Mollie and Sprague's wife, Marion, took Marni to the hospital, where she passed into a coma, awakening only once to call to Mollie. She died on the afternoon of September 26.[28] The funeral took place in Stamford three days later. Sprague brought her ashes to their beloved Greensboro, where they were buried in a hillside cemetery at the end of the north shore road overlooking Caspian Lake.

Lucy did not attend Marni's funeral. On that sunny Monday afternoon, Clark Kerr presented her with the degree of honorary doctor of laws, the University's highest award. The citation read:

First Dean of Women at the University of California, self-styled "first such creature west of the Rockies"; sympathetic friend and wise counselor of students; far-seeing proponent of wider educational opportunities for women; leader in the theory and practice of elementary instruction; founder of the Bank Street College of Education; charming author; understanding mother; devoted life-partner of eminent economist Wesley Clair Mitchell; one of our greatest professors of half a century ago.[29]

Several family members and friends noted with mixed feelings that this distinguished educator, honored for her pioneering work for women and children, missed her daughter's funeral to receive her tribute. Perhaps they underestimated the cost to Lucy. At eighty, barely recovered from a serious heart attack, a trip cross-country might have been fatal to her. But those who condemned her believed her actions reflected her priorities. In Lucy's life, had not work always mattered more than children?

It was months before Lucy could openly express her grief for Marni. Only on Christmas Day, the time that she and Marni had often spent together, did her tears for her daughter finally flow. In years to come, Lucy would frequently break down when she thought of Marni or came across one of her belongings, asking trusted friends why her life could not have been taken before Marni's. She never could fully confront her daughter's alcoholism. The final cause of death had been an aneurysm, caused by a portal vein that had probably been defective from birth, Lucy reported to her family. The implication was that Marni's problem had been one for which Lucy and Wesley, her adoptive parents, were not responsible.[30]

Arnold and Jean had urged Lucy to come to California when she became a widow, even though one of the reasons they had moved cross-continent was to build a life of their own. When she settled three blocks away, they saw her regularly, for an hour or so each day, or for dinner. She indicated that she wanted intimacy, Jean recalled, but at the same time she didn't allow it. Often on their visits together she would be holding a sheaf of papers—letters from friends, business letters, household matters, a manuscript on which she was working, perhaps a book she was reading—that she wanted to share. With a drink in one hand and a cigarette dangling from the other, she would go over her documents, from the top of the pile down, handing each to Arnold as she finished but hardly allowing time for a reply. She was the chairman of the cocktail hour.[31]

If Lucy worried about her relationship with her children, there is no evidence of it in her papers. The "sonnets" written after Marni's death indicate that she felt each of her three sons had achieved a new stage of maturity after difficult times. She felt comfortable with all three and especially appreciative of the fact that she was made welcome by Arnold and his family.

Lucy was a proud and doting grandmother, often vying with colleagues and friends as to whose grandchildren were the most adorable. She loved Sprague's twins and their young sister and Jack's three boys, and visited them frequently when she lived in Stamford. Now in California, she was happily absorbed by Arnold and Jean's four young children, occasionally jotting down an especially vivid phrase or story, still fascinated by children's artful uses of language.

But Lucy, in her colorful long skirts and embroidered blouses and wearing her favorite Chinese snake necklace and the scarab pins from ancient Egypt, was "not like any other grandmother," her grandchildren thought. Like their parents, Lucy's ten grandchildren responded to her in different ways. Some found her distant and remote. But for others, Lucy was enchanting, creating an influence that lasted throughout their lives.[32]

Aside from her family, Lucy saw few people in Palo Alto other than a few old friends like Rosie Bliven, who with her husband, Bruce, former editor of *The New Republic*, had moved to Stanford, and some new friends who, like Rosie, were involved with Bank Street's West Coast Associates, an organization of alumnae and friends of Bank Street that Lucy had helped establish.[33] Lucy worked actively with the Associates, planning workshops and helping to raise money for Bank Street. One bad moment, albeit a brief one, came after she had lectured to a two-week workshop on children's language given to the Associates by Claudia Lewis. She found she no longer had confidence in her powers as a teacher, and she felt "adrift again . . . near the breaking point," yearning for her earlier life.[34]

A more serious decline in Lucy's spirits began in November, 1960 when, at the urging of Arnold and Jean, she began to consider leaving her house to move to a retirement home. The family had grown anxious about her health, for she continued to refuse practical help. Concerned neighbors would see her tottering down the street, laden with shopping bags, stooped and fragile. She appeared almost hunchbacked, much smaller than her full five feet seven inches. Once she fell at home, cracking a rib. Finally, to relieve the children ("for I love you better than you have known," she wrote in a poem at this juncture), she reserved an apartment at Channing House, a planned apartment complex for the elderly to be constructed only a few blocks from her home.[35]

The thought of moving caused Lucy great anxiety, recorded in a new stage of her writing to Robin. A series of fully realized sonnets expressed both her deepest agonies and her surges of exultation. Noting her inconstancy, she was disturbed by the months of fluctuation. "I rise on the crest of exaltation; I fall to the trough of depression," she acknowledged, "yet I never move forward." She recognized that her mood swings reflected both poles of her self-esteem—her "vanity" and her "mock-modesty"—the traits that Robin had identified during their courtship fifty years before. Both patterns were "irrational" and self-deluding. To be gentle with herself, not lashing herself with blame for the "dramatic vagaries" that Robin had accepted and loved, was "the final step in gentleness." She kept his example constantly before her as she rehearsed her inadequacies in her own terms and sought to amend them in practice.[36]

Despite these reverses, Lucy found that a strange, peaceful "sense of waiting" had come to her during the two years that Channing House was being built. She was calmed by her garden and by her writing to Robin, which eventually took on a joyous quality, no longer full of stark grief and self-pity. She could express their love as a "vital flowing," without pained reminiscences of special moments, missed opportunities, or guilt.[37] In Camus, Brecht, and Agee, whose works she read avidly at this time, she found the same struggle and ultimate victory over despair. "In the middle of winter, I found there was in me an invincible summer," Camus had written. And so in her old age there seemed to lurk the possibilities of positive growth and the sustaining force of love.[38]

One of the happiest encounters of Lucy's declining years came in January, 1962, when she heard Mary Bunting, president of Radcliffe College, speak at the Radcliffe Club of San Francisco. Bunting told of a new experimental program—the Radcliffe Institute for Independent Study— which she had established at the college in 1960 for a five-year trial basis. Concerned that a "climate of unexpectation" was causing a "waste of highly talented educated women-power," Bunting set up the institute as a "laboratory" where talented married women could pursue self-directed projects in scholarship or the creative arts on a part-time basis, aided by small stipends, access to Harvard's libraries and laboratories, and office space. The institute also sponsored research to investigate the plight of highly educated women in America, and instituted a guidance program to help deal with the problem of college women's entry and re-entry into the job market. Lucy thought these programs inspired. "What a fine *woman!* . . . so simple and yet imaginative," she wrote to Sally Kerlin. "She seems to be an influence not only on Radcliffe but on *all* college women—indeed, on women in our culture."[39]

Eight months earlier, in an informal talk to the Radcliffe Club of San Francisco, Lucy had observed that in spite of the excellent education she had received at Radcliffe more than a half century before, she had been disappointed that the experiences of women and children had been totally excluded from its curriculum. Now, delighted at the pioneering Institute for Independent Study, she decided to ask Bunting to join a new group of Bank Street sponsors. "From the beginning in 1916," she wrote:

Bank Street has stood for experimental education. This makes us peculiarly appreciative of your fresh thinking about women's education and your courage in launching a radical experiment. Of course it rejoices me that this experiment emanates from my Alma Mater . . . I am glad to have lived to see this new step in the progress of education![40]

Radcliffe, in fact, had not forgotten Lucy Mitchell. Unable to bestow honorary degrees, it established its own award for graduates who had been leaders in their professions. In 1956, Lucy Mitchell had been awarded the Radcliffe Graduate Chapter Medal for Distinguished Achievement, the tenth recipient of the medal and the first person in education to be so honored.

The conflict between Lucy's desires for continued professional work and the satisfactions of a life privately lived—between "service" and "self," as Lucy called it—was never fully resolved.[41] Shortly after her retirement and move to Palo Alto, Lucy had begun a new book on the subject of "human geography." The book was to consist of a roughly chronological grouping of her own previous writings and some new ones, supplemented by materials from Bank Street colleagues. The manuscript—titled at various times *Young Explorers and Their Teachers* and *Children of the World*—was sent off to Lucy's three closest friends at Bank Street, Irma Black, Barbara Biber, and Charlotte Winsor, directors of the Divisions of Publications, Research, and Teaching, respectively. But these colleagues found the writing turgid and grandiose. Lucy's earnestness and idealism now appeared merely sentimental, a product of her advancing age and her growing concerns about the worsening international political scene, particularly in regard to underdeveloped nations. More than ever, she idealized children as creatures of innocence whose universal traits might point the way to a world free from selfishness and war.

Lucy's colleagues and John Niemeyer delayed confronting her with Bank Street's decision not to publish the book. When at last she was told, she was distraught, feeling that she had been betrayed by these friends who "killed [her] book-child." To face her colleagues without vindictiveness or injured pride would be the most "serious test" of her life. She endeavored to persuade them of the value of her ideas, even though she conceded that her powers of expression were not what they once were. To publish the book elsewhere would "spoil the brag" of Bank Street's cooperative work style. Any break with Bank Street, moreover, would "disorient [her] utterly."[42] In the end, the book was not published; instead, Charlotte Winsor wrote a new introduction to a revised edition of *Young Geographers* and Lucy discharged her anger on Charlotte. The whole episode left a deep scar. Lucy was to recall it bitterly in the last years of her life, even though her relations with Niemeyer and with Charlotte remained strong.

Lucy moved to Channing House at the end of 1963. She had two handsome rooms on the tenth floor with a balcony facing east looking out over the Bay and coastal mountain range. The other side of the apartment overlooked the rolling green hills of Palo Alto and the Stanford campus. Indoors, the wall facing her bed was covered with photos of Robin, her children, grandchildren, and first great-grandchild.

Channing House was "beautiful" and "comfortable." Nevertheless, she wondered if she could make it a home. It was Lucy's good fortune that the apartment next door was occupied by a retired schoolteacher who knew Lucy's work and had long worshipped her from afar. With much to talk about, the two became friends.[43]

Only once during the first year at Channing House did Lucy write to Robin. "What am I at 86?" she asked. "Have I shrunk to fit a shrunken world?" Though she wrote that she could not find herself nor Robin in her new quarters, she was not unhappy or negative, she stated, but merely sought some way to become more active. Perhaps here her "work job" was to learn from her new "colleagues"—the old people around her—learning to "give" to them and "take" from them.[44]

In 1965, however, a fire in Lucy's apartment, started by a cigarette, had a destructive effect on her morale. Many of her papers and some of her cherished mementoes were burned, but even more frightening was this palpable sign of her declining powers.

"She changed so much so fast," recalled Robin Mitchell after her grandmother's move to Channing House.

She had always taken great pride in being an independent woman, and all at once that was taken away from her. She couldn't be that any more. . . . She cried easily, which was a side of grandmother I had never seen, and was always getting confused and couldn't remember things.[45]

Robin and other grandchildren were upset when Lucy talked about dying and asked them to select their favorite things to be mentioned in her will. Several of them remember her pleading for death to come.[46]

In the fall of 1966, she suffered a stroke, which temporarily left her without mobility or speech. Former Bank Street students who visited her in January 1967 found that she had won the struggle to regain her powers; she was the "same Mrs. Mitchell, with her marvelous Lucy-clothes

and beads . . . her quick eyes and the sharp life to her." She walked with
two canes, precariously but triumphantly.[47]

Before moving to Channing House, Lucy had gone through her files to
discard materials she did not want to take with her. Among them, she
came upon endless notes to herself and to Robin about her life experiences.

I felt like a spectator watching a kind of montage of my long life where the backdrops of successive periods have been my diverse environments, both geographic
and social. Yet simultaneously, I felt that inside I had always been the same kind
of person and that the successive experiences I was able to take in and then give
out again in action were growth stages that made me more like my essential self.
In the younger stages of learning of dependent childhood and responsible middle
years, I found clues that helped me to understand and to accept—even enjoy—
what I had become in old age.[48]

This discovery led her to arrange the written records of her past according to her concept of the stages of learning. In the early months of
1967, at the age of eighty-eight, this is what she was up to, a project begun purely for "personal pleasure," or perhaps, in mimeographed form, to
serve as an "informal chat" for friends, colleagues and family.

Lucy titled the manuscript "Becoming More So: Stages of Learning in
My Long Life." "Becoming more so" was a phrase she had used repeatedly
in conversations with friends and neighbors during her seventies and
eighties. She had discovered that despite the wide range of personalities
she saw among her contemporaries, each had grown not merely old, but
"more so." That is, she explained, something deep in one's personality
that had not a chance to flower fully in earlier life stages finds a new
chance in old age to become more like "one's essential self."

I saw my present self as a kind of crazy quilt composed of habits that had definitely been put over on me as a child and adolescent, mixed in with native impulses and interests some of which had been inhibited and crusted over with
guilt, but not killed. These I found matched to an astonishing degree the things
that I now longed to do. And it came to me almost as a discovery that the sense
of one's age is insignificant in comparison with the sense of one's self. [Though
older,] I still feel just like myself!"[49]

Indeed, old age had become an opportunity for self-discovery. As in
every stage, she believed that the learning process in this period was
composed of the two interlocking experiences she had noted many times
before: taking in and giving out. In her declining years, she had begun to

unlearn some of the inhibitions that had been imposed upon her by her early environment. By taking into her life the living things of nature and the great earth forces, she had found a peace based on personal experience and intuition rather than fact or science. The second step in the learning process of old age, she now understood, had been writing for herself, not for "service" reasons but for the sheer pleasure it gave her. At last in her eighties, she was "liberated" to record her experiences, feelings, "even . . . phantasies," a kind of dramatic play that she felt paralleled the child's play with words. Writing to Robin was thus not merely a sign of dependency, guilt or "therapy," but a positive reflection of her deepest urges. "Taking time to observe and enjoy the wonder of the world around me, and writing for myself have filled me with the sense of the miracle of growth and a sense of being a part of the living world where death arises from life and life arises from death. . . . I am no longer fighting myself," she wrote. "I have, I suppose, accepted myself."[50]

The discovery of these truths, and her understanding of the learning that is possible in old age, came to Lucy as an "amazing adventure." Subject and object were joined as they had been throughout her life: her own experiences became the most pregnant sources for understanding the wider processes of growth in the last stage of life, while her pursuit of the general case helped her come to terms with her own condition. Suddenly, as she gathered the records of her experiences, she wanted to explain to others her understanding of the stages of lifelong learning. "Once more the irresistible urge to write grips me," she wrote. "Hurrah!"[51] But following a mild infection that put her in the infirmary for two weeks, she died of a heart attack on October 15, 1967, a few months past her eighty-ninth birthday. She had written an introduction and arranged the list of contents, but the book was never completed. Before her death, she had given it a new title—"Every Stage of Life Has Its Song: My Song Has Been a Woman's Song."

Epilogue

"I've had a wonderful life," Lucy Sprague Mitchell declared as she presented her personal "credo" on Edward R. Murrow's radio show, *This I Believe*, in 1955. She told listeners that "human beings have undeveloped power to think, to enjoy, to create, to care for the other fellow. . . . Development of these powers is society's best chance for its own improvement. . . . education is society's chief tool." Despite the "long, groping years" of her childhood and extended adolescence, she had found meaningful work which allowed her to pursue that vision. She was struck by the extent to which prevailing ideas about the education of children had changed, and even more impressed by the momentous changes in women's roles. At every stage of her own life she had struggled against the conventional attitude of her father's generation that "women belonged only in the home, which meant that their education was unimportant, their work outside the home unseemly."[1]

By the 1950s, Lucy believed that the traditional thinking which had shaped her own girlhood was being swept back once and for all into the historical past. The assumption that women belong in the home, and that daughters belong to their families, was giving way to the idea that "daughters are human beings with the same rights to live a satisfactory life as men"; and that "women belong in the world inside and outside the home." While educated women of her own generation had been oddities, in the 1950s women attended college because it was the "thing to do." And professional women were no longer viewed with the definite suspicion that had greeted them in earlier decades.[2]

Of all the changed attitudes that she had lived to see, Lucy felt, "that towards the roles of husband and wife stands out above all others." Dur-

ing her lifetime, she said, she had experienced two marital "extremes"—
the "authoritarian attitude" of her father toward her mother and her own
"companionate" marriage with Wesley Mitchell. Her marriage had not
been typical, but she believed that it represented a general trend—the
breakdown of the "old sharp separation of human society into two
worlds," male and female. By mid-century, women had "successively entered fields that had hitherto been reserved for men," while men—at
least a minority—had developed new attitudes toward their roles as husbands and fathers. "It might be said that 'men have entered the home'
rather than that 'women have left it.'"[3]

Lucy was keenly aware of the double burden carried by women with
careers as well as families. Working women "want and need and love and
feel responsible for their children as much as women . . . with little or no
contact with the world's problems except vicariously through their husbands," she observed. Technology had lightened housekeeping burdens
but on the other hand the new thinking about children called for more
rather than less attention to their needs. Concern for her children made
it difficult for a working mother to "unify her life" and kept her "anxious
and usually tired." "It is a conflict I have long lived with," Lucy wrote.[4]

"Of course I had the advantage of having money," Lucy acknowledged
in her autobiography. But "a mother's job with her children is scarcely affected by her income. Money helps with the housekeeping but does not
help one to be in two places at the same time—with her children and on
her job."[5] At a time when most women in her social class employed servants to extend their leisure, Lucy's use of household help was part of a
considered strategy without which she would have had to renounce her
work. Despite the egalitarian principles that structured both Lucy's marriage and her professional work, her solution to the problem of child care
was a hierarchical one, dependent upon the service of other women and
available only to a privileged class. In some respects, because of the unusual combination of housing, office, and school that Lucy's money and
ingenuity had made possible, she was very nearly able to be in two places
at the same time. But in general, Lucy insisted, "money helps but it does
not solve the problem for a woman."[6]

On a societal level, Lucy understood that the goal of balancing work
and family interests could not be attained until it was no longer seen
solely as a "woman's problem." Adjustments in family life, child care pro-
visions, and labor conditions were each necessary. "Fathers will have to
take a more active and more personal part in the responsibilities of

bringing up children, which will be good for both them and the children," she wrote. "More help for housekeeping and for the adequate care of children out of the home"—through "nursery schools . . . child care centers" and "after school activities"—was required. Finally, women's place in the work force had to be upgraded. Women needed to be sought as workers "for the value of their work, not merely because they will work for less pay than men." "The world's problems need working on by trained women as well as men," she asserted. And "sharing the world's problems should make [women] better mothers."[7]

Yet, while Lucy felt that she had largely solved the problem of unity— that her work did not hurt the children and in fact helped her understand them better—her children believed otherwise. When I interviewed her sons for this book, their recollection was that they had often felt like grist for her mill, guinea pigs in the laboratory of progressive education.[8] The Mitchell children recalled very little of their mother's actual presence in their lives, focusing on her distance rather than her involvement. Sometimes there seemed to be two totally different versions of family life: hers and theirs. The children were quite surprised when I told them that their mother sewed and knitted for them, stayed home when they were ill, took them to doctors and lessons, met with teachers, and did many of the other things that concerned mothers do for their growing children. But they remembered, and resented, her close observations of their behavior because these seemed to spring from her professional interest in them, not from affection.

To her children, Lucy seemed cerebral rather than spontaneous, remote rather than intimate. Though she was more changeable in her emotions than her husband, in her relationship to her children Lucy was always controlled. "You know, in all my life, I've never lost my patience with a child," she told a daughter-in-law. As one son put it: her reactions were "not those of sudden tears to the eyes or goose pimples." Her natural reserve and her intellectuality partly explain this; and yet with adults she was often impetuous and expressive. No doubt the generalized perspective of a professional educator further restricted her direct responses to her own children.

The Mitchells' sons were generally more critical of their mother than of their father, even though two of them believed that he was the more remote. Just because it was she, not Wesley, who was more involved with their daily routines and crises, it was she who disappointed them more by her lack of intimacy and spontaneity. Perhaps, too, even in this household, the double standard had its force: less was expected of Wesley Mitchell as a father according to traditional mores, and the outcome was that he was less resented. The children nonetheless took pride in Lucy's artistic and writing talents and the diversity of her interests as much as in Wesley's academic brilliance. And despite their anger at their mother's emotional limitations, they acknowledged that she had had to contend with the burden of a difficult past. "She did the very best she could possibly do," Arnold conceded.

The tacit message both Mitchells transmitted to their children emphasized integrity, honor, independence, and achievement in areas of public good. As progressive educators, they encouraged their children to make their own choices and to take responsibility for the consequences. Yet the children often wanted more direct advice—about small daily decisions as well as more weighty ones.

Both Lucy and Wesley valued intellectual attainments highly. Given Lucy's antipathy to her father's values, a career in business was not what was expected of their sons. Marni also felt that her equestrian pursuits did not meet their expectations. Yet both parents consistently supported their children's decisions and were sympathetic with their difficulties. For example, when Jack in his late fifties confided to Lucy that he felt like a failure because he was still trying to complete his Ph.D., she responded as always by encouraging him to accept the talents he had.

Lucy's work was an important element in the children's resentment. Not only did she have a full-time career when most mothers of school-age children did not, but it was a very notable career, and one that was ever-present because of the close connection of the Mitchell home to the children's schools. This connection had its practical advantages for all; on the other hand, the children's jealousy of this neighboring institution that absorbed so much of their mother's energies and resources is understandable.

Lucy's solution to the problem of her absences from home—a reliable, sympathetic housekeeper—succeeded only too well. The children wound up deeply attached to Mollie, and seem to have been more critical of their mother by comparison. "Mollie Cotter was my real mother," Arnold admitted. And in spite of Lucy's real devotion to Marni in her last illness, it was in Mollie's arms that Marni died.

The relationship of the Mitchell children toward their parents was complicated by the fact that two of the four, Jack and Marni, were adopted. While all the children went through unhappiness and stress, the adopted ones seem to have fared the worst. Certainly Jack was the most resentful of all the children toward his mother. He and Marni were not treated as different from the others in any way; but they were told at an early age that they were adopted, and they may well have been more vulnerable to feelings of inadequacy because they knew they did not belong by nature to this demanding and achieving family. They may have also been troubled by fantasies, inflated or ignominious, about their true identities.

In the end, it is easy to understand how all the children of such competent and illustrious parents might have felt limited in their own talents, character, and options. "It's difficult to stand in the shadows of a pretty tall column, you see. Somehow or other," Arnold observed, "it was taken away from us to create our own world."

But if, despite her best intentions, Lucy's mothering lacked warmth and supportiveness, in the classroom she was communicative and enabling. It is "no coincidence," she wrote, "that my mature work has been concentrated on trying to understand what goes on inside a child and what kinds of experiences free him to be himself." She had been brought up to feel guilty that "I was the kind of person I was," and in all aspects of her work she held to the concept that "children are persons in their own right—immature, but still persons to be respected."[9]

Teaching was the work that Lucy did best. "If a big word [is] necessary," she once wrote, "I'd rather [be] called an 'educator,' though to me the best title is 'teacher.'"[10] She taught teachers how to teach by the force of her own example. In the same way, her own wide-ranging curiosity helped children discover that learning could be exciting. As Mary Phelps and Margaret Wise Brown recalled, she could make any subject interesting, from "the habits of the octopus" to "the economic history of potatoes. . . . Invariably she calls out an adventurousness and an insight at least something like her own."[11] One former student summed up Lucy's effect on her students when she remarked that Lucy, in her eclectic "'Madwoman of Chaillot' clothes" wasn't "just a teacher, she was an Experience."[12] By her own life Lucy promoted the idea that those who teach must consistently learn. To make teaching into a respected profession with opportunities for continued growth became one of the most urgent objectives of her mature career.

Yet writing—the "secret sin" of her childhood—was the activity to which Lucy gave her deepest allegiance. While she never felt that she was a talented author, she was happiest with a pencil in her hand: "Writing is my personal gyroscope." The habit of recording her thoughts— even "half-thoughts"—about anything that entered into her current experience lasted throughout her life.[13] But until her final years, her desire to express herself, unless it was linked to professional work, remained a source of guilt. At Bank Street, her engagement in writing and her passion for teaching came together in the innovative and influential Writers' Laboratory.

As an administrator, the role she liked least, Lucy established a supportive and cooperative working environment which allowed Bank Street's teaching, writing, and research staff to participate directly in its management. She always balked at being called Bank Street's "leader." "Don't make me into a myth!" she admonished a growing coterie of admiring colleagues. She insisted that her share in creating Bank Street was "no greater than that of many others."[14]

Lucy brought her passionate intensity to bear on even the smallest detail of administrative work. With little time for small talk, her attention always on the matter at hand; to some Bank Streeters she seemed brusque and impersonal. Many were frightened by her manner, her reputation, and her seemingly overwhelming competencies. But others found her, as one secretary put it, "immediate, comforting and enabling."[15]

While in many respects Lucy's executive work as well as her writing and teaching drew on the artistic talents she believed she inherited from her mother, she recognized that the constraints of her Puritan father never lost their grip on her.[16] Industrious, conscientious, and thrifty to a fault, she was usually unable to tolerate a moment's idleness or the slightest waste, whether of effort or money. Not only did she use the backs of old manuscripts for writing paper, but to the desperation of editors, secretaries, and this biographer, she would augment her first drafts in a tiny hand between the typed lines and all up and down the narrow margins. She was always the first to arrive at a meeting and became impatient at any delay. But more than Lucy's frugality and punctuality were instilled by her father. Her love of learning and the discipline with which she approached it were also inheritances from Otho Sprague.

Lucy's early life and her inherited sense of wealth had given her, along with a many-layered and hampering sense of guilt, something that in the long run went even deeper. It turned out that it had not been "taken away from her to create her own world." She was not burdened by expectations: Otho's example as an entrepreneur had never been held up to her, but perhaps, just for that reason, she was able to draw strength from it.

With hard work, single-mindedness, and shrewd organization, she transformed her vision into a life work that motivated other pioneers committed to educational innovation. Otho had built his mercantile empire by personal contacts: by inspiring confidence and knowing whom to trust. Lucy was unhesitating in her appeals to the imagination and energy of others, and not the least of her achievements was the quality of her colleagues.

Her friends were struck by the fact that Lucy had so little class sense: she judged everyone not by background but by potential, and was democratic to a fault in her appraisals. But she was aristocratic in her complete freedom from social fear. Even in her early adult life, when she methodically underestimated herself in relation both to her tasks and to others whom she admired, she expected and got consideration; she knew the power of her "personality." It would have been in poor taste for her to acknowledge that her beauty was part of it, still less her wealth. Her bohemian style of dress was a rejection of the conventional signals of class, but one that a woman of more modest background, with professional ambitions, might not have allowed herself.

One staff member who joined Bank Street after Lucy's retirement remembers the day he met her for the first time on one of her periodic visits to the college. Though she was then nearly eighty-five, she was dressed in the same striking clothing and wore her distinctive handwrought silver jewelry. When she spoke, it was in the measured, elegant, though by now slightly quavering tones of a highly educated gentlewoman of great refinement.[17]

In her mature years, the combination of her informal style with her authoritative bearing was disconcerting but eloquent: it was a declaration of Lucy's essential program, her insistence on carrying the "primaries" of poetry and humanity into public and institutional life. The costs were high—to her family and herself, and sometimes to her colleagues—and the triumph was less than perfect; but in the end, this was her achievement. If education in the United States is committed in our time to a concern for individual development, to the encouragement of curiosity and understanding rather than rote learning, to acquainting children with their environment—above all to a respect for the child's own pleasure in activity—very much credit must go to the institution and programs Lucy Sprague Mitchell created; they played a major role in bringing these "progressive" notions into the mainstream of education.

Lucy's own view of her work was unabashedly positive. Deemphasizing Bank Street's occasional failures as she did her own shortcomings as a parent, she never relinquished the optimistic, progressive vision that had shaped both her work and family life. Less and less through her life was she willing to acknowledge the dark side of events or the personal vices and frailties that caused suffering and error. In her student years she had rejected the notion of free will and written of life as governed by suffering and helplessness; but as she gained control and satisfaction in her own life, she accepted the universe as open and responsive to purposeful endeavor. An allegory with which she ended her remarks on Murrow's *This I Believe* attested to her abiding faith in human nature and the possibilities of social change. Set in her country retreat in Stamford, it recalled Robin's last vision from their joint home.

I have a big window looking out on a stretch of woods and hills. Some of my visitors see the view, some see the flyspecks on the window. So it is in life. Some people center their attention on social flyspecks, on debunking and anti-crusades. I believe that we need to see beyond our human failures, to feel a lift at the broader view of human progress and human potentialities. We all need to have faith in the works of the world. We are working on human problems that my parents' generation didn't even recognize as problems, working in fumbling ways as happens in these situations, but we are learning. Thus, the most fundamental clause of my personal and institutional credo is: While we are learning, there is hope.[18]

Lucy's idealism propelled her activism, even though it also contributed to her tendency to deny unpleasant truths. Her excitement in learning nourished both her personal and professional life, and she in turn nourished others.

Abbreviations

BEE	Bureau of Educational Experiments
BL	Bancroft Library, University of California
BS	Bank Street
CC	City and Country Archives
CHS	Chicago Historical Society
CP	Caroline Pratt
ESC	Elizabeth Sprague Coolidge
ESCP	Elizabeth Sprague Coolidge Papers, Library of Congress
LS	Lucy Sprague
LSM	Lucy Sprague Mitchell
LSMP	Lucy Sprague Mitchell Papers, Columbia University
NAS	Nancy Atwood Sprague
NASD	Nancy Atwood Sprague Diaries, Schlesinger Library, Radcliffe College
OCOS	*Our Children and Our Schools* (LSM)
PIE	*Pioneering in Education* (LSM oral history)
RCA	Radcliffe College Archives
TL	*Two Lives* (LSM)
UA	Unpublished autobiography (LSM)
VHS	Vermont Historical Society
WCA	Wellesley College Archives
WCM	Wesley Clair Mitchell
WCMD	Wesley Clair Mitchell Diaries
WCMP	Wesley Clair Mitchell Papers, Columbia University

Notes

INTRODUCTION

1. Of all the women who received the Ph.D. degree between the years 1877 and 1924, 75 percent never married. Emilie J. Hutchinson, *Women and the Ph.D.* (Greensboro, N.C.: North Carolina College for Women, 1930), pp. 178–79. The marriage rates of white women who graduated college between the years 1908–1912 was about 62 percent. Mary E. Cookingham, "Combining Marriage, Motherhood, and Jobs before World War II: Women College Graduates, Classes of 1905–1935," *Journal of Family History* 9, no. 2 (Summer 1984): 179. Also see William H. Chafe, *The American Woman: Her Changing Social, Economic, and Political Role, 1920–1970* (New York: Oxford University Press, 1974), p. 100; Mary Van Kleeck, "A Census of College Women," *Journal of the Association of Collegiate Alumnae* 11 (May 1918): 557–91.
2. See, for example, Elaine Showalter, ed., *These Modern Women: Autobiographical Essays from the Twenties* (Old Westbury, N.Y.: The Feminist Press, 1978.)
3. See Joyce Antler, "Feminism as Life Process; The Life and Career of Lucy Sprague Mitchell," *Feminist Studies* 7 (Spring 1981): 134–57; also see Antler, "Lucy Sprague Mitchell," in Barbara Sicherman and Carol Hurd Green, eds., *Notable American Women: The Modern Period* (Cambridge: Harvard University Press, 1980), pp. 484–87; Ernestine Evans, "A Happy Family Album," *New York Herald Tribune Book Review*, June 14, 1953, p.4.
4. LSM, *Two Lives* (New York: Simon and Schuster, 1953).
5. Louis M. Hacker, "A Man, a Woman and a Vision," *The New York Times Book Review*, July 5, 1953.
6. This view is presented in Joyce Antler, "Was She a Good Mother? Some Thoughts on a New Issue for Feminist Biography," in Barbara J. Harris and JoAnn K. McNamara, eds., *Women and the Structure of Society: Selected Research from the Fifth Berkshire Conference on the History of Women* (Durham, N.C.: Duke University Press, 1984), pp. 53–66.
7. On the relation of public to private lives, see Justin Kaplan, "The Naked Self and Other Problems," in Marc Pachter, *The Biographer's Art* (Philadelphia: University of Pennsylvania Press, 1981).

8. See, for example, William L. O'Neill, *Everyone Was Brave: A History of Feminism in America* (Chicago: Quadrangle Books, 1969), p. 274; Chafe, *The American Woman*, p. 37; and Lois W. Banner, *Women in Modern America: A Brief History* (New York: Harcourt, Brace and Jovanovich, 1984), p. 39.

9. Most settlement women did not marry, though many shared their personal lives with close female friends. An exception was the Mitchells' good friend, Mary Simkhovitch, who co-founded Greenwich House with her husband Vladimir in 1902. Mary directed the settlement, but attributed much of its distinctiveness to her husband, an economist who taught at Columbia University. The couple lived in an apartment on the upper floor of Greenwich House. See Mary Simkhovitch Papers, SL.

10. Ruth Benedict, Notebook on "Adventures in Womanhood," Benedict Papers, Vassar College.

1: CHICAGO GIRLHOOD

1. On the Sprague family, see VHS: Edward George Sprague, *The Ralph Sprague Genealogy* (Montpelier, Vt.: Capital City Press, 1913); *The New England Historical and Genealogical Register* (Boston: New England Historical and Genealogical Society, 1909), 63: 147–51; George Walter Chamberlain, *The Spragues of Malden, Massachusetts* (Boston: privately printed, 1923); Richard Soule, Jr. *Memorial of the Sprague Family* (Boston: J. Munroe & Co., 1847).

2. Chamberlain, *The Spragues of Malden*, p. 49.

3. Along the route, he stopped at Hanover, New Hampshire, where he built one of the buildings of the new Dartmouth College. The innovative "square rule" technique Sprague used in designing the structure attracted widespread comment at the time and confirmed his reputation as a master carpenter. Abby Maria Hemenway, ed., *The Vermont Historical Gazeteer* (Burlington, Vt.: privately printed, 1871) 2:1044.

4. The village lay on the route of the Randolph Turnpike, a popular overland highway, and became the locus of a thriving trade between Vermont and Boston. See Leigh Wright, *Potash and Pine: The Formative Years in Randolph History* (Randolph, Vt.: Randolph Historical Society, 1977); Harry Cooley, *Randolph Vermont Historical Sketches* (Randolph, Vt.: Randolph Historical Society, 1978).

5. *Ralph Sprague Genealogy*, p. 97; interview with Claire Riford, East Randolph, Vermont, July 1981. On the Free Will Baptists, see William G. McLoughlin, *New England Dissent 1630–1833: The Baptists and the Separation of Church and State* (Cambridge: Harvard University Press, 1971).

6. In 1903, the Free Will Baptist Church of East Randolph united with the Vermont Baptist Association and became known as the Baptist Church of East Randolph. Today it is called the East Randolph Alliance Church and meets in the same building that Ziba and his neighbors constructed in 1848.

7. Town Records, Randolph, Vermont.

8. Evelyn M. Wood Lovejoy, *History of Royalton, Vermont with Family Genealogies* (Burlington, Vt., 1911).

9. NAS, *Pleasant Memories of My Life* (privately printed, 1911), NASP, SL.

10. Ibid., p. 90.

11. July 13, 1871, NASD.

12. On Chicago's development during these years, see Bessie Louise Pierce, *A History of Chicago* (Chicago: University of Chicago Press, 1957), 3: *The Rise of a Modern City, 1871–1893*; David F. Burg, *Chicago's White City of 1893* (Lexington: University Press of Kentucky, 1976).

13. PIE, pp. 19–20. Courtesy, The Bancroft Library. TL, p. 63.

14. Oct. 8, 9, 11, 1871. NASD.

15. "O. S. A. Sprague," *Encyclopedia of Biography of Illinois*, 2:86–89; *Graphic News*, Sept. 24, 1887; Sprague Warner & Co. history; Pierce, *A History of Chicago*, 3:18; Oct. 7–11, NASD.

16. Not only the variety, but the quality of Sprague Warner products became a major selling point. In an age of impure food, the company sold its reliability, boasting that not one item in its entire line of preserved foods contained any added chemical preservative. See 1885 catalogue, Sprague Warner & Co., Sprague Warner History, p. 57; CHS; *Graphic News*, Sept. 24, 1887; "Albert Sprague," *Encyclopedia of Biography of Illinois*, 1:270–71.

17. Hugh Dalziel Duncan, *The Rise of Chicago as a Literary Center from 1885 to 1920: A Sociological Essay in American Culture* (Totowa, N.J.: The Bedminster Press, 1964), p. 33.

18. See "O. S. A. Sprague," *Encyclopedia of Biography of Illinois*; "O.S.A. Sprague," obituaries, *Chicago Tribune*, Feb. 22, 1909, *Pasadena Daily News*, Feb. 23, 1909; "Albert A. Sprague," *Encyclopedia of Biography of Illinois*.

19. UA.

20. John J. Glessner, "Some Friends of Mine among the Earlier Members of the Commercial Club" (Chicago: privately printed, n.d.). p. 30, CHS.

21. UA; TL, pp. 61–62.

22. "O. S. A. Sprague," *Chicago Tribune*, Feb. 22, 1909; *Chicago Evening Post*, Feb. 22, 1909. "No one has more friends at Chicago than you," wrote Walter Gresham to Otho on June 16, 1894, "and I am glad to say that no one deserves more friends," CHS.

23. Helen Lefkowitz Horowitz, *Culture and the City: Cultural Philanthropy in Chicago from the 1880s to 1917* (Lexington, Ky.: The University of Kentucky), p. 41.

24. The Citizens' Asociation extended its program beyond its original goal of securing better fire protection to include charter, tax, and tenement reform. The Citizens' League worked to decrease juvenile crime by prohibiting the sale of alcohol to minors. See Pierce, *A History of Chicago*, 3:281, 301, 345, 459.

25. Nan's diaries record supper parties for 75, luncheon parties for 20 ladies, musicales, whist parties, and dinner dances. See, for example, Feb. 13, 1880, April 1882, Feb. 1, 1886, Jan. 2–3, 1891, May 1, 1891, Mar. 7, 1893.

26. PIE, p. 13; TL, pp. 34, 50; Untitled notes, LSMP.

27. Ibid.

28. On the health of nineteenth century women, see Ann Douglas Wood, "'The Fashionable Diseases': Women's Complaints and Their Treatment in Nineteenth-Century America," and Carroll Smith-Rosenberg and Charles Rosenberg, "The Female Animal: Medical and Biological Views of Woman and Her Role in Nineteenth Century America," in Judith Walzer Leavitt, ed., *Women and Health in America* (Madison, Wisc.: Univ. of Wisconsin Press, 1984).

29. TL, p. 69.
30. PIE, p. 15.
31. School theme, "Thanksgiving," 1890, LSMP.
32. UA.
33. Notes, LSMP.
34. TL, p. 47.
35. PIE, pp. 28–29.
36. UA.
37. TL, p. 41.
38. Ibid., p. 42; Glessner, "Some Friends of Mine," p. 30.
39. See Schlesinger Library, Radcliffe College, Nancy Atwood Sprague diaries, Sept. 20, 1872.
40. TL, p. 43.
41. UA.
42. TL, pp. 50, 41, 48.
43. UA.
44. TL, pp. 46–47, 50–51.
45. UA.
46. TL, p. 49.
47. Apr. 1, 1889, NASD.

2: COMING OF AGE

1. Perhaps no event was more characteristic of the neighborhood's celebration of its wealth than the Mikado Ball, given by Marshall Field in January 1886 to honor two of his children, at a cost of more than $75,000. Catered by Sherry's of New York, which transported supplies, equipment, and staff to Chicago in two specially equipped railroad cars, the ball was attended by 500 guests from Prairie Avenue. See Robert Pruter, "The Prairie Avenue Section of Chicago: The History and Examination of Its Decline " (master's thesis, Roosevelt University, 1976), pp. 1–2.
2. Arthur Meeker, cited in Pruter, "The Prairie Avenue Section of Chicago," p. 9.
3. UA.
4. See Pruter, "The Prairie Avenue Section of Chicago"; Homer Hoyt, *One Hundred Years of Land Values in Chicago* (Chicago: Chicago University Press, 1933); *The Elite Dictionary and Club List of Chicago* (Chicago: Elite Publishing Co., 1887).
5. PIE, p. 30.
6. TL, p. 66.
7. Ibid.
8. Ibid., p. 59.
9. PIE, pp. 30–31.
10. Albert Sprague to Amelia Sprague, May 2, 1889, LS Scrapbook, courtesy of Barbara Mitchell.
11. Burg, *Chicago's White City*, pp. 95–100.
12. Ibid., pp. 217–18, 221.
13. TL, pp. 71–72.

14. See Burg, *Chicago's White City*, pp. 207–09; also Jeanne Madeline Weimann, *The Fair Women* (Chicago: Academy Chicago, 1981).
15. TL, p. 67.
16. Ibid., p. 69.
17. Ibid., p. 72. On the University of Chicago, see Thomas W. Goodspeed, *A History of the University of Chicago: The First Quarter Century* (Chicago: University of Chicago Press, 1916); Steven J. Diner, *A City and Its Universities: Public Policy in Chicago, 1892–1919,* (Chapel Hill, N.C.: University of North Carolina Press, 1980).
18. TL, p. 74; UA.
19. See Patricia A. Palmieri, "In Adamless Eden: A Social Portrait of the Academic Community at Wellesley College 1875–1920" (Ed.D. thesis, Harvard Graduate School of Education, 1981).
20. George Herbert Palmer, *The Life of Alice Freeman Palmer* (Boston: Houghton Mifflin Co., 1908), pp. 233–35. On the life of Palmer, see Barbara Miller Solomon, "Alice Elvira Freeman Palmer," in Edward T. James and Janet Wilson James, *Notable American Women: A Biographical Dictionary* (Cambridge: Harvard University Press, 1971), 3:4–8.
21. TL, p. 73.
22. Anne Firor Scott, "Jane Addams," in *Notable American Women*, 1:16–22; also see Allen F. Davis, *American Heroine: The Life and Legend of Jane Addams* (New York: Oxford University Press, 1975).
23. In this, she thought he was the opposite of his brother, who was tender and understanding toward those he knew personally but unmoved—especially financially—by "humanity in the mass" (UA).
24. July 5, 1894, NASD.
25. July 11, 1894, NASD.
26. UA; PIE, pp. 23, 25.
27. TL, p. 60.
28. Ibid., p. 63.
29. Ibid., p. 60.
30. Ibid.; UA.
31. TL, p. 64.

3: DUTIFUL DAUGHTER

1. Jan.–Feb., Nov. 30, 1890; Apr.–May 1891; Apr. 4, 1892, NASD.
2. TL, p. 69; Aug. 9–18, 20–21, 1893, NASD.
3. July 26, 1893, NASD.
4. Apr. 11, Oct. 2, 9, 24, 1893, NASD.
5. Dec. 25, 1894; Jan., Feb. 11–13, 1895, NASD. Albert graduated from Harvard in 1898. He then began a business career at Sprague, Warner & Co., becoming president in 1915. He resigned two years later to enlist as a private in World War I. He saw service overseas with the 86th Division and was promoted to the rank of lieutenant colonel. After the war, he was made chairman of the board of Sprague, Warner & Co. One of the founders of the American Legion, Albert gained national prominence for his work in veterans' affairs. In 1924, he became the Democratic candidate

for senator in Illinois, but lost in the Republican landslide to former Gov. Charles Deneen. A member of the board of directors of many corporations, he held major public offices in Chicago and was active in civic and philanthropic work, serving as Commissioner of Public Works, Chairman of the Chicago Plan Commission, Director of the John Crerar Library and of the Chicago Natural History Museum, President of the Medical Center Commission, and Vice-President of the Museum of Science and Industry. See Memorials to Albert Arnold Sprague, CHS, and *Chicago Tribune*, Oct. 18–19, 1924.

6. LSM, "Credo."
7. Mar. 1895, NASD.
8. UA.
9. Ibid.
10. Apr. 18, 1894, NASD; TL, p. 102.
11. John E. Baur, *The Health Seekers of Southern California* (San Marino, Calif.: Huntington Library, 1959), pp. 34–59.
12. TL, p. 105.
13. Untitled notes, LSMP.
14. UA.
15. TL, pp. 108–09.
16. Ibid., pp. 109–10.
17. Ibid., p. 110.
18. Ibid.
19. Descriptions of the school which follow are taken from Marlborough School Scrapbooks, Marlborough School, Los Angeles.
20. TL, p. 111.
21. Something of Mary Caswell's ideas about deportment can be gleaned from the list of "Marlborough Don'ts" posted on each boarder's door. The girls were advised not to use grammatical "barbarisms," to eat politely and quietly, to prepare their dress and toilette carefully. There were rules like "don't talk through your nose," "don't giggle, shout, scream, or laugh loudly," "don't take your soup noisily," "don't look about you in church," and "don't walk about the halls half-dressed." Marlborough School Papers.
22. "A girl should learn something," she told her charges, "as a clever boy learns a business. If she were taught to administer her father's household affairs in a business way, practicing method, punctuality, self-reliance and arithmetic, whatever Fate requires of her later would be better done because of it." Marlborough School Papers.
23. TL, p. 111.
24. Ibid., p. 112.
25. Ibid.
26. Frederic Hart to the author, Oct. 18, 1978; UA.
27. TL, p. 113.
28. UA.
29. Sept. 24, 1894, NASD.
30. UA.
31. Ibid.
32. TL, p. 115.

33. Ibid.
34. Ibid.
35. Ibid., p. 116.
36. Interview with Elizabeth Coolidge Winship, June 1983.
37. Untitled notes, LSMP.
38. TL, p. 116.

4: MEANING AND MEANINGLESSNESS

1. LS, "Class History," *Radcliffe College, Class of 1900*, p. 7, RCA.
2. On the history of women's higher education, see Joyce Antler, "Culture, Service and Work: Changing Ideals of Higher Education for Women," in Pamela J. Perun, ed. *The Undergraduate Woman: Issues in Educational Equity* (Lexington, Mass.: D.C. Heath and Co., 1982), pp. 15–41; Helen Lefkowitz Horowitz, *Alma Mater: Design and Experience in the Women's Colleges from Their Nineteenth-Century Beginnings to the 1930s* (New York: Alfred A. Knopf, 1984); Mabel Newcomer, *A Century of Higher Education for American Women* (New York: Harper Brothers, 1959); Barbara Miller Solomon, *In the Company of Educated Women* (New Haven: Yale University Press, 1985); Thomas Woody, *A History of Women's Education in the United States*, 2 vols. (New York: Science Press, 1929).
3. On the history of Radcliffe, see Joseph B. Warner, "Radcliffe College," *Harvard Graduates' Magazine* (March 1894): 329–45; David McCord, *An Acre For Education* (Cambridge: Radcliffe College, 1938); Sally Schwager, "Harvard Women: A History of the Founding of Radcliffe College" (Ed.D. diss., Harvard University, 1982).
4. TL, p. 117; Mabel Wolcott Richardson Brown, in *Thirty-Fifth Anniversary Report of the Class of 1900, Radcliffe College, 1900–1935*, RCA.
5. TL, p. 117.
6. Agnes Repplier, *Agnes Irwin: A Biography* (Garden City, N.Y.: Doubleday, Doran & Co., 1934), p. 70.
7. "Awestruck in her presence and unfriendly out of it," commented one undergraduate (Repplier, p. 75). She was down on the "twentieth century girl," another student put it, "and not afraid to say so" (Blanche Bonnelle Church Papers, RCA). Also see Edith Puffer Howes, "The Golden Age," *Radcliffe Quarterly*, 21, no. 2 (May 1937): 15.
8. Going to the Harvard Library was another formidable experience. When one professor sent Fuller to the Library to work on her senior thesis, she persuaded her grandmother to accompany her. Later she recalled her "own hot shame lest someone should see me . . . and Grandmother, uncomfortably knitting on one of the hard wooden chairs in the little upstairs alcove . . . sighing unconsciously now and then, but steadfast till my work was finished." Lucy Fuller, Jan. 27, 1934, in *My Tenth Anniversary*, Ada Comstock Scrapbook, RCA.
9. These rules changed slowly. Even in the 1930s, it was considered "wild and dashing" to use Widener Library, and hats were to be worn at all times in Harvard Square. See Marian Cannon Schlesinger, "Across the Common," in Diana Dubois, *My Harvard, My Yale* (New York: Random House, 1982), pp. 18–19.
10. Constitution, By-Laws and Minutes, Class of 1900, RCA.

11. Radcliffe College, *Annual Report of the President and Treasurer of Radcliffe College,* *1899–1900*, pp. 22–23; TL, p. 119; Mabel Richardson Brown, June 16, 1950, 50th Reunion Address, Blanche Bonnelle Church Papers, RCA.
12. TL, p. 119; E. Kathleen Jones, in *Thirty-fifth Anniversary Report of the Class of 1900.*
13. William Byerly, "Radcliffe College Thirty Years After," *Harvard Graduates' Magazine* (Dec. 1909): 5.
14. Once, some years later, a classmate of Lucy met Gates on Brattle Street in the midst of a heavy snowstorm. "Isn't it cosmic?" he asked her. Had she been prepared, she would have replied, she told her classmates, "Yes, but hard on lyrical interludes in long skirts." Mabel Cilley Fiske, in *Thirty-Fifth Anniversary Report of the Class of 1900.* Gates taught English 22 (English Composition), a standard course for many Radcliffe sophomores. Lucy took the course with Gates in her second year.
15. Schwager, "Harvard Women," pp. 276, 290.
16. LSM, in *Fiftieth Anniversary Report of the Class of 1900, Radcliffe College, 1935–1950,* RCA; UA.
17. UA, TL, p. 118.
18. TL, p. 122.
19. Patricia Ann Palmieri cites Palmer's use of this phrase in "In Adamless Eden."
20. Palmer, *Life of Alice Freeman Palmer,* pp. 125, 148, 150, 159.
21. "[Alice Freeman] married at the age of thirty-two, and apparently entered on a wholly new career," remarked President Eliot of Harvard. "The opponents of the higher education of women had always argued that such education would tend . . . to dispossess the family as the cornerstone of society. Alice Freeman gave the whole force of her conspicuous example to disprove that objection. She illustrated . . . the supremacy of love and of family life in the heart of both man and woman." Charles William Eliot, *A Service in Memory of Alice Freeman Palmer Held by Her Friends and Associates in Appleton Chapel, Harvard University, Jan. 31, 1903* (Boston: Houghton Mifflin, 1903), p. 38.
22. LS to George Herbert Palmer, Feb. 14, 1912, WCA.
23. See Alice Freeman Palmer, *A Marriage Cycle* (Boston: Houghton Mifflin Co., 1914). The Palmers' courtship correspondence is collected in *An Academic Courtship: The Letters of Alice Freeman and George Herbert Palmer, 1886–1887* (Cambridge: Harvard University Press, 1940).
24. TL, p. 122.
25. Ibid., p. 121; UA.
26. Ibid.
27. TL, p. 122. Bruce Kuklick notes that Palmer, "a canny evaluator of men," had "no equal in placing graduate students." Kuklick, *The Rise of American Philosophy: Cambridge, Massachusetts, 1860–1930* (New Haven: Yale University Press, 1977), p. 250.
28. Ibid., pp. 238–42.
29. Charles Bakewell, "The Philosophy of George Herbert Palmer," in *George Herbert Palmer, 1842–1933: Memorial Addresses* (Cambridge: Harvard University Press, 1935), p. 41.
30. Faculty Minute on the Life and Service of Professor Palmer, Harvard University, Harvard University Archives, p. 79.

31. TL, p. 124.
32. Ibid., p. 121.
33. Ibid.
34. See Radcliffe College, *Annual Report, 1899–1900*, pp. 9–19.
35. Notable members of the class of 1900 included writers Katharine Fullerton Gerould and Rebecca Hooper Eastman, and composer Mabel Wheeler Daniels. Members of Lucy's Radcliffe club from the class of 1899 included Josephine Sherwood Hull, Dora Drew Babbitt, and Cornelia James Cannon. On Cannon, a novelist and essayist, see Marion Cannon Schlesinger, *Snatched from Oblivion: A Cambridge Memoir* (Boston: Little Brown, 1979).
36. Radcliffe College, *Annual Report, 1900–1901*, pp. 25–26.
37. LS, "Class History," pp. 14–15.
38. In her first year, Lucy chose History I (Medieval and Modern European history), a standard choice that caused almost as many agonies as freshman English; physics; literature; mathematics; and French. In her sophomore year, she took another course in English literature and courses in government, history, fine arts, chemistry, and philosophy. In her junior and senior years, she took various courses in geology, economics, music and philosophy.
39. Ethel Puffer Howes, "The Golden Age," *Radcliffe Quarterly*, p. 15.
40. UA; TL, p. 119.
41. TL, pp. 120–21.
42. Comment on LS, "Knowledge and Reality; Their Relations to Beauty," Dec. 18, 1899, LSMP.
43. LS, "Knowledge and Reality."
44. LS, "The World and the Individual," Feb. 19, 1900; also see LS, "The Problem of Evil and Its Solution by the Mystic and the Idealist," May 28, 1900, LSMP.
45. LS, "To What Extent Am I Free?" Mar. 23, 1899, LSMP.
46. LS, Thesis for Honors, May 14, 1900, LSMP.
47. LS, Thesis for Honors.
48. LS, "The World and the Individual." Royce had reason to be pleased by Lucy's challenge. Years before he had suggested that "the true difficulty" of women studying philosophy was "rather a moral than intellectual one: it is a certain fear of standing alone, of being eccentric, of seeming unduly obstinate in thought. This fear makes them, in the long run, too docile followers of a teacher or of an author, and so hinders their feedom of constructive thought." Royce to Abigail Williams May, Jan. 5, 1886, in May-Goddard Family Papers, SL. I am grateful to Barbara Miller Solomon for this reference.
49. Comment on LS, "The World and the Individual." On pragmatism, see William James, *Pragmatism* (Cambridge: Harvard University Press, 1975); David A. Hollinger, "The Problem of Pragmatism in American History," *Journal of American History* 67 (June 1980): 88–107; and Morton White, in *Pragmatism and the American Mind* (New York: Oxford University Press, 1973).
50. William James, "Dilemmas of Determinism," in *The Will to Believe and Other Essays on Popular Philosophy* (New York: Dover Publications, 1956), p. 152. Among the Radcliffe women whom James influenced most strongly was Gertrude Stein, who received her A.B. in 1898. Stein observed that "She went to Radcliffe and had a very

good time. . . . She was the secretary of the philosophical club and amused herself with all sorts of peole. She liked making sport of question asking and she liked equally answering them. She liked it all. But the really lasting impression of her Radcliffe life came through William James." *The Autobiography of Alice B. Toklas* (London: John Lane, The Bodley Head, 1933), p. 104.

51. Notes on Talk to Radcliffe Club, May 1956, LSMP.

52. Written Jan. 27, 1934, for Comstock's *My Tenth Anniversary*.

53. See, for example, Carol Gilligan, *In A Different Voice: Psychological Theory and Women's Development* (Cambridge: Harvard University Press, 1982); and Jean Baker Miller, *Toward A New Psychology of Women* (Boston: Beacon Press, 1975).

54. Schwager, "Harvard Women," p. 285.

55. Grace Burroughs Palmer, in *Fiftieth Anniversary Report of the Class of 1900*.

56. LS, "The Forms and Results of Student Social Activities," *Journal of the Association of Collegiate Alumnae*, 3, no. 18 (Dec. 1908): 50–53.

57. TL, p. 119.

5: STASIS

1. Mabel Richardson Brown, 50th Reunion Address, in Blanche Bonnelle Church Papers, RCA.

2. See, for example, Karen Blair, *The Clubwoman as Feminist: True Womanhood Redefined, 1868–1914* (New York: Holmes & Meier, 1980); Mari Jo Buhle, *Women and American Socialism, 1870–1920* (Urbana, Ill.: Univ. of Illinois Press, 1981); Barbara Leslie Epstein, *The Politics of Domesticity: Women, Evangelism and Temperance in Nineteenth Century America* (Middletown, Conn.: Wesleyan University Press, 1981); Mary P. Ryan, *Womanhood in America: From Colonial Times to the Present* (New York: New Viewpoints, 1975).

3. By 1900, the General Federation of Women's Clubs, formed eight years earlier, numbered 150,000 members. Ten years later, a million members belonged to the association, making it the largest women's organization of the period. On the club movement, see William O'Neill, ed., *The Woman Movement: Feminism in the United States and England* (Chicago: Quadrangle Books, 1969).

4. Vida Scudder to Louise Manning Hodgkins, Dec. 27, 1889, Scudder Papers, WCA.

5. *Chicago Tribune*, Dec. 1, 1900.

6. *Boston Evening Transcript*, June 20, 1900.

7. At many women's schools, however, the suffrage cause was to peak and decline as rapidly as it had risen. Commenting on the "latest thing in radicals," *The Vassar Quarterly* noted in 1916, for example, that "socialism and suffrage are passé." Dorothy A. Plum, compiler, *The Magnificent Enterprise: A Chronicle of Vassar College* (Poughkeepsie, New York: Vassar College, 1961), p. 49.

8. Palmer, *Life of Alice Freeman Palmer*, p. 242.

9. "Class Prophecy," *Class of 1900*, RCA.

10. On Class Day activities, see *The Harvard Graduates' Magazine*, 9 (Sept. 1900): 52–53: *Boston Transcript*, June 27, 1900.

11. UA.

12. TL, p. 126.

13. UA.
14. TL, pp. 126–27.
15. Addams, "Filial Relations," in Anne Firor Scott, ed., *Democracy and Social Ethics by Jane Addams* (Cambridge: Harvard University Press, 1964), p. 83.
16. Jane Addams, *Twenty Years at Hull House* (New York: Macmillan Co., 1910; New American Library ed., 1961), p. 94.
17. Helen Ekin Starrett, *After College, What?* (New York: Thomas Y. Crowell, 1896).
18. Hilda Worthington Smith, "The Remembered Way," Autobiographical typescript, Hilda Smith Papers, SL. For further discussion of this problem, see Joyce Antler, "'After College, What?': New Graduates and the Family Claim," *American Quarterly* 32 (Fall 1980):409–34.
19. UA.
20. Ibid.
21. TL, pp. 127–28.
22. Ibid., p. 41.
23. See, for example, Mar. 16, 1894, NASD.
24. News clipping, Lucy Sprague Scrapbook, courtesy of Barbara Mitchell.
25. June 7–8, 1901, NASD.
26. June 16, 1901, NASD.
27. Lucy was a bridesmaid with Florence Field; they wore "white muslin and pink tulle hats." June 19, NASD.
28. Lucia Sprague to NS, Aug. 28, 1901, NASD.
29. Sept. 1, 1901; also see July 14, Aug. 30, 1901, NASD.
30. Sept. 1, Oct. 6, 1901, NASD.
31. To honor Lucia's memory, Otho built a 36-bed hospital in Pasadena.
32. Feb. 20, Mar. 7, Mar. 9, 1902, NASD.
33. TL, pp. 128–29.
34. During this period, chlorosis, a form of anemia, was widely reported (often self-diagnosed) in American girls. Its symptoms included loss of appetite and strength, difficulty in breathing, and a supposed greenish tinge of the skin. Historians believe chlorosis was a culturally constructed disease related to women's family roles. See Joan Jacobs Brumberg, "Chlorotic Girls, 1870–1920: A Historical Perspective on Female Adolescence," *Child Development* 53 (1981): 1468–77.
35. Mar. 9, 1902, NASD; TL, p. 129. "Lucy is very weak and sick. She cannot keep anything [down]," Nan wrote on her arrival. Apr. 12, 1902. Also see May 11, 1902, NASD.
36. TL, p. 129.
37. Ibid.; Aug, 7, 18, 19, 30, Sept. 14, 15, 25, 1902, NASD.
38. UA.
39. Ibid.
40. TL, p. 130.
41. UA.
42. "A young woman cannot hold herself apart from a needy family, as a young man can," she once reported to the Association of Collegiate Alumnae. "We need to strengthen women to devote themselves to high, persistent work . . . there is too lit-

tle proper sentiment in America about the sacredness of their time." Palmer, *Life of Alice Freeman Palmer*, p. 273.

43. TL, p. 133.
44. LS, Class of 1900, *Decennial Report*, p. 34, RCA.
45. UA.
46. TL, p. 133.
47. UA.
48. June 20, 29, 1903, NASD.
49. UA.
50. TL, p. 134.

6: A "HEART CULTURE" FOR WOMEN STUDENTS

1. TL, p. 146.
2. TL, p. 143.
3. George Rieber to LSM, June 30, 1944, LSMP. As for Rieber, he was for all "for 'triangulating the universe with a good theodolite' and Robin was all for keeping the talk at the level of intelligent language." Ernest Hocking to LSM, Aug. 18, 1949, LSMP.
4. TL, p. 150; UA.
5. TL, p. 161.
6. On the history of the University of California see Verne A. Stadtman, ed.; *The Centennial Record of the University of California* (Berkeley, Calif.: University of California Press, 1967).
7. See Lynn Gordon, "Women with Missions: Varieties of College Life in the Progressive Era" (Ph.D. diss., University of Chicago, 1980). Also see Florence Howe, *Myths of Coeducation: Selected Essays, 1964–1983* (Bloomington: Indiana University Press, 1984.)
8. Even enlightened administrators did not include women as fundamental to their definition of a university. As Benjamin Wheeler noted: "The whole purpose of the university is to provide men with the means of seeing into things themselves, so that they shall not be dependent, but independent" (Benjamin Wheeler, *Memorial Exercises*, University of California, Oct. 3, 1927). David Starr Jordan, president of Leland Stanford Jr. University, remarked that "the college is the place for . . . the development of personal manners and manliness. . . ." ("The University and the College," *Journal of the Association of Collegiate Alumnae*, 3, no. 18 [Dec. 1908]:79).
9. Widely known as a moral and religious thinker, at Cornell Wheeler lectured to a Bible class numbering over 800 students. *Daily Californian*, Feb. 9, 1911.
10. Stadtman, *Centennial*, pp. 180–81. See Wheeler, *Memorial Exercises*.
11. Inauguration of Benjamin Ide Wheeler, Oct. 25, 1899, in *University Chronicle* (Berkeley University Press, 1899), 2:27–28.
12. Berkeley, *Blue and Gold*, 1914, p. 43.
13. See *The Prytaneans: An Oral History of the Prytanean Society, Its Members and Their University*, 2 vols. (Berkeley, Calif.: The Prytanean Alumnae Association, Inc., 1970, 1977).

14. Hearst financed kindergarten associations in the San Francisco region and in Washington, D.C., where she founded the National Cathedral School for Girls. In the late 1890s, she helped establish the National Congress of Mothers. She provided funds for an international competition for the best comprehensive plan for the University of California campus at Berkeley, the Hearst Memorial Mining Building, a university museum and other projects. "Phoebe Hearst," BL; Rodman Wilson Paul, "Phoebe Hearst," *Notable American Women*, 2:171-73.
15. See Mary Bennett Ritter, M.D., *More Than Gold in California, 1849-1933* (Berkeley, Calif.: University of California Press, 1933).
16. UA.
17. Lucy Sprague's work as dean is presented in the "Report of the Dean of Women," in *Biennial Report of the President of the University on behalf of the Board of Regents, 1906-08, 1908-10, 1910-12,* University Archives, BL.
18. In her survey and focus on cooperative housekeeping, Lucy followed the path of Dr. Mary Ritter, who had worked to improve housing for women students.
19. See LS to Benjamin Wheeler, Mar. 11, Apr. 11, 1911, Benjamin Wheeler to LS, Apr. 10, 13, 1911, Records of the President of the University of California, University Archives, BL.
20. The other six buildings were named for University of California alumnae, including Lucy's friends May Cheney and Jessica Peixotto. At the time of the University's Centennial in 1968, Mitchell Hall housed 80 men. Later, it became an apartment complex for student families. Stadtman, *Centennial*, p. 58.
21. She recalled on that occasion that the idea of dormitories had met with strenuous opposition. "Don't coddle the girls," she remembered being told. "If they want an education, let them work hard at it and live where they can." Notes on Talk for Groundbreaking Ceremony, Mar. 10, 1958, and news clipping, "Groundbreaking Paves Way for UC Student Hall," LSMP.
22. LS, "The Pan-Hellenic," Berkeley *Key* (n.d.), LSMP.
23. LS, "The Pan-Hellenic."
24. Edna Watson Bailey, cited in Eunice Mitchell Lehmer to Evelyn Seely Stewart, Jan. 30, 1956, LSMP.
25. LS, "The Forms and Results of Student Social Activities," pp. 50-53.
26. LS, "Report of the Dean of Women," 1910.
27. PIE, p. 50.
28. TL, p. 198.
29. LS, "Report of the Dean of Women," 1906.
30. UA; TL, p. 194.
31. LS, "Report of the Dean of Women," 1910.
32. TL, p. 196; PIE, pp. 48-53. *The Bard of the Dimbovitza: Roumanian Folk Songs* (New York: Charles Scribner's Sons, 1891; complete edition, 1902) were collected "from the peasants" by Helene Vacaresco.
33. Anna Rearden Baeck typescript, "I Remember Lucy Sprague," BL.
34. PIE, pp. 50-53; TL, pp. 189-90; Sinclair Lewis, *Ann Vickers*, cited in Allen F. Davis, *Spearheads for Reform: The Social Settlements and the Progressive Movement* (New York: Oxford University Press, 1967), p. 17.
35. Stadtman, *Centennial*, p. 133. See *Essays in Social Economics in Honor of Jessica*

Peixotto (Berkeley, Calif.: Univ. of California Press, 1935). Foreword by Wesley Clair Mitchell.

36. TL, p. 193.
37. PIE, p. 42.
38. TL, pp. 192–93.
39. *New York Times*, Oct. 24, 1911. Lucy was attending the 13th Annual Convention of the Association of Collegiate Alumnae at the Hotel Martinique.
40. *San Francisco Call*, Oct. 13, 1911.
41. LS to WCM, Oct. 29, 1911, LSMP.
42. Lucy Stebbins to LSM, Sept. 21, 1953, LSMP. Also see Stebbins to LSM, Apr. 15, 1947, LSMP.
43. Like Lucy Sprague and Lucy Stebbins, most of these deans held academic rank, either as regularly teaching faculty or as nonteaching members of faculty councils and senates. One contemporary female dean suggested, however, that teaching appointments were generally given to deans of women either to strengthen their administrative influence or as a "sop to Cerberus" and were regarded by male faculty with "tolerant condescension." See Gertrude S. Martin, "The Position of Dean of Women," *Journal of the Association of Collegiate Alumnae* 4, no. 2 (Mar. 1911): 65–78.
44. In another sense, the professionalization of the deans signified their declining academic status. Few of the later deans of women possessed the high academic credentials of the earlier ones, many of whom, unlike Lucy Sprague, had doctorates. By the 1920s, the position had become almost entirely administrative. See Lulu Holmes, *A History of the Position of Dean of Women in a Selected Group of Co-Ed Colleges and Universities in the United States* (New York: Teachers College, Bureau of Publications, 1939).
45. LS to WCM, Oct. 29, 1911, LSMP.

7: SIERRA VISIONS

1. TL, p. 211.
2. "Symbol of A New Career," LSMP.
3. TL, p. 200.
4. See John C. Burnham, "The Progressive Era Revolution in American Attitudes toward Sex," *Journal of American History* 59 (Mar. 1973): 885–908: David Pivar, *Purity Crusade* (Westport, Conn.: Greenwood, 1973); Linda Gordon, *Woman's Body, Woman's Right: A Social History of Birth Control in America* (New York: Penguin Books, 1977).
5. TL, p. 200; Dr. Mary Ritter taught a course in "Hygiene and Home Sanitation" for freshmen women before 1905. Ritter, *More Than Gold*, pp. 204–06.
6. TL, p. 150.
7. Ibid., p. 191.
8. "Boulder Creek, 1904," LSMP.
9. Untitled sonnet, LSMP.
10. Untitled sonnet, LSMP.
11. Untitled sonnet, LSMP.
12. Other guests included novelist Robert Herrick and his wife, Harriet, who were the

Millers' closest friends, poet William Vaughan Moody, and J. Laurence Laughlin, chairman of the Economics Department, called "Uncle Larry" by students (privately, Mary called him the "Medicine Box," for she thought he smelled of antiseptic).

13. LSM, "Robin," Nov. 1948, LSMP.
14. UA; TL, p. 150.
15. UA.
16. TL, p. 83; see WCM, "Thorstein Veblen, 1857–1929," *The New Republic*, Sept. 4, 1929, in Joseph Dorfman, ed., *Thorstein Veblen: Essays, Reviews and Reports* (Clifton, N.J.: Augustus M. Kelley, 1973), p. 607.
17. Cited in TL, pp. 86, 88.
18. LSM, "John Dewey," Oct. 21, 1949, LSMP.
19. Frederick C. Mills, "Wesley Clair Mitchell, 1878–1948," LSMP.
20. WCM, "Fifty Years as an Economist," in TL, p. 86.
21. See, for example, Nov. 24, 1907, WCMD.
22. Mar. 17, Apr. 17, Apr. 27, 1905; Jan. 21, Oct. 5, 28, Nov. 1, 1906, WCMD.
23. Jan. 19, Feb. 6, Mar. 1, 9, 29, 1907, WCMD.
24. May 3, 8, 1907, WCMD.
25. May 8, 1907, WCMD; UA.
26. UA; TL, p. 147.
27. May 10, 1907, WCMD; "The Dancer," LSMP.
28. May 31, June 1, 12, 30, Sept. 26, Nov. 1, 1907, Jan. 26, Feb. 1, 3, 6, Mar. 4, 14, 1908; WCMD; TL, pp. 214–15.
29. Apr. 4, 6, 1909, WCMD.
30. WCM to LS, Oct. 18, 1911, LSMP; see Nov.–Dec. 1908, Jan.–June 1909, WCMD.
31. Aug. 9, 15, 23, 1909, WCMD.
32. Jan. 27, 1908, Mar. 1908, NASD.
33. Apr. 1, 15, 17; Aug. 2, 1908, NASD.
34. Apr. 28, 1909, Feb. 18–26, 1909, NASD.
35. Nicholas Murray Butler to LS, May 28, 1909, LSMP.
36. Nicholas Murray Butler to LS, July 14, 1910, LSMP.
37. TL, p. 204.
38. After Otho's death, Lucy arranged Nannie's care in institutions or with private nurses and visited her regularly.
39. Wheeler delivered a lecture series on "The Sources of Public Opinion in America." See *The California Alumni Weekly*, 2, Sept. 11, 1909.
40. TL, p. 205, 207. George Palmer wrote to Lucy that Professor Munsterberg "is continually hearing your praises sung in Berlin and that much of President Wheeler's great success there is attributed to you." George Palmer to LS, Dec. 2, 1909, LSMP.
41. UA.
42. Notes, LSMP.
43. UA; TL, p. 206.
44. Notes, LSMP.
45. TL, p. 206.
46. Ibid., p. 207.
47. Ibid.

48. Wheeler spoke on "Recent Readjustments in the College Course." Edith Abbot, Katharine Coman, Jessica Peixotto, and Susan Kingsbury presented papers at a session on the "Economic Efficiency of Women." Lucy spoke the next day at a session on "Social Values in College Life" ("The Forms and Results of Student Social Activities"). *Journal of the Association of Collegiate Alumnae,* 3, no. 17 (Jan. 1908).
49. Adolph Miller to NS, Jan. 16, 1909, NASD; TL, p. 207.
50. Sept. 25, Oct. 6, Oct. 30, Dec. 6, 1910, Feb. 15, 1911, WCMD; TL, p. 216.
51. May 8, 11, 18–20, 26, June 1, 3, 1911, WCMD; TL, p. 216.
52. TL, pp. 216–17.
53. Ibid., p. 217.
54. Ibid., pp. 217–18.
55. Ibid., p. 220.
56. Ibid., pp. 218–20; UA.
57. TL, p. 221.
58. WCM to LS, Oct. 30, 1911, LSMP.

8: NEW YORK APPRENTICESHIPS

1. Charlotte Perkins Gilman, "The Passing of Matrimony," *Harper's Bazaar* 40 (June 1906):495–98.
2. Ibid., p. 496.
3. Roosevelt coined the term "race suicide" in 1903. See David M. Kennedy, *Birth Control in America: The Career of Margaret Sanger* (New Haven: Yale University Press, 1971), p. 42. Hall's remarks are cited in May Cheney, "Will Nature Eliminate the College Woman?" *Journal of the Association of Collegiate Alumnae* 3, no. 10 (Jan. 1905): 3. Also see Frances M. Abbott, "A Generation of College Women," *Forum* 20 (1895–96): 377–84; Millicent Washburn Shinn, "The Marriage Rate of College Women," *Century Magazine* 50 (Oct. 1895): 946–48; and Charles Franklin Emerick, "College Women and Race Suicide," *Political Science Quarterly* 24 (1909): 269–83.
4. M. Carey Thomas, "The College Woman of the Present and Future," *McClure's* Syndicate Reprint, pp. 4–5. Thomas Papers, Bryn Mawr College Archives.
5. See A. S. Ethridge, "The Modern Woman and Matrimony," *The Vassar Miscellany* 25 (Nov. 1895): 47–51; "Why Do Not Educated Women Marry?" *Independent* 67 (1909): 966–69; 1193–94; and Anne O'Hagan, "The Confessions of A Professional Woman," *Harper's Bazaar* 41 (Sept. 1907): 848–54.
6. LS to WCM, Oct. 16, 1911, LSMP.
7. LS to "Round Robins," Oct. 17, 1911, LSMP.
8. Ibid.
9. Mary Howard gave a supper to honor Santayana following this address, which Wesley Mitchell, and presumably, Lucy, attended. Aug. 25, 1911, WCMD. For Santayana's talk, see "The Genteel Tradition in American Philosophy," *University of California Chronicle* 13 (1911): 357–80; reprinted in Douglas L. Wilson, ed., *The Genteel Tradition: Nine Essays by George Santayana* (Cambridge: Harvard University Press, 1967).
10. *Twenty Years at Hull House,* chap. 6. On women and the settlement movement, see

Kathryn Kish Sklar, "Hull House in the 1890s: A Community of Women Reformers," SIGNS 10, no. 4 (Summer 1985): 658–77; Jill K. Conway, "The First Generation of American Women Graduates " (Ph.D. diss., Harvard University, 1969); Davis, Spearheads for Reform; Davis, American Heroine: The Life and Legend of Jane Addams; Ellen Lagemann, A Generation of Women: Education in the Lives of Progressive Reformers (Cambridge: Harvard University Press, 1979); John P. Rousmaniere, "Cultural Hybrid in the Slums: The College Woman and the Settlement House, 1889–1894," American Quarterly 22 (1970): 45–66; Barbara Sicherman, Alice Hamilton: A Life in Letters (Cambridge, Harvard University Press, 1984); and Christopher Lasch, The New Radicalism in America: The Intellectual As a Social Type (New York: Alfred A. Knopf, 1966), chap. 1.

11. See, for example, Brooks's The Social Unrest (New York: The Macmillan Co., 1903); American Syndicalism (New York: The Macmillan Co., 1913); and Labor's Challenge to the Social Order (New York: The Macmillan Co., 1920). Because of his opposition to anarchism and syndicalism, contemporary historians locate Brooks within the tradition of democratic liberalism rather than radicalism.

12. Lucy recalled Brooks as full of "boundless energy and warmth, with a zeal for understanding human behavior." See her remarks in John Graham Brooks/Helen Graham Brooks: A Memorial (Boston: privately printed, 1940), pp. 35–36.

13. See Robert Bremner, "Lillian Wald," Notable American Women, 3: 526–29; Lagemann, A Generation of Women, chap. 3.

14. TL, p. 208.

15. LS to WCM, Nov. 8, 1911, LSMP.

16. LS to WCM, Oct. 29, 1911, LSMP.

17. See Joyce Antler, "Florence Kelley," Women and Health 1 (1976): 1–2; Dorothy Rose Blumberg, Florence Kelley: The Making of a Social Pioneer (New York: Kelley, 1966); Josephine Goldmark, Impatient Crusader: Florence Kelley's Life Story (Urbana: University of Illinois Press, 1953); Louise C. Wade, "Florence Kelley," Notable American Women, 2:317–19.

18. Her book, Some Ethical Gains through Legislation (New York: Macmillan Co., 1905), asserts strategic goals which focused on the achievement of social reconstruction through broadly based organization for legislative reform.

19. TL, pp. 208–09; PIE, p. 79.

20. TL, p. 209; PIE, p. 81.

21. Her book Social Diagnosis (New York: Russell Sage Foundation, 1917), which followed Friendly Visiting among the Poor (New York: Macmillan Co., 1899) and The Good Neighbor in the Modern City (Philadelphia: J.B. Lippincott Co., 1907), represented the first full formulation of theory and methods of social investigation, and became a classic text in social work where it was regarded as a reflection of the field's growing professionalization. See "Mary Richmond," Encyclopedia of Social Work, 2: 1224–25; and Muriel W. Pumphrey, "Mary Richmond," Notable American Women, 3: 152–54.

22. Mary E. Richmond and Fred S. Hall, A Study of Nine Hundred and Eighty-Five Widows Known to Certain Charity Organization Societies in 1910 (New York: Russell Sage Foundation, 1913).

23. TL, p. 209. See "Pauline Goldmark," in Encyclopedia of Social Work 1: 509–10.

24. Among the junior fellows at the time were Frances Perkins, who later would become Secretary of Labor under President Franklin D. Roosevelt, and the nation's first female cabinet member, and Lawrence K. Frank, who was to play a vital role in the child development movement after 1925.

25. TL, p. 208.

26. *West Side Studies* (1914: Russell Sage Foundation; Reprint ed., Arno Press, 1974), under Pauline Goldmark's direction.

27. Ibid., pp. 209–10.

28. PIE, p. 80.

29. Ibid., p. 81.

30. Ibid., pp. 81–82.

31. Yet a local petition to transfer "this self-constituted censor of our morality" out of the district was unsuccessful. On Richman's life, see William Brickman and Paul Boyer, "Julia Richman," *Notable American Women*, 3:150–52.

32. See Selma C. Berrol, "Julia Richman: Agent of Change in the Urban School," *Urban Education* (Jan. 1977): 361–81; and Martha Kransdorff, "Julia Richman's Years in the New York City Public Schools: 1872–1912" (Ph.D. diss., University of Michigan, 1979).

33. TL, p. 210.

34. Mary Van Kleeck, "A Census of College Women," *Journal of the Association of Collegiate Alumnae* 11 (May 1918): 560; Class of 1900 Decennial, Thirty-Fifth, and Fiftieth Anniversary Reports, RCA.

35. LS to WCM, Oct. 29, 1911, LSMP.

36. Lillian Wald to LS, Dec. 19, 1911, LSMP. As a token of affection, Wald sent a pair of brass candlesticks that Lucy had admired on to Berkeley. Wald to LS, Jan. 3, 1912, LSMP. Also see Wald to LS, Nov. 27, 1911.

37. LS to WCM, Nov. 30, 1911, LSMP.

38. LS to WCM, Dec. 8, 1911, LSMP.

39. LS to WCM, Dec. 9, 1911, LSMP.

40. Notes, Dec. 11, 1911, LSMP.

41. See The Vice Commission of Chicago, Inc., *The Social Evil in Chicago: A Study of Existing Conditions* (Chicago: 1911), pp. 36–37, 45, 56–61.

42. LS to WCM, Dec. 24, 1911, LSMP.

43. LS to WCM, Dec. 24, 1911, LSMP.

44. Lucy conducted a session on "The Nature and Extent of Instruction in Personal Hygiene" for 25 deans of women who were attending the annual conference of the Association of Collegiate Alumnae in New York at the end of October 1911. The deans passed a resolution that instruction in hygiene, reproduction, and venereal diseases be given for credit in the freshman year. See "Proceedings of the Association," *Journal of the Association of Collegiate Alumnae*, 5, no. 2 (Mar. 1912): 193–208.

9: A PASSIONATE WOMAN

1. WCM to LS, Nov. 14, 1911, LSMP.

2. On patterns of American courtship, see Ellen Rothman, *Hands and Hearts: A History of American Courtship* (New York: Basic Books, 1984).

3. WCM to LS, Oct. 18, 1911, LSMP.
4. WCM to LS, Oct. 18, 1911.
5. LSM to WCM, Oct. 29, 1911, LSMP.
6. LS to WCM, Oct. 26, 1911, LSMP.
7. WCM to LS, Nov. 1, 1911, LSMP.
8. LS to WCM, Nov. 6, 1911, LSMP.
9. LS to WCM, Oct. 29, 1911, LSMP.
10. LS to WCM, Oct. 29, 1911.
11. WCM to LS, Nov. 3, 1911, LSMP.
12. WCM to LS, Nov. 6, 1911, LSMP.
13. WCM to LS, Nov. 6, 1911.
14. WCM to LS, Nov. 6, 1911.
15. LS to WCM, Nov. 8, 1911, LSMP.
16. WCM to LS, Nov. 12, 1911, LSMP.
17. WCM to LS, Nov. 15, 1911, LSMP.
18. WCM to LS, Nov. 18, 1911, LSMP.
19. LS to WCM, Nov. 20, 1911, LSMP.
20. LS to WCM, Nov. 27, 1911, LSMP.
21. WCM to LS, Nov. 26, 1911, LSMP.
22. WCM to LS, Nov. 26, 1911.
23. LS to WCM, Dec. 2, 1911, LSMP.
24. LS to WCM, Dec. 3, 1911, LSMP.
25. LS to WCM, Dec. 18, LSMP.
26. WCM to LS, Dec. 9, 1911, LSMP.
27. LS to WCM, Dec. 2, 1911, LSMP. Mary Howard suggests that differences of "background" may have been connected with Lucy's misgivings. Mary Howard to LS, Nov. 28, 1911, UC.
28. WCM to LS, Dec. 7, 1911, LSMP.
29. WCM to LS, Nov. 29, 1911, LSMP.
30. WCM to LS, Dec. 7, 1911, LSMP.
31. WCM to LS, Dec. 7, 1911.
32. WCM to LS, Dec. 7, 1911.
33. LS to WCM, Dec. 12, 1911, LSMP.
34. WCM to LS, Dec. 19, 1911, LSMP.
35. LS to WCM, Dec. 18, 1911, LSMP.
36. WCM to LS, Dec. 23, 1911, LSMP.
37. WCM to LS, Dec. 23, 1911.
38. LS to WCM, Dec. 20, 1911, LSMP.
39. LS to WCM, Dec. 23, 1911, LSMP.
40. LS to WCM, Dec. 25, 1911, LSMP.
41. LS to WCM, Dec. 26, 1911, LSMP.
42. WCM to LS, Dec. 11, 1911, LSMP.
43. WCM to LS, Dec. 31, 1911, LSMP.
44. WCM to LSM, Dec. 20, 1911, LSMP.
45. LS to WCM, Dec. 27, 1911, LSMP.
46. LS to WCM, Dec. 29, 1911, LSMP.

10: A MASQUE OF MAIDENHOOD

1. Mary Howard to John Galen Howard, July 11, 1912, BL.
2. TL, p. 230.
3. WCM to LSM, Nov. 6, 1911, LSMP.
4. See Stebbins' report in *Report of the President of the University*, 1914, Files of the Office of the President, University of California Archives, BL. Also see Gordon, "Women with Missions." At the University of California as at other coed schools, home economics as a solution to the vocational dilemmas inherent in women's higher education combined traditional and innovative ideas. Such programs provided vocational opportunities for women yet hardened sexual segregation. See, for example, Margaret Rossiter, *Women Scientists in America: Struggles and Strategies to 1940* (Baltimore: Johns Hopkins University Press, 1982), pp. 70–71.
5. Feb. 4, 1912; and LS to NAS, Feb. 9, 1912; NASD.
6. Feb. 25, 1912, NASD.
7. ESC to LS, n.d., LSMP.
8. E. H. Wells to Albert Sprague II, Feb. 15, 1912, NASD.
9. Albert Sprague II to Albert Sprague, Feb. 17, 1911, NASD.
10. Albert Sprague to LS, Feb. 8, 1912, LSMP.
11. March 16, 1912, NASD.
12. Mar. 28, 1909, WCMD.
13. June 12, 1912, NASD.
14. LS to NAS, Mar. 3, 1912, NASD.
15. LS to NAS, Feb. 26, 1912, NASD.
16. Mary Caswell to LS, n.d., LSMP.
17. Marion Jones Farquhar to LS, n.d., LSMP.
18. George Herbert Palmer to LS, March 3, 1912, LSMP.
19. Jacques Loeb to LS, Mar. 9, 1912, LSMP.
20. Agnes Hocking to LS, LSMP.
21. Jessica Peixotto to LS, n.d., LSMP.
22. Florence Kelley to LS, May 1, 1912, LSMP.
23. Dr. Henry Stehman to LS, Feb. 29, 1912, LSMP.
24. LS, "The Forms and Results of Student Activities," p. 50.
25. TL, pp. 196–97.
26. Anna Rearden Baeck, "The Incipient Idea of an All-Woman Masque," handwritten report, BL.
27. Florence Doyle, "Report of the Partheneia," Associated Women Students, Apr. 6, 1912, BL.
28. Anna Rearden Baeck to Eunice Lehmer, Feb. 5, 1950, BL; also see *The Daily Californian*, Nov. 17, 1911.
29. Anna Rearden Baeck, typescript, "I Remember Lucy Sprague," LSMP.
30. Anna Rearden, "The Partheneia: A Masque of Maidenhood," Berkeley, Calif.: University of California, 1912, BL.
31. Baeck, "I Remember Lucy Sprague."
32. *The San Francisco Examiner*, April 7, 1912.
33. *Examiner*, Apr. 7, 1912.
34. Ibid.

35. *The San Francisco Call*, Apr. 7, 1912.
36. Apr. 6, 1912, NASD.
37. Porter Garnett sent a copy of Rearden's *Partheneia* to Katharine Lee Bates of Wellesley, who replied: "I recognize in reading it the resemblance pointed out to our Wellesley Tree Day festivities, but it seems to me the poetic qualities of the lines is exceptionally fine. There is a peculiar beauty in the theme, too, and a certain personal loveliness of spirit over the whole" (Sept. 3, 1912 [Anna Rearden Baeck Papers, BL]). In later years, the Partheneia's "usual assortment of dancing nymphs and personified abstractions" came in for occasional campus criticism. *Daily Californian* (n.d., 1922), BL.
38. Baeck, "The Incipient Idea of an All-Woman Masque."
39. Agnes Steel, *The Awakening of Everymaid*, 1913, BL.
40. Baeck, "The Incipient Idea of an All-Woman Masque."
41. Baeck, "I Remember Lucy Sprague."
42. LS to NAS, Apr. 20, 1912, NASD.
43. Apr. 7–19, 1912, NASD.
44. LS to NAS, Apr. 20, 22, 1912, NAS Diaries.
45. LS to NAS, Apr. 20, 1912, NASD.
46. WCM to NAS, Apr. 21, 1912, NASD.
47. WCM to NAS, Apr. 24, 28, 30, 1912, NASD.
48. Mary Miller to NAS, May 4, 1912, NASD.
49. LS to NAS, May 1, 1912, NASD.
50. Apr. 20, 1912, NASD.
51. Eleanor Atwood to NAS, n.d., NASD.
52. Nan Rearden to LSM, Jan. 19, 1913, BL. As a wedding gift, the senior class at the university sent Lucy an old silver coffee pot with the inscription, "To Lucy Sprague, Beloved even more for herself than for her gracious years of unfailing service." NASD.
53. LS to NAS, May 11, 1912; May 11–13, 1912; NASD.
54. LSM to NAS, May 11, 1912, NAS Diaries.
55. Mary Miller to NAS, May 8, 1912, NASD.
56. LSM to NAS, May 10, 1912, NASD.
57. May 25, 1912, NASD.
58. May 27, 1912, NASD.
59. WCM to NAS, May 29, 1912, NASD.
60. LSM to NAS, July 14, 1912, NASD.
61. LSM to NAS, July 12, 1912, NASD.
62. "Till Hitler polluted it," she added later ("Robin").
63. Alvin Johnson to WCM. Aug. 24, 1912, WCMP; TL, p. 233.
64. UA.
65. TL, p. 212.
66. LSM, "Robin."

11: GETTING STARTED

1. Mary Howard to John Galen Howard, May 7, 1913, BL.
2. LSM to "Robins," May 12, 1913, LSMP. Also see LSM, "To Robin, " Aug. 5, 1913, LSMP.

3. UA.

4. Allen Churchill, *The Improper Bohemians* (New York: E.P. Dutton, 1959), pp. 22, 25.

5. Frederick J. Hoffman, *The 20s* (New York: The Free Press, 1965), pp. 34–35; Caroline Ware, *Greenwich Village, 1920–1930: A Comment on American Civilization in the Postwar Years* (Boston: Houghton Mifflin, 1935). Also see Judith Schwarz, *Radical Feminists of Heterodoxy: Greenwich Village, 1912–1940* (Lebanon, N.H.: New Victoria, 1982), p. 29.

6. Feb. 5, 8, 17–18, Mar. 7, 11, 1913, WCMD. Wesley Mitchell attended Henri Bergson's lecture on intuition at Columbia University, another milestone in America's prewar cultural rebellion. See Henry May, *The End of American Innocence: A Study of the First Years of Our Time, 1912–1917* (New York: Alfred A. Knopf, 1959).

7. TL, p. 254.

8. They also attended the Pooles' "salon." Dec. 2, 1913, WCMD.

9. "Films and Births and Censorship," *The Survey*, April 3, 1915, p. 5.

10. Scholars have argued that despite their declarations of sexual radicalism, both female and male Village feminists—including Eastman, Floyd Dell, and Hutchins Hapgood—were bound by traditional, middle-class Victorian morality. See Ellen Kay Trimberger, "Feminism, Men and Modern Love: Greenwich Village, 1900–1925," in Ann Snitow, Christine Stansell, and Sharon Thompson, *Powers of Desire: The Politics of Sexuality* (New York: Monthly Review Press, 1983); and Leslie Fishbein, "The Failure of Feminism in Greenwich Village before World War I," *Women's Studies*, 9 (1982): 275–89.

11. Dec. 10, 1916, WCMD. On the early years of *The New Republic*, see Ronald Steel, *Walter Lippman and the American Century* (New York: Vintage Books, 1980).

12. Lucy owned several of Davies' allegorical paintings, set in the California background of Carmel and Sierra. TL, p. 243. On one occasion, Davies came to see the "children's drawings"—Apr. 3, 1917, WCMD. See *Dream Vision: The Work of Arthur B. Davies* (Boston: Institute of Contemporary Art, 1981.)

13. Among Lucy's close friends in New York were her Radcliffe classmate, Sally Eaton Mower, a singer then in the process of separating from her husband, and Norah Hamilton, an artist who worked at the Henry St. settlement when she was not living in Chicago at Hull House. Norah and her older sister Alice Hamilton visited Lucy often; Lucy helped care for Norah on occasions when she was hospitalized because of nervous illness. See 1913–16 passim, WCMD.

14. On Feb. 28, 1915, for example, at dinner with the Deweys and Max Eastman the conversation concerned "Isadora Duncan and Freud." Also see Feb. 6, Mar. 14, Oct. 17, 1913; Feb. 20, Dec. 21, 1914, WCMD.

15. Jan.–Dec. 1913, WCMD.

16. Mary Howard to John Galen Howard, May 13, 1913, UC; Edward H. Collins, "Smuggling and Taxes: A Study of Some Lectures of the Late W.C. Mitchell and Applications Today," *The New York Times*, Apr. 28, 1958; obituary of WCM, *The New York Times*, Oct. 30, 1948.

17. "Realism is Allah, and Mitchell is his prophet. Paradise may be around the corner," wrote Paul Homan in a somewhat critical view of Mitchell's progressivism. Homan, *Contemporary Economic Thought* (Freeport, N.Y.: Books for Libraries Press, Inc.,

1928), pp. 435–36. For another view of Mitchell's *Business Cycles*, see Arthur F. Burns, *Wesley Mitchell and the National Bureau of Economic Research* (New York: National Bureau of Economic Research, 29th Annual Report, 1949), p. 23: "No other work between Marshall's *Principles* and Keynes' *General Theory* has had as big an influence on the economic thought of the Western world."

18. John Dewey, *Democracy and Education* (New York: Macmillan Co., 1916; Free Press ed., 1966), pp. 37, 76, 333–46. Also see Lawrence Cremin, *The Transformation of the School: Progressivism in American Education, 1876–1957* (New York: Vintage Books, 1964), pp. 121–26.

19. LSM, "John Dewey," Oct. 21, 1949, and draft of letter to Sidney Ratner, Mar. 19, 1959, LSMP; also see LSM, "John Dewey," *The New Republic*, Oct. 17, 1949, p. 30. In 1959, Lucy served on the Honorary Committee for the Observation of John Dewey's Centenary.

    On one visit to the Dewey's Greenlawn home, Wesley received multiple bee stings helping Alice Dewey hive a swarm of bees. ("One always obeyed Alice Dewey.") TL, p. 254; May 30–31, 1913, WCMD.

20. On Thorndike, see Merle Curti, chap. 14, in *The Social Ideas of American Educators* (Totowa, N.J.: Littlefield, Adams & Co., 1974); Cremin, *The Transformation of the School*, pp. 110–15; and Geraldine Joncich Clifford, *The Sane Positivist: A Biography of Edward L. Thorndike* (Middletown, Conn.: Wesleyan University Press, 1968).

21. TL, p. 243.

22. See Sol Cohen, *Progressivism and Urban School Reform: The Public Education Association of New York City, 1895–1954* (New York: Bureau of Publications, Teachers College, 1964), pp. 70ff.

23. On the Visiting Teachers Project see Harriet M. Johnson, *The Visiting Teacher in New York City* (New York, Public Education Association), 1916; John Oppenheimer, *The Visiting Teacher Movement* (New York, Public Education Association, 1924); Eleanor Hope Johnson, "Social Service and the Public Schools," *Survey* 30 (May 3, 1913), pp. 173–78; Julia Richman, "A Social Need of the Public Schools," *Forum* 43 (Feb. 1910): 161–69; and Howard W. Nudd, "The Contribution of the Visiting Teacher To Child Adjustment," *Progressive Education* 3 (Jan.–Mar. 1925): 26–30.

24. Cohen, *Progressivism and Urban School Reform*, pp. 75–76.

25. LSM to "Robins," May 12, 1913, LSMP.

26. TL, p. 250. There is no biography of Harriet M. Johnson. See the brief biographical account in Barbara Biber, ed., *School Begins at Two: A Book for Teachers and Parents*, (1936: rev. edition, New York, Agathon Press, 1970), pp. ix–xi. This book presents a number of Johnson's unpublished manuscripts.

27. Mar. 23, Mar. 30, Apr. 14, May 14, 1913, Mar. 26, Apr. 12, 1914, WCMD.

28. LSM to "Robins", May 12, 1913.

29. LSM, "The Public's Schools and the Public's Ideals," LSMP.

30. LSM, "School Children and Sex Idealism," *Survey* 32, no. 2 (June 20, 1914): 327–28.

31. LSM to "Robins," May 12, 1913.

32. Lucy "wrestled" with accepting the chairmanship of the City Club's Committee on Education; she eventually refused it after discussion with Alice Dewey, Caroline

Pratt, and Elisabeth Irwin; Mar. 5–6, WCMD; the incident with Suzzallo is discussed in UA.

33. UA; Mar. 14, 1914, WCMD. In 1915, Suzzallo left Columbia to assume the presidency of the University of Washington.

34. March 1913, WCMD. On the Gary Plan, see Ronald D. Cohen and Raymond A. Mohl, *The Paradox of Progressive Education: The Gary Plan and Urban Schooling* (Port Washington, N.Y.: Kennikat Press, 1979).

35. Thousands of school children in the Bronx and Brooklyn went on strike against the Gary Plan, attacking schoolmates who tried to cross picket lines. They burned books, threw stones at police and the schools, and marched in anti-Gary parades. Several children were arrested; hundreds of others were expelled, suspended, or put on probation. The participation of young children in these strikes was variously blamed on Socialist agitators, older students, and parents. But mothers interviewed by police blamed the trouble on the Gary system itself, particularly the longer school day. Cohen and Mohl, *The Paradox of Progressive Education*, pp. 52–59.

36. Lucy spoke on behalf of the Gary Plan at an "uproarious" meeting of the Board of Education; Apr. 7, 1916, WCMD; and *New York Times*, Apr. 8, 1916. The Wirts dined with the Mitchells on May 31, 1916. Also see Mar. 15, 20, Apr. 5, May 18, 1914; Dec. 5, 16, 24, 27, 1916, WCMD. On Mar. 1, 1917, Alise Gregory of The Gary School League wrote to Lucy that "there is in New York City no other group of people so keenly in sympathy with the Gary School work [as the Bureau of Educational Experiments]." BEE Papers, CC.

37. Later known as the Committee on Hygiene of School Children, the committee was led by social workers Eleanor Johnson and Elisabeth Irwin.

38. H. H. Goddard, director of the Vineland School in New Jersey, an institution for "defective" individuals, published a translation of Binet's 1905 scale; in 1911, he translated Binet's 1908 revisions. These were the tests in use until 1915, when Yerkes published revisions of the Binet scale and especially, until the Stanford Revision of the Binet-Simon Intelligence Test was made in 1916 under the direction of Lewis M. Terman at Stanford. The Mitchells celebrated their fourth anniversary at a "New York University Feeble-Minded Dinner" at which Johnson of Vineland spoke. May 8, 1916, WCMD.

39. Helen Thompson Woolley received her Ph.D. summa cum laude from the University of Chicago in 1900, preparing a thesis on "the mental traits of sex." After marriage to Paul Woolley and the birth of two daughters, she was appointed director of the Bureau for the Investigation of Working Children in Cincinnati and later director of the Cincinnati Vocational Bureau, which became part of the Cincinnati Public Schools. For a discussion of Woolley's early work on sex roles see Rosalind Rosenberg, *Beyond Separate Spheres: Intellectual Roots of Modern Feminism* (New Haven, Yale University Press, 1982), chap. 3. Also see Marguerite W. Zapoleon and Lois Meek Stolz, "Helen Bradford Thompson Woolley," *Notable American Women*, 3:657–60.

40. See, for example, Oct. 14, 16, 20, 29, Nov. 4, 1914, WCMD.

41. On Irwin's life and career, see Patricia Albjerg Graham, "Elisabeth Irwin," in *Notable American Women*, 2:255–57; Schwarz, *Heterodoxy*, p. 68.

42. Woolley was attempting to survey various motor and mental capacities of 1000–

1500 14- to 18-year-olds, with the objective of developing a percentile ranking system and final scale. See Helen T. Woolley, *Journal of Educational Psychology* 7 (1916):431–33; idem, *An Experimental Study of Children* (New York: Macmillan, 1926); Oct. 11, 1915, WCMD.

43. On the Psychological Survey, see 1914–16 passim, WCMD.

12: A COOPERATIVE CAREER

1. Mar. 28, 1916, WCMD.
2. Apr. 14, 1916, WCMD. On Coolidge's life, see Gillian Anderson, "Elizabeth Penn Sprague Coolidge," in *Notable American Women: The Modern Period*, pp. 160–62; William Charles Bedford, "Elizabeth Sprague Coolidge: The Education of a Patron of Chamber Music, the Early Years " (Ph.D. diss., University of Missouri, 1964); Jay C. Rosenfeld, "Elizabeth Sprague Coolidge " (pamphlet, 1964); and Coolidge's own *Da Capo* (Washington, D.C.: The Library of Congress, 1952).
3. PIE, p. 90; see Apr. 13, 25, May 4, 1916, WCMD; *The New York Times*, Feb. 1, July 28, 1915. Later that year, Elizabeth Sprague Coolidge began to underwrite a Chicago chamber music group. The group, which she renamed the Berkshire String Quartet, gave concerts at her home in Pittsfield, Mass. Later she moved the performances to a Temple of Music and a 500-seat auditorium she built at nearby South Mountain, where she sponsored summer festivals. In 1925, she established the Elizabeth Sprague Coolidge Foundation at the Library of Congress, which played a leading role in the support of modern music.
4. Apr. 14–15, 1916, WCMD. Lucy's sister Mary had taken a different path. In 1914, President Wilson appointed Adolph Miller to the Federal Reserve Board, in which position he served until 1936. The Millers became part of an informal club consisting of the new assistant secretary of the navy, Franklin Delano Roosevelt, and his wife, Eleanor, and Secretary of the Interior, Franklin Lane, and his wife. After a visit to the Millers in 1914, Elizabeth Coolidge wrote to her mother that "Mary and Adolph are already among the very most prominent people here . . . they are receiving attentions from those highest in office and entertaining or being entertained . . . in a bewildering way. . . . Isn't it lovely to see her expanding into her birth right, and at last learning to enjoy her money and put it to use!" ECS to NAS, Mar. 25, 1914, NASD.
5. LSM to ECS, Apr. 15, 1916, ESCP.
6. May 6, 17, 1916, WCMD.
7. PIE, p. 90; UA.
8. By-Laws and Papers of Incorporation, BEE Papers, CC.
9. Minutes of the Working Council, Jan. 8, 1917, BEE Papers, CC.
10. Papers of Incorporation, March 5, 1917. On the early planning phase of the Bureau, see LSM to Jean Hunt, Nov. 14, 1916; Jean Lee Hunt, Report of the Dept. of Information, Oct. 12, 1916, BEE Papers, CC; Oct. 16, 26, Nov. 13, 16, WCMD. The BEE's first headquarters were at 71 Fifth Ave.
11. The publications of the Bureau in 1916–17 included *Playthings*, no. 1; *Study of Animal Families in Schools*, no. 2; *Experimental Schools: The Play School*, no. 3; *Experimental Schools: The Children's School; Teachers College Playground, The Gregory School,*

no. 4; *Experimental Schools: The Stony Ford School, The Home School, Sparkill, N.Y.*, no. 5. They are collected in Charlotte Winsor, ed., *Experimental School Revisited: Bulletins of the Bureau of Experimental Education* (New York: Agathon Press, Inc., 1973).

12. Hollingsworth, who had completed her Ph.D. under Thorndike at Teachers College, had long been engaged in studying gifted children, and was a friend and collaborator of Working Council member Elisabeth Irwin. See LSM to ESC, Sept. 8, 1916, ESCP; LSM, Chairman's Report of the BEE Working Council, 1917; Evelyn Dewey, Report to Working Council, 1917; Eleanor Johnson, Report on the Laboratory School, and Frederick Ellis and Eleanor Johnson, Statement for the Executive Committee on the Laboratory School, Mar. 31, 1917, BEE Papers, CC.

13. Jean Lee Hunt, Secretary's Report, BEE, Oct. 12, 1916, CC; July 14, 1916, WCMD.

14. LSM, "A Trial Outline," n.d., BEE Papers, CC.

15. In addition to plans suggested by working council members, plans were submitted by William Heard Kilpatrick and Edward Thorndike (research in progress tests); Robert and Delia Hutchinson (for the Stony Ford School); Rita Morgenthau of the Henry St. Settlement (vocational education); Alice Boughton (household arts teaching); Laura Garrett (a civic center for children); Alyse Gregory (The Gary School League); Meredith Smith (School of Childhood, University of Pittsburgh). BEE

16. LSM, "Plan on Welfare Work and Cooperation of Public Agencies," Jan. 1917, BEE Papers, CC.

17. Harriet Johnson, "The Administration of Social Service Activities within a School," Jan. 1917, BEE Papers, CC.

18. Harriet Forbes, "Proposed Study of Nutrition," BEE Papers, CC.

19. Harriet Johnson, "Plan for Bureau to Put in Next Year's Program," n.d., BEE Papers, CC.

20. After working for the BEE for several years, Harriet Forbes left to become associated with a cooperative residential service that offered meals and laundry services to professional women.

21. LSM, 1917 Chairman's Report, BEE Papers, CC.

22. On vocational ideas, see Rita Wallach Morgenthau to LSM, Mar. 8, 1917, Helen Marot, Proposal on Educational Aspects of Military Training in Public Schools, Mar. 8, 1917; Working Council Minutes, Mar. 12, 1917; and Reasons for Undertaking a Department of Vocational Education; BEE Papers, CC.

23. "Plans for Emergency Studies to Be Undertaken by the Dept. of Information," BEE Papers, CC.

24. See *Camp Liberty: A Farm Cadet Experiment*, BEE, Bulletin no. 7 (1918). Similar programs were to be developed on a national scale in the 1930s, when President Roosevelt established the Civilian Conservation Corps.

25. LSM, 1917 Chairman's Report.

26. Ibid.

27. See Joyce Antler, "Female Philanthropy and Progressivism in Chicago," essay review of Gilbert A. Harrison, *A Timeless Affair: The Life of Anita McCormick Blaine*, *History of Education Quarterly*, 21, no. 4 (Winter 1981): 461–69.

13: "A KIND OF MIRACLE"

1. LSM, "Robin"; Notes, LSMP.
2. TL, p. 541.
3. LSM, "Robin."
4. UA.
5. TL, p. 540. Wesley spoke in favor of woman suffrage, Feb. 11, 1915, WCMD. There is no record that he participated in the Men's League for Women Suffrage of New York, although his friends John Dewey, Vladimir Simkhovitch, and Max Eastman served as officers.
6. TL, p. 21.
7. Medora's father, James McClellan, left Chautauqua County, New York for Chicago, where in 1834 he became editor of *The Western Citizen*, Illinois' leading abolitionist newspaper. A participant in the underground railroad, McClellan stumped the state for antislavery with the Reverend Elijah Lovejoy, editor of an abolitionist newspaper in nearby Alton who was later murdered by a mob while defending his press. UA.
8. TL, p. 27.
9. Ibid.
10. Ibid.
11. TL, p. 16.
12. TL, p. 5.
13. Alvin Johnson to LSM, Nov. 4, 1948, LSMP.
14. Vladimir Simkhovitch to LSM, Nov. 21, 1948, LSMP.
15. Walter Hart to LSM, Jan. 20, 1949, LSMP.
16. John McClellan Mitchell to LSM, July 22, 1950, LSMP.
17. Sadie Gregory to LSM, Feb. 25, 1949; Elsa Ueland to LSM, July 11, 1948, LSMP.
18. Interview with Arthur Burns, July, 1978.
19. Ellen Reese to LSM, Oct. 30, 1948, LSMP.
20. Horace Taylor to LSM, Nov. 29, 1948, LSMP.
21. V. Simkhovitch to LSM, Nov. 21, 1948.
22. UA.
23. TL, p. 387.
24. Ibid.; C. Reinold Noyes to LSM, Nov. 1, 1948, LSMP.
25. George Noyes to LSM, Feb. 8, 1949, LSMP.
26. LSM, "Robin."
27. UA.
28. Lucy McClellan Mitchell to LSM, n.d., LSMP.
29. ESC to NAS, Mar. 11, 1914, NASD.
30. Benjamin Wheeler to LSM, Mar. 24, 1913, LSMP.
31. *The New York Times*, Apr. 1, 1914.
32. See Joyce and Stephen Antler, "Social Policy and the Family: The Progressive Vision," Conference on Historical Perspectives on the Scientific Study of Fertility in the United States, American Academy of Arts and Sciences, Boston, 1977.
33. WCM to LSM, Mar. 13, 1914, LSMP.
34. Nov. 16, 18, 1914, NASD.

35. Lucy McClellan Mitchell to WCM, Mar. 25, 1915, LSMP.
36. March 24–28, 1915, WCMD.
37. Lucy McClellan Mitchell to WCM, Apr. 7, 1915, LSMP.
38. See July 15–Aug. 5, 1915, WCMD.
39. WCM to LSM, July 11, 1915, LSMP.
40. WCM to LSM, July 16, 1915, LSMP.
41. Aug. 3, 1915, WCMD.
42. WCM to LSM, Aug. 20, 1918, LSMP.
43. Dec. 25, 1919; Nov. 4, 1917, WCMD; WCM to Medora Mitchell, June 23, 1918, LSMP.
44. WCM to LSM, Nov. 11, 1918, LSMP.
45. ESC to LSM, Oct. 21, 1945, ESCP.
46. TL, p. 259.

14: REAL PLAY AND REAL WORK

1. TL, p. 288.
2. CP, *I Learn from Children* (New York: Cornerstone Library, 1948), p. viii.
3. A daughter of Charles Henry Marot, a Philadelphia bookseller and publisher, and Hannah Marot, both of Quaker stock, Helen Marot was educated at Friends' schools and began her career in Philadelphia as a librarian. Sol Cohen, "Helen Marot," in *Notable American Women*, 2:499–501.
4. The investigation of the custom tailoring trade changed Marot's life by engaging her directly in the problems of the working class, particularly those of women and children. From a "studious librarian of pacifist tendency" there emerged a "belligerent activist." Cohen, "Helen Marot," p. 499.
5. The strike transformed the International Ladies' Garment Workers Union from a small, ineffective organization into a major union, heralding a revolution in women's unionism. See Helen Marot, "A Woman's Strike—An Appreciation of the Shirtwaist Makers of New York." *Proceedings of the Academy of Political Science in the City of New York* 1 (1910):119–28, and Marot, "Revolution of the Garment Trade," *The Masses* (Aug. 1916):29. Also see Nancy Schrom Dye, *As Equals and as Sisters: Feminism, the Labor Movement, and the Women's Trade Union League of New York* (Columbia, Mo.: University of Missouri Press, 1980).
6. Her book *American Labor Unions* (New York: Henry Holt, 1914) praising the IWW, created a considerable stir. She became an editor of the *Masses*, serving until it was suppressed in December 1917 for its antiwar policies. The following year she joined the editorial board of the *Dial*, helping to convert it into a radical journal of opinion.
7. CP, *I Learn from Children*, p. 29.
8. Ibid., p. 16.
9. UA.
10. CP, *I Learn from Children*, p. 59.
11. The Play School is described in John and Evelyn Dewey, *Schools of Tomorrow* (New York: John Day & Co., 1915), pp. 118–19.
12. City and Country *Bulletin*, 1922–23, p. 7. Also see CP, "Making Environment Meaningful," *Progressive Education* 4 (Apr.–June 1927):103–08.

13. CP, ed., *Experimental Practice in the City and Country School* (New York: E.P. Dutton & Co., 1924), p. 53.

14. BEE, Bulletin no. 3, CP, *The Play School Experiment in Education*, p. 15.

15. See CP to Lloyd Marcus, Nov. 20, 1947, in Marcus, "The Founding of American Private Progressive Schools, 1912–1921" (Honors Thesis, Harvard University, 1948), p. 131; also see Maxine Emelia Hirsch, "Caroline Pratt and the City and Country School: 1914–45" (Ed.D. diss., Rutgers University, 1978).

16. See, for example, John Dewey, *The Child and the Curriculum* (Chicago: University of Chicago Press, 1902); Dewey, *The School and Society* (Chicago, 1899); John and Evelyn Dewey, *Schools of Tomorrow*; Cremin, *The Transformation of the School*, pp. 204–14; and Harold Rugg, *The Child-Centered School: An Appraisal of the New Education* (Yonkers-on-Hudson, N.Y.: World Book Co., 1928), pp. 5, 37.

17. Lawrence Cremin notes that the social reformist strain in progressive education was generally mute after the First World War. He views Pratt as the author of "a pedagogical version of the expressionist credo" which released an "extraordinary flow of genuinely first-rate student art" in the hands of such "artist-teachers" as Lucy Sprague Mitchell. Cremin believes, however, that the "doctrine of creative self-expression" resulted in "shoddiness and self-deception" when applied by less capable educators. See Cremin, *The Transformation of the School: Progressivism in American Education*, pp. 206–07.

18. CP, draft on "Socialist Education," CC.

19. Ibid.

20. LSM, 1917 Chairman's Report, BEE Papers, CC.

21. This point has not been noted by educational historians, who claim, to the contrary, that progressive educators perpetuated sex-role stereotypes in their classrooms. See, for example, Sari Knopp Biklen, "The Progressive Education Movement and the Question of Women," *Teachers College Record*, 80, no. 2 (Dec. 1978): 316–35.

22. CP, *Experimental Practice in the City and Country School*, pp. 7–8; *I Learn from Children*, p. 48.

23. City and Country, *Bulletin*, 1919.

24. CP, *I Learn from Children*, p. 68.

25. "Many of these teachers believed in the common ownership of the means of production and stood ready to join any promising movement towards attaining this end," Pratt observed. "In analyzing what they wanted for their children, [they] found that the aims for a rational adult society were not very different from those of children. That is, in both cases, the effort was to order the social element so that it should contribute to the objectives of the individual." CP, "As to Indoctrination," *Progressive Education* 11 (Jan.–Feb. 1934): 107.

26. Among the works on progressive education, see Robert Holmes Beck, "American Progressive Education, 1875–1930" (Ph.D. diss., Yale University, 1941); Cremin, *The Transformation of the School*; John and Evelyn Dewey, *Schools of Tomorrow*; Patricia Albjerg Graham, *Progressive Education from Arcady to Academe: A History of the Progressive Education Association* (New York: Teachers College Press, 1967); Katherine Camp Mayhew and Anna Camp Edwards, *The Dewey School* (1936; New York: Atherton Press; rev. ed. 1966). An important symposium on "The New Education, 10 Years After," in *The New Republic*, June and July 1930, presents the

viewpoints of John Dewey, Caroline Pratt, Carl Bode, and Francis Mitchell Froelicher.

27. Shady Hill was founded in Cambridge, 1915; Oak Lane Country Day School, Philadelphia, 1916; Moraine Park School, Dayton, Ohio, 1917; Unquowa School, Bridgeport, 1917. See Stanwood Cobb to Lloyd Marcus, May 20, 1947, in Marcus, "The Founding of American Private Progressive Schools," pp. 111–14.

28. Lucy added that the term "progressive" eventually covered a wide gamut of people—"from anarchists who thought any amount of freedom was good, to people who thought having dolls in the kindergarten was radical." PIE, p. 98. Charlotte Winsor distinguishes between "progressive" schools concerned with formal pedagogic improvements to teach students more efficiently, and more open, "inner-directed" schools which focused on process rather than content. Ruth Dropkin and Arthur Tobier, eds., *Roots of Open Education in America* (New York: City College Workshop Center for Open Education, 1976), pp. 138–40. The first bulletin prepared by the BEE's Department of Information concerned the Play School. In 1918 the BEE published Marot's *The Creative Impulse in Industry.* The Play School was also described in chapter 5 of the Deweys' *Schools of Tomorrow.*

29. Mary Marot, Helen's older sister, a social worker who had been one of the first visiting teachers in New York, served as Recorder for the BEE and Play School. Pratt credited her with teaching teachers to write records for groups of children as a whole, rather than solely for individual children.

30. "To be playful and serious at the same time . . . defines the ideal mental condition," Dewey had asserted, a sentiment which Pratt quoted prominently in the BEE bulletin, *Children in the Play School.* See Winsor, *Experimental Schools Revisited*, p. 17.

31. CP, *Experimental Practice*, p. 54.

32. TL, p. 412.

33. UA.

34. Ibid.

35. TL, pp. 412–13; UA.

36. UA.

37. Pratt wrote a foreword briefly describing Mrs. Mitchell's "new method of approach to literature for young children." She noted that Lucy Mitchell "is having an influence in the school which has not been altogether unlooked for." LSM, *The Here and Now Story Book* (New York: E.P. Dutton & Co., Inc., 1921), pp. xi–xii.

15: CHILDREN AND THE HERE-AND-NOW

1. See, for example, Milton Schwebel and Jane Ralph, *Piaget in the Classroom* (New York: Basic Books, 1973).

2. LSM, *The Here and Now Story Book*, p. 45.

3. Ibid., pp. 71, 66.

4. Ibid., p. 20.

5. Ibid., p. 22.

6. Ibid., p. 20.

7. Ibid., pp. 35–36.

8. Ibid., p. 16.

9. See, for example, Rose Oliver, "Whatever Became of Goldilocks?", *Frontiers*, 2 (1977):85–93; Karen E. Rowe, "Feminism and Fairy Tales," Bunting Institute Working Paper, Mar. 1978. A different view is taken in Alison Lurie, "Fairy Tale Liberation," *The New York Review of Books*, 15 (Dec. 17, 1970), pp. 42–44.
10. Oct. 1, 3, Nov. 6, 7, 22, 27, 1920, WCMD.
11. "No doubt it will fearfully upset our writers of Primers and School Readers, 50-foot shelves of which are still being published each year," Rugg wrote. "If they will only read Mrs. Mitchell's introduction, they will at least dimly see the why and wherefore of all the change." *Journal of Educational Psychology*, (Mar. 1922):186–87.
12. *New York Post Literary Review*, Nov. 7, 1921.
13. Mary Lamberton Becker, "Reader's Guide," *New York Post Literary Review*, Dec. 3, 1921; Apr. 10, 1922. Among other journals which reviewed *The Here and Now Story Book* were *The New York World; Pedagogical Seminary; The American School; The Survey; The British Journal of Psychology; The New York Times; The New Republic.*
14. The book "contains the very best stories for young children that I have ever seen," Dell wrote.

> Stop right now and look on your shelf and find the book I am talking about, and turn to "The Many-Horse-Stable," and read about the "many g-r-e-a-t- b-i-g wagons and the one little-bit-of-a-wagon, and see if you don't think that is first-rate story telling! Then turn to "Marni Gets Dressed in the Morning," and see if it doesn't have exactly the same kind of excitement that Knut Hamsun's "Growth of the Soil" has—an excitement about the significance of small and familiar things. . . . Think how much fun it would be to tell the fog-boat story, tooting away in all the different keys your voice can command! That is the lovely thing about these stories—things happen in terms of sound, not of bare idea. . . . Mother's shoes go pat, pat, pat, downstairs, and then you hear the front door close, Bang! and out on the street a g-r-e-a-t- b-i-g horse goes clumpety-lumpety bump! thump!
> "It's a great book!" Dell concluded. "I haven't had such a fine time in years."

Dell noted one flaw in an otherwise perfect compendium: giving a cat a dog's name ("How Spot Found a Home"); *New York Post* clipping, BS.
15. The book was popular for many years. Reprinted and translated into Russian 24 times, Norwegian, and Swedish, the *Here and Now Story Book* was followed by a number of similar works. The *Here and Now Primer; Home from the Country,* published in 1924, went through four printings, and *Another Here and Now Story Book,* published in 1937, enjoyed six printings in a year and a half. *Believe and Make Believe* was published in 1956. On the Russian translations of here-and-now stories, see Vera Fediaevsky to LSM, Nov. 19, 1927, Mar. 28, 1929, LSMP; Fediaevsky, "Here and Now Stories in Russia," *Elementary School Journal* 26 (Dec. 1925): 278–89.
16. Margaret Wise Brown (1910–52) graduated from Hollins College in Virginia in 1932; after taking a writing course at Columbia University she felt she would never master the technique of plotting short stories. She then enrolled in the BEE's teacher training program, and encouraged by Lucy Sprague Mitchell to write for children, joined the staff of the BEE's Writers' Laboratory. Under her own name and several pseudonyms, she wrote more than 100 books, including the *Noisy Book* series, *Cotton-tails,* and *Wait Till the Moon is Full.* See Bruce Bliven, Jr., "Margaret Wise Brown," *Notable American Women: The Modern Period,* 113–14; and Bliven, "Child's Best Seller," *Life,* Dec. 2, 1946: 59–62. Bliven notes that although Brown's

first book, *When the Wind Blew*, (about an old lady who lived alone by the side of a sea with a toothache, seventeen cats and one grey-blue kitten who comforted her), represented a protest on behalf of fantasy, here and now principles influenced much of her later work.

17. In the 1948 edition, it is a Puerto Rican boy named Beno.

18. Alison Lurie contrasts fairy tales in which women are more powerful than men to Mitchell's stories. See "Fairy Tale Liberation." The stories in the 1921 *Here and Now Story Book* are more stereotypical in regard to race than gender. Negroes singing while picking cotton appear in "The Children's New Dresses." Racial stereotypes are used in "Peter, Please! It's Pancakes," by Mary McB. Green, in *Another Here and Now Story Book* (1937).

19. For one criticism of the book, see Karl M. Bowman, in *Mental Hygiene*, 5 (1921): 631–32. Not until some fifty years later did this argument reach its penultimate form. In *The Uses of Enchantment: The Meaning and Importance of Fairy Tales* (New York: Alfred Knopf, 1976), Bruno Bettelheim provides a psychoanalytic defense of fairy tales. Bettelheim asserts that by symbolically presenting such universal conflicts as oedipal and sibling rivalries, pubertal awakenings, and traumas of adult sexuality, fairy stories allow children to cope subconsciously with struggles that would otherwise terrify them. Also see Lurie, "Fairy Tale Liberation."

20. By "Journeyman," in *The Freeman*, May 17, 1922, pp. 231–32.

21. LSM, *The Here and Now Story Book* (New York: E.P. Dutton & Co., Inc., 1921; new ed., 1948; second printing, 1971), pp. 10–11. In her oral history, Lucy observed that her claim had always been that "fantasy is a child's natural way of thinking and that you should not give really historic material until the child has a grasp of what is fantasy and what is reality." PIE, p. 132.

22. TL, p. 285.

23. Ibid., p. 288.

16: "UNITY"

1. Dorothy Bromley, *Harper's Magazine*, 1927, cited in Showalter, *These Modern Women*, p. 4.

2. See Solomon, *In the Company of Educated Women*, p. 185.

3. Howes received a doctorate in philosophy from Radcliffe in 1902. She taught at Radcliffe, Simmons, and Wellesley, but following her marriage in 1908 and the birth of two children found few professional opportunities. Her experience was not unusual. "Marriage ended a woman's career or, at the very least, severely crimped it," concluded Bruce Kuklick from a survey of the careers of women trained by Harvard's philosophy department through 1930 (*The Rise of American Philosophy*, p. 591). Rosenberg also notes that academic jobs usually went to unmarried women with no other means of support (*Beyond Separate Spheres*, p. 232).

4. See, for example, Eva B. Hansl, "What about the Children? The Question of Mothers and Careers," *Harper's Monthly Magazine*, January 1927, pp. 220–27. Frank Stricker, in "Cookbooks and Law Books: The Hidden History of Career Women in Twentieth Century America," *Journal of Social History* 10 (Fall 1976): 1–19, argues against the notion that after 1920, educated women became disillusioned with ideals

of economic independence and meaningful careers as they turned towards marriage and domesticity. Though balancing marriage, family, and job was difficult, Stricker notes that fewer career women went home than stayed on the job.

5. Howes, "The Institute for the Coordination of Women's Interests," *Progressive Education* 3, no. 1 (Jan.–Mar. 1925): 57–58. Also see Howes, "Accepting the Universe," *Atlantic Monthly* 129 (1922): 444–52.

6. On the Institute, see Judy Jolley Mohraz, "The Institute for the Coordination of Women's Interests: A Solution to the Either / Or Issue," presented to the Berkshire Conference on the History of Women, June 1981, and the Morgan-Howes Family Papers, SL.

7. For discussions of part-time work and other strategies pursued by working mothers, see Mary Ross, "Can Mother Come Back?" *The Survey* 57, no. 5 (Dec. 1, 1926): 38–39; Katharine Angell, "Home and Office," *The Survey* 57, no. 5 (Dec. 1, 1926): 318–20. On the problems of working-class working mothers, see *Mothers Who Must Earn* (New York: Survey Associates, 1914). Also see Lynn Y. Weiner, *From Working Girl to Working Mother: The Female Labor Force in the United States, 1920–1980* (Chapel Hill: University of North Carolina Press, 1985).

8. LSM, "Introduction," to Harriet M. Johnson, *A Nursery School Experiment*, 2d ed., New York: BEE, 1924, p. 27.

9. Eunice Fuller Barnard, "The Child Takes a Nurse," *The Survey* 57, no. 5 (Dec. 1, 1926): 326. The National Society for the Study of Education formed a committee on preschool and parental education in 1925: two years later the National Committee of Nursery Schools was formed. Only during the New Deal, however, did publicly supported nursery schools become available to large numbers of working-class families. See Christine Heinig, "The Emergency Nursery Schools and the Wartime Child Care Centers: 1933–1946," in James L. Hymes, Jr., *Early Childhood Education: Living History Interviews* 3, (Carmel, Calif.: Hacienda Publishers), 1978.

10. 1910, 1935, 1950 Classbooks, Class of 1900, RCA; Cookingham suggests that 1910 marked a turning point in employment participation rates for educated women ("Combining Marriage, Motherhood and Jobs Before World War II").

11. In this survey of 3362 Radcliffe alumnae, 2000 answered the question about combining career and family life. Of these, only 14 percent were certain that they could be combined, although almost 50 percent responded that they hoped it was possible. Only 9 percent of respondents were both married and working at the time of the survey. Solomon, *In the Company of Educated Women*, pp. 182–83.

12. Virginia MacMakin Collier, *Marriage and Careers: A Study of One Hundred Women Who Are Wives, Mothers, Homemakers and Professional Workers* (New York: Bureau of Vocational Information, 1926), p. 10.

13. Collier, *Marriage and Careers*, p. 37. On Sidonie Gruenberg, see Roberta L. Wollins, "Educating Mothers: Sidonie Matsner Gruenberg and the Child Study Association of America, 1881–1929" (Ph.D. diss., Univ. of Chicago, 1983).

14. Collier, *Marriage and Careers*, p. 47.

15. Fewer than ten of the 100 women worked because of financial need. Ibid., pp. 23–25, 44–45.

16. Ibid., p. 121.

17. TL, p. 258.

18. UA.
19. UA.
20. TL, p. 484.
21. LSM, "Robin."
22. TL, p. 259.
23. Wesley noted that "with Mollie gone the care of the children takes more of [Lucy's] time." Aug. 16, 1924, WCMD. The Mitchells employed a German "Fräulein" during the 1930s. In the 1940s, when the children were grown, Lucy took over the housekeeping, and never again had a regular maid.
24. Oct. 23, 1915, WCMD.
25. LSM, *Our Children and Our Schools*, p. 9.
26. Ibid., p. 9.
27. LSM, "Arnold Mitchell," May 23, 1922, LSMP.
28. LSM, "Sprague Mitchell," June 12, 1918; Notes on Jack Mitchell, June 12, 14, 1918; "Arnold Mitchell," Nov. 26, 1919, LSMP. Wesley also "whipped" summer guest David Farquhar "several times" for wetting himself. Aug. 31, Sept. 1, 1914, WCMD.
29. UA; LSM, "Jack Mitchell," Jan. 26, 1921; "Arnold Mitchell," May 23, 1922, Notes on Jack Mitchell, June 14, 16, 1918, LSMP.
30. Report on Marian Mitchell, BEE Nursery School, June 2, 1919, LSM, "Arnold Mitchell," Nov. 26, 1919; May 23, 1922; "Marian Mitchell," Nov. 26, 1919; Jan. 5, 1920; "Sprague Mitchell," Mar. 1920; "Jack Mitchell," Jan. 26, 1921; WCM, "Sprague Mitchell," Feb. 6, 1921, "Arnold Mitchell," Feb. 17, 1921, LSMP.
31. June 1918, LSMP.
32. WCM, "Sprague Mitchell," Feb. 6, 1921.
33. Yet in 1919 she decided to reverse matters and give baths to the younger ones, a response to the "mutual devotion and dependence" of eighteen-month-old Arnold and his nurse, Mary. Lucy worried that she had become an "outsider" to Arnold, who rejected her "advances." LSM, "Arnold Mitchell," Oct. 1918, LSMP.
34. In cases of serious illness, Lucy supervised the care of the Farquhar children and Polly Forbes-Johnson. She cared for Caroline Pratt, Norah Hamilton, and other of her own friends when taken ill.
35. See WCMD passim. In December 1916, Lucy submitted a "Plan Concerning Mr. Alexander's Work" to be considered as one of the first experimental projects the BEE might undertake. BEE Papers, CC. On Alexander's appeal to progressive educators, see Frank Pierce Jones, "The Work of F. M. Alexander as an Introduction to Dewey's Philosophy of Education," in *The Alexandrian* 1, no. 4 (Spring/Summer 1982): 2, 6.
36. LSM, "Arnold Mitchell," Jan. 5, 1920.
37. LSM, "Arnold Mitchell," Jan. 5, 1920; May 23, 1922; "Sprague Mitchell," Mar. 1920.
38. LSM, "Jack Mitchell," Jan. 26, 1921.
39. Interview with Elizabeth Coolidge Winship; Margaret Coolidge, Feb. 1978.
40. On child-rearing in the twentieth century, see Lucille C. Birnbaum, "Behaviorism in the 1920s," *American Quarterly*, vol. 7 (Spring 1955): 15–30; Geoffrey H. Steere, "Freudianism and Child-Rearing in the Twenties," *American Quarterly* 20 (Winter

1968): 759–65; William Graebner, "The Unstable World of Dr. Spock: Social Engineering in a Democratic Culture, 1917–1950," *Journal of American History* 67 (Dec. 1980): 612–29; Michael Zuckerman, "Dr. Spock: The Confidence Man," in *The Family in History*, ed. Charles Rosenberg (Philadelphia, University of Pennsylvania Press, 1975); and Nancy Pottishman Weiss, "Mother, the Invention of Necessity: Dr. Benjamin Spock's *Baby and Child Care*," *American Quarterly* 29 (Winter 1977): 519–46.

41. June 1, 1917, WCMD. The Mitchells celebrated their wedding anniversary that year by "working as usual: L office hrs at BEE A.M., committee work P.M. I read masters thesis, carpentry class; Miss Marot came 5:30 to see babies in bath, discuss boys on farm Marion F dined with us." May 8, 1917, WCMD.

42. Interview with Margaret Coolidge, July 1978, and Arnold Mitchell, February 1978.

43. Sept. 16, 26, Nov. 29, 1925, Jan. 17, 1926, WCMD; letter to author from Orlin Donaldson, May 1979.

44. UA.

45. Marion and Robert Farquhar separated in 1918. After driving an ambulance in France during World War I, Marion returned to New York, where she lived with her children and mother on West 11th Street in Greenwich Village, frequently entertaining her friends at musical evenings. Marion's older sister, Alice, married to sculptor Frederic MacMonnies, lived nearby. Lucy became a "second mother" to Marion's children, helped Marion through various illnesses, and aided her when she suffered financial reverses during the Depression.

But in 1941, the long friendship between the women came to an abrupt end. According to Lucy's children, Marion's liaison with composer-pianist Frederic Hart, of which Lucy apparently disapproved, may have caused the rupture. But Hart believes there had been a dispute over Marion's children, whom Lucy had sought to protect from their high-strung mother. According to Hart's account, Lucy reacted angrily when Marion tried to obtain information from Lucy about her son Colin, hospitalized after a nervous breakdown. Though Lucy was cordial afterwards, Marion remained cool. Frederic Hart to author, Oct. 18, 1978.

46. TL, p. 267.

47. Orlin Donaldson to author, May 1979.

48. Ibid.

49. LSM to "Robins," Mar. 1924, LSMP.

50. UA; TL, p. 260.

51. TL, p. 540.

17: GREENSBORO

1. TL, pp. 306, 308, 316; UA.

2. *St. Johnsbury Caledonian*, Aug. 18, 1915. Also see *St. Johnsbury Caledonian*, Aug. 11, 1915. On Greensboro's history, see Peter Watson, "North Shore Summers: Memories of Greensboro in the 1920s and 1930s" (1981); S. Whitney Landon, "Early Memories of Caspian Lake"; Constance Votey, "Growing Up with Aspenhurst, 1897–1917," (1975); Bliss Perry, "Greensboro: The Place Itself," *St. Johnsbury Caledonia*, Aug. 18, 1915. Interview with Lewis Hill, July 1978.

3. Natives of the neighboring town of Hardwick say that Hardwick merchants began building summer cottages on the lake shores in the 1870s and 1880s. Another faction claims that Vermonters from Randolph, Burlington, Barre and Montpelier established the first fishing camps at Caspian. See Allen Davis, "Caspian's Lake—Hardwick's Summer Resort," *The Hazen Road Dispatch*, 4 (Summer 1979):1–3.

4. Other notable vacationers included Alfred H. Barr, Jr. director of the Museum of Modern Art, novelist William Maier, Glenn Alvero Olds, president of Kent State University, Margaret Mead, visiting her friend and collaborator Rhoda Metraux in nearby Craftsbury, and Supreme Court Justice William Rehnquist.

5. TL, p. 307.

6. UA.

7. TL, p. 315.

8. Aug. 24, 1923, WCMD. Wesley was equally precise with statistics on height, weight, and for himself, hat and collar size, which he recorded in the diary once a year. (Wesley was 5 feet 7 1/2 inches, and Lucy, 5 feet 7 1/16 inches tall; he usually weighed around 147, with Lucy a pound or so less).

9. TL, p. 317; LSM, "Jack Mitchell," Jan. 26, 1921, LSMP; Interview with Joan Daudon Coolidge, Aug. 1985.

10. Interviews with Mrs. Albert S. Cook and Ellen Day Patterson, July 1978; Joan Hocking Kracke, Feb. 1978. Another neighbor family was the O. M. W. Spragues (no relation) and their children, Theodore and Katherine. Oliver Sprague was professor of Banking and Finance at Harvard Business School.

11. May Sarton, *I Knew a Phoenix: Sketches for an Autobiography* (New York: Rinehart & Co., 1954), pp. 101–14. Mrs. George Day, wife of the Yale professor, called Agnes Hocking "westwind" after Shelley's Ode.

12. A favorite story about Mrs. Hocking was that, discovering in the Harvard Square subway station one day that she had no money with her, she walked right past the gate, telling the collector, "Ernest Hocking will give you five cents tomorrow." The anecdote is told by Sarton in *I Knew a Phoenix*, p. 104.

13. Interview with Katherine Sprague, July 1978.

14. Elizabeth Day describes the school and her Greensboro summers in "My Life," an autobiographical typescript, courtesy of Ellen Day Patterson. See "My Life," pp. 208–09, 215.

15. Amey Watson received a doctorate from Bryn Mawr in 1924. She taught at the Pennsylvania School of Social Work from 1915 to 1926, and was active in child study and parent education groups in Philadelphia.

16. UA.

17. UA; TL, p. 310.

18. Margaret Coolidge graduated from Radcliffe, taught briefly at the Shady Hill School in Cambridge, and was a founder and member of the Cambridge Nursery School and the Mother's Study Club of Cambridge.

19. Louis Kesselman and his wife Esther are memorialized in Wallace Stegner's novel *Second Growth* (Boston: Houghton Mifflin, 1947).

20. Reacting to Sprague Coolidge's avowed socialism, the Library of Congress denied him a place on the board of directors of the Coolidge Foundation, the philanthropy established by his mother and administered by the Library to benefit chamber music.

21. Interviews with Margaret Coolidge, Joan Hocking Kracke, Ellen Day Patterson, Peter and Roger Watson, Arnold, Sprague, and John Mitchell, Katherine and Peter Sprague.

18: A SCIENTIST BY CONVICTION

1. See Mitchell's 1918 presidential address to the American Statistical Association, "Statistics and Government," in WCM, *The Backward Art of Spending Money and Other Essays* (New York: Augustus M. Kelley, 1950).
2. WCM to LSM, July 16, 1918, TL, p. 334. Veblen spent seven years in New York, teaching at the New School from 1919 to 1926, and was a frequent visitor at the Mitchell household. Lucy recalled that the usually shy man took great pleasure in the Mitchell children, who crawled into his lap and "fired their everlasting questions at him" (TL, p. 265).
3. WCM, "The New School for Social Research," letter printed in the *New York Evening Post*, Mar. 31, 1920, TL, p. 337. WCM to LSM, Nov. 11, 1918, LSMP. WCM, "The New School for Social Research," Aug. 14, 1920, WCMP.
4. WCM, "The National Bureau of Economic Research and Its Work," Mar. 1, 1923, WCMP. The NBER received its charter in 1920.
5. WCM, *Business Cycles: The Problem and the Setting*, (New York: National Bureau of Economic Research, 1927).
6. See Homan, *Contemporary Economic Thought*, pp. 424, 427; Burns, "Wesley Clair Mitchell," and Frederick Mills, "Wesley Clair Mitchell," LSMP; TL, p. 350.
7. See *The Decennial Report of the Social Sciences Research Council, 1923–1933* (New York: Social Sciences Research Council, 1934); Pendleton Harrington to LSM, Oct. 29, 1948, LSMP. On the growth of the social sciences see Thomas L. Haskell, *The Emergence of Professional Social Science: The American Social Science Association and the Nineteenth Century Crisis of Authority* (Urbana, Ill.: University of Illinois Press, 1977) and Charles M. Bonjean, Louis Schneider, and Robert L. Lineberry, *Social Sciences in America: The First 200 Years* (Austin: University of Texas Press, 1976).
8. UA; TL, pp. xviii–xix.
9. TL, pp. 545, 538.
10. Cremin, *The Transformation of the School*, pp. 179–85.
11. Joseph Featherstone, "Rousseau and Modernity," *Daedalus*, 107 (Summer 1978): 167–92.
12. See, for example: Dewey, *The Child and the Curriculum*; Rugg and Schumaker, *The Child-Centered School*, and Cremin, *The Transformation of the School*.
13. LSM, Chairman's Report, BEE *Annual Report*, 1919, BS.
14. LSM, draft on the BEE, written for the Associated Experimental Schools, circa 1935, LSMP.
15. LSM, Chairman's Report, BEE *Annual Report*, 1919.
16. Ibid.
17. TL, pp. 250–51.
18. LSM, "Harriet M. Johnson: Pioneer, 1867–1934," *Progressive Education* 11 (1934): 427–29.

19. Harriet Johnson, *Children in "The Nursery School"* (New York: Agathon Press, 1972, 1st ed., 1928), p. 61.
20. Harriet Johnson, "Report on the Nursery School," Bureau of Educational Experiments, *Annual Report*, 1924–1925, CC. For example, the Merrill-Palmer School focused on "habit formation and the correction of undesirable forms of reaction." The Institute of Child Welfare Research at Teachers College developed an elaborate inventory of the habits of preschool children: See Ruth Andrus, *An Inventory of the Habits of Children from Two to Five Years of Age* (New York: Teachers College, 1928).
21. Johnson, *Children in "The Nursery School,"* p. 61.
22. Johnson did much to popularize the view that common play objects were superior to didactic materials (like those used by Montessori schools) in encouraging children's growth. See Harriet Johnson, "Educational Implications of the Nursery School," *Progressive Education* 2 (Jan.–Mar. 1925); and Johnson, "Mental Hygiene of Younger Children," Proceedings of the National Conference of Social Work, Toronto, June–July 1924; Barbara Biber, "Introductory Essay," in Johnson, *Children in "The Nursery School,"* pp. vii–xxvii.
23. See Biber, "Introductory Essay," in Johnson, *Children in "The Nursery School."*
24. LSM, "Harriet Johnson," p. 428; MSS notes, Aug. 14, 1954, LSMP.
25. UA.
26. Rugg and Schumaker suggest that educational pioneers at experimental schools were primarily artists rather than scientists or technicians *The Child-Centered School*, p. 116. Also see Cremin, *The Transformation of the School*, pp. 201–15.
27. Alice Dewey read a paper on the Lab School at a BEE meeting at the Mitchells', Feb. 5, 1917. Also see Nov. 18, 28, 1916, WCMD. Lucy thought that record-keeping at the Deweys' school had been inadequate. UA.
28. In 1921, The Iowa Child Research Station, established in 1917, inaugurated a laboratory school to study the psychological development of preschool children. The Merrill-Palmer School was established in 1920 with a three-million-dollar bequest from Lizzie Palmer. In 1922, it opened a preschool nursery to train women in the care of young children but also to conduct research about child devlopment. Along with the BEE, it was one of only a few schools not affiliated with a university that collected comprehensive data about children's growth.
29. Ruml, president of the LSRM, had worked with Lucy on the Psychological Survey. His assistant, Lawrence K. Frank, masterminded the Memorial's strategies to promote child development and parent education. Frank, an economist, came to know Wesley Mitchell when working at the New York Telephone Company, later joining Wesley on the War Industries Board in 1917. He served as business manager of the New School for Social Research before coming to the Rockefeller Memorial. According to child development specialist Milton Senn, who interviewed Frank, the influence of Lucy Mitchell on Frank was "even more remarkable" than that of her husband; it was "profound," "lasting and vital." Frank sent his own children to the BEE Nursery School and served on its board of trustees. See Milton Senn, *Insights on the Child Development Movement in the United States*, Monographs of the Society for Research in Child Development 40 (1975): 12–14. The influence of Lucy Sprague Mitchell and the BEE on Frank is also cited in the Oral History of Lois Meek Stolz,

p. 52, Child Development Archives, Library of Congress. For an excellent discussion of Frank's role in the child-development movement see Steven Schlossman, "Philanthropy and the Gospel of Child Development," *History of Education Quarterly*, 21 (Fall 1981): 275–99.

30. On the origins of child-development research in the 1920s, see Steven L. Schlossman, "Philanthropy and the Gospel of Child Development," *History of Education Quarterly* 21 (Fall 1981); idem, "Before Home Start: Notes toward a History of Parent Education in America, 1897–1929," *Harvard Educational Review* 46 (August 1976): 436–37; Ruby Takanishi, "Childhood as a Social Issue: Historical Roots of Contemporary Child Advocacy Movements," *Journal of Social Issues* 34 (Summer 1978): 8–16; idem, "Notes on the Historiography of Child Development Research, 1920–1975," paper presented at the biennial meeting of the Society for Research in Child Development, San Francisco, 1979; Robert S. Woodworth, "Historical Antecedents of the Present Child Study Movement," *Progressive Education* 3 (Jan.–Mar. 1926): 3–6; Senn, *Insights on the Child Development Movement*; Dorothy Bradbury, "The Contribution of the Child Study Movement to Child Psychology," *Psychological Bulletin* 34 (1937): 21–38; Lawrence Frank, "Research in Child Psychology: History and Prospect," in *Child Behavior and Development*, ed. Robert G. Barker, Jacob S. Kounin and Herbert F. Wright (New York: McGraw-Hill, 1943), pp. 1–16; and idem, "The Beginnings of Child Development and Family Life Education in the Twentieth Century," *Merrill-Palmer Quarterly* 8 (1962): 207–27.

31. LSM to trustees of the Laura Spelman Rockefeller Memorial, May 6, 1925, Laura Spelman Rockefeller Memorial Collection, Rockefeller Archive Center, Pocantico Hills, New York. I am grateful to Steven L. Schlossman for this reference.

32. PIE, p. 94. TL, p. 460.

33. TL, pp. 250–51.

34. UA. At the time the Bureau was founded, Lucy Mitchell had offered behavioral scientist John B. Watson a position as bureau psychologist. Watson accepted on the condition that Johns Hopkins give him a leave of absence, but he never joined the Bureau. "We used to wonder what would have happened" if Watson had come, Lucy admitted, since, as an avid behaviorist, Watson "attacked the demonstrative parent" and counseled that "scientific" nursery school teachers must act in a completely impersonal manner. See May 19, 1917, WCMD; TL, p. 463.

35. The Bureau's distinctive "hybrid" position was highlighted by the fact that the individuals associated with it in the early period played leading roles in both the progressive education and child development movements. Gertrude Hartman, a member of the bureau staff in its first years, became the first editor of *Progressive Education*, a position she held from 1924 to 1930, while bureau psychologist Buford Johnson became the first editor of *Child Development*, serving from 1930 to 1938. Under Bureau auspices, Gertrude Hartman published *The Child and His School: An Interpretation of Elementary Education as a Social Process* (New York: E.P. Dutton, 1922). Harold Rugg noted (in "A New Hand Book of Modern Education for Teachers," *Journal of Educational Psychology* 13 [March 1922]: pp. 187–88): "This book is an example of what the Bureau of Educational Experiments is doing. It combines the use of a broad philosophic interest in child life and the improvement of society with the

scientific foundations of these in biology, psychology, and sociology." On Hartman's role as editor of *Progressive Education*, see Graham, *From Arcady to Academe*, pp. 39, 86.

Buford Johnson was co-author of *Health Education and the Nutrition Class* (New York: E.P. Dutton, 1922) and author of *Mental Growth of Children in Relation to the Rate of Growth in Bodily Development* (New York: E.P. Dutton, 1925), both of which reported on BEE work.

36. BEE, *Annual Report*, 1925–26, BS.

37. TL, p. 461; draft on the BEE, Associated Experimental Schools. Also see Buford Johnson's *Mental Growth of Children*.

38. PIE, p. 96. Lucy asked Robert Woodworth to conduct an analysis of BEE records. Dec. 29, 1928, WCMD. Later she hoped he would edit a collection of articles about the BEE's work on physical and mental growth, but the volume did not materialize. Notes, LSMP.

39. Dec. 2, 1928, WCMD.

40. After graduating from Barnard, where she was deeply influenced by her studies with Franz Boas, Biber worked for the Amalgamated Clothing Workers Union in New York for two years. She received a Ph.B. in psychology from the University of Chicago in 1926. See, "Barbara Biber: 50 Years at Bank Street College, 1928–1978," BS.

41. UA; TL, p. 462; PIE, p. 95; draft on the BEE, Associated Experimental Schools.

42. See Takanishi, "Notes on the Historiography of Child Development Research," p. 24.

43. "Realism is Allah, and Mitchell is his prophet," wrote Paul Homan. "Paradise may be around the corner." See his *Contemporary Economic Thought*, pp. 424, 427, 435–36.

44. WCM, *The Backward Art of Spending*, pp. 338–39.

45. UA.

19: A WORLD OF RELATIONSHIPS

1. Untitled notes, LSMP.

2. TL, p. 431.

3. Dec. 1–12, 1921; July 4–5, WCMD.

4. LSM, "Making Young Geographers instead of Teaching Geography," *Progressive Education*, 5, no. 3 (July–Sept. 1928): 218. As a visiting teacher at Shady Hill in 1926, Lucy took a class of eight-year-olds studying the Vikings to the Custom House Tower at Boston Harbor where they worked with pilot maps. Back at school, they created a map of the harbor and city out of sheet rock cement. Having acquired some knowledge about navigation, they then constructed oil-cloth maps depicting the Vikings' route.

5. LSM, *Horses Now and Long Ago* (New York: Harcourt, Brace and Co., Inc. 1926), p. ix.

6. TL, pp. 423–24; Oct. 22, Nov. 4, 1924, WCMD.

7. TL, p. 427.

8. The *New Republic* called the book "a gorgeous contribution to the study of history and geography . . . dramatic, thrilling"; the *Chicago Post* found it "unique in concep-

tion and execution, combining simple naturalness of narrative with a sure dramatic touch"; the *New York Times* praised its "wisdom and subtlety of method," observing that children would enjoy the tales "while unconsciously they absorb the feeling and significance of other days" (clippings, BS). Lucy commented years later that the book was flawed because the exposition section seemed geared to an older group than the stories. PIE, 133.

9. LSM, *North America: The Land They Live In for the Children Who Live There* (New York: The Macmillan Co., 1931). Twenty years after the book was written, Ona Bramfield of the New Lincoln School complained to the publisher about its use of racial stereotypes. Lucy replied that she would consider a revised edition if she felt that stories created a "wrong attitude," but the book was not reissued. LSM to Doris Patee, Aug. 2, 1950, LSMP.

10. LSM and Clara Lambert, *Manhattan, Now and Long Ago* (New York: The Macmillan Co., 1934). Clara Lambert served as director of the Summer Play School's Association in New York in the early 1940s. In 1942, she completed an extensive survey of the outdoor play activities of urban children.

11. LSM, *Young Geographers* (New York: The John Day Co., 1934). It was reprinted by Basic Books in 1963 and the Bank Street Publications Division in 1971. Lucy cites the example of a group of nine- and ten-year-olds who built an 80-foot-wide map of the U.S. with Rocky Mountains five feet high (p. 49). During the years 1939–41, Lucy tried to market her smaller maps, but without success. At the time, the cost of producing them commercially seemed prohibitive.

12. LSM, *Young Geographers*, pp. 31–32.

13. See Irma Simonton Black and Joan Blos, "Introduction" to PIE, and Emily Pond Matthews, "Lucy Sprague Mitchell: A Deweyan Educator" (Ed.D. diss., Rutgers University, 1970), for perceptive discussions of Lucy Mitchell's educational ideas.

14. Interview with Mary Phelps, Feb. 1979; *Another Here and Now Story Book*, p. 242.

15. "Language Notes," LSMP; LSM, "Children's Experiments in Language," *Progressive Education* 5, no. 1 (Jan.–Mar. 1928).

16. Lucy's review of Piaget's book appeared in *Progressive Education* 4, no. 2 (Apr.–June 1927). In a review of two anthologies of poetry for children, Louis Untermeyer's *This Singing World* and Walter de la Mare's *Come Hither*, she asserted that the authors knew their craft better than they did children. While she liked the selections, she criticized the organization of both books. The review appeared in *Progressive Education* 1, no. 2 (July–Sept. 1924), pp. 115–17.

17. LSM, *The Here and Now Primer*. American artists first began to explore illustration as a medium of expression in children's books in the 1920s. Only in the 1930s and 1940s did developments in photo-offset lithography make popular editions of inexpensive, illustrated books possible. See Cornelia Meigs, Anne Eaton, Elizabeth Nesbitt, Ruth Hill Viguers, *A Critical History of Children's Literature* (New York: The Macmillan Co., 1953), pp. 436–38.

18. TL, pp. 408, 411; PIE, p. 97.

19. TL, pp. 412–13; UA.

20. LSM to CP, May 21, 1930, memorandum on meeting with LSM, CP, Harriet Johnson, Leo Huberman, Feb. 8, 1930, CC. I am grateful to Patricia Carlton for this reference.

21. CP, memorandum of Feb. 8, 1930 meeting.

22. TL, pp. 413–14.
23. LSM to Basil Bass, June 29, 1940, BS.
24. Oct. 7, 1928, WCMD.
25. *New York Times*, May 7, 1932.
26. Irwin explained that the experimental group only learned to spell words it encountered in daily experience, while the control group had been drilled on standard grammar book words which appeared in the test. Elisabeth Irwin, "The Youngest Intellectuals," *The New Republic*, Nov. 10, 1926, BEE reprint.
27. LSM, "Young Explorers and their Teachers," unpubl. MSS., LSMP.
28. TL, p. 416.
29. TL, p. 417.
30. TL, pp. 419–20.
31. TL, p. 421.
32. *New York Times*, May 7, 1932.
33. Ibid.
34. Tuition at Little Red was $125 per year, compared to $600 at most private progressive schools. Per capita cost in the public system was approximately $101 per year. "Progressive Training vs. Pupil Cost," *New York Times*, Sept. 25, 1932.
35. UA; PIE, p. 129.
36. TL, p. 422.

20: 69 BANK STREET

1. On the Depression and American cultural ideals, see Richard H. Pells, *Radical Vision and American Dreams* (New York: Harper & Row, 1973); and Robert Crunden, *From Self to Society, 1919–1941* (Englewood Cliffs, N.J.: Prentice Hall, 1972).
2. TL, p. 469.
3. The BEE's five-year research plan culminated in June 1931 without producing a program for future studies. In September 1931, the Working Council voted to terminate the program, and a "new organization" came into being. "Origin of the Working Council," Dec. 17, 1931, BS.
4. Participating in initial discussions were Harriet Johnson, Alvin Johnson, director of the New School for Social Research and a BEE trustee, Jessie Stanton, Elisabeth Irwin, Elsa Ueland, president of Carson College, a residential school for orphan girls in Philadelphia, and Ellen Steele, director of the Rosemary Junior School in Old Greenwich, Connecticut. See Jan.–Mar. 1930, WCMD. Also see LSM, "A Cooperative School for Student Teachers," *Progressive Education* 8 (Mar. 1931):251.
5. LSM, "A Cooperative School for Student Teachers," p. 253.
6. TL, pp. 470–71; "A Cooperative School for Student Teachers," p. 251.
7. On Kilpatrick's ideas and influence, see Cremin, *The Transformation of the School*, pp. 215–21. Along with Lucy Sprague Mitchell and Alvin Johnson, Kilpatrick gave an address at Bank Street's official "housewarming" on April 24, 1931.
8. CSST, *Annual Report*, 1934–1935, and "The Nursery and Elementary School Teacher-Education Curriculum of the Cooperative School for Student Teachers," BS.
9. The CCST considered practice-teaching and formal course work to be "simultaneous"

experiences in "reciprocal interaction." Students began teaching at the beginning of their school experience, earlier than most other training institutes. "The Nursery and Elementary School Teacher-Education Curriculum."

10. The course was then taught by Louise Woodcock.
11. See Elizabeth Healy, "Once a Week for Five Years," 69 *Bank Street*, 3, no. 4 (Jan. 1937): 1–9; interviews with Barbara Biber, Feb. and Nov. 1978; Claudia Lewis, Feb. 1978; Sally Kerlin, July 1979; Mary Phelps, Mary Ellen Gilder.
12. On the arts at Bank Street, see LSM, "An Approach to the Arts for Teachers and Other Lay Adults," 69 *Bank Street*, 2, no. 5 (Feb. 1936), and TL, pp. 471–72.
13. Trained in Germany, Polly Korchien made an impressive debut in New York in 1934. Ralph Pearson, a graduate of Chicago's Art Institute, won numerous prizes for his etchings throughout the United States. He was the author of numerous books on modern art and lectured at the New School for Social Research, where he directed a Design Workshop. Charlotte Perry was a director and choreographer and author of several published plays.
14. The link between the New School and the CSST was strengthened by occasional lectures which Lucy Mitchell presented about her work to the New School. Alvin Johnson was the keynote speaker at a Bank Street conference on methodology in the social sciences, Jan. 26–27, 1934.
15. Healy, "Once a Week for Five Years."
16. Interview with Mary Ellen Gilder, Feb. 1978.
17. *Cooperative School for Student Teachers*, BS.
18. LSM, "Making Real Teachers," *Educational Outlook* 20 (Jan. 1946): 52–63. Teachers' "class thinking" and the CSST's attitude toward social policy and political questions were discussed at Bank Street on May 22, 1931, Jan. 19, May 30, Oct. 19, 1935, WCMD.
19. Notes taken in Lucy Mitchell's language class, 1932–33, Bank Street; LSM, "Language," 69 *Bank Street*, 2, no. 5 (Feb. 1936).
20. TL, p. 443.
21. Posey Hurd, *Lucy Sprague Mitchell, 1868–1967*, BS, Dec. 1, 1967, BS.
22. LSM, "Extending the Environment: An Experiment," 69 *Bank Street*, 1, no. 8 (May 1935): 1; UA.
23. LSM to WCM, Oct. 18, 1931, LSMP.
24. LSM to WCM. Nov. 22, 1931, LSMP.
25. LSM to Jack Mitchell, Apr. 23, 1932, LSMP.
26. LSM to WCM, May 15, 1932, LSMP.
27. LSM to WCM, Apr. 6, 1932, LSMP.
28. LSM to WCM, Apr. 5, 1932, LSMP.
29. LSM to Jack Mitchell, Apr. 13, 1932, LSMP.
30. LSM to Jack Mitchell, Apr. 23, 1932, LSMP.
31. LSM to WCM, May 7, 1932; May 15, 1932, LSMP.
32. LSM to Jack Mitchell, Apr. 23, and May 1, 1932, LSMP.
33. LSM to WCM, Apr. 6, 1932.
34. LSM to WCM, Apr. 5, 1932.
35. WCM to LSM, Apr. 16, 1932, LSMP, TL, p. 388; Nov. 8, 1932, WCMD.
36. LSM to WCM, Feb. 24, 1934, LSMP.

37. LSM to WCM, Apr. 23, 1933, LSMP.

38. Nov. 19, 1934, WCMD.

39. BEE Working Council minutes, Dec. 20, 1935, BS. Bank Street also rented space to a CIO Union at $25/month. Working Council minutes, May 10, 25, 1938. In 1920, the BEE received a gift from Mrs. Hunt, a sculptress, of stocks and bonds amounting to about $32,000, which it shared with City and Country. The Hunt securities fund helped the BEE underwrite deficits during the Depression.

40. According to Lucy, Walden emphasized children's emotional needs, while City and Country with its jobs program felt that the only psychology that counted was the "therapy of work." Hessian Hills and the Manumit School, organized by trade unionists, focused more on community-minded work activities than on an expressive curriculum. Little Red and Bank Street, the only schools that participated in both the CSST and AES, recognized the educational importance of each kind of program. The "common aims" of the AES included: learning as a process of "experimentation"; a focus on the child's "total" needs at each growth stage; the need to establish a "cooperative" classroom atmosphere; the absence of grades and marks; the use of "laboratory methods," trips, source materials, and discussions; provision of "real jobs" that had "social meaning"; and creation of opportunities to extend the child's "social horizon" and stimulative creative work in the arts. "The Associated Experimental Schools," 69 Bank Street 2, no. 6 (Mar. 1936): 6–7.

41. Though it had hoped to stimulate the cooperative production of goods—encouraging unemployed city mothers to produce children's work clothing, for example—and had at one point contemplated buying only cooperatively produced items, the AES found this policy impractical. AES Papers, CC.

42. See, for example, 69 Bank Street, 2, no. 5 (Feb. 1936), 3, no. 1 (Oct. 1936), and 3, no. 3 (Dec. 1936.)

43. UA; on Bank Street's organizational problems, see, for example, Working Council Minutes, May 5, 1941, May 10, 1948, BS.

44. Nov. 12, 1934, WCMD.

45. Other members of the committee were John Dewey and Dean William Russell of Teachers College. Jessie Stanton set up the nursery school at Arthurdale (or Reedsville, as the resettlement project was sometimes called). On the Arthurdale program, see Joseph P. Lash, Eleanor and Franklin (New York: W.P. Norton & Co., 1971), chap. 37.

46. See Elizabeth Whitney Walther's account of the 1935 long trip in 69 Bank Street 1, no. 8 (May 1935):3–10; Elsa Ueland, "Eight Days," in 69 Bank Street 2, no. 5 (Feb. 1936). Interviews with Claudia Lewis, Sally Kerlin, Mary Phelps. Also see Charlotte Winsor's description of the trips, cited in Courtney Cazden, "Charlotte Winsor as Social Studies Teacher," unpublished paper, Bank St. College, May 1983.

47. An especially favored stop was the Highlander Folk School in the Cumberland Mountains of Tennessee. Established in 1932, the school trained leadership for the Southern labor movement, teaching courses in union work as well as "cultural" courses in dramatics, economics, folk dancing, group singing, and history. Claudia Lewis, one of the CSST's first graduates, became director of the nursery school at Highlander, as well as "janitor, parentworker, cook and school bus-driver." Highlander Folk School bulletin, BS.

48. Willy Barton Kraber to "Lucy," Nov. 1967, BS.
49. Interview with Mary Ellen Gilder; Jane Prescott, '48, in Eleanor Bowman Hogan Memorial Book, lent to the author by Mary Ellen Gilder.
50. Marguerite Hurrey Wolf to author, May 7, 1979; Elizabeth Helfman to author, May 21, 1979.
51. Marguerite Wolf to author.
52. Transcript of taped discussions on LSM with Irene Prescott, Charlotte Winsor, Irma Black, Barbara Biber (n.d.), LSMP.
53. Sally Morrison Kerlin, *Children and the Environment*, Lucy Sprague Mitchell Memorial Conference (New York: BS, 1971):75.
54. *Lucy Sprague Mitchell, 1878–1967*, p. 11.
55. See WCM, *Recent Social Trends in the United States: Report of the President's Research Committee on Social Trends* (New York: McGraw-Hill, 1934). He had also served as the director of a study undertaken by the National Bureau of Economic Research at the behest of President Hoover on *Recent Economic Changes in the United States*. See the brief accounts in TL, p. 367, and Burns, *Wesley Mitchell and the National Bureau*, p. 52.
56. Wesley notes in a brief reference that the dinner was a "touching occasion." Dec. 17, 1934, WCMD.
57. In the summer of 1934, he gave the Hitchcock Lectures at the University of California, and in 1935, the Messenger Lectures at Cornell, on the subject of planning.
58. WCM to Herbert Hoover, Dec. 24, 1934; TL, pp. 370, 372.
59. Mar. 1933, Oct., Nov. 1934, Feb. 1935, WCMD.
60. "Robin." Wesley's diaries reported a few exchanges with his sons about the "conduct of life" or the "world at large." Victories over the boys in chess were also recorded: Arnold recalled that his father did not like to lose. Jan. 4, 1931; July 5, Sept. 4, 1932, WCMD.
61. Jack suffered a nervous breakdown during his first year at Harvard. After spending a few years at Oxford University, he completed his bachelor's degree at Columbia.
62. Interview with Polly Forbes-Johnson, Feb. 1985.
63. TL, pp. 485.
64. Marguerite Hurrey Wolf to author.
65. Interview with Mary Ellen Gilder.
66. TL, pp. 430, 487; Notes, LSMP.
67. Edith Hurd, *Lucy Sprague Mitchell, 1878–1967*, p. 5. Early members included Margaret Wise Brown; Madeline Dixon, author of *High, Wide and Deep*; Ruth Krauss, author of *The Carrot Seed*; Louise Woodcock, author of *The Smart Little Boy and His Smart Little Kitty*; Leone Adelson, author of *The Blowaway Hat*; Cathleen Schurr, of *The Shy Little Kitten*; Nina Scheider, co-author with her husband of a series of science books for children. Later members of the Writers' Laboratory, which continues to this day, included Marguerite Rudolph, Eve Merriam, Helen Kay, Jane Siepmann, and Elizabeth Helfman.
68. *Lucy Sprague Mitchell, 1878–1967*, pp. 2–6.
69. Helfman to author; "The Writers' Laboratory," June 1958; June 1961; LSMP; interviews with Betty Miles, July 1979, Mary Phelps.
70. Interview with Betty Miles. Irma Black, who formerly worked as a nursery school

teacher and research worker with elementary age children, wrote 16 children's books and three books for adults, along with many articles on child development for national magazines. Other Bank Street staff members who participated in the workshop included Claudia Lewis, Betty Miles, and Carl Memling, Ruth Sonneborn, and Joan Winsor Blos.

71. Agnes Snyder of Adelphi College and Blanche Kent Verbeck of Otterbein College provided detailed teaching guides for the series.

72. UA. She considered "The Americas: North and South," the sixth-grade reader which was never published, to be the best piece of writing she ever did.

73. The Writers' Laboratory was associated with several additional Bank Street projects—among them, the Bank Street Golden Books, (*The Taxi That Hurried; The New House in the Forest; Fix-It Please; A Year in the City,* and *A Year on the Farm*); and *Believe and Make-Believe,* a collection of poems and stories for children from three to seven. Eventually it became less of a production cooperative and more of an informal "authors' club" where writers met to talk over their work, aided by Bank Street staff.

74. For an analysis of the documentary impulse in the 1930s, see William Stott, *Documentary Expression and Thirties America* (New York: Oxford University Press, 1973). Also see Pells, *Radical Visions and American Dreams;* and Warren Susman, "The Thirties," in Stanley Coben and Lorman Ratner, eds., *The Development of an American Culture* (Englewood Cliffs, N.J.: Prentice-Hall, 1970), pp. 179–218.

75. "The best substitute for sharing lives alien to our own," she wrote, "is through dramatic identification with the 'other fellow,' that strange monetary taking of of another's personality or problem as one's own which takes place in the reader or auditor whenever the novel, story or play moves him." LSM, Eleanor Bowman, and Mary Phelps, *My Country 'Tis of Thee* (New York: The Macmillan Co., 1940), pp. v, vi.

76. Lucy did most of the writing, Bowman and Phelps wrote parts of the background material and surveyed source material.

77. Ibid., p. 313.

78. Ibid., p. vii.

79. Ibid.

80. In 1931, the University of the State of New York granted the Bureau of Educational Experiments a Provisional Charter incorporating the organization as an educational institution "for the purpose of maintaining and operating a progressive experiment in nursery and primary school, and to engage in experiments and research work relevant . . . thereto." The charter was amended in 1935 to authorize the education of teachers for nursery, kindergarten, and elementary schools.

81. Barbara Biber, in BS, *Lucy Sprague Mitchell, 1878–1967,* p. 21.

82. For the reactions of a public school principal, see the remarks of Marion Clark, ibid., pp. 12–17.

83. Biber, ibid., p. 21.

84. Charlotte Winsor, ibid., p. 12.

85. *Our Children and Our Schools* became a Book Find Club selection and was widely used by public school administrators and schools of education.

86. LSM, Foreword, to Harriet M. Johnson, "The Modern Teacher," unpublished writings, *69 Bank Street,* 1, no. 2 (Nov. 1934).

87. On Biber's work, see Barbara Biber, *Early Education and Psychological Development*

(New Haven: Yale University Press, 1984). Interviews with Barbara Biber, Nov. 1978, Feb. 1979, Jan. 1984.

88. LSM, Notes for Speech on Jessie Stanton, LSMP; *Our Children and Our Schools*, p. xi; Marcia S. Schaab "'We Had Such an Elegant Time!': Jessie Stanton's Career in Early Childhood Education" (master's thesis, Bank Street College 1973); interview with Evelyn Beyer, June 1985.

89. Interview with Barbara Biber, Nov. 1978.

90. Barbara Biber to Eleanor Bowman Hogan, June 14, 1961, Hogan Memorial Book.

91. Biber, *Children and the Environment*, pp. 70–71.

92. Black, Taped Discussions on LSM; Winsor, *Lucy Sprague Mitchell, 1878–1967*, p. 10. In their introduction to PIE, Black and Joan Blos noted that Lucy was not a "headstrong individualist running a one man show. . . . those who worked with her speak with feelings not unlike those of the little boy who called her a genius" (pp. xi–xii).

93. Interview with Barbara Biber, Nov. 1978.

94. Interviews with Biber, Nov. 1978, Feb. 1979, Jan. 1984.

95. Interviews with Elizabeth Gilkerson, July 1979; Sally Kerlin; Mary Phelps; Betty Miles; Claudia Lewis; Barbara Biber; Charlotte Winsor; Mary Ellen Gilder; and Biber, taped discussions on LSM. The importance of Lucy's vision in shaping Bank Street as an innovative educational institution is cited in Esther Raushenbush, "Three Women: Creators of Change," in Helen S. Astin and Werner Z. Hirsch, eds., *The Higher Education of Women: Essays in Honor of Rosemary Park* (New York: Praeger, 1978).

21: SEPARATIONS

1. Each program began with an announcer stating that "even in this world at war, the care, the training, the development of our children, are as essential to true victory as every bullet fired at the front." The program was terminated after a year for lack of sponsors. See Baby Institute papers, CC and LSMP.

2. Roger Howson to Frederick Mills, Oct. 17, 1949, LSMP.

3. TL, p. 494.

4. Ibid., 497.

5. Ibid., pp. 499–504; interview with Arnold Mitchell, Feb. 1978.

6. TL, p. 498.

7. LSM, "Robin"; "In Your Stamford Study"; TL, pp. 504–05.

8. TL, p. 517.

9. Ibid., p. 522.

10. LSM, "Robin."

11. Ibid.

12. Paul H. Douglas, President of the AEA, to WCM, TL, p. 522.

13. Cited in "Robin." Wesley Mitchell had served as president of the American Economic Association, the American Statistical Association, the Econometric Society, and the Academy of Political Science. He received honorary degrees from the universities of Paris, Chicago, Columbia, California, Princeton, Harvard, Pennsylvania, and the New School for Social Research. Burns, *Wesley Mitchell and the National*

Bureau, p. 51. Also see Arthur Burns, ed., *Wesley Clair Mitchell: The Economic Scientist* (New York: National Bureau of Economic Research, 1952).

14. TL, p. 506.
15. "You," Feb. 1961; "Hold Me Tight, Darling," Nov. 2, 1960, LSMP.
16. TL, p. 534.
17. Margaret Wise Brown (Brownie) to LSM, n.d., LSMP.
18. LSM, "Robin"; TL, p. 531.
19. Interview with Arthur Burns, July 1978.

22: "BECOMING MORE SO"

1. Alvin Johnson wrote: "When we set before us his towering intellect, his epoch-making scholarly contribution, we feel that there was something greater than this in our beloved friend and master: a gentle and sympathetic soul, a tender and true heart, a just and merciful judgment of the honest efforts, the successes and failures of those who came before his intellectual court" (*New School Bulletin*). An editorial in the *New York Times* commented on Wesley Mitchell's "kindness, the courtesy and the genuine humility" that made him loved by innumerable friends and acquaintances. LSM, "Robin."
2. "The Wonder of Your Love Is with Me," Nov. 25, 1949; "The Best Gift," Oct. 15, 1950, LSMP.
3. LSM, "Robin."
4. LSM to Jean and Arnold Mitchell, Jan. 18, 1951, LSMP.
5. "October 29, 1950," LSMP.
6. "The Auction Block," Fall 1959, LSMP.
7. LSM to Basil Bass, Oct. 23, 1949, BS.
8. The 500-page *Our Children and Our Schools* included discussions of Bank Street's educational theories as well as curriculum outlines, notes of discussions with children and teachers, and other firsthand materials.
9. "I thought that only Senator McCarthy tried to ruin people with whom he disagreed," wrote Marion Ascoli in a letter to Lucy, protesting the trustees' decision. Trustee Minutes, June 17, 1953, BS. Other members of the parent group who supported Eleanor Brussel, director of the nursery school, were attorney Robert Morgenthau and Judge Justine Wise Polier. Among the Bank Street trustees who opposed Brussel were Lawrence Frank, Arthur Rosenthal, founder of Basic Books, and Trude Lash, executive director of the Citizens Committee for Children of New York.
   In the fall of 1954, the nursery school, renamed the School for the Nursery Years, moved to East 90th Street. A new Bank Street School for Children opened that fall for 65 youngsters, aged two to six, later expanding to the primary grades. The school became a cooperating member of the Bank Street community, participating in all aspects of research and teaching. Interviews with Eleanor Reich Brussel, Jan. 1984, Elizabeth Gilkerson, John Niemeyer, Feb. 1978, Claudia Lewis, Charlotte Winsor.
10. Minutes of Board of Trustees Meeting, Nov. 16, 1954, BS; interview with John Niemeyer. Bank Street honored Lucy at a dinner at the Biltmore Hotel on Feb. 2, 1957. Lucy read a prose poem, "Everychild," she had written for the occasion.
11. LSM to Sally Kerlin, Aug. 6, 1961. I am grateful to Mrs. Kerlin for letting me share her correspondence with Lucy Mitchell.

12. Frederica Barach, *Children and the Environment*, p. 23.
13. LSM to Sally Kerlin, Oct. 2, 1956; also LSM to Kerlin, Nov. 4, 1961. Over the years, Bank Street expanded its traditional concern with young children and the education of teachers to offer training for a variety of schools, families, and communities. In 1968, it inaugurated Follow Through, a federally funded research and development program to extend the Bank Street approach to children in low-income families, and sponsored fourteen Follow Through projects throughout the country. Bank Street also offers training and research programs concerned with parent education, community leadership, day care services and youth tutoring. Recently, it has been involved in research and evaluation concerning computer training for children. Its own word-processing program, *The Bankstreet Writer*, is widely used in schools and homes. Bank Street has also extended its graduate program to such new areas as special education, administration and supervision, human development, and bilingual and bicultural education.
14. LSM to ESC, Oct. 17, 1943, ESCP.
15. Interview with Elizabeth Coolidge Winship.
16. Mollie Casey to LSM, Aug. 24, 1949; LSM to Mollie Casey, Aug. 30, 1949, Mar. 17, 1950, LSMP.
17. Interview with Margaret Coolidge.
18. "I Called Her the Princess," Apr. 20, 1957, LSMP.
19. "California Again," Aug. 5, 1955; untitled, Oct. 18, 1955, LSMP.
20. "Song of Old Age," Aug. 5, 1957; "Old Age I; "A Precious Patch of the Cosmos," June 1959; "One Does Not Live by Mind Alone," Jan. 1, 1960; "The Geranium Pioneer," Apr. 1960; "My Companions," May 1960, LSMP.
21. "I Can Talk to You Again," July 1958.
22. LSM to Sally Kerlin, Dec. 18, 1955.
23. LSM, "All Is Not Guilt That Jitters," LSMP.
24. Interview with Bernie and Lora Atherton, August 1984.
25. "I Can Talk to You Again," July 1958; "Another Christmas," Dec. 18, 1958, LSMP.
26. "I Can Talk to You Again."
27. LSM to Irma Black, n.d., LSMP.
28. Mollie Casey to LSM, Oct. 1958, LSMP.
29. News release, Office of Public Information, UC, Sept. 29, 1958.
30. "Christmas Day, 1958," Dec. 30, 1958; interviews with Arnold Mitchell, Margaret Coolidge.
31. Interview with Jean Schuyler, Feb. 1978.
32. Interviews with Beverly Corbett, Joan Watrous, Andrew and Jack Mitchell, July 1978; Robin Mitchell to author, Mar. 3, 1978; Gregory Mitchell to author, Mar. 1978.
33. Rose Emery Bliven graduated from the CSST, taught at various progressive schools, and worked as a volunteer at Bank Street for 12 years.
34. "I Am Adrift Again," Aug. 1960, LSMP.
35. "Hold Me Tight, Darling," Nov. 1, 1960, LSMP.
36. "The Final Test," n.d.; "Chart of Rationality," n.d.; "The Final Step in Gentleness," Aug. 1960, LSMP.
37. Untitled, May 1961, LSMP.
38. "Waiting—For What?" Nov. 1961; "Another Year, 1962," Jan. 1962; "The Sense of

Being Blessed," Easter 1962; "Home and Horizons," Nov. 1962; "Something Strange Is Happening," Jan. 3, 1963; untitled, May 1961; "Invincible Summer," Apr. 1962, LSMP.

39. LSM to Sally Kerlin, Jan. 9, 1962; on the Bunting Institute, see "The Mary Ingraham Bunting Institute," Bunting Institute, Radcliffe College.
40. LSM to Mary Ingraham Bunting, Feb. 13, 1962, courtesy Sally Kerlin.
41. LSM to Sally Kerlin, Feb. 4, 1961.
42. "Another Big Test," Sept. 12, 1963, LSMP.
43. "Can I Build One More Home?" Feb. 22, 1964, LSMP; interview with Jean Schuyler, Feb. 1978.
44. Untitled fragment, LSMP.
45. Letters to the author from Robin Mitchell and Gregory Mitchell.
46. Gregory Mitchell and Robin Mitchell to author; interview with Jack Mitchell, July 1980.
47. Marjorie Graham Janis, "A Visit with Lucy Sprague Mitchell," Jan. 1967, BS.
48. LSM, "Retrospection and Memories in Old Age," 1967, LSMP.
49. Untitled typescript, LSMP. Also see LSM, "Becoming 'More So,'" *Children Here and Now* 3 (1955):2–4, BS.
50. LSM, Notes on Old Age, LSMP.
51. Ibid.

EPILOGUE

1. LSM, recording of "This I Believe," Nov. 1955, BS.
2. UA.
3. TL, p. 542.
4. Ibid.; UA.
5. UA.
6. Ibid.
7. Ibid., TL, p. 543.
8. The following account derives from the author's interviews with John McClellan Mitchell, Jan. 1978; Arnold Mitchell, Feb. 1978; and Sprague Mitchell, July 1978. Also see Antler, "Was She a Good Mother?"
9. Untitled notes, LSMP; TL, p. 539.
10. LSM to Sally Kerlin, Aug. 26, 1961.
11. Mary Phelps and Margaret Wise Brown, "Lucy Sprague Mitchell," *Horn Book Magazine*, May–June 1937.
12. Willy Barton Kraber to John Niemeyer, Nov. 1967, BS.
13. UA.
14. LSM to Sally Kerlin, Oct. 2, 1956.
15. Notes on Lucy Sprague Mitchell, Alma Weisberg, Nov. 1967, BS.
16. She described these as "obedience, promptness, orderliness, a pervasive conscientiousness that enabled me to work hard, to crush expression, to carry heavy responsibilities." Notes, LSMP.
17. Interview with William Hooks, June 1980.
18. LSM, "This I Believe."

Archival Sources

MANUSCRIPT COLLECTIONS AND UNPUBLISHED SOURCES

Berkeley. University of California, Bancroft Library
  University Archives
  Presidential papers
  "Pioneering in Education." Oral history conducted 1960 by Irene M. Prescott, Regional Oral History Office, The Bancroft Library, University of California, Berkeley, 1962
  Records of the Partheneia
Cambridge. Radcliffe College Archives
  Blanche Bonnelle Church Papers
  Class of 1900 papers
  Ada Comstock papers
  Mary Coes papers
  Edith Rotch papers
Cambridge. Radcliffe College. The Arthur and Elizabeth Schlesinger Library on the History of Women in America
  Nancy Atwood Sprague papers
  Mary Simkhovitch papers
  Hilda Worthington Smith papers
Chicago Historical Society
  Sprague family papers
  Sprague, Warner & Co. papers
Los Angeles. Marlborough School Archives
Montpelier, Vermont. Vermont Historical Society
  Sprague and Atwood genealogies
New York. Bank Street College of Education
  Board of Trustee minutes
  Working Council minutes
  Bulletins of the Bureau of Educational Experiments
  69 *Bank Street*
  Miscellaneous papers and publications

New York. City and Country School Archives
    Associated Experimental School papers
    Baby Institute papers
    Bureau of Educational Experiments papers
    Caroline Pratt papers
New York. Columbia University. Rare Book and Manuscript Library
    Lucy Sprague Mitchell papers
    Wesley Clair Mitchell papers
Poughkeepsie. Vassar College Library
    Ruth Benedict papers
Randolph, Vermont
    Town records
Washington, D.C. Library of Congress
    Elizabeth Sprague Coolidge papers
Wellesley. Wellesley College Archives
    Alice Freeman Palmer papers

Works by Lucy Sprague Mitchell

UNPUBLISHED

Autobiography (miscellaneous drafts, n.d., n.p., 1944–45).

BOOKS FOR ADULTS

Know Your Children in School.
New York: Macmillan Co., 1954.
My Country 'Tis of Thee: The Use and Abuse of Natural Resources (with Eleanor Bowman and Mary Phelps). New York: Macmillan, 1940.
Our Children and Our Schools. New York: Simon and Schuster, 1950.
The People of the U.S.A.: Their Place in the School Curriculum (with Johanna Boetz and others) New York: Progressive Education Association, 1942.
Two Lives: The Story of Wesley Clair Mitchell and Myself. New York: Simon and Schuster, 1953.
Young Geographers: How They Explore the World and How They Map the World. New York: John Day, 1934. Reprint. New York: Basic Books, 1963.

BOOKS FOR CHILDREN

Another Here and Now Story Book. New York: E. P. Dutton, 1937.
Believe and Make-Believe. New York: E. P. Dutton, 1956.
Guess What's In The Grass. New York: William R. Scott, 1945.
The Here and Now Primer: Home from the Country. New York: E. P. Dutton, 1924.
The Here and Now Story Book. New York: E. P. Dutton, 1921. Revised 1948.
Har och nu: Sagobok för Barn. Stockholm: Kooperativa Förbundets Bokforlag, 1939.
Her og nå eventyr. Oslo: Anders, Kjaer, 1948.
Horses Now and Long Ago. New York: Harcourt-Brace, 1926.
Manhattan Now and Long Ago (with Clara Lambert). New York: Macmillan, 1934.
North America: The Land They Live In for the Children Who Live There. New York: Macmillan, 1931.
Red, White and Blue Auto. New York: William R. Scott, 1944.
Skyscraper (with Elsa H. Naumburg and Clara Lambert). New York: John Day, 1933.

SERIES

Golden Books (Bank Street Series) New York, 1946–48.
  The Taxi That Hurried (with Irma Simonton Black and Jessie Stanton)
  The New House in the Forest
  A Year on the Farm
  A Year in the City
  Fix It, Please
Stories for Children under Seven. New York: John Day, 1933.
  Streets
  Trains
  Boats and Bridges
Our Growing World. New York: D.C. Heath, 1945. Revised 1954.
  Farm and City
  Animals, Plants and Machines
  Our Country

ARTICLES IN JOURNALS AND BOOKS

"Ages and Stages," *Child Study* 15 (February 1938): 144–47.
"Becoming 'More So'"; *Children Here and Now* 3 (1955): 2–5.
"Children as Geographers," *Education* 52 (April 1932): 446–50.
"Children's Experiments in Language," *Progressive Education* 5, no. 1 (Jan.–Mar. 1928): 21–27. (Also in Gertrude Hartman and Ann Shumaker, eds., *Creative Expression: The Development of Children in Art, Music, Literature and Dramatics*. For the Progressive Education Association. New York: John Day Co., 1932.)
"A Cooperative School for Student Teachers," *Progressive Education* 8 (March 1931): 251–55.
"Everychild: The Miracle of Growth," *Children Here and Now*, 40th Anniversary Issue, chap. 5 (1957): 2–8.
"Five-Year Old's First Language Work," *American Childhood* 2 (April 1926).
"The Forms and Results of Student Social Activities," *Publications of the Association of Collegiate Alumnae Magazine* 3, no. 18 (Dec. 1908): 50–53.
"Geographic Thinking," *New Era* 12 (July 1931): 245–48.
"Geography for Children," *New Republic* 52 (November 16, 1927): 355–57.
"Geography for Children," *Saturday Review of Literature* 5 (November 24, 1928): 414.
"Geography with Five-Year-Olds," *Progressive Education* 6 (Sept.–Nov. 1929): 232–37.
"Harriet M. Johnson: Pioneer, 1867–1934," *Progressive Education* 11 (November 1934): 427–29.
"Imagination in Realism," *Childhood Education* 8 (November 1931): 129–31.
"Jimmy Wonders How Things Work," *Children Here and Now* 2 (1954): 13–15.
"Making Real Teachers," *Education Outlook* 20 (January 1946): 52–63.
"Making Young Geographers instead of Teaching Geography," *Progressive Education* 5 (July–Sept. 1928): 217–23.
"Map Making in the School," *American Childhood* 15 (November 1929): 5–8.

"Maps as Art Expression," *Progressive Education* 3 (Apr.–June 1926): 150–53. Also in Hartman and Shumaker, *Creative Expression*, p. 41.

"Margaret Wise Brown: 1910–1952," *Children Here and Now* 1 (1953): 18–20.

"Natural Regions of the United States: Their Work Patterns and Their Psychologies," *Progressive Education* 15 (March 1938): 187–209.

"Play Based on Neighborhood Work: Harriet Johnson Nursery School and Little Red School House," *Nursery Education Digest* 3 (1945): 2–5.

"Programming for Growth at P.S. 186," *Childhood Education* 22 (December 1945): 173–78.

"Research on the Child's Level: Possibilities, Limitations, and Techniques" 31st Annual Schoolmen's Week Proceedings, University of Pennsylvania bulletin, 1944, pp. 111–19.

"School Children and Sex Idealism," *Survey* 32 (June 20, 1914): 327–28.

"Social Studies and Geography," *Progressive Education* 11 (January 1934): 97–105.

"Social Studies for Future Teachers," *Social Studies* 26 (May 1935): 289–98.

"Tribute to a Pioneer [Elisabeth Irwin]," *Progressive Education* 20, no. 2 (February 1943): 65.

Index

ACA. *See* Collegiate Alumnae, Association of

Adams, Mrs. Milward, 28

Addams, Jane, 70, 140, 157; "Filial Relations," 75; and Hull House, 30–31; influence on Lucy, xix, 31–33, 156–58, 327; Pullman strike (1894), 31–33; *Twenty Years at Hull House*, 75

AES. *See* Associated Experimental Schools

After College, What? 75

Agassiz, Elizabeth, 51–52

Age-behavior relationship, 248, 292, 334, 356–57

Allen, Evelyn, 112

American Association for the Advancement of Science, 221

American Economic Association, 37, 283

American Geographic Society, 296

American Statistical Association, 283

Animals, Plants and Machines (Mitchell, L., Brown, M. W.), 323

ASC. *See* Associated Students of California

Associated Experimental Schools, 315, 317, 327

Associated Students of California, 97–98

Associated Women Students, 98, 184–85

Association of Collegiate Alumnae, 102, 111, 130, 213

Atherton, Bernie, 348–49

Atherton, Lora, 348–49

Atwood, Eleanor (cousin), care of Otho, 38, 79–80, 125–26

Atwood, Lucia. *See* Sprague, Lucia Atwood (mother)

Atwood, Nancy. *See* Sprague, Nancy Atwood (aunt)

AWS. *See* Associated Women Students

"The Baby Institute," 333

Bancroft, Dr. Eleanor, 116

Bank Street, xviii–xx, 328–30, 344, 354; *69 Bank Street*, 316; and City and Country School, 316; effect of Depression on, 314–16; Golden Books, 343; Little Red School House, 302–06, 316; nursery school, 308, 316–17; Public School Workshop, 325–27, 329; School for Children, 344; teacher training program, 325; West Coast Associates, 352; Working Council, xix, 220; Writers' Laboratory, 322–25, 329. *See also* Bureau of Educational Experiments

Bank Street College of Education, xiii, 343, 416n–17n; *See also* Bureau of Educational Experiments

Bank Street Readers, 344

"Becoming More So: Stages of Learning in My Long Life," 356

BEE. *See* Bureau of Educational Experiments

Education (*continued*)
 with industry, 222–23, 242; research
 and the function of, 285, 290–93; social aspects of, 157, 207–08, 212; socialist theory of, 239, 241–42; and standardized testing, 149; of teachers, 212,
 325–27; Thorndike's theory on, 208;
 through play, 236, 244; vocational,
 130–31, 223; of "whole" child, 149–
 50, 211–12, 241; and the "whole"
 teacher, 309; of women, 30, 41, 50–52,
 66, 67, 71, 95, 104–05, 358, 382n,
 388n
Educational measurement, 284
Educational Psychology (Thorndike), 208
Edwards, George C., 100
Eliot, Charles W., 53
Ellis, Frederick, 215, 216, 219, 220, 291,
 292
Environmentalism, 231–32, 262
Equal Rights Amendment, xviii, xix
Equal Suffrage Association, 71
Eugenics movement, 231
"Every Stage of Life Has Its Song: My Song
 Has Been a Woman's Song," 357
Experimental education, xix, 221, 243,
 284–85, 302–06, 412n; Associated Ex-
 perimental Schools, 315, 317, 327;
 Lucy's view of, 329–30; and national
 planning, 320; need for teachers, 308;
 place of art and politics in, 316
Expressionism, 203, 284

Farm and City, (Mitchell, L., Brown,
 M. W.), 323
Farm labor camps, 223
Farquhar, Marion Jones, 86, 117, 123,
 176, 192, 268, 274; friendship with
 Lucy, 44–45, 403n; reaction to Lucy's
 engagement, 182
Farquhar, Robert, 86
Farrell, Elizabeth, 215
Fathers: role in modern family, 359–60; in
 Victorian household, 11–14
Feminism: after 1920, xviii; as "life pro-

cess," xiv; relationship to mothering,
 xvii. *See also* Suffrage; Women
"Filial Relations" (Addams), 75
Forbes, Harriet, 209–10, 219, 337; and
 nutrition experiment, 222; and Psycho-
 logical Survey, 217
Forbes-Johnson, Polly, 224, 268, 274, 321
Frank, Lawrence K., 406n
Freeman, Alice. *See* Palmer, Alice Free-
 man
Freudianism, 284
Freud, Sigmund, 203, 205, 252; *Psycho-
 analysis*, 252
Fuller, Lucy, 60, 66

Garnett, Porter, 185, 186, 187
Garrett, Laura, 210, 219, 220
Gary Plan, 214–15, 220, 221, 223, 392n
Gender: issues of, xvi, xx, 64–68, 109–
 10, 242–43; traditional education and,
 xx
General Federation of Women's Clubs, 70
Gesell, Arnold, 253, 288
Gesell, Beatrice, 253
Gilligan, Carol, 66
Gilman, Charlotte Perkins, 135, 256
Golden Books, 343
Goldmark, Pauline, 140, 147–48, 205;
 education of, 147; influence on Lucy,
 157
Greenwich House, 205, 209, 220
Gregory, Sarah Hardy (Sadie), 93, 122,
 123, 132, 162, 193, 229, 340
Guilt, 15, 348

Hall, G. Stanley, 288
Hart, Walter, 94, 122, 132, 229
Hartley House, 209, 238
Harvard Annex. *See* Society for the Colle-
 giate Instruction of Women
Harvard University: development of phi-
 losophy department, 57–58; Radcliffe
 College, 50–51; professors' treatment of
 women, 53–54
Harvey, Marie Turner, 220
Haymarket Riot (1886), 32

women, 55; influence on Lucy, 29–30, 47–48, 54–59, 83, 88; marriage/career, 30, 56; *A Marriage Cycle*, 56, 84; on suffrage, 71

Palmer, George Herbert, 29, 35, 141; attitude toward suffrage, 71; European sabbatical, 81–83; growing dependency on Lucy, 84–86; influence on Lucy, 82–84, 88; and love for Alice, 55; marriage/career, 30, 56; marriage proposal to Lucy, 85–86; and promotion of Harvard's philosophy department, 57–58; reaction to death of Alice, 83–84; writings on George Herbert, 58, 81–83, 85

Pankhurst, Emmeline, 195

Park, Maud Wood, 71

"Partheneia: A Masque of Maidenhood" (Rearden), 186–91; reviews of, 188; symbolic of Lucy's life, 190; as tribute to womanhood, 186

Pearson, Ralph, 311

PEA. *See* Public Education Association

Peixotto, Jessica, 116, 122, 142, 162, 183, 194; influence on Lucy, 107, 109

Perry, Bliss, 272, 280

Perry, Charlotte, 311

Phelps, Mary, 319, 323, 324, 362

Philanthropy, 137–38, 147, 165, 225

Piaget, Jean: *The Language and Thought of the Child*, 299–300

Pine Ridge, 220

Play, education through, 236, 244

Play School, 219, 237, 238, 239–44; development of, 238; and education of "whole" child, 241; goal of, 240–41; Lucy's support of, 239–40, 243; program of, 240–41, 249; staff, 243–44. *See also* City and Country School; Pratt, Caroline

Pode, Ernest, 203, 205

Pratt, Caroline, 219, 315; differences from Lucy, 245–46, 295; education, 237; and equality of sexes, 242–43; friendship with Lucy, 244–46; influence of Helen Marot, 237–38; influence on

Lucy, 239–40, 305; Play School, 219, 237, 238, 239–44; rejection of Lucy's language and geography programs, 300–01; as socialist, 241–42; theory of education, 236–39

Preschools, 257; and women's careers in, xviii. *See also* Early childhood education; Nursery school

President Hoover's Research Committee on Social Trends, 319–20

Progressive education, 243, 397n, 398n, 412n; Bank Street, 325; and Bureau of Educational Experiments, 290; college curriculum, 106; educational measurement and scientism, 284; Edward Thorndike and, 207–08; and expressionism, 284; John Dewey and, 207–08; Lucy's trademarks in, 156; and psychological testing, 215–17; and sex education, 155–58; and study of geography, 295; and study of history, 295

Progressive Education Association, 243

Progressive Era, 69–70

Progressive reform: in economics, xv; in education, xv; and public and private morality, 156; and sex education, 155–58; women in, 106

"Project method," 309

Psychoanalysis, 203, 204, 205

Psychoanalysis (Freud), 252

Psychological Association, National, 221

Psychological Clinic. *See* Psychological Survey

Psychological growth, theory of, 291–93

Psychological Survey, 216–17, 225

Psychological testing, 215–17, 219, 220, 223, 287

Psychology (Dewey), 119

Public education, 149–51

Public Education Association (PEA), 208–09, 213, 215, 216, 302, 304

Public school: differences from City and Country school, 303; experimental education in, 302–06

Public School Workshop, 325–27, 329, 336